Alienation

Cambridge Studies in the History and Theory of Politics

EDITORS

MAURICE COWLING

G. R. ELTON

E. KEDOURIE

J. G. A. POCOCK

J. R. POLE

WALTER ULLMANN

Alienation

MARX'S CONCEPTION OF MAN
IN CAPITALIST SOCIETY

BERTELL OLLMAN

Associate Professor
Department of Politics, New York University

SECOND EDITION

CAMBRIDGE UNIVERSITY PRESS

CAMBRIDGE

LONDON   NEW YORK   MELBOURNE

Published by the Syndics of the Cambridge University Press
The Pitt Building, Trumpington Street, Cambridge CB2 1RP
Bentley House, 200 Euston Road, London NW1 2DB
32 East 57th Street, New York, NY 10022, USA
296 Beaconsfield Parade, Middle Park, Melbourne 3206, Australia

First published 1971
Reprinted 1972, 1973, with corrections 1975
Second edition 1976
Reprinted 1977

Printed in the United States of America
Typeset by The Fuller Organization, Inc., Philadelphia, Pa.
Printed and bound by R.R. Donnelley & Sons Co.,
Crawfordsville, Ind.

Library of Congress Cataloging in Publication Data
Ollman, Bertell
Alienation
(Cambridge studies in the history and theory of politics)
Bibliography: p.
Includes index.
1. Alienation (Social psychology)   2. Communism
and society   3. Marx, Karl, 1818-1883   I. Title
HM291.O58   1976   301.6′2   76–4234
ISBN 0 521 21281 2 hard covers
ISBN 0 521 29083 X paperback
(First edition:
ISBN 0 521 08086 X hard covers
ISBN 0 521 09813 0 paperback)

Contents

PART IV   CONCLUSION

Preface to the second edition

A book like *Alienation* is never truly finished; its arguments are only more or less ready to be read. Under the sometimes forceful prodding of critics and other readers, I have tried to improve its readiness by filling in bothersome gaps, providing occasional clarifications and otherwise strengthening positions that events have shown to be wanting.

Most of the critical comment, both favorable and unfavorable, directed at *Alienation* has had to do with my attributing to Marx a philosophy of internal relations and the conclusions I drew from this. That this was in part foreseen is evidenced by the appendix to the first edition in which I tried to respond, before the fact, to expected criticisms. This was clearly insufficient, as these same and similar objections fell upon me from all sides, including the side of those who had much praise for the book. I would like to take advantage of this second edition to return to the fray and offer a more extended defense for my interpretation, especially since I consider it to be absolutely central to what is of value not only in this book but in the book I am now writing on Marx's method. The response to my critics on the question of internal relations is found in Appendix II of this edition.

Two other major additions to *Alienation* are the systematic discussion of Marx's theory of ideology (now Chapter 32), elements of which were formerly dispersed throughout the book, and an attempt to set the treatment of political alienation in the framework of Marx's broader theory of the state (now Section III of Chapter 30). The latter is also offered as a model of how an approach based on internal relations can be used to integrate various apparently contradictory interpretations of Marx's views.

Finally, I should also like to draw the attention of those familiar with the first edition – whose comments, after all, provoked most of these revisions – to my efforts at clarifying the political implications of holding that Marx did or did not have an ethics (pp. 46-7, 50-1), the basis for his inconsistent use of the concept 'class' (pp. 120-2), the sense in which one can and cannot speak of alienation in the 'communist' countries (perhaps the most frequently asked of all questions) (pp. 252-3), and the theoretical status of Marx's vision of communism and the means and criteria for judging it (pp. 49, 118-9, 238-9). While all these additions/changes and the many minor ones have not by any means made *Alienation* into a new book, I have no doubt that they have helped make it into a better one.

Paris, France
May 1976

BERTELL OLLMAN

Note on translations

The English translations of Marx's works have been used whenever they were available. Where I had doubts about the translation of a particular expression I checked the German original. For the very involved *Economic and Philosophic Manuscripts of 1844*, which occupies a central place in my study, I have used Martin Milligan's translation (Moscow, 1959) in preference to the more recent one by T. B. Bottomore (London, 1963) and Ria Stone's little known mimeographed translation (n.p., 1949).

Though very difficult to follow, it is my impression that Milligan's effort is a more faithful rendering of what Marx wrote than either of the others. Bottomore's work, in particular, in attempting to simplify, has often chosen the better known English expression over the accurate one. On p. 157, for example, he translates *Wesen* as 'significance', while Milligan renders it as 'essence' (p. 103); on p. 153, Bottomore translates *abstrahieren* as 'eliminates', while Milligan renders it as 'abstracts' (p. 99); and there are many such instances. The importance of these differences, which may seem trivial now, will become clear as my interpretation develops.

Furthermore, in preparing his translation of the text which appears in the *Gesamtausgabe,* Milligan made use of the recent corrections (1956) of typographical and other errors that had found their way into the first edition. Some of these changes are not without importance, such as the substitution on several occasions of *Genuss* (happiness) for *Geist* (spirit).

In my own efforts at translating Marx's texts, I have tried to follow as far as possible the pattern set by Milligan. Thus, for example, *Wesen* is generally rendered by 'essence', 'nature' or 'being'; *Kraft* is generally rendered by 'power', and *Wesenskraft* by 'essential power'. Again, the significance of these English expressions, and others which I regularly substitute for Marx's originals, will become clear later.

The attempt to be consistent has also meant that I have had, on occasion, to alter words in the English editions of Marx's other works. Any change considered significant is mentioned in the footnotes. The footnotes are also used to comment on problems that arise in translating particular terms when these terms make their appearance in the text. In this respect, the present 'Note on translations' is only an introduction to the subject of translating Marx which is dealt with in more detail in the pages to come.

Acknowledgements

Whatever its achievements and failures, this work stands as a tribute to Isaiah Berlin without whose aid as a teacher and friend it could never have been completed. It gives me great pleasure to acknowledge the debt I owe to his wisdom and kindness. Among the many people who have read portions and offered helpful criticisms, Marshall Berman, Ann Spackman, Richard Gombrich, Norman Pollach, Z. A. Pelczynski, Graeme Duncan, Peter Sedgwick, Steven Lukes, Charles Taylor, Peter Waterman, Paul Sweezy, David McLellan, Shlomo Avineri, Colwyn Williamson and, in particular, Maximilien Rubel and John Plamenatz deserve special thanks. None of the above, of course, bear any responsibility for the judgements expressed. Financially, the task of research was considerably eased through the generosity of the Ford Foundation and of St. Antony's College (Oxon.), and I would like to thank them for their help as well.

General introduction

'Marxism' is essentially Marx's interpretation of capitalism, the unfinished results of his study into how our society works, how it developed, and where it is tending. Men in their relations with each other, their products and activities are the primary subject matter of this study. It is *men* who fight on both sides of the class struggle, men who sell their labor-power, men who buy it, and so on. Though Marx generally organizes his findings around such non-human factors as the mode of production, class and value, his theory of alienation places the acting and acted upon individual in the center of this account. In this theory, man himself is offered as the vantage point from which to view his own relations, actual and potential, to society and nature; his conditions become an extension of who he is and what he does, rather than the reverse. To expound the analysis of capitalism made from this vantage point, an analysis that remains little known despite the current preoccupation with the term 'alienation', is the task of this book.

Marx's individual, however, is himself a product of theory. Marx has a conception of how men appear, what they feel and think, what motives influence them and how much, and – on another plane – what they are capable of, both in existing and in new conditions. Without these qualities, they could not or would not respond to events in the manner Marx posits. For even if we accept that material conditions are as he describes them, there is no need for people to react as Marx says they do and will unless they bring to their situation such qualities as make other action impossible or extremely unlikely. Consequently, any account of alienation as an explanatory social theory focusing on the individual must begin by clarifying what is distinctive in Marx's conception of human nature.

Marx seems to have been aware of the significance of other writers' views on man and, to some extent, of man's status in their broader theories, but he was only partially and intermittently aware of his own. He notes, for example, that 'our philosophic consciousness is so arranged that only the image of man that it conceives appears to it as the real man', but this barb of wisdom is never pointed inward.[1] The 'True Socialists' are condemned because they take the 'German petty philistine' as the typical man, and see his

xi

qualities in everybody.[2] Bentham is accused of doing the same thing with his ideal, the English shopkeeper.[3]

However, Marx's chief objection to these writers' views is that they are unhistorical, that they fail to take account of the transformations in human character that follow changes in social conditions. Taking the individual simply for what he appears, as something given, of the same order as the earth and the sky rather than as a product of his time, is declared by Marx to be an illusion characteristic of each epoch in history.[4] For him, variations in human nature are also produced by the diverse conditions of life found inside the same society. For example, the contrasting qualities of capitalists and workers are said to be due to differences in the circumstances in which each class lives. Obviously, a conception of human nature which does not take these factors into account is faulty at its inception, but to take them into account, as Marx does, is not the same as being without a conception of human nature. It merely complicates this conception with the addition of these new factors.

Marx's own conception of human nature was most fully, if not carefully, worked out in the *Economic and Philosophic Manuscripts of 1844* and in *The German Ideology* (1846). Yet, the form of presentation makes coming to grips with this conception an involved and cumbersome task. Relevant material on the subject of man can also be found throughout Marx's writings, but it is not nearly so concentrated as in these early works, neither of which was published. Two questions arise: why did Marx not present his conception of human nature in a more ordered fashion? And why did he not publish the *1844 Manuscripts* and *The German Ideology*? The latter question, which is also asked by critics who would like to dismiss these works as 'immature', must be taken first.

To begin with, Marx did try to publish *The German Ideology,* and only failed because conditions in Germany did not allow it. He tells us in the aftermath that he did not mind abandoning this work 'to the gnawing criticism of the mice' because it had achieved its main purpose – self-clarification.[5] Marx always wrote to obtain specific ends, and, once the philosophies he attacked as pernicious in *The German Ideology* began to decline, the purpose – other than self-clarification – for which he wrote this early work became obsolete. Furthermore, Marx was constantly revising his exposition, and he must have soon realized that the form in which he first presented his positive views was unfathomable to the working class people he most wanted to understand them.[6]

Like *The German Ideology*, but even more so, the *1844 Manuscripts* is an exercise in self-clarification. In much less space it manages to cover much more ground. While *The German Ideology* is essentially an historical and philosophical work, one cannot classify the *1844 Manuscripts,* despite the label that has been attached to it, in the same way. History, philosophy, economics, psychology, anthropology, ethics, religion and sociology crisscross each other in an amazingly complex pattern as Marx's intellect ranges across the whole terrain of what he knows. In this work, Marx provided himself with the brave outlines of a new system, but he was surely aware that this first statement of his views would convince no one and that few would even comprehend what he was saying.

In explaining why Marx did not publish *The German Ideology,* I have also accounted in part for why Marx did not present his conception of human nature in a more ordered fashion. Human nature was an important topic when he wanted to put his own house in order, but he hesitated to give it the same prominence when his purpose was to explain his views and to convince others. Proletarian class consciousness could be better affected by emphasizing environmental factors which are open to direct kinds of evidence and which can be developed in discussion. Whereas talk about human nature, as Marx recognized, is too often a means of putting an end to discussion.

Moreover, and this is probably as important, in the years immediately following 1844 Marx was engaged in a series of political and ideological disputes with a number of petty bourgeois and socialist thinkers whose favorite expressions were 'human nature', 'humanity' and 'man in general'. In combating the 'True Socialists', Stirner, Feuerbach, Krieg and others, Marx was driven to distinguish his own theories by the relative absence of terms which were their main stock in trade and to formulate the thoughts they contained in another manner.

Yet, despite the fact that anthropology and psychology cease to be major subjects, man continues, of necessity, to occupy a central position in Marx's theories. And the men who act and interact in

Marx's later writings are no different from those who appear in his early works. The conception of human nature with which he began has hardly altered. Thus, while the framework and categories used in *Alienation* are borrowed for the most part from the *1844 Manuscripts* and *The German Ideology,* their content, as my quotations will amply show, is not so limited.

Before trying to reconstruct Marx's conception of human nature, there are problems concerning his broader philosophy that must be considered. In particular, one must make an author's peace with Marx's unusual terminology, a preliminary task which is too often shirked, to insure that no more or other is made of his expressions than he intends them to convey. The path from Marx's use of language leads directly to the view of reality which underlies it, and from here to the methods of inquiry and exposition that he felt this view required. These matters are dealt with in the opening Part. I would not devote much space to Marx's general philosophy in a work on alienation if this subject were treated adequately elsewhere. Unfortunately, I do not believe this is the case.

The organization of this book, therefore, is as follows: Part I deals with the philosophical foundations of Marxism, primarily with how Marx views all of reality; Part II deals with Marx's conception of human nature, or the ties Marx sees between man and nature, viewed in the above manner; and Part III with the theory of alienation, or what happens to these ties in capitalism, again viewed in the above manner. In erecting this pyramid of concerns, I have tried to keep necessary repetition, the presentation of familiar relations in new and more complex guises, to a minimum.

My treatment of Marxism also differs from that of most other writers in this field in being 'unhistorical' in three different senses: little attention is given to the development of Marx's ideas; not much time is spent on their genesis; and no attempt is made to set Marxism in the perspective of other ideas before and since. As for the first, I do not emphasize alterations in Marx's thinking because I do not see many there, especially when compared to the essential unity in Marxism from 1844 on. Consequently, to gain an understanding of these views, it is far more important to treat all Marx's writings as expressions of a single theoretical scheme than to give an undeserved emphasis to the relatively few and minor changes that occur. The latter approach only enhances the difficulty of grasping the interrelations present.

Even the concession which is always made regarding the new terminology Marx adopted after 1844 is overdone. The 'Hegelian' and 'Feuerbachian' language of the *1844 Manuscripts* is only partly replaced by another one better suited to presenting Marx's ideas and getting them accepted. As for the rest, Marx's specialization in the fields of politics, history and economics did not require a terminology which had been used primarily in discussions of philosophy and anthropology. Even in his later works, however, whenever connections across disciplines had to be made, he frequently resorted to these 'older' terms; though, as we shall see, their meanings may have altered somewhat through the change of context.

The view which holds that Marx's ideas must be partitioned according the period in which they appear, each period taken as a radical departure from what came before, requires evidence of a kind that has nowhere been offered. First, one must show that Marx was aware of such a break, that he actually and clearly refers to his earlier views as incorrect. Second, one must show that what Marx either approves or disapproves of in his first works is treated in a contrary manner later on. And third, one must show that a significant number of early concepts do not enter into later works at all.

Though we find numerous allusions to developments and minor changes in theories and ways of presenting them, neither Marx nor Engels ever points to a change of mind that qualifies for the term 'break'. On the contrary, it was Marx's habit to return to his earlier notebooks in drafting his later works. Engels informs us, for example, that in writing *Capital* Marx used his notebooks of 1843-5.[7] The *Grundrisse* (1858), which served as Marx's first draft for *Capital,* contains many pages which could have been lifted bodily from the *1844 Manuscripts.*[8] Even in the published version of *Capital,* there is much more of Marx's 'earlier' ideas and concepts than is generally recognized. The chapters on Marx's economic theories in the middle of Part III are my attempt to document this thesis.

But if Marx's theories cannot conveniently be separated into periods, how can the many small changes and developments which did occur be accounted for? Clearly, I do not wish to say that

Marx's views were always the same, or that 'true' Marxism is only what appears in the *1844 Manuscripts,* or in *The Communist Manifesto,* or in *Capital.* Instead, my position is that there is an *evolution* in Marx's thinking which is already present in the logic of his earliest commitments and knowledge, and that from the moment he began writing seriously about man and society his views progressed in a direction from which he never turned aside. As we shall see, the new areas he came to study, together with the results of his research are responsible for most of this theoretical development. The writings of 1842, 1844, 1846 and 1848 show the most significant alterations, but the essential unity of all the main ideas advanced must not be lost. In the following pages I treat the developments and changes in Marx's theories and expressions whenever they are relevant to the subject under discussion.

Relatively little time is devoted to the origins of Marx's ideas (hence, too, to their originality), not because this point is unimportant, but because I believe the prior task is to establish what these ideas are. The origins of any theoretical system can only be studied after one grasps it well enough to know what does and does not count as origins. This grasp is not achieved by seeking bits and pieces of Marxism in the works of other thinkers, but only by fitting together the relations in Marxism itself. Only after we know Marx's major theories, which includes their mutual relations as parts of a system, can we know what we are looking for. Otherwise, superficial similarities may be taken for influences, with the result that Marx's ideas are often made more difficult to understand by the very preparations made to understand them.

Finally, I do not set Marxism alongside other theories that have been expounded before and since, first, because until we know what Marxism is it makes little sense to provide it a niche in the history of ideas; and, second, because I admit to having a prejudice against accounts of Marxism which rely on analogies with other theories. It is the intellectual's disease – a disease from which I am not wholly immune – to treat one thing by discussing everything which bears the slightest resemblance to it. When applied to Marxist exegesis, this means that Aristotle, Locke, Hegel, Feuerbach, Rousseau, the Roman Catholic Church and many more people, ideas and things are used in extended analogies to highlight Marx's meaning. But all analogies have a tendency to be misleading both for the writer and his readers. The writer is tempted to substitute his understanding of the analogy for an understanding of his subject, and to trim the edges of the latter whenever necessary to facilitate comparison. The reader is tempted and often urged to do the same. To assert that Marx, like Aristotle, had a teleology, or that, like Rousseau, he believed man a social animal, or that, like Locke, he wanted man to be free is to mislead people into thinking that the similarity is more than that of a lowest common denominator. Marxism, understood as Marx's interpretation of capitalism, did not exist before Marx, nor in its pure form does it exist anywhere outside his writings. What Marx said is the raw material to be used in explaining Marxism.

What, then, of Engels? As Marx's intimate collaborator for almost forty years of his life and his literary executor after death, Engels is usually taken as a co-equal spokesman with Marx for the theories of Marxism. For most purposes, this procedure is perfectly justifiable. Certain small differences, however, do exist on the subject of man and alienation so that to deal fully with both men would require many exacting distinctions. Consequently, I have restricted my evidence for Marx's conception of human nature and the theory of alienation to Marx's own words. Yet, the marginal possibility of error in using Engels is not enough for me to ask readers to do the same. Occasionally (the section on philosophical foundations is replete with such instances), the forthrightness of Engels' speech on points where there is complete agreement with Marx supplants all other considerations, and he finds his way into the text as a totally reliable witness. A more detailed defense of Marx's and Engels' unity of views is offered in the forthcoming discussion of the dialectic, which has been the center of most of the controversy surrounding this unity.

Criticism, no matter how penetrating, if it comes at the wrong time is also out of place, and can be as effective a barrier to understanding as the most rigid stupidity. The threads of any argument, especially one so intricate as Marxism, should not be submitted to any definite pronouncements until a substantial piece of the cloth has been woven. Otherwise, one cannot be sure that what is under attack is 'what Marx really meant'. I am only too conscious of the fact that, generally, what is being disputed in the avalanche of exegetic material on Marxism is not what this socialist thinker said

– the evidence of his writings particularly today is readily available – but what he was 'trying to say'. Therefore, Marx must be allowed sufficient time unimpeded by constant interruptions to establish his views. For this reason I have delayed my own more important critical comments until the end.

Throughout *Alienation* I have tried not to make Marxism more consistent than it really is, while at the same time stressing its essential unity. Marx is always the architect, this writer but the archaeologist of his ideas.

PART I

Philosophical introduction

1. *With words that appear like bats*

The most formidable hurdle facing all readers of Marx is his 'peculiar' use of words. Vilfredo Pareto provides us with the classic statement of this problem when he asserts that Marx's words are like bats: one can see in them both birds and mice.[1] No more profound observation has ever been offered on our subject. Thinkers through the years have noticed how hard it is to pin Marx down to particular meanings, and have generally treated their non-comprehension as a criticism. Yet, without a firm knowledge of what Marx is trying to convey with his terms, one cannot properly grasp any of his theories.

How, for example, are we to understand the startling claim that 'Value *is* labor' (my emphasis), or Marx's assertion that the 'identity of consumption and production . . . appears to be a threefold one', or his allusion to theory which under certain circumstances becomes a 'material force'?[2] Marx's statements frequently jar us, and instances of obscurity in his work, occasions where two or more interpretations seem equally applicable, are more numerous still.

Engels was well aware of the trouble people had in coming to grips with Marx's terminology. In his Preface to the English edition of *Capital* I, he says, 'there is, however, one difficulty we could not spare the reader: the use of certain terms in a sense different from what they have, not only in common life, but in ordinary political economy.' But, according to Engels,

this was unavoidable. Every new aspect of a science involves a revolution in the technical terms of that science . . . Political economy has generally been content to take, just as they were, the terms of commercial and industrial life, and to operate with them, entirely failing to see that by so doing, it confined itself within the narrow circle of ideas expressed by those terms . . . It is, however, self-evident that a theory which views modern capitalist production as a mere passing stage in the economic history of mankind, must make use of terms different from those habitual to writers who look upon that form of production as imperishable and final.[3]

Whether the necessity which forced Marx to adopt his peculiar use of language is 'self-evident', as Engels claims, is open to question, but to question it now would be to depart from my chosen inquiry. What Engels is saying is that words express the understanding of a period and as this understanding progresses these words and/or their meanings must give way to new ones. To use only terms that are current or only the accepted meanings of such terms is to confine oneself to expressing ideas which are also current. In Marx's case, viewing capitalism as a passing phase is said to demand different concepts from those used by people who consider capitalism to be the eternal mode of production.

Eight years later, in his Introduction to *Capital* III (after a considerable volume of misinterpretation had passed under the bridge), Engels returns to this subject, mentioning yet another difficulty in Marx's use of words. It seems that Marx's terminology, besides being new and unusual, is also inconsistent, the same word meaning different things at different times. Rather than seeing this as a fault, Engels proclaims it a virtue, and says this was necessary to express Marx's understanding of the society he describes. Engels argues that we should not expect to find

fixed, cut-to-measure, once and for all applicable definitions in Marx's works. It is self-evident that where things and their interrelations are conceived, not as fixed, but as changing, their mental images, the ideas, are likewise subject to change and transformation, and they are not encapsulated in rigid definitions, but are developed in their historical or logical process of formulation.[4]

According to Engels then, Marx's words are meant to express a conception of 'things and their interrelations . . . not as fixed, but as changing', and, consequently, the definitions of these words must also change.

It is tempting at this point to call a halt to the 'jargon', and declare Engels and Marx with him confused and incapable of full clarification. There is a tradition in the English speaking world going at least as far back as George Bernard Shaw which warns readers of Marx to 'never mind the metaphysics' and blames his slight exaggerations or gaping errors, depending on the critic's political complexion, on his 'animistic philosophy'.[5] Another more difficult path to follow is the one which leads from Marx's terminology to the picture of the world he was trying to convey. Engels' comments have not solved the mystery, but they point the direction in which research must proceed. In Marx's conception of social reality lies the solution to the riddle which some readers have discovered in his terminology.

With few exceptions, Marx's critics have avoided any serious investigation of his conception of social reality. This has not relieved them, however, of the necessity of having a position on this subject, of making an assumption about the way in which Marx views the world and, consequently, of believing (generally without ever making it explicit) that whatever he knows is of a certain character. In so doing, whether aware of it or not, they are prescribing the real limits to what he could be saying; Marx's terms are forced into the mold of what they must mean, given this view of the world. Consequently, to launch directly into a discussion of Marx's theories, in so far as one is not content simply to repeat his expressions, is almost invariably to adopt by default ordinary language criteria for deciding on his meaning. It is to assume that what we take to be 'common sense' is an adequate foundation on which to build an understanding of Marxism, that there is no fundamental difference between his conception of social reality and our own.* Engels has already said enough to indicate the dangers in making this assumption, but I should also like to show its influence on at least one standard interpretation of Marx's theories. By this means, too, I hope to justify the amount of time devoted to epistemological inquiry in the coming chapters.

II

Perhaps nothing Marx ever said has been more frequently echoed than the claim that 'The mode of production of material life determines the social, political, and intellectual life process in general.'[6] This is declared true not only of the present but 'across' time, such that any major development in the mode of production brings about changes in these other sectors as well. So much every student

---

* Common sense is all that strikes us as being obviously true, such that to deny any part of it appears, at first sight, to involve us in speaking nonsense. In this work, I shall use 'common sense' as well to refer to that body of generally unquestioned knowledge and the equally unquestioned approach to knowledge which is common to the vast majority of scholars and laymen in Western capitalist societies.

of Marxism knows. The questions which remain to be answered
are – what exactly is included in the mode of production, and in
what sense is it said to determine these other factors? Or, we may
ask, how is Marx using the expressions 'mode of production' and
'determine'?

John Plamenatz offers a concise statement of the most widespread interpretation of Marx's claim which he formulates as a
series of 'Fundamentalist' assumptions. According to Plamenatz,
Marx's view

> assumes in the first place, that men's activities recorded by the historian
> have been properly classified, that they have been divided into a
> number of mutually exclusive classes or 'factors'. It assumes, in the
> second place, that the activities called fundamental change their char-
> acter more or less independently of the others. And, lastly, it assumes
> that changes in the character of the activities called fundamental pro-
> duce, directly or indirectly, corresponding changes in the characters of
> all the other activities.[7]

On this interpretation, Marxism offers an easy target for criticism on each of these three counts. To begin with, Marx did not
succeed in dividing the social reality with which he was concerned
into 'a number of mutually exclusive classes or "factors" '. Thus
'ideology', for example, refers at times to all ideas, sometimes to
normative and other ideas which are considered unscientific, and
sometimes to such ideas only in so far as they serve the interests of
a class. Using a still sharper knife, Georges Gurvitch claims to have
found thirteen meanings of 'ideology' in Marx's writings, and is
able to provide supporting evidence.[8] Differences of an equal magnitude can be found in Marx's use of 'class' and of many other
important concepts.[9]

But if Marx often uses the same expression to refer to different
things, he is equally capable of using different expressions to refer
to what appears to be the same thing. In the passage in his Preface
to the *Critique of Political Economy* where he speaks of the mode
of production determining 'the social, political, and intellectual life
process in general', the same role is attributed to 'relations of production', 'forces of production', 'economic structure of society',
'social existence' and the 'economic foundation'.[10] Not only do
these expressions have different referents (in the case of 'social
existence' the contrast would seem to be considerable), but some

of them appear to include in their meaning part of the reality which Marx says they 'determine'. Thus, property relations as a system of legal claims comes under the heading of superstructure, but they are also a component of the relations of production which 'determines' this superstructure. The same difficulty arises with class struggle, which constitutes part of the political life of society while also being an element in the economic structure that is said to 'determine' political life. Such inconsistency and sloppy conceptualization (if that is what it is) has come under heavy critical fire.[11]

If we accept that Marx's theory requires a separable determining factor carefully distinguished from what it is supposed to determine, we arrive by a process of elimination at productive technology, not because it satisfies all the conditions but because it does so better than other possible factors. What is popularly known as 'economic determinism' becomes on this interpretation technological determinism, and it is in this manner that Plamenatz, Popper, Bober, Carew-Hunt and Acton – to name some of the more prominent representatives of this school – have understood Marxism.[12] The sustaining model for their interpretation is supplied by Marx's claim that 'The hand mill gives you society with the feudal lord; the steam mill society with the industrial capitalist.'[13]

Having reduced 'economic structure' and 'relations of production' to technology, the second basic assumption of Marxism – treated as "Fundamentalism' – can hardly stand careful examination. Can the technology of any society 'change its character more or less independently' of the social, economic and political factors it is supposed to determine? It does not require a profound knowledge of history to see that technological development is invariably a function of the level of science, the laws of a country, the policies of a regime, consumer demand and much else. Thus, technology is *obviously* dependent in numerous important ways on the character and changes occurring in those areas of life which it is supposed to determine, something that the Fundamentalist model rules out as impossible. In levelling this kind of criticism against Marxism then, the claim is not simply that Marx is wrong but that he is ignorant of the elementary facts of social life. Nothing less – except, perhaps, dishonesty in the service of his political aims – can account for such gross misrepresentation.

The third basic assumption of Marxism, according to this interpretation, that development in technology produces corresponding changes in all other activities and institutions, is equally open to question. Again it is not necessary to probe very deeply into history to remark that Christianity and Roman Law, to mention only the most obvious instances, have outlasted the productive technology which is said to be responsible for their appearance. Yet, taken together, these three criticisms – that the elements in Marx's system are inconsistently defined, that what is called the economic factor is vitally affected by the factors it is supposed to determine and that changes in the 'superstructure' do not automatically follow upon developments in the 'base' – make up the great bulk of the attacks levelled against Marx's materialist conception of history.

Having made such criticisms, most of the same commentators readily admit that in his concrete political and economic studies Marx is guilty of none of the errors prefigured in the second and third assumptions of his 'Fundamentalist' theory.[14] That is to say, when dealing with real situations, Marx does not offer the development of technology or any other version of the economic factor as self-generating, but as the result of a cluster of factors coming from every walk of life and from every level of social analysis. Likewise, when concerned with actual events, Marx does not treat political and cultural progress as an automatic response to changes in technology; his explanation is invariably complex, and it is not always economic factors which play the leading role. However, the conclusion which is most often reached is that he is inconsistent, or that he does not know how to use his theories – in short, that Marx is a bad Marxist. Popper has even suggested that Marx does not always take his system seriously.[15]

III

An alternative conclusion is that this interpretation of Marxism as 'Fundamentalism' drawn exclusively from general theoretical statements is erroneous. In order to take this stand, however, it must be possible to interpret Marx's theoretical claims in a manner which is compatible with the kind of social interaction that characterizes his description of real events. In other words, when Marx says 'The mode of production of material life determines the social, political, and intellectual process in general', we must try to understand this claim in a way that allows the latter group of factors to vitally affect the mode of production, and in a way that removes the automatic dependence of the social superstructure on the economic base. We must do this, because this is how Marx used his theories in practise. Engels advised a correspondent who had asked about Marx's materialist conception of history to read *The Eighteenth Brumaire of Louis Bonaparte* as a practical case of Marx's use of this theory.[16] This elementary suggestion has seldom been followed.

Likewise, numerous statements by the elderly Engels on the role of non-economic factors are generally written off as attempts to extricate himself from an untenable position. For example, he calls it a fatuous notion 'that because we deny an independent historical development to the various ideological spheres which play a part in history we also deny them an effect upon history'.[17]

In this light, 'Economic Determinism', an expression Marx himself never applied to his ideas, appears to be a caricature foisted upon Marxism by readers who misread his general claims. And if 'Economic Determinism' is a caricature, then so are 'Historical Materialism' and 'Dialectical Materialism', other popular labels for his views that have not originated with Marx. Essentially, these are limiting expressions which tend to foreclose on what Marx is saying before he has said it, restricting before research is done the number of possibilities inherent in any historical situation. As caricatures, they vary widely and always indicate the writer's specific limitations in coming to grips with the complex reality presented in Marx's works. Engels, particularly in correspondence after Marx's death, does mention 'Historical Materialism', though he usually sets it between quotation marks; it is, after all, someone else's expression.[18] Like Marx, he prefers to speak of 'the materialist conception of history', a much looser construction or, quite simply, 'our view of history'.[19]

I do not believe that thinkers of stature are never inconsistent or incapable of putting their theories to work. But when such a thinker is shown, practically at every turn, to have strayed from his general conception, there is every likelihood that it is we who have misinterpreted him. In political theory, a case which is too well made is often no case at all against the real views of our opponent. The difficulty in exhibiting such normal caution where Marx is concerned is that it is not immediately apparent what interpretation could be given to his theoretical statements which would also account for his workaday descriptions. If the mode of production is said to determine the character and development of other social factors, each of which is regarded as mutually exclusive, then the self-generation of the former and the automatic response to its changes by the latter follow naturally.

What remains to be shown, however, is that Marx treats the components in the initial equation as mutually exclusive. This is the unsupported premise on which the entire logical structure of the interpretation of Marxism as Fundamentalism stands. Rather, all the evidence is that Marx manipulates the size of his factors, alters his classificational boundaries, to suit his changing purposes. An extreme instance of this, which starkly sets out the dimensions of our problem, is his claim that 'religion, family, state, law, morality, science, art, etc.' are 'particular modes of production'.[20] What is left of the Fundamentalist interpretation in the wake of this assertion? And though Engels admits that Marx's definitions are never fixed, this practise, as I have indicated, is generally cited in criticism. That Marx had to obtain consistent, mutually exclusive categories is simply taken for granted.

In most cases, this aim is taken for granted because of the philosophical assumption, made explicit by Acton, that if there is no means of separating out social factors which interact there is no way of testing the validity of a theory which holds that one of them is the 'prime causal agency'.[21] But, it is just what is meant by calling one factor 'primary', or 'basic' or 'determining' that is at question here, and we shall not be able to arrive at a satisfactory answer until we grasp why Marx *did not* clearly separate out his social factors.

Acton has simply turned the real problem around, using what is in effect an ordinary language interpretation of 'primary' to impose upon Marx a common sense conception of social reality. He is saying, 'Given Marx understands "primary" in this way [Acton's way], he must group social phenomena into easily separable units in order that one (or one set of them) can be held to be primary.' If this is Marx's basic conception, then the Fundamentalist interpretation of his theories is correct and all the criticism based on it is valid. However, Marx's 'ambiguous' practise has made an ordinary language interpretation of his key expressions, at the least, highly dubious, and suggests that until we understand his conception of social reality and, consequently, what he could be saying, we shall not be able to comprehend clearly what he is, in fact, saying.

The problem is more serious still. For if Marx often uses the same expression to refer to what we would consider different things and, as he often does, different expressions for what we think of as the same thing, how can we grasp what it is he is referring to on *any* occasion without knowing what lies behind this practise?[22] Preferring to interpret Marx's theories in the light of how he used them, the task is to discover how he could take such liberties not only with the generally accepted classificational boundaries of his subject matter, but with the boundaries he himself seemed to lay down on various occasions. I wish to understand Marx with the aid of his voluminous writings, and not in spite of them. With this declaration of intent, let us return to the original formulation of the problem: Marx's words are like bats. They have meanings, according to Engels, which are not only new and unusual but also inconsistent. This was said to result from viewing 'things and their relations . . . not as fixed but as changing'. It is this conception which made it impossible for him to operate with mutually exclusive social factors. What, then, is this conception?

2. Social relations as subject matter

The only extensive discussion of Marx's concepts (or categories) and the conception of social reality which finds expression in them appears in his unfinished Introduction to the *Critique of Political Economy*. This seminal work, which was first published by Karl Kautsky in 1903, has been unjustly ignored by most Anglo-Saxon writers on Marxism.[1] Here we learn that 'In the study of economic categories, as in the case of every historical and social science, it must be borne in mind that as in reality so in our mind the subject, in this case modern bourgeois society, is given and that the categories are therefore but forms of expression, manifestations of existence, and frequently but one-sided aspects of this subject, this definite society.'[2] This distinction between subject and categories is simple recognition of the fact that our knowledge of the real world is mediated through the construction of concepts in which to think about it; our contact with reality, in so far as we become aware of it, is contact with a conceptualized reality.

What is unusual in Marx's statement is the special relation he posits between categories and society. Instead of being simply a means for describing capitalism (neutral vehicles to carry a partial story), these categories are declared to be 'forms', 'manifestations' and 'aspects' of their own subject matter. Or, as he says elsewhere in this Introduction, the categories of bourgeois society 'serve as the expression of its conditions and the comprehension of its own organization'.[3] That is to say, they express the real conditions necessary for their application, but as meaningful, systematized and understood conditions. This is not merely a matter of categories being limited in what they can be used to describe; the story itself is thought to be somehow part of the very concepts with which it is told. This is evident from Marx's claim that 'The simplest economic category, say, exchange-value, implies the existence of population, population that is engaged in production within determined relations; it also implies the existence of certain types of family, class, or state, etc. It can have no other existence except as an abstract one-sided relation of an already *given concrete and living aggregate*' (my emphasis).[4]

12

One of the more striking results of this approach to language is that not only the content but also the categories are evaluated by Marx in terms of 'true' and 'false'. Thus, in criticizing Proudhon, Marx claims that 'political-economic categories' are 'abstract expressions of the real, transitory, historic, social relations', and they '*only remain true* while these relations exist' (my emphasis).[5] By deciding to work with capitalist categories, Proudhon, according to Marx, cannot completely disassociate himself from the 'truths' which these categories contain. According to the common sense view, only statements can be true or false, and to use this same measure for evaluating concepts seems unwarranted and confused.

Three conclusions stand out from this discussion: that Marx grasped each political–economic concept as a component of society itself, in his words as an 'abstract one-sided relation of an already given concrete and living aggregate'; that it is intimately linked with other social components to form a particular structure; and that this whole, or at least its more significant parts, is expressed in the concept itself. If these conclusions are unclear, it is because the kind of structure they take for granted is still vague and imprecise. To properly understand concepts which convey a particular union, we must be at ease with the *quality* of this unity, that is, with the way its components combine, the properties of such combinations, and the nature of the whole which they constitute. Only by learning how Marx structures the units of his subject matter, only by becoming aware of the quality and range of what is known when he considers he knows anything, will the relations between concepts and reality that have been set out in these conclusions become clear.

II

What is distinctive in Marx's conception of social reality is best approached through the cluster of qualities he ascribes to particular social factors. Taking capital as the example, we find Marx depicting it as 'that kind of property which exploits wage-labor, and which cannot increase except on condition of getting a new supply of wage-labor for fresh exploitation'.[6] What requires emphasis is that the relation between capital and labor is treated here as a function of capital itself, and part of the meaning of 'capital'. This tie is extended to cover the worker as well, where Marx refers to him as 'variable capital'.[7] The capitalist is incorporated into the same whole: 'capital is necessarily at the same time the capitalist . . . the capitalist is contained in the concept of capital'.[8] Elsewhere, Marx asserts that 'the means of production monopolized by a certain section of society', 'the products of laborers turned into independent powers', 'money', 'commodities' and even 'value that sucks up the value creating powers' are also capital.[9] What emerges from these diverse characterizations is a conception of many tied facets, whose sense depends upon the relations Marx believes to exist between its components: property, wage-labor, worker, his product, commodities, means of production, capitalist, money, value (the list can be made longer still).[10]

It is insufficient to accuse Marx of loose and misleading presentation for, as we shall see, all social factors are treated in the same manner. But if it is not incompetent writing, then Marx is offering us a conception of capital in which the factors we generally think of as externally related to it are viewed as co-elements in a single structure.

It is this system-owning quality of capital that he has in mind when he refers to it as a 'definite social relationship'. This conception is contrasted with Ricardo's where capital 'is only distinguishable as "accumulated labor" from "immediate labor" '. In the latter case, where capital 'is something purely material, a mere element in the labor process', Marx claims, 'the relation between labor and capital, wages and profit, can never be developed'.[11] Marx believes he is only able to trace out these connections because they are already contained in his broad conception of capital. If they were not, he would, like Ricardo, draw a blank. *Every factor which enters into Marx's study of capitalism is a 'definite social relationship'*.

III

The relation is the irreducible minimum for all units in Marx's conception of social reality. This is really the nub of our difficulty in understanding Marxism, whose subject matter is not simply society but society conceived of 'relationally'. Capital, labor, value, commodity, etc., are all grasped as relations, containing in themselves, as integral elements of what they are, those parts with which we tend to see them externally tied. Essentially, a change of focus has occurred from viewing independent factors which are related to viewing the particular way in which they are related in each factor, to grasping this tie as part of the meaning conveyed by its concept. This view does not rule out the existence of a core notion for each factor, but treats this core notion itself as a cluster of relations.

According to the common sense view, a social factor is taken to be logically independent of other social factors to which it is related. The ties between them are contingent, rather than necessary; they could be something very different without affecting the vital character of the factors involved, a character which adheres to that part which is thought to be independent of the rest. One can logically conceive, so the argument goes, of any social factor existing without its relations to others. In Marx's view, such relations are internal to each factor (they are ontological relations), so that when an important one alters, the factor itself alters; it becomes something else. Its appearance and/or function has changed sufficiently for it to require a new concept. Thus, for example, if wage-labor disappeared, that is, if the workers' connection to capital radically changed, capital would no longer exist. The opposite, naturally, is also true: Marx declares it a 'tautology' that 'there can no longer be wage-labor when there is no longer any capital'.[12] Max Hirsch is clearly right, therefore, when he points out that if 'capital' is defined as a 'means of exploitation and subjection of the laborer', a machine used by a farmer who owned it would not be capital, but it would be capital if he hired a man to operate it.[13] Rather than an obvious criticism, which is how Hirsch intends it, this paradox merely illustrates the character of capital as a social relation.

In this study, I shall use the term 'relation' in two different senses: first, to refer to the factor itself, as when I call capital a relation, and also as a synonym of 'connection', as in speaking of the relation between different factors. Marx and Engels do the same. Besides calling capital a 'social production relation' (*Verhältnis*), Marx refers to money as a 'relation of production', the mode of production itself as the 'relation in which the productive forces are developed', and the list of such remarks is far from complete.[14] His use of 'relation' as a synonym of 'connection' is more extensive still, with the result that *Verhältnis* probably occurs more frequently than any other expression in Marx's writing, confounding critics and translators alike.[15] It is not entirely satisfying to use 'relation' to convey both meanings but, rather than introduce a new term, I accede to Marx's practise, with this single change: I intend to capitalize 'relation' (henceforth 'Relation') when it refers to a factor, as opposed to the connection between factors, to aid readers in making this important distinction. Besides, such obvious alternatives to 'Relation' as 'structure', 'unit' and 'system' suggest a closed, finished character which is belied by Marx's treatment of real social factors. 'Relation' appeals to me, as it must have to him, as the concept which is better adapted to take account of the changes and uncertainties that constitute so large a part of social life.

I V

The outlook presented here must not be confused with the view that has found great favor among sociologists and others, which holds that social factors are *unintelligible* except in terms of relations. It is important to realize that Marx took the additional step indicated in his claim that society is 'man himself in his social relations'.[16] On one occasion, Marx specifically berates apparent allies who accuse economists of not paying enough attention to the connections between production and distribution. His complaint is that 'this accusation is itself based on the economic conception that distribution exists side by side with production as a self-contained sphere'.[17] Marx's own version of this relationship is presented in such claims as 'Production is . . . at the same time consumption, and consumption is at the same time production.'[18]

For the average social scientist – starting with a conception of factors as logically independent of one another – the conjunction of parts in his analysis is mechanical, an intrusion; it exists only where found and disappears once the investigator's back is turned, having to be explained and justified anew. One result is the endless attempts to account for causality and the accompanying need to distinguish between cause and condition. In such studies, one side of the interaction invariably wins out over the other ('comes first') leading to 'economic determinism' or 'existentialism' or other partial positions.

In Marx's case, all conjunction is organic, intrinsic to the social units with which he is concerned and part of the nature of each; that it exists may be taken for granted. On this view, interaction is, properly speaking, *inner*action (it is 'inner connections' which he claims to study).[19] Of production, distribution, consumption and exchange, Marx declares, 'mutual interaction takes place between the various elements. Such is the case with every organic body'.[20] What Marx calls 'mutual interaction' (or 'reciprocal effect' or 'reciprocal action') is only possible because it occurs within an organic body. This is the case with everything in Marxism, which treats its entire subject matter as 'different sides of one unit'.[21]

It is in this context that we must place Marx's otherwise confusing and confused use of 'cause' and 'determine'. There are not some elements which are related to the factor or event in question as 'causes' (meaning among other things that which does not condition) and others as 'conditions' (meaning among other things that which does not cause). Instead, we find as internally related parts of whatever is said to be the cause or determining agent everything that is said to be a condition, and vice versa. It is this conception which permits Engels to say that the whole of nature has 'caused' life.[22]

In practise, however, 'cause' and 'determine' are generally used to point to the effect produced by any entity in changing one or more of the relations that make up other entities. But as each one develops with the direct and indirect aid of everything else, operating on various levels, to single out any aspect as the determining one can only be a way of emphasizing a particular link in the problem under consideration. Marx is saying that for this factor, in this context, *this* is the influence most worth noting, the relation which will most aid our comprehension of the relevant characteristics.[23]

V

The whole at rest which I have been examining is but a limiting case of the whole in movement, for, in Paul Lafargue's words, Marx's 'highly complicated world' is 'in continual motion'.[24] Change and development are constantly occurring; structure is but a stage in process.

To introduce the temporal dimension into the foregoing analysis, we need only view each social factor as internally related to its own past and future forms, as well as to the past and future forms of surrounding factors. Capital, for Marx, is what capital is, was and will be. He says of money and commodities, 'before the production process they were capital only in intention, in themselves, in their destiny'.[25] It is in this manner, too, that labor is seen in the product it will soon become and the product in the labor it once was. In short, development – no matter how much facelifting occurs – is taken as an attribute of whatever undergoes development.

The present, according to this relational model, becomes part of a continuum stretching from a definable past to a knowable (if not always predictable) future. Tomorrow is today extended. To speak of such a relation between the present and the future within the context of formal logic would indicate belief in a vitalistic principle, divine will or some other metaphysical device. But, here, all social change is conceived of as a coming to be of what potentially is, as the further unfolding of an already existing process, and hence, discoverable by a study of this process taken as a spacial–temporal Relation. The 'destiny' of money is rooted in its existing structure. So is the 'destiny' of any society. What will become of it (or, more accurately, what is likely to become of it) is pieced together by an examination of the forces, patterns and trends that constitute the major existing Relations. It is the result of such research into any particular factor or set of factors that is conveyed by Marx's concept 'law'.[26]

The common sense view recognizes two types of laws: inductive laws, which are generalizations based on the results of empirical research, and deductive laws, which are *a priori* statements about the nature of the world. For the first, evidence is relevant, and the predictions it occasions are never more than probable. For the second, evidence is irrelevant and the predictions occasioned are necessary. Marx's laws possess characteristics that we associate with both of these types.

Like inductive laws, Marx's laws are based on empirical research. Unlike them, however, his laws are not concerned with independent events whose ties with each other and with surrounding circumstances are contingent. Marx says that in political economy 'law is chance'; the elements related have no ties other than those actually uncovered by research.[27] Whereas, for Marx, the relations he discovers are considered already present as real possibilities in the relations which preceded them (they exist there as temporally internal relations).

As regards deductive laws, Marx's laws also deal with the nature of the world, but do so on the basis of evidence, and are forever being modifed by evidence. As a result, they cannot be encapsulated in simple formulae which hold true for all time. Still, strictly speaking, all Marx's laws are tautologies: given these are 'A's' relations, this is what 'A' must become and, in the becoming, 'A' may be said to obey the law of its own development. Such laws express no more necessity than that contained in the particular group of relations for which they are standing in. The very uncertainties in the situation are their uncertainties. Yet, by including within the law all possible developments prefigured by the relevant relations, the law itself may be said to be necessary. All that happens to a factor is the necessary working out of its law. Consequently, rather than coloring Marx's findings in any way, it is his findings which lend these laws their entire character.

The relations bound up in any factor generally make one kind of development more probable than others, and Marx often uses 'law' to refer to this development alone. 'Law' in this sense is the same as 'tendency', and on one occasion, Marx goes as far as to say that all economic laws are tendencies.[28]

VI

Until this point, the discussion has been limited to social factors which are generally recognized as such – capital, labor, class, etc. – though Marx's interpretation of them was shown to be highly unusual. However, in seeking favourable vantage points from which to analyze capitalism, a system contained relationally in each of its parts, Marx sometimes felt obliged to create new parts. This was simply a matter of mentally carving up the whole in a different manner for a particular purpose. The result is, in effect, a new social factor, a new unit in which to think about and refer to society. Perhaps the most important new social unit created in this way is the 'relations of production', the core of which lies in the complex interaction of production, distribution, exchange and consumption. Another is 'surplus-value'. These two Relations occupy a central position in Marx's work.

The novelty of having the relations of production as a subject matter becomes evident when we consider the limited concern of most capitalist economists. The latter are interested in studying (more particularly, in measuring) what goes on in the 'economy', a sector of life artificially separated from other sectors, whose necessary links with human beings as regards both means and results are seldom investigated.

What *kind* of productive activity goes on in a society where people obtain what they want through the exchange of value equivalents? What *kind* of political, cultural, religious, and social life fosters such exchange and is, in turn, fostered by it? These questions are beyond the bounds of relevance established by capitalist economics, but they are well within the boundaries set by Marx. He tells us in *Capital* I, for example, that he wants to examine '*Why* is labor represented by the value of its product and labor-time by the magnitude of that value?'[29] (My emphasis.) This is really a question about how the particular 'economy' which capitalist economists are content to describe came into existence and how it manages to maintain itself. By conceptualizing his subject matter as 'relations of production', as a union of the main processes involved (as a factor centering upon this union), Marx facilitates his efforts to deal with this wide ranging problem. The result, *Capital,* is not properly speaking an economic treatise, but– as many readers have noted – a work on social praxis.

VII

Returning to Marx's discourse, the problem of misinterpretation arises from what might be called his practise of making definitions of all his descriptions. Whatever Marx discovers about any factor, particularly if he considers it to be an essental characteristic, is incorporated into the meaning of its denoting term, becomes a part of its concept. Marx's concepts, then, are meant to convey to us the already structured information they express for him; it is in this way that they acquire a 'truth value' distinct from that of the statements which embody them.[30]

Therefore, whatever Marx understands about his society, including its processes of change and the projections he has made from them, is already contained in each of the major concepts he uses to explain what it is he understands. Such meaning lies heavy on Marx's terms. It is this which allows Marx to equate 'economic categories' with 'historic laws', and which makes 'logic' a synonym for 'law' in Marxism.[31] 'Law' refers to relations in the real world; while 'logic', as Marx ordinarily uses it, refers to these same relations as reflected in the meanings of the relevant concepts.

Marcuse offers the same insight when he claims that Marx's

categories are negative and at the same time positive: they present a negative state of affairs in the light of its positive solution, revealing the true situation in existing society as the prelude to its passing into a new form. All the Marxian concepts extend, as it were, in these two dimensions, the first of which is the complex of given social relations, and the second, the complex of elements inherent in the social reality that make for its transformation into a free social order.[32]

That readers make any sense of Marx's terminology at all suggests that many of the relations he sees in reality correspond, more or less, to our 'common sense' view of the world (which is not much to assume), and that it is these relations which constitute the core meanings of most of his concepts.

Though each of Marx's major concepts has the theoretical capacity to convey the entire analysis made with it, in practise Marx's current interest governs the degree to which the relations bound together in any social factor (and hence the meaning of its covering concept) extended. As Marx moves from one problem to the next, whole new areas inside each social Relation become relevant, and some areas which were relevant in the previous context cease being so. In this way, what was formerly assumed is expressed directly and what was expressed is now assumed. Class, for instance, has a vital role in explaining the state, but only a small part in accounting for exchange, and the size of the Relation, class, in Marx's thought (and the meaning of 'class' in Marx's writing) varies accordingly.

It is this practise which is responsible for what was referred to earlier as Marx's 'manipulation' of classificational boundaries, both those which were generally accepted and those which he himself seemed to lay down elsewhere in his work. Yet, each such restriction of the social whole is merely practical, a means of allowing Marx to get on with his current task. Should he ever want to extend the size of any factor, and hence the meaning of its concept, to its relational limits, he can do so. Thus, we learn, 'Man, much as he may therefore be a particular individual . . . is just as much the totality – the ideal totality – the subjective existence of thought and experienced society present for itself.'[33]

V I I I

If each of Marx's concepts has such breadth (actual or potential), and includes much of what is also expressed by other concepts, how does Marx decide on any given occasion which one to use? Why, for example, call interest (which, for him, is also capital) 'interest' and not 'capital'? This is really the same problem approached from the other side. Whereas before I accepted Marx's nomenclature and tried to find out what he meant, I am now asking – given his broad meaning – why does he offer the names that he does? The unorthodox answer given to the first question has made this second one of special importance.

It may appear that I have only left Marx a nominalist way out, but this is not so. The opposition between the view that the world gives rise to our conceptions and the view that naming is an arbitrary process is, in any case, a false one. The real problem is to discover the various precise ways in which what actually exists, in nature as well as in society, affects the ways we conceive of and label it; and how the latter, in turn, reacts upon what exists, particularly upon what we take to be 'natural' structures. In short, this is a two-way street, and to be content to travel in only one direction is to distort. Marx's own practise in naming takes account of both the real world as it is, and his conceptualization of it which decides (as distinct from determines) what it can be. The former is seen in Marx's acceptance of the core notion of each factor, which is simply what the factor, being what it is, strikes everyone that it is (the idea is of necessity quite vague); and the latter stands out in the decisive importance he attributes to the function of each factor (grasped as any part of its core notion) in the particular sub-system of society which he is examining.

In setting out what can and cannot be called 'fixed capital', Marx says 'it is not a question here of a definition, which things must be made to fit. We are dealing here with definite functions which must be expressed in definite categories'.[34] Thus, capital in

a situation where it functioned as interest would be called 'interest', and vice versa. However, a change in function only results in a new name (as opposed to a descriptive metaphor) if the original factor is actually conceived to be what it is now functioning as. That is, capital can only *act as* or *appear to be* interest and, hence, never really deserve its name unless we are able to conceive of the two as somehow one. This, of course, is just what Marx's relational conception allows him to do. Through its internal ties to everything else, each factor is everything else viewed from this particular angle, and what applies to them necessarily applies to it, taken in this broad sense. Thus, each factor has – in theory – the potential to take the names of others (of whatever applies to them) when it functions as they do, that is, in ways associated with their core notions.

When Marx calls theory a 'material force', or when Engels refers to the state as an 'economic factor', they are misusing words only on our standard.[35] On the basis of the relational conception, theory and state are being given the names of their own facets whose core functions they are performing. Thus, Marx says, in the instance quoted, that theory becomes a material force 'once it gets a hold of men', that is, once it becomes a driving factor in their lives, strongly influencing character and actions. This role is generally performed by a material force, such as the mode of production, but theory can also perform it, and when it does it becomes a 'material force'.

To understand Marx's nomenclature, however, it is not enough to know that naming attaches to function, which in turn is conceived of within a relational whole. The question arises whether the particular function observed is objective (actually present in society) or subjective (there because Marx sees it to be). The answer is that it is both: the functions, according to which Marx ascribes names, exist, but it is also true that they are conceptualized in a manner which allows Marx to take note of them. Other people viewing the same 'raw facts' with another conceptual scheme may not even observe the relation he has chosen to emphasize (this, as we shall see, is the main obstacle to grasping Marx's theory of alienation).

For example, when Marx calls the worker's productive activity 'variable capital', he is labelling a function that only he sees; in this case, because this is how such activity appears 'from the point of view of the process of creating surplus-value', a unit that Marx himself introduced.[36] It is only after we finish reading *Capital* and accept the new concept of surplus-value that 'variable capital' ceases to be an arbitrary name for labor-power. Generally speaking, we understand why Marx has used a particular name to the extent that we are able to grasp the function referred to, which in turn depends on how similar his conception of the relevant factors is to our own.

Marx's concepts, it is clear, have been tailored to fit both his unique vision of capitalism (as Engels says) and his unusual conception of social reality. The great lesson to be drawn from all this is that Marx's concepts are not our own, no matter how much they may appear so. In short, the fact that Marx uses the same words as we do should not mislead us into believing that he has the same concepts. Words are the property of language and are common to all who use this language. Concepts, or ideas about the world which find expression in words (or words in so far as they contain such ideas) are best grasped as the property of the individuals concerned. Expressing what he knows as well as how he knows it, Marx's concepts tell us much more (often), much less (sometimes), and much different (always) than we think they do. Hence Engels' reference to the novel meanings Marx gives to familiar terms.

Moreover, as if this were not enough, the very sense conveyed by Marx's concepts is unstable. What he understands at any given time of the interrelations which make up social reality is reflected in the meanings of the words he uses. But these interrelations are constantly changing, and further, Marx is forever learning more about them through his research. Hence, Engels' pointed warning that we should not expect to find any 'fixed, cut-to-measure, once and for all applicable definitions in Marx's works'.[37]

The lack of definitions (that is, of statements obviously meant as definitions) in Marx's writings has often been belabored, but it should now be clear what difficulty he had in providing them. Viewing the world as devoid of the clear cut classificational boundaries that distinguish the common sense notion, Marx could not keep a definition of one factor from spilling over into everything. For him, any isolating definition is necessarily 'one-sided' and probably misleading. There are critics, such as Sartre, who have accepted

Engels' dictum.[38] More typical, on the other hand, is the reaction of Carew-Hunt who is so convinced of the impossibility of such an approach to meaning that he claims (against the evidence) that Marx does not manipulate language in this way, though his dialectic, according to Carew-Hunt, requires that he do so.[39] Basically unaware of Marx's relational conception, most critics simply cannot take the concepts which are entailed by this conception for what they are.[40]

I X

What emerges from this interpretation is that the problem Marx faces in his exposition is *not* how to link separate parts but how to individuate instrumental units in a social whole which finds expression everywhere. If I am right, the usual approach to understanding what Marx is getting at must be completely reversed: from trying to see the way in which labor produces value, we must accept at the outset a kind of equation between the two (the two social Relations express the same whole – as Marx says, 'Value is labor'), and try instead to see the ways in which they differ.[41] Marx's law of value is concerned with the 'metamorphosis of value', with the various forms it takes in the economy, and not with its production by labor. This, and not what Smith and Ricardo had said before, is the economic theory illustrated in the massive volumes of *Capital*.

So, too, instead of seeking a strict causal tie between the mode of production and other institutions and practises of society which precludes complex social interaction, we must begin by accepting the existence of this interaction and then seek out the ways in which Marx believes that the effects proceeding from the mode of production and other economic factors (narrowly understood) are more important. Such interaction, as we have seen, is a necessary part of each social Relation. This, and not technological determinism, is the conception of history illustrated in *all* Marx's detailed discussions of political and social phenomena. If Marx is at ease with a foot on each side of the fence, it is because, for him, the fence does not exist. In light of this analysis, most of Marx's opponents are guilty of criticizing him for answers to questions he not only did not ask, but – given his relational conception of reality – could not ask. Marx's real questions have been lost in the process; they must be rehabilitated.

3. *The philosophy of internal relations*

Marx's scholarly concern was with capitalism, and in studying this society he naturally operated with *social* Relations, his vocabulary reflecting the real *social* ties which he uncovered. What remains to be explained, however, is how Marx could conceive of social factors as Relations where physical objects are involved. For in his discussions, machines, the real articles produced, the worker's person, etc., are all components of one social Relation or another. We learn, for example, that 'capital is, among other things, also an instrument of production, also past personal labor'.[1] According to the definition given earlier, every such component is itself a Relation. It follows from this that Marx conceives of *things* as Relations. Unless this conclusion can be defended, the interpretation I have offered of social Relations will have to be drastically altered. By drawing together the relevant evidence and tracing the history of the broad philosophical position that underlies Marx's practise, I shall try in this chapter to provide such a defense.

Most modern thinkers would maintain that there cannot be relations without things just as there cannot be things without relations. Things, according to this 'common sense' view, constitute the basic terms of each relation and cannot themselves be reduced to relations. However, this objection only applies to Marx if what he is doing is caricatured as trying to reduce the terms of a relation to that which is said to stand between them. But his is not an attempt to reify 'between' or 'together'. Instead, as we saw in the previous chapter, the sense of 'relation' itself has been extended to cover what is related, so that either term may be taken to express both in their peculiar connection.

No one would deny that things appear and function as they do because of their spacial–temporal ties with other things, including man as a creature with physical and social needs. To conceive of things as Relations is simply to interiorize this interdependence – as we have seen Marx do with social factors – in the thing itself. Thus, the book before me expresses and therefore, on this model, relationally contains everything from the fact that there is a light on in my room to the social practises and institutions of my society which made this particular work possible. The conditions of its existence are taken to be part of what it is, and indicated by the fact that it is just this and nothing else. In the history of ideas, where every new thought is invariably an old one warmed over, this view is generally referred to as the philosophy of internal relations.[2]

There are four kinds of evidence for attributing a philosophy of internal relations to Marx. First, Marx makes statements which place him on the side of those who view things as Relations. He declares, for example, that 'the thing itself is an objective human relation to itself and to man'.[3] Marx also calls man (who, after all, has a body as well as a social significance) the 'assemble [aggregate] of social relations'.[4] Elsewhere, this same creature is said to be 'a natural object, a thing, although a living conscious thing'.[5] Marx can refer to man as a thing as well as an assemble of social relations, because he conceives of each thing as a Relation, in this instance, as the assemble of social relations. Engels' comments are often more explicit still, as when he maintains that 'the atom itself is nothing more than a Relation'.[6]

To be sure, Marx also speaks – particularly when treating the fetishism of commodites – of social relations which are taken for things. However, it is not difficult to interpret these instances as attempts to make a distinction between two kinds of Relations, one of which (in conformity with ordinary usage) he calls 'things'. The view I am proposing does not require that Marx should cease speaking of 'things', only that they should also be grasped as Relations. While statements indicating the existence of things can be interpreted relationally, his statements which present things as Relations cannot as easily be interpreted in a way that accords the former their customary independence.

Second, even if Marx's direct comments on the subject of things as Relations are ambiguous, his treatment of man and nature (or its material components) as Relations with internal ties to one another is not: 'That man's physical and spiritual life is linked to nature means simply that nature is linked to itself.'[7] Likewise, when he declares that man 'is nature' or that his objects 'reside in the nature of his being', the ties to which our attention is drawn are clearly *not* external ones.[8] Rather, the individual is held to be in some kind of union with his object; they are in fact relationally contained in one another, which requires that each be conceived of as a Relation.

The same inner tie is presented from the other end when Marx declares that he views 'the evolution of the economic foundations of society' as a 'process of natural histoɪy', or includes among the forces of nature 'those of man's own nature' along with 'those of so-called nature'.[9] Unless we accord Marx a conception of things as Relations, those comments (of which I have quoted but a few) which reveal man as somehow an extension of nature, and nature as somehow an extension of man can only be understood metaphorically or as poetic utterances.[10]

Third, if we take the position that Marx drew an indelible line between things and social Relations we are left with the task of explaining what kind of interaction he saw in the physical world and how the two worlds of nature and society are related. Does Marx view natural development on the model of cause and effect? He specifically states his opposition to seeking for first causes in economics and religion, where it is the relations in which the so-called first causes stand that still require explanation.[11] In a rare instance where he records the connection he sees between two physical objects, his adherence to a philosophy of internal relations is evident. 'The sun', he says, 'is the object of the plant – an indispensable object to it confirming its life – just as the plant is an object of the sun, being an expression of the life awakening power of the sun, of the sun's objective essential power.'[12] The sun's effect on the plant, which most of us are inclined to treat causally, is considered by Marx to be an 'expression' of the sun itself, a means by which it manifests what it is and, in this way, part of it.

To clarify this, Marx adds that 'A being which does not have its nature outside itself is not a natural being, and plays no part in the system of nature.'[13] Each physical object, by virtue of being a natural object, is more than whatever part of it is apparent or easier to isolate. As natural objects, the sun and the plant have their natures – as Marx puts it – outside themselves, such that the relation between them is conceived as appertaining to each, and is part of the full meaning conveyed by their respective concepts.[14]

It is not only the difficulty of attributing to Marx a causal explanation of physical phenomena but also – as I have indicated

– the problems raised by combining a common sense view of nature with his conception of social relations which argues for his having a philosophy of internal relations. Sidney Hook offers the arresting case of a critic who makes a clean break between Marx's social relations, of which he gives one of the better accounts, and the objects of nature. Hook claims 'the Marxian totality is social and limited by other totalities', and that 'For Marx there are wholes not the whole'.[15] This raises the practical problem of how to explain the effect of the physical world on social phenomena. For example, how are we to interpret Marx's claim that the mode of production determines what occurs in other social sectors when the mode of production includes machines and factories (physical objects) as well as the way people use these objects and cooperate among themselves (social relations)? The former suggests a causal interpretation of this claim, for this is the kind of explanation into which physical objects generally enter; while the latter suggests one that emphasizes reciprocal action between the parts, for this is the kind of explanation into which social relations generally enter.[16]

In *From Hegel to Marx* and *Towards the Understanding of Karl Marx* Hook wavers between these two incompatible explanatory models. Under pressure to choose, in his most recent work, *Marx and the Marxists,* he has finally settled on a causal account, and Marx's conception of history is declared a 'monistic theory' with the mode of production held solely responsible for all major social developments.[17] In the last analysis, the division of Marxism into separate wholes simply did not allow Hook to use his own considerable insights into Marx's social relations to explain the complex interaction which he knows is there. This is not to dismiss the fact that for a variety of reasons Hook's views on Marxism have changed over the years. I have simply indicated the position taken in his early works which allowed for and even rendered likely this later development.

Fourth and last, I believe I am justified in ascribing a philosophy of internal relations to Marx because it would have required a total break with the philosophical tradition in which he was nourished for this not to be so. Hegel, Leibniz and Spinoza had all sought for the meanings of things and/or of the terms which characterize them in their relations inside the whole (variously referred to as 'substance', 'nature', 'God', etc); and, judging by his voluminous notebooks, there are thinkers the young Marx studied with the greatest care.[18]

It is chiefly because the philosophy of internal relations is currently held in such disrepute that it is assumed Marx could not have accepted it, and, consequently, that the burden of proof rests upon me to show that he did. In presenting evidence from Marx's writings which places him in this tradition I have agreed to play the role of prosecutor. I should now like to suggest, however, that if Marx inherited this conception from his immediate predecessors, the burden of proof rests with those who believe he discarded it; in which case we are also entitled to know the conception of things and social factors with which he replaced it – an atomist outlook, such as is implied in the interpretation of Marxism as 'Fundamentalism', or something completely different for which no name exists as Althusser claims, or what? In the remainder of this chapter (and Appendix I) I shall briefly sketch the history of the philosophy of internal relations, and respond to some of the 'devastating' criticisms which have kept writers of all persuasions from even taking seriously the possibility that Marx might have shared this view.

II

The philosophy of internal relations, which can be traced as far back as the early Greek philosopher Parmenides, first came into prominence in the modern period in the work of Spinoza. Spinoza's own version of this philosophy is constructed upon Aristotle's definition of 'substance' as that which is capable of independent existence. Since only nature taken as a whole is capable of independent existence, it is, according to this view, the sole substance. It is such a unified nature which Spinoza labels 'God'. All components of this single substance, whether material things or thoughts, are conceived of as its transient forms, as its 'modes' of being and, hence, expressive of the sum of interrelations which determines their individual characters. For Spinoza, who accents the totality, the parts are strictly adjectival.[19]

Leibniz, on the other hand, puts his emphasis on the parts and devotes little attention to the whole he sees reflected in each. Not one, but an infinite number of substances exist for him. By asserting that these substances, which he calls 'monads', have individual qualities but no extension, Leibniz is refusing to treat what we ordinarily take to be things as the basic units of reality. However we understand the queer mental construct which is Leibniz's monad, what stands out clearly from his account is the relational tie that exists between each one and the universe. Hence, he can claim, 'there is no term so absolute or so detached that it doesn't enclose relations and the perfect analysis of which doesn't lead to other things and even to everything else, so that one could say that relative terms mark expressly the configuration which they contain'.[20]

Coming a century later, Hegel was perhaps the first to work through the main implications of the philosophy of internal relations and to construct in some detail the total system which it implied. In this he was aided – as is often the case in philosophy – by the character of the impasse bequeathed to him by his immediate predecessor, Kant. The latter had convincingly demonstrated that things are no more than the qualities by which we know them, but found such a conclusion unacceptable. Determined to believe that what appears is something more than (really, for him, something behind) what actually strikes our senses, Kant invented the nebulous 'thing in itself' which remains the same through all changes in the entity.

Hegel exhibited less timidity before Kant's first conclusion, that things dissolve upon inspection into their qualities, but considered that the decisive task is to show how this conclusion must be understood. Setting aside for the moment the idealistic content of Hegel's philosophy, his main contribution consists of providing the context of the whole, or 'Absolute', in which to place both Kant's problem and answer. Thus, for Hegel, the thing under examination is not just the sum of its qualities but, through the links these qualities (individually or together in the thing) have with the rest of nature, it is also a particular expression of the whole. To a great extent, the distinctiveness of Hegel's system lies in the various means used to maintain our awareness of the whole while he sets about distinguishing between its parts. His formidable vocabulary receives most of its character from this task. For example, when Hegel refers to things as 'determinations', 'moments' or 'phenomena', he means to suggest something partial and unfinished, something whose full analysis requires that it be conceived of as including far more (both in space and through time) than is immediately apparent.

In establishing the identity of each thing in its relation to the whole, as a mode of expression of the Absolute, Hegel altered the notion of identity used by Kant and of truth itself. Mathematical equality ($1 = 1$) is replaced as the model for comprehending identity by what may be called 'relational equality', where the entity in question is considered identical with the whole that it relationally expresses. For Hegel, 'Self-relation in essence is the form of identity', where 'essence' refers to just such extended relations.[21] However, identity in this sense is clearly a matter of degree; small, simple things possess less identity with the whole than large, complex ones. For most modern philosophers, this proposition is manifestly absurd, but Hegel not only embraces it but uses it as a central thesis on which to construct other notions.

Thus, he maintains that truth 'is the whole'.[22] If things are more or less identical with the whole that they express, then what can be said about them is more or less true, depending on how much of what can be truly said of the whole is said about them. Each thing being relationally identical with the whole, all that is true of the latter is its entire truth; and everything short of that – which means all that we say about particular things (determinations, moments, etc.) – is partial truth. Hegel himself registers the practical effect of this interpretation for his phenomenological undertaking when he declares that knowledge 'can only be set forth fully . . . in the form of system'.[23] To state what is known about any one thing is to describe the system in which it exists; it is to present, as Hegel invariably did, each part as a facet of the whole. Returning to Kant's dilemma, Hegel, while denying the existence of a 'thing in itself' behind observed reality, affirms that through their interrelations things are more than they appear.

Is this the aspect of Hegel's philosophy which Marx disparaged as idealist? I think not. Hegel constructed the framework described here in order to treat ideas, characterizing what I have called the 'whole' as 'Absolute Idea' or 'Reason'. Marx's criticism is always directed against how Hegel chose to apply this framework and his preferred subject matter, and *never* against the relational quality of his units or the fact of system which this entails.[24] Essentially, his complaint is that having produced the category of 'Absolute Idea' from the real world by generalizing from the thinking of living men, Hegel produces the real world, the actual thoughts of men, out of this category. Individual ideas are given a mystical significance by representing them as moments in the development of a generalization which they themselves have given rise to.

After reversing the real relation between ideas and their concept, Hegel is led to reverse the real relation between ideas and nature – it is impossible for nature to effect the immanent unfolding of what is absolute. There is nothing left for the material world to be but an externalization and profanation of what people think about it. Without ever stating explicitly that ideas create matter (there has been considerable confusion over this point), by presenting real developments as following upon and reflecting what occurs in the realm of ideas, this is the general impression that Hegel conveys. Marx pinpoints his error as that of 'considering the real as the result of self-coordinating, self-absorbed, and spontaneously operating thought'.[25] There is no contradiction between opposing the role Hegel gives to ideas and their concept and accepting his relational views. Feuerbach – from whom Marx derived much of his criticism of Hegel – did just this.[26] And, indeed, Marx's silence on Hegel's relational conception, while criticizing so much of what he wrote, speaks eloquently in favor of this interpretation.[27]

Marx's philosophical rebellion began with his refusal to accept the independent development of ideas, a refusal in which he was by no means unique. In his case, this led to study which showed that social change generally preceded Hegel's vaunted history of ideas. He concluded that it was just these 'material' relations, relegated by Hegel to the backside facets of all pervasive thesis, which required the closest investigation in order to comprehend both ideas and the real world. What has been insufficiently recognized, however, is that in stressing social factors Marx does not dispense with the broad philosophy of internal relations in which he was initially introduced to them. Naturally, a new focus of interest as well as the real ties he uncovers in research required the adoption of some fresh concepts, but they too were incorporated into this relational scheme.

It is hardly remarkable (though seldom remarked upon) that whenever any system-owning attribute of a factor is at question, Marx generally relies on Hegel's vocabulary. 'Identity', 'abstract', 'essence' and 'concrete', for example, are all used by Marx, as they were by Hegel, to mark some aspect of the whole in the part, to refer to an ontological and not a logical relation. These terms which appear in rich profusion throughout Marx's writings – late as well as early – cannot be consistently interpreted in any other way. Likewise, it is clear that the unusual approach to meaning which was attributed earlier to both these thinkers is a necessary result of the relational conception they shared.

One of the more significant effects of Marx's refusal to countenance the independent development of ideas is that the concept of the whole, which in the form of Absolute Idea served Hegel as the source of its particular expressions, no longer has a role to play in the system it represents. It remains the sum of all relations and that which is expressed in each, but does not help, as a distinct concept, in elucidating any one of them. The real world is too complex, diffuse and unclear in its detail to be a help in explaining any event that goes on in it. One result is that whereas Hegel offers a large assortment of terms in which he attempts to capture the whole – 'Absolute Idea', 'Spirit', 'God', 'Universal', 'Truth' – Marx does not offer any (unless we choose to consider 'history' in this light). It is likely that this difference is at least partly responsible for the belief that Marx did not hold a philosophy of internal relations. However, what essentially characterizes this view is the internal nature of the tie between the parts (whatever parts), and not the function of the whole *qua* whole in clarifying these ties. In this same tradition, some thinkers, such as Spinoza and Hegel, devote considerable attention to what they take to be the totality, and others, such as Leibniz and Marx, do not.

Naturally the conception of change and development embedded in Marx's 'materialistic' philosophy of internal relations differs significantly from its counterpart in Hegel's philosophy. The reconciliation that Hegel foresaw as the eventual outcome of history was the World Spirit becoming conscious of itself. In this context, development could only be the self-discovery of the greater ideational form of whatever is developing. The individual himself is reduced to passivity, except in so far as he partakes in his thoughts of the understanding that properly belongs to the World Spirit.

Even before Marx, the school of Young Hegelians led by Bruno Bauer replaced Hegel's World Spirit as subject with man. In the early works of this group, reconciliation was understood, however imprecisely, in terms of revolutionary activity. Disappointed by the failure of the Radical movement, they adopted by 1843 the pose of

'Critical Criticism' for which they are better known, holding that reconciliation occurs through 'right interpretation', through people coming to understand the world.[28] Marx, who was a close friend of Bauer's during his student days in Berlin, developed the Young Hegelians' early perspective: if man is the subject, the way to reconcile himself with the world, now understood as his object (actual or potential), is actively to change it. Change becomes a matter of man transforming his existence. From being a passive observer of development, as in Hegel, the individual has become the actor whose daily life brings it about.

Even from this brief outline, it is apparent that Marx's Hegelian heritage is too complex to allow simple characterization. Hegel never ceased being important for Marx, as Lenin, for example, perceived when he wrote in his notebook in 1914, 'It is impossible completely to understand Marx's *Capital,* and especially its first chapters, without having thoroughly studied and understood the whole of Hegel's *Logic.* Consequently, half a century later none of the Marxists understood Marx.'[29] To those who argue that Marx made his break with Hegel, in 1842, 1844 or 1848, my reply is that there was no such break. This does not mean that I would like to join the ranks of critics who maintain that Marx was a Hegelian, with its connotations of idealist bias, foreshadowed behavior and metaphysical posturing. In my opinion, the choice offered by these two positions is not the real one. If by 'theory' we mean – as I think we should – an explanation in general terms of particular events or phenomena, it is doubtful whether Marx in any period of his life, going back to university days, ever agreed with any of Hegel's theories, which gave to the World Spirit and ideas generally a role that he found unacceptable.[30] However, as regards the epistemological decision concerning the form in which any and all subject matter is considered, Marx never wavered from the relational conception bequeathed to him by Hegel.*

Of what then does Marx's movement away from Hegel, which practically all writers on this subject have noted, consist? If we rule

---

* Most discussions of the link between Hegel and Marx center around the dialectic, a notion I have thus far studiously avoided. This is not because I disagree. On the contrary, in the philosophy of internal relations I have isolated a central facet of Hegel's and Marx's dialectic. However, it is only by clarifying this facet that a full and fruitful discussion of other elements in the dialectic becomes possible. (See below, Chapters 5 and 6.)

out Hegel's concrete theories (which Marx always rejected) and
the philosophy of internal relations (which he always accepted),
this development could only involve the meaning of the concepts
Marx borrowed as well as those new ones he introduced. By transferring his attention to the real world Marx instills the concepts
taken from Hegel with fresh meaning while removing their idealistic content. This upheaval was not accomplished in a moment; it
had to be worked out, and this took time.

Likewise, by progressively shifting his main area of concern
from philosophy to politics and then to economics, the information
and ties Marx uncovered became parts – and sometimes the major
part – of the sense conveyed by these same concepts. I have
already noted that the meanings of Marx's concepts were extended
through his research, and that their particular denotations were
determined by what was relevant to the problem under consideration. But Marx's research never ceased, and new problems were
constantly arising out of actual events and his study of them. It is
in the developing meanings of Marx's concepts, which reacted upon
his system but left its relational features intact, that we can best
observe his growing estrangement from Hegel. The character of
this *evolution,* which began when Marx the student read Hegel and
registered his first uncertainties, is seriously distorted by any talk of
'breaks' and even of 'stages' and 'periods'.

III

Marx never dealt with the special problems raised by the materialist content he gave to the philosophy of internal relations. No doubt
this would have been part of the work he wanted to do on Hegel,
but the pressing claims of his social and economic studies and of
political activity never allowed him to begin. Provided that he
could successfully operate with his relational view, he gave low
priority to its elaboration and defense. This task was undertaken to
some degree by Engels, particularly in his writings on the physical
sciences, but more directly by the German tanner, Joseph Dietzgen.
'Here is our philosopher,' Marx said on introducing Dietzgen to the
Hague Congress of the First International.[31] Yet, despite further
eulogies by Engels, Dietzgen's work remains relatively little known,
especially in the non-communist countries.[32] However, Dietzgen's

views provide a necessary supplement to Marx's own. The relationship between these two thinkers is clearly set out by Anton Pannekoek, who claims that Marx demonstrated how ideas 'are produced
by the surrounding world', while Dietzgen showed 'how the impressions of the surrounding world are transformed into ideas'.[33]

Mindful of the dangers of using what one thinker says to support
an interpretation of another, I shall limit my comments to features
which Marx could not have missed in praising Dietzgen's work.
Like Hegel, Dietzgen affirms that the existence of any thing is manifested through qualities which are its relations to other things.
Hence, 'Any thing that is torn out of its contextual relations ceases
to exist'.[34] So, too, Dietzgen declares – in almost the same words
as Hegel – 'The universal is the truth,' meaning that the full truth
about any one thing includes (because of its internal relations) the
truth about everything.[35] But unlike Hegel – and Marx too – who
proceeds from these foundations to an investigation of the whole in
each part, Dietzgen's inquiry is directed toward how such parts get
established in the first place. For Hegel's and Marx's approach suggests that the preliminary problem of deciding which units of the
whole to treat as parts has already been solved. Yet, it may legitimately be asked whether the unity posited by this conception does
not preclude the very existence of those separate structures in which
they claim to have caught sight of this unity. This is essentially the
problem of individuation, and it constitutes a major stumbling
block for any philosophy of internal relations.

Dietzgen's contribution to the solution of this problem is his
account of what can occur in individuation and what does occur.
He asks, 'Where do we find any practical unit outside of our
abstract conceptions? Two halves, four fourths, eight eighths, or an
infinite number of separate parts form the material out of which the
mind fashions the mathematical unit. This book, its leaves, its letters, or their parts – are they units? Where do I begin and where do
I stop?'[36] His answer is that the real world is composed of an
infinite number of sense perceptible qualities whose interdependence makes them a single whole. If we began by applying the relational conception to social factors and then to things, we see now
that it can also apply to qualities. Because the process of linking up
qualities may be stopped at any point between the individual quality and the whole, the ways of dividing up the latter into distinct

parts called 'things' is endless. One result is that what appears as a thing here may be taken as an attribute of some other thing there. Every quality can be conceived of as a thing, and every thing as a quality; it all depends where the line is drawn. So much for what is possible.[37]

What actually occurs, that is the construction of units of a *particular* size and kind out of the 'formless multiplicity' presented to our senses, is the work of the human mind. In Dietzgen's words, 'the absolutely relative and transient forms of the sensual world serve as raw material for our brain activity, in order through abstraction of the general or like characteristics, to become systematized, classified or ordered for our consciousness'.[38] The forms in which the world appears to our senses are 'relative' and 'transient', but they are also said to possess the 'like characteristics' which allow us to generalize from them. 'The world of the mind', we learn, finds 'its material, its premise, its proof, its beginning, and its boundary, in sensual reality.'[39] In this reality, like qualities give rise to a single conception because they are, in fact, alike. This is responsible, too, for the wide agreement in the use of concepts, particularly of those which refer to physical objects. Yet, it is only when we supply these similar qualities with a concept that they become a distinct entity, and can be considered separately from the vast interconnection in which they reside.

According to Dietzgen, therefore, the whole is revealed in certain standard parts (in which some thinkers have sought to re-establish the relations of the whole), because these *are* the parts in which human beings through conceptualization have actually fragmented the whole. The theoretical problem of individuation is successfully resolved by people in their daily practise. The fact that they do not see what they are doing as individuating parts from an interconnected whole is, of course, another question and one with which Dietzgen does not concern himself. He is content to make the point that, operating with real sense material, it is the conceptualizing activity of people that gives the world the *particular* 'things' which these same people see in it. Even mind, we learn, results from abstracting certain common qualities out of real experiences of thinking; they become something apart when we consider them as 'Mind'.[40]

Dietzgen's practical answer to the problem of individuation suggests how structures can exist within a philosophy of internal relations, something which Althusser for one has declared impossible.[41] Yet, if individuation is not an arbitrary act but one governed by broad similarities existing in nature itself, there is a necessary, if vague, correlation between such natural similarities and the structures conveyed by our concepts. This is how the study of any conceptual scheme, whether based on a philosophy of internal relations or not, teaches us something about the real world (unfortunately, this cannot be pressed – as many insist on doing – beyond what is common to all conceptual schemes). That Marx, through his study of capitalism, came to stress certain social relations as more important does not in any way conflict with his conception of each part as relationally containing its ties of dependence to everything else. The fact that some ties are preferred and may, for certain purposes, be viewed as forming a structure is no more surprising than any other act of individuation (conceptualization) based on real similarities.

The significant service Dietzgen renders Marx is to show how a proper balance can be reached on a relational view between accepting the reality of the external world (including, too, the general trustworthiness of sense perception) and holding that the conceptual activity of human thought is responsible for the *precise* forms in which we grasp the world. Marx's support for Dietzgen and, more so, his own practise in conceptualizing new social units show clearly that he accepted such a balance. Yet, by stressing the first part (in criticism of his idealist opponents) and neglecting to develop the second, he left his epistemology open to misinterpretation as a kind of 'naive realism'; and it is this belief, as we saw, that lies behind the widespread, mistaken use of ordinary language criteria to understand his concepts.[42]

IV

The line of reasoning which I have followed so far in this work may be summarized as follows: either Marx means what he seems to (what common sense and ordinary language strongly suggest he means) or he does not. If he does, the interpretation of his theories as Fundamentalism is inescapable, and Marx is not only guilty of ridiculous exaggeration but of a gross ignorance of history and the simplest facts of economic life. Furthermore, he frequently wrote sentences which are utter nonsense, and was wise enough to avoid his own theories when describing any concrete situation. The attempt by some 'vulgar' Marxists to defend the master while accepting this Fundamentalist interpretation is vulnerable at every point.

If Marx did not mean what we ordinarily mean in using the same terms, it is incumbent upon those who take this view to offer not only an alternative interpretation but also another basis for their interpretation than common sense. It is not enough to claim that words in Marxism have unusual meanings (no matter what we take them to be) without making clear how Marx could use words in this way. In undertaking the latter task, I followed a thread leading from Marx's *actual* use of concepts to the way in which he referred to concepts, his view of them as social components, his treatment of social components as Relations, his use of Relations as meanings and, finally, to his belief in a philosophy of internal relations which served as the necessary framework for these practises.

Besides placing Marx in this tradition, I have also tried to make the point that the relational conception shared by such thinkers as Spinoza, Leibniz, Hegel and Marx cannot be rejected out of hand. Yet, holding that it can be defended is not quite the same as defending it. This is an important distinction, and it is one readers should bear in mind in going through the appendix on criticisms of this view.* Only after examining the role the relational conception plays in some of Marx's theories, have I tried to offer an evaluation of it.

---

* Those who wish to pursue this discussion further should see the two appendixes on the philosophy of internal relations at the end of the book.

4. *Is there a Marxian ethic?*

I

The question Marx set out to answer in *Capital* is 'Why is labor represented by the value of its product and labor-time by the magnitude of that value?'[1] If Marx had succeeded in writing the work he planned to do on ethics, I believe the question which would have occupied most of his attention is 'Why are approval and condemnation represented in our society as value judgements?' Marx's critique of the capitalist economy is essentially an explanation of how existing forms of production, distribution, exchange and consumption arose, and how they are dependent on one another and on the character of human activity and achievement in areas far removed from the economy proper. Any critique of ethics would likewise have concentrated on showing how the distinctive forms of our ethical life, such as treating approval and disapproval as value judgements, are internally related to the whole social fabric out of which they arose. Why is this aspect of reality organized in this manner, into these forms?

Such an approach is already apparent in some of Marx's brief comments on this subject. He says, for example, that in bourgeois ethics speaking and loving lose their characteristic significance and 'are interpreted as expressions and manifestations of a third artificially introduced Relation, the Relation of utility'. According to Marx, 'something is demanded of the individual's power or capacity to do anything which is a foreign product, a Relation determined by social conditions – and this is the utility Relation'.[2] In short, a social relation has become a thing in the form of a principle, and moreover a thing which exerts important influence over people's thinking and action.

Unfortunately, this approach to the problem of ethics has received little attention from Marxist scholars. Instead, they have generally been content to elaborate on the following claims: '(1) moral values change; (2) they change in accordance with society's productive forces and its economic relations; and (3) the dominant moral values at any given time are those of the dominant economic class'.[3] As part of this case, concepts such as 'good', 'right'

41

and 'justice' are shown to derive their very meaning from the conditions of life and corresponding interests of the men who use them.[4]

One result of avoiding the larger question of why acts of approval and condemnation in capitalist society appear as value judgements, as deductions from absolute principles, is that Marx's own acts of approval and condemnation defy easy classification. Without wishing to probe too deeply into what is a vast and growing subject, the unorthodox position taken in the last two chapters requires some clarification of what have been called 'value judgements' in Marx's own works. Is there a Marxian ethic, no doubt different from other ethical systems in what it is based on and in what it advocates but constructed like them and performing the same general function? The debate on this subject has been badly marred by the existence of several different (and not always recognized) standards for deciding. Depending on which one or few are chosen, Marx may be taken as being, or not being, or both being and not being an ethical thinker. For example, if we are asking whether Marx considered he had ethical views and/or used such stock ethical terms as 'good', 'bad', 'evil', 'value judgement', etc., clearly the answer is that Marx is not an ethical thinker. We come quickly to the same conclusion if our standard is whether Marx is moralizing, that is concerned with scolding and praising as ends in themselves.

On the other hand, if we are asking whether Marx expresses feelings of approval and disapproval in his works, the answer can only be that Marx is an ethical thinker. The same answer applies if the standard is whether Marx takes sides with one of the classes he is describing, and again, if it is a matter of whether he uses his writings to incite people to act. But perhaps the most important standard that has been used concerns the character of Marx's own personal commitment. Is Marx motivated, it is asked, by some idea of the 'good'? Phrased in this manner, once more I am inclined to respond – though with some hesitation – that Marx is an ethical thinker. However, unlike most writers who adopt this position, I find it difficult to decide just what is his idea of the 'good'. Is Marx's morality a matter of defending the interests of the proletariat, whom he thinks of as 'the hardest working and most miserable class'?[5] Does he believe that whatever contributes to their interests is 'good' and whatever harms them is 'bad'? Or is humanity the cause Marx believes he must serve? Lafargue recounts Marx's statement that scientists should 'put their knowledge to the service of humanity'.[6]

There are still third and fourth possibilities (among the more plausible interpretations), which I shall treat as one – as do most writers who offer them. Is it communist society and the human fulfillment which occurs there that Marx regards as 'good' and 'just'? An affirmative reply has recently been given by Charles Taylor who claims that 'Marxism has a definite standard of value, of higher and lower . . . The basis of this standard of value lies in the teleological notion of human nature: a stage or form of society is higher than another because it involves a greater realization of human goals.'[7] My own difficulty with all these questions is not that I find it hard to answer 'yes', but that I find it hard to answer 'no' to any of them. In other words, if Marx's theories – including too his statements of approval and disapproval, his siding with the proletariat, and his incitements to action – rest on some prior moral commitment, I believe that this commitment can be stated equally well in terms of working class interests, humanity, communism and human fulfillment. With this admission, however, where have we arrived? We have simply arrived back at the theories from which we had originally set out. That is, once what is taken to be the 'good' involves us with so many factors, the relations between these factors needs to be explained, and the explanation situates us within the very theories from which we thought to stand apart. What is the link, for example, between serving working class interests and serving humanity, and between either, or both, and the social and human achievements of communism? In answering such questions one must offer the very theories on man and society which, on this model, are supposed to be the *results* of Marx's ethical views.

There is still another objection to ascribing an ethic to Marx on the basis of his commitment to human fulfillment or any of the other goals listed. This is that it is easily mistaken for a description of what Marx actually and daily does, rather than a way of viewing his work. Neither Taylor nor Maximilien Rubel, who takes a similar position, sees Marx measuring each new question as it comes up alongside an absolute standard and deciding which position to take accordingly.[8] Yet, both men have been misunderstood in this way.

This misunderstanding arises because what is called 'ethics' is generally taken to involve a conscious choice; to act on the basis of a principle, under any guise, is to decide to do so. An ethic assumes that for each question studied there was a period before the standard was applied when one's attitude was neutral, or at least less certain than afterwards; and also that there is a possibility that one could have chosen otherwise.

Robert Tucker rightly remarks that ethical inquiry (and hence ethics) is only possible on the basis of a suspended commitment. But Marx never suspends his commitments; nor does he ever consciously choose to approve or disapprove; nor does it make any sense to say of the matters he studied that he might have judged otherwise. Tucker's conclusion is that Marx is not an ethical, but a religious thinker with a 'vision of the world as an arena of conflict between good and evil forces'.[9] However, if expressing approval and favoring certain goals are insufficient grounds for ascribing an ethics to Marx, his conception of class struggle coupled with his vision of the future society are hardly enough to burden him with a religion. But if Tucker is unlucky in the alternative he offers, his criticism of attempts to treat Marxism as an ethical theory or as the product of an ethical theory remains valid.

The foregoing remarks may be summarized as follows: all ethical systems, that is all those ways of thinking which are generally accepted as such, have a basis for judgement which lies outside that which is to be judged. This results in a suspended commitment until the 'facts' have been gathered and their relation to the standard for judgement clarified. The evaluation, when it comes, is a matter of conscious choice. Our problem then reduces itself to this: do we want to say of Marxism, where none of these things apply, that it either is or contains an ethical theory? One might, but then the limited sense in which this claim is meant would have to be made explicit.[10]

II

I prefer to say that Marx did not have an ethical theory. But how then to explain the approval and disapproval which he expresses in his works, the fact that he sided with the proletariat and incited them to overthrow the system? How, too, it may be asked, do I account for his attachment to the cause of humanity and to the ideas of communism and human fulfillment? In asking such questions, however, one must be careful not to assume at the outset the form the answer must take. For this is what happens if one is saying, 'Here are two worlds, facts and values; how do you link them?' But to accept that reality is halved in this way is to admit failure from the start. On the contrary, the relational conception which was discussed in the last two chapters required that Marx consider what was known, advocated, condemned or done by everyone, himself included, as internally related. Every facet of the real world, and people's actions and thoughts as elements in it, are mutually dependent on each other for what they are, and must be understood accordingly.

The logical distinction which is said to exist between facts and values is founded on the belief that it is possible to conceive of one without the other. Given a particular fact, the argument runs, one may without contradiction attach any value to it. The fact itself does not entail a specific value. Historically the view that moral beliefs are contingent has tended to go along with the view that they are also arbitrary. On this model, all judgement depends in the last instance on the independent set of values which each individual, for reasons best known to himself, brings to the situation. The ethical premiss is not only a final arbiter but a mysterious one, defying sociological and even psychological analysis. Though some recent defenders of orthodoxy have sought to muddle the distinction between fact and value with talk of 'context', 'function', 'real reference', 'predisposition', etc., the logical line drawn in conception remains. Yet, if one cannot conceive of anything one chooses to call a fact (because it is an open ended relation) without bringing in evaluative elements (and vice versa), the very problem orthodox thinkers have set out to answer cannot be posed.

Moreover, on Marx's view, the real judgements which are made in any situation are a function of that situation and the particular individuals active in it. Thus, the very notion that it is logically permissible to take any attitude toward a given 'fact' is itself a judgement inherent in the circumstances out of which it emerges. Rather than being logically independent of what is, any choice – as well as the idea that one has a choice – is linked by innumerable threads to the real world, including the life, class interests, and character of the person acting. Judgements can never be severed, neither practically nor logically, from their contexts and the number of real alternatives which they allow. In this perspective, what is called the fact–value distinction appears as a form of self-deception, an attempt to deny what has already been done by claiming that it could not have been done or still remains to do.

Marx would not have denied that the statements 'This is what exists' and 'What exists is good' or 'This is what should exist', mark some distinction, but he would not have called it one of fact and value. If we define 'fact' as a statement of something known to have happened or knowable, and 'value' as that property in anything for which we esteem or condemn it, then he would maintain that in knowing something, certainly in knowing it well, we already either esteem or condemn it. As man is a creature of needs and purposes, however much they may vary for different people, it could not be otherwise. Because everything we know (whether in its immediacy or in some degree of extension through conditions and results) bears some relation to our needs and purposes, there is nothing we know toward which we do not have attitudes, either for, against or indifferent.

Likewise, our 'values' are all attached to what we take to be the 'facts', and could not be what they are apart from them. It is not simply that the 'facts' affect our 'values', and our 'values' affect what we take to be the 'facts' – both respectable common sense positions – but that, in any given case, each includes the other and is part of what is meant by the other's concept. In these circumstances, to try to split their union into logically distinct halves is to distort their real character.

Followers of Marx have always known that what people approve or condemn can only be understood through a deep-going social analysis, particularly of their needs and interests as members of a class. What emerges from the foregoing is that the forms in which approval and condemnation appear – like setting up absolute principles or values – must be understood through the same kind of analysis. This is not the place to undertake such an analysis, but it may be useful to sketch its broad outlines. The attempt to establish values which apply equally to everyone results, to a large extent, from the need to defuse growing class conflict arising from incompatible interests in a class-ridden society. To apply values equally is to abstract from the unequal conditions in which people live and the incompatible interests that result. The main effort of capitalist ideology has always been directed to dismissing or playing down this incompatibility. The abstractions with which such ideology abounds are so many attempts to sever the class-affected 'facts' from the judgements and actions that ordinarily follow upon their comprehension.

Marx goes so far as to suggest that the fact—value distinction is itself a symptom of man's alienation in modern capitalist society: 'It stems from the very nature of estrangement that each sphere applies to men a different and opposite yardstick – ethics one and political economy another.'[11] A chief characteristic of alienation, as we shall learn, is the separation of what does not allow separation without distortion. The organic unity of reality has been exchanged for distinct spheres of activity whose interrelations in the social whole can no longer be ascertained. Removed from their real context, the individual's relations with nature and society, taken one at a time, appear other than they are. As part of this process, many, often contradictory yardsticks for measuring achievement come into existence for different areas of life, making all broad plans of reform seem 'illogical' or 'irrational' in some respect or other. In this context, it would appear that altogether too much attention has been paid to the biased and false message in capitalist ideology and too little to what is predisposed in the forms of thought themselves, to the class advantage contained in accepted rules of thinking. For any attempt to universalize a moral code, whatever its content, by undercutting the reality of class conflict only succeeds in serving capitalist ends.

As far as Marx's own work is concerned, those remarks which strike us as being an evaluative nature are internally related facets of all he says and knows, which in turn are internally tied to his life and all surrounding circumstances – not as an exception, but because everything in the world is related in this way. However, being conscious of this, Marx integrated his remarks of approval and disapproval more closely into his system then have most other thinkers, making any surgical division into facts and values so much more destructive of his meaning. For example, Marx claims that when a communist stands in front of 'a crowd of scrofulous, overworked and consumptive starvelings', he sees 'the necessity, and at the same time the condition, of a transformation both of industry and of the social structure'.[12] Marx is asserting that for those who share his outlook these 'facts' contain their own condemnation and a call to do something about them. If an individual chooses otherwise, it is not because he had made a contrary moral judgement, but because the particular relations in which he stands (the class to which he belongs, his personal history, etc.) have led him to a different appreciation of the facts.[13]

Such internal relations between what others take to be factual and evaluative elements are also apparent in an early comment Marx makes on the import of religious criticism: 'The criticism of religion ends', he says, 'with the doctrine that man is the supreme being for man. It ends, therefore, with the categorical imperative to overthrow all those conditions in which man is an abased, enslaved, abandoned, contemptible being'.[14] Marx's analysis of what religion is does not prepare us for an evaluation but includes it. And he believes that to fully accept one is necessarily to accept the other – because the latter, the judgement, is internally related to the whole set of information which makes it both possible and necessary. Though it is not always so obvious, all Marx's descriptions may be treated in a similar manner. There are no 'morally neutral' statements in Marxism (which is no more than he would claim for the statements of any other thinker).

What then is the best way to characterize what are taken to be evaluative elements in Marx's works? On the basis of the preceding analysis, I would say they are straightforward descriptions of the factor or factors before him which he makes on the basis of its function in the problem under consideration, set in the larger context of what he knows to be true of the world. Such knowledge, as indicated earlier, includes where things are tending as well as where they have come from. Alternatively, one may say Marx is individuating from the whole information which contains elements that are ordinarily placed in each sphere, rather than relating logically independent facts and values. With the philosophy of internal relations, the problem is never how to relate separate entities but how to disentangle a relation or group of relations from the total and necessary configuration in which they exist.

Thus, in asserting that the workers are degraded, Marx is not making an evaluation on the basis of what he sees but describing what the workers are; but what they are is a Relation which includes, among other things, their ties to other classes who are suffering less, the state of poor people before capitalism, and the achievements which everyone will be capable of under communism. Viewed in this perspective, that is conceiving what we would consider external objects of comparison as parts of the workers themselves, the assertion that the workers are degraded is a fair description of their condition.

Treating the achievements of people in communism as one part of what workers are depends not only on conceiving of workers as a Relation that incorporates both their real past and future potential but on analysing this potential in a manner that uncovers these communist achievements. Projecting present patterns and trends forward, given the new priorities that would be established by a socialist government, Marx's study of the past is likewise an inquiry into the future, into the probable destiny of mankind. He then uses this vision of communism, along with the other comparisons mentioned, to help orient himself to the problems of his day.

Finally, what applies to Marx's statements applies equally to his concepts. That is, as his ideas about the world which find expression in his terms, Marx's concepts convey the real relations which he takes to be in the world; and, in so far as these relations include elements which some would consider of an evaluative nature, these concepts can be said to convey in what they mean the very 'judgements' that Marx ordinarily makes with them. It is in this way, we will recall, that concepts were said to have a truth value apart from the statements in which they are found. Marx's concept 'proletariat', for example, contains as part of its meaning the same degradation and other 'moral' qualities which he uncovered in his analysis of the Relation, proletariat. The truth value of this concept, therefore, depends on the validity of this analysis.

It should now be possible to understand Marx's otherwise confusing admission in *The Communist Manifesto* that 'the theoretical conclusions of the Communists are in no way based on ideas or principles that have been invented, or discovered by this or that would-be universal reformer. They merely express, in general terms, actual relations springing from an existing class struggle, from an historical movement going on under our very eyes.'[15] Marx is concerned to explain why capitalist economic, political and ideological forms appear when they do and what general attitudes result from people's interests as members of a particular class. He never, however, goes beyond stating the relations involved when he himself approves or condemns anything, or when he concludes from a situation what must be done. It is no coincidence that other thinkers who possess a philosophy of internal relations – Spinoza, Leibniz, Hegel, Dietzgen, etc. – have likewise foresworn the fact–value distinction; for partaking of this philosophical tradition any value judgment would have to be understood as internally related to what they know, and hence as an expression of all that makes it both possible and necessary. In these circumstances, 'Marxian ethics' is clearly a misnomer in so far as it refers to Marx as opposed to certain 'Marxists' who came afterwards.

As with any misnomer in the human sciences, 'Marxist Ethics' is not without its ideological consequences. For to accept that Marxism either is or contains an ethic, to admit that Marx operated from fixed principles (whatever content one gives them), is to put Marx on the same logical plane as his opponents. It is to suggest that Marx, for all his effort at historical explanation and despite his explicit denial, criticized them because he favored different principles. In which case, the capitalist ideologist easily removes the noose Marx has placed around his neck by the simple device of rejecting what passes for the latter's principles. Either he declines the honor of serving the goals of communism or of human fulfillment as understood by Marx because he doesn't consider this state of affairs possible, or he refuses to serve the interests of the proletariat or of humanity because – for reasons best known to himself – he prefers other ends, whether of this or the next world. To berate such refusals as irrational only begs the question, as it uses the very ends put aside as guides to what is rational. The crucial fault comes earlier in accepting that Marx's position, and the criticism evolved from it, is based on any principles whatsoever.

It is in this manner, by permitting Marx's opponents to free themselves from the untenable position in which his criticism places them, that attributing an ethic to Marxism inevitably serves the ends of the bourgeoisie. This is the real danger, for example, in espousing 'Marxist Humanism' (quite apart from its dubious standing as a 'scientific concept'), whatever the short-term political benefits in Eastern Europe of this reformulation.[16]

The debate between Marx and the ideologists of capitalism is and could only be a debate carried on at cross purposes, and this fact must not be lost sight of through a too facile use of labels. Properly speaking, there is no clash of judgements or goals involved here. While capitalist thinkers belabor Marx for an over-emphasis on economic factors and – without noticing any inconsistency – for idealism, Marx tries to trace their beliefs and principles (including the forms taken) and the arguments based on them to the real world out of which they arose. Marx's object is, in the broadest sense, to show that they have done something other than they think, that what they have said generally results from and functions other than they know, and through this analysis itself to bring readers to another kind of understanding and action. The enormous critical power inherent in Marxism is diluted whenever its scientific character is misrepresented.[17]

5. *Dialectic as outlook*

All I have described in terms of relations can also be presented in the language of the dialectic; for above all else Marx's dialectic is a way of viewing things as moments in their own development in, with, and through other things. The vocabulary of the dialectic – 'moment', 'movement', 'contradiction', 'mediation,' 'determination', etc. – was Marx's preferred mode of expression, more so in his early than in his later writings. However, as the assignment of priorities has indicated, I consider that the basic scaffolding of Marxism is best constructed of 'relations'. 'Relation', too, is a term out of the vocabulary of the dialectic but its broad and easily understood meaning – at least when compared to other terms in this vocabulary – permits it to play this special role.

Besides a way of seeing things, Marx's dialectic is also his approach to the study of problems which concentrates on looking for relationships, not only between different entities but between the same one in times past, present and future. Finally, the dialectic is Marx's method of exposition; this includes how he organizes his topic as well as the terms he chooses to clothe his views. Much confusion over Marx's dialectic, and Hegel's also, has been due to the inability to grasp that it has these three distinct functions.

It is Engels in his later philosophical and scientific writings, rather than Marx, who provides us with the most explicit statements of the dialectic as a means of viewing the world.[1] Marx was wholly familiar with Engels' views on this subject, and in my opinion fully endorsed them. Early in their partnership, the two men co-authored two books, *The German Ideology* and *The Holy Family,* which could never have been written unless they shared the same dialectic. Afterwards, Marx and Engels were in constant touch, either personally or through correspondence, and the dialectic was a major subject of discussion. Evidence can be found for their disagreement on other topics but not on this one. Engels even tells us that he read the whole of *Anti-Dühring,* which contains his fullest treatment of the dialectic, to Marx before he published it – not sent it, but *read* it to him.[2]

Was Marx too sick, too preoccupied with finishing *Capital* and with personal matters, as a recent critic has suggested, to take much notice of Engels' 'revision' of his views?[3] Even if we accept this unlikely explanation for the period 1877 (the writing of *Anti-Dühring*) to 1883 (Marx's death) – a period in which the two friends saw a lot of each other – this explanation assumes that Marx was unaware of what Engels was thinking about a crucial subject during the previous thirty-five years of their partnership. In reality, Engels sprung no surprises, not even in works that Marx never saw. Engels outlined, for example, some of the major themes which were to appear in the posthumously published volume, *Dialectics of Nature* (1925), in a letter to Marx as early as 1858.[4]

On the other hand, Marx's own interests in the physical sciences were sufficiently strong to bring him regularly to the lectures of Liebig and Huxley. Darwin, to whom he wanted to dedicate *Capital* I, was a constant fascination. And though he never wrote on the physical sciences (other than in letters), there are a number of remarks which indicate clearly his agreement with Engels' dialectical approach to nature. Such, for example, is his claim that the law of the transformation from quantity to quality (to be dealt with shortly) provides the basis of the molecular theory in chemistry; and elsewhere, referring to the same law, he says, 'I regard the law Hegel discovered . . . as holding good both in history and in natural sciences.'[5]

The problem of taking such statements at their face value and allowing that Marx saw the dialectic operating in nature is that this 'nature dialectic' is generally taken to stand apart from what is called the 'social dialectic', the former being both analytically and synthetically prior to the latter.[6] But if nature and society are internally related (Marx explicitly denies nature and history are 'two separate things'), an examination of any aspect of either involves one immediately with aspects of the other.[7] The priority suggested above cannot exist if the parts are not logically independent. As a way of viewing reality, there is one dialectic because there is one reality; and Engels, using examples from every field, offers the best account of it.[8]

According to Engels, 'When we reflect on nature, or the history of mankind, or our own intellectual activity, the first picture presented to us is of an endless maze of relations and interactions, in which nothing remains what, where and as it was, but everything moves, changes, comes into being and passes out of existence.'[9] He claims that the dialectical outlook already existed among some philosophers in ancient Greece, but as long as the details were not properly understood the general picture remained vague. In order to get at the details, processes had to be examined in isolation from each other, the interconnections broken up into artificial pieces and these pieces placed into classes. This work was begun by the ancient Greeks themselves and was continued, with certain lapses, up to the nineteenth century. Unfortunately, says Engels, 'this method of investigation has also left us . . . the habit of observing the natural objects and natural processes in their isolation, detached from the whole vast interconnection of things'.[10] Bacon and Locke are named as the villains of the piece who brought this limiting outlook from the natural sciences over into philosophy.

Hegel's dialectic is declared a return to the early Greek view of reality, but a return based on a knowledge of the details garnered in the intervening period. Where Hegel goes wrong is in believing that the interconnections he sees in the material world are mere copies of relations existing between ideas. By turning Hegel, who was 'standing on his head', right side up, Marx corrects this error.

Over two millennia of research into details enabled Hegel, and Marx and Engels after him, to offer some broad generalizations on the kinds of relations which exist in nature. Beyond stating that everything is interconnected and forever in flux, the dialectic expresses what some of these connections and changes are. According to Engels, the dialectic is 'the science of the most general laws of all motion. This implies that its laws must be valid just as much for motion in nature and human history as for the motion of thought.'[11] Engels is using 'motion' here as the equivalent of 'change in general' and 'mutual interaction'.[12] The most important dialectical laws are said to be 'transformation of quantity to quality – mutual penetration of polar opposites and the transformation into each other when carried to extremes – development through contradiction or negation – spiral form of development'.[13]

'Transformation of quantity to quality' is a way of stating that an increase or decrease in the amount or number of any entity (meaning any one of the relations bound up in it) will at some point transform this entity into a qualitatively new one. By 'qualitatively new' I mean that the altered relations make the entity appear as something different, or enable it to do new things or to be done to in ways that were not possible before. At what point in adding more of the same this change occurs will differ with the entity and the particular quality involved. As we saw, Marx declares that this law provides the basis for the molecular theory in chemistry where the addition of atoms to a molecule, one by one, produces successively different compounds.[14]

Engels also offers the notorious instance of water which assumes a liquid, solid or gaseous state depending on the temperature.[15] This example has been attacked on the grounds that the quantity affected here is heat and not water, but this objection overlooks the relational view of reality on which this dialectical law is based, which allows temperature to be treated as a component relation of water. Hence, it remains a case where a change in the quantity of one component relation results in the overall entity exhibiting qualities it did not have before. With all entities viewed as sums of relations, the 'transformation of quantity to quality' is a fair if not always enlightening, way to describe one kind of change.[16]

The law regarding the 'mutual penetration of polar opposites' has 'identity and difference', 'necessity and chance', 'cause and effect', 'positive and negative', 'love and hate', 'good and bad', 'north and south' and other like opposites for its subject matter. Engels is asserting here that qualities which 'appear' opposite and distinct are in reality joined by internal relations; they are not logically independent of one another. So far this is only a re-statement of the dialectic as a way of seeing all of nature. This law goes further, however, to make the point that the truth of any contrasting observation depends on the angle or point of view of the observer. Viewed in another way, for other purposes, on the basis of other values, or in connection with other things, what was identical is seen to be different, what was north is now south, what was a cause is now an effect, what was good is now bad. Identical twins have different times of birth; the North Pole seen from the North Star is south; inflation is good for debtors and bad for creditors, and so on.

No matter how appropriate a label for an entity may appear, to follow through the internal relations of this entity, its real ties within a concrete situation, will bring one to instances where the opposite label must be applied. In Engel's words, the dialectic knows no 'either-or', to it everything is 'both this and that'. In the dialectic there are no hard and fast lines between the classes we construct in any sphere of reality. What appears as an element in one class now may appear in the opposite class later.[17]

II

The third dialectical law, 'development through contradiction', refers to what was dealt with earlier under the temporal relations of an entity to itself. Like all laws of the dialectic, the law of contradiction is rooted in Marx's conception of a world which is internally related and in flux. Engels points out that

> So long as we consider things as static and lifeless, each one by itself, alongside of and after each other, it is true that we do not run up against any contradiction in them. We find certain qualities which are partly common to, partly diverse from, and even contradictory to each other, *but which in this case are distributed among different objects and therefore contain no contradiction* . . . But the position is quite different as soon as we consider things in their motion, their change, their life, their reciprocal influence on one another. Then we immediately become involved in contradictions (my emphasis).[18]

What are ordinarily taken as different objects are being conceived of here as components of the same one; only then, Engels says, can they be in contradiction. Either one grants that Marx and Engels subscribe to a philosophy of internal relations and then tries to discover the particular ways things are related in their system, or the ways they say things are related will appear manifestly absurd. Hence the abuse leveled by most critics at Marx's dialectical method.

The temporal relations of any entity, as we saw, are its ties to what it was and will be conceived of as its component parts. Each component of an entity is itself a Relation whose development is a function of the particular configuration of circumstances in which it stands. It is the result of all these different developments (viewed as occurring within the entity) that determines what the entity as a whole will become. 'Contradiction' is a way of referring to the fact that not all such developments are compatible. In order to progress further in the direction made necessary by its own links of mutual dependence, a component may require that the probable course of change of another component be altered. The developments of the two (as internally related elements in the same covering structure) stand in contradiction, and it is through the working out of such contradictions that the larger entity takes on the form it does.

When one component of an entity is forced by what it is and must become to predominate over another it incorporates (or 'sublates') certain characteristics, generally subordinate relations, of the latter and carries them, now appropriately altered, into the next stage. Marx and Engels usually treat this transition as a sharp one. Contradiction never completely destroys what is contradicted but merely refashions it to suit new ends. Naturally, the way in which this process occurs varies considerably from case to case. As Engels says, 'Each class of things . . . has its appropriate form of being negated in such a way that it gives rise to a development, and it is just the same with each class of conceptions and ideas.'[19]

Capital, for example, includes the proletariat and the capitalists among its components, but these two components cannot progress together toward the goals inherent in their respective relations. It is in the nature of capitalists to exploit workers, and it is equally in the nature of workers to resist such exploitation. This is a contradiction existing in capital, growing in it as these relations develop (as the power of each capitalists and workers increases), and when this contradiction is resolved, capital will have become something else.[20] What finally results will have taken something from both of these conflicting elements, though from one more than the other. The resolution of this contradiction is sometimes called 'the negation of the negation', referring to the fact that capital itself emerged out of similar contradictions in the entities that preceded it.

Closely related to this third law is the last law mentioned – 'spiral form of development'. The claim that development is spiral rather than linear is a claim that progress is not uniform or free of all retarding effects and influences. With change occurring through contradiction, as I have explained it, it is possible to view succeeding stages of any entity as reactions to what went before. It is this way of viewing development that makes Engels say 'repulsion is the really active aspect of motion and attraction the passive aspect'.[21] The reaction to a reaction ('the negation of the negation'), however, brings us back to where we began, but for Marx and Engels this is a return with a difference. Witness Engels' account of the advance in dialectical thought from ancient Greece to Hegel, and what was said of sublation in discussing contradiction. As stage 'three' bears a remarkable resemblance to stage 'one', 'spiral development' serves as a striking metaphor for what has taken place.

The four laws which Engels lists as the most important laws of the dialectic are some of the broad patterns in which he and Marx, following upon Hegel, saw change occurring in the world. Each entity with which Marx came into contact was viewed as internally related to numerous others in a setting that was forever fluctuating; it was seen as something which experiences qualitative change with an alteration at some point in quantity; as something which appears quite different, even the opposite, of what it does now when looked at from another angle or for another purpose; and as something which progresses through repeated conflicts between its parts, conflicts that are taken to constitute a series of reactions against what went before.

To make them applicable to all spheres of reality, the laws of the dialectic were purposely tailored to fit very loosely. They were not meant to offer any details, information true for only certain entities, since this would limit their application to a single realm. These laws are best viewed as a synthesis and reformulation of what Marx and Engels took to be everyone's experience with reality, though people were forever distorting this reality by separating the inseparable. Engels tells us that when these laws are explained, they often seem obvious and commonplace to the very people who condemned them earlier as metaphysical and incomprehensible.[22] They, clearly, are obvious to Marx, who never felt it necessary to discover these laws anew or to collect supporting evidence. Since he grasped everything which could possibly serve as evidence dialectically from the start, it is impossible to say what would constitute contrary evidence for him. Like his relational view of the world, of which they are in effect a reformulation, Marx's dialectical laws can be neither proven nor disproven.

Nothing is more difficult in writing about Marx than to keep the dialectic on the 'commonplace' level to which I have assigned it. The temptation among friends and foes of Marxism alike is to use the dialectic as a means of proving and predicting things.[23] For it to perform these functions they endow it with a body and content it does not have. 'Development through contradiction' and 'spiral development' are the laws most amenable (one is tempted to say too amenable) to such treatment. The classic result is the construction of a rock ribbed triad of thesis, anti-thesis and synthesis, whose strict lines allow prediction even before the facts have been gathered. But this degrades the dialectic to a guessing game: starting from a recognized thesis and anti-thesis, how do we decide which of two or more suggested syntheses is the correct one? Before the synthesis has occurred, how can we be sure that what has been labelled 'anti-thesis' is really such? And again, before the synthesis has occurred, how do we know that what we have isolated as the thesis is really the central thesis in our situation or period?*

Prior to all these questions, and perhaps more important than any, is the problem of defining the boundaries for each part of the triad. Amid the welter of relations which constitutes each entity, how do we decide which relation or set of relations makes up a thesis, which an anti-thesis and which a synthesis? Where, and on the basis of what standard, do we draw the line between them? There is no way of arriving at conclusive answers for any of these questions.

When used for predictions, the dialectic can never be shown wrong, only foolish and worthless. If the synthesis predicted does not occur, it is easy to change to another synthesis – what is to stop one? – or to talk of a time lag. Like a balloon, when hit in one place, it bulges out in another. The real fault lies in harnessing the dialectic for predictive purposes in the first place. The same kind of difficulty arises when the dialectic is used to prove something. There is no way of getting agreement on what constitutes the thesis, the anti-thesis and the synthesis in any given problem, even among people who claim to view the world dialectically. Marx himself does not share in this guilt. He never rests a proof on the grounds that an entity is the 'negation of the negation', or says some partic-

---

* Among the reasons responsible for the heavy and undeserving emphasis placed upon this triad, along with the natural desire to make the dialectic 'produce', is the need most people feel to focus their attention on something unchanging even when the object of their gaze is change itself. Those who cannot view reality dialectically require hooks on which to hang the dialectic. Unfortunately, once installed, these hooks, which may render some initial service, are almost impossible to remove.

ular event must happen because 'spiral development' requires it.

In criticism of Dühring, Engels says that when Marx characterizes the capitalist production process

> as the negation of the negation ... Marx does not dream of attempting to prove by this that the process was historically necessary. On the contrary: after he has proved from history that in fact the process has partially already occurred, and partially must occur in the future, he then also characterizes it as a process which develops in accordance with a definite dialectical law. That is all.[24]

As part of his theoretical apparatus for viewing reality, the laws of the dialectic radically affect Marx's approach to his subject matter and how he organizes what he finds there. Besides serving as a prism by means of which change itself is brought into focus, they predispose him in any situation to pay special heed to developments which might otherwise be missed, or noticed only tangentially. But it is what he finds through his research, the real relations of specific entities, rather than the dialectic, which is the substance of all his proofs and projections. When the laws of the dialectic remain on the level of the 'commonplace', as descriptions of the broad patterns in which change occurs, the embarrassing questions asked above never arise. After the facts have been gathered, dialectically to be sure, the tags 'thesis', 'anti-thesis' and 'synthesis', may then be used to facilitate exposition. Marx and Engels prefer *not* to use them.[25]*

---

* By subsuming the laws of the dialectic under the philosophy of internal relations, I have already indicated my belief that these specific laws are not as important for Marx as their broad framework. I do not emphasize these laws in this study because I feel Marx's conception of human nature and theory of alienation can be reconstructed just as effectively and with fewer difficulties on the more general plane of relations.

6. *Dialectic as inquiry and exposition*

Besides a way of viewing the world, the dialectic also serves Marx as a method of inquiry and as a type of organization and set of forms in which to present his findings. Marx points to the difference between these latter two roles (he assumes here the function of the dialectic as a way of seeing things) when he says, 'of course the method of presentation must differ in form from that of inquiry. The latter has to appropriate the material in detail, to analyse its different forms of development, to trace out their *inner connections*'.[1] (My emphasis.) Nothing that was said regarding the philosophy of internal relations was meant to deny the empirical character of Marx's method of inquiry. Marx does not deduce his knowledge about capitalism from the meanings of terms, but, like a good social scientist, does research to discover what is the case. Marx even delayed finishing *Capital* II, in part because he wanted to see how the crisis about to break out in England would develop.[2]

The dialectical method of inquiry is best described as research into the manifold ways in which entities are internally related. It is a voyage of exploration that has the whole world for its object, but a world which is conceived of as relationally contained in each of its parts. The first question this raises is how to decide on the parts in which and between which one will seek for relations. The need to divide up reality into what are, in effect, instrumental units was spoken of earlier as the need to individuate, and declared a common problem for all thinkers who ascribe to a philosophy of internal relations. This is the problem Marx tries to solve by what he calls the 'force of abstraction'.[3]

An 'abstraction' is a part of the whole whose ties with the rest are not apparent; it is a part which *appears* to be a whole in itself.[4] According to Marx, to hold that the world is actually composed of such 'abstractions' is evidence of alienation (see Part III below). However, believing otherwise does not release Marx from the requirement of operating with units; it simply gives him more latitude in conceptualizing what these will be and in deciding how much of what is relationally contained in them to bring forward at any one time. The results of Marx's method of abstraction are not only such new factors as the relations of production and surplus-value, but as well all the other factors that come into his investigation. They have all been individuated out of the whole which is relationally contained in each. And again, which group of qualities Marx chooses to treat as a unit is determined by the real similarities he sees in reality together with the particular problem under consideration.

But if Marx may be said to abstract all the units with which he deals in order to be able to deal with them at all, he does not refer to every one as an 'abstraction'. Instead, this term is generally used to refer to those units whose ties with reality are fully obscured, where the particular society in which they exist has been completely lost sight of. Thus, labor – which, as labor in general, Marx takes to be a special product of capitalism – is spoken of as an 'abstraction' because most people consider that it existed in all social systems. In so far as productive activity is particularized as slave labor, indentured labor, wage-labor, etc., the conditions in and through which it must exist are brought into the open with the result that it can no longer be treated as a complete abstraction.

Because the internal relations of labor are less evident than those of wage-labor, Marx believes the former offers a better jumping-off point from which to begin an analysis of any third factor (or the social system as a whole). To start with wage-labor, one would have to explain why it is *wage*-labor, which would involve us in the capitalist system before we had made ready to study it. Consequently, Marx would have us begin with the 'general abstract definitions which are more or less applicable to all forms of society', and then proceed to forms that are more clearly products of the society in question.[5] In this manner, Marx begins his own study of capitalism with the abstractions, labor and value. However, he never forgets that these abstractions are themselves internally related to the full picture he is trying to reconstruct with them. Referring to the assumptions he made in Section I of *Capital* I, Marx writes to Engels, 'this is the only possible way to avoid having to deal with everything under each particular Relation'.[6]*

---

* Marx's method of abstraction is treated in more detail in examining the particular abstractions made. See especially the chapters on Marx's economics in the section on alienation. Light is also shed on this subject later in the present chapter in discussing how Marx sought to expose his views.

Once a decision was made on his units, Marx's next task was to examine the manifold ways in which these units are related, either as mutually dependent wholes or as components in some larger whole – usually both. In examining their interaction, he began with each part in turn, continuously altering the perspective in which their union was viewed. Thus, capital (generally the core notion of 'capital') served as one vantage point from which to work out the intricacies of capitalism; labor served as another, value as another, and so on. In each case, while the interaction studied is the same, the angle and approach to it differ.[7]

Marx assumed that the patterns of change embodied in the laws of the dialectic were universal, and they served him as the broad framework in which to look for particular developments. However, the real crisscrossing influences at work in any situation were his proper subject matter. The enormous difficulties involved in extricating himself from such a maze required the kind of genius for grasping connections which Marx is reputed to have had in great abundance.[8] The maze itself is revealed in all its complexity in an early appraisal Marx made of his task: 'We have to grasp the essential connections between private property, avarice, and the separation of labor, capital, and landed property; between exchange and competition, value and the devaluation of man, monopoly and competition, etc.; the connection between this whole estrangement and the money system.'[9]

The task Marx pursues of grasping the 'essential connections' of capitalism is what makes Marxism a science. It is the relations which Marx considers crucial for understanding any system or factor that are convened in 'essence' (*Wesen*).[10] Marx often contrasts 'essence' with 'appearance', or what we can observe directly. Actually, essence includes appearance but transcends it in every direction in which what is apparent acquires its importance. Since what Marx takes to be crucial in understanding anything, however, depends in part on the problem under consideration, what he considers its essence will also vary. What is the essence of man? Some of Marx's comments indicate it is his activity, others that it is his social relations and still others that it is the part of nature he appropriates.[11] The compromise, that it is all these in their interrelations, misses the point that it is through this category that Marx has chosen to emphasize one or the other. This is the chief difficulty in the way of adopting the common sense translation of

Wesen as 'core' or – as is now popular in France – 'structure', with their connotation of unchanging stability, and makes the popular equation of the term 'essential' with 'economic conditions' impractical.[12]

As the work of uncovering essences, science is primarily concerned with those major relations which are not open to direct observation; it is a matter of extending the ties between entities, conceived of as internally related to one another, further than we do in ordinary life. If to know anything is to know its relations, or in Engels' words: 'to allocate to each its place in the interconnection of nature', to know anything scientifically is to grasp its place in nature more fully than is possible without specialized research.[13] As Marx says, the 'hidden substratum' of phenomena 'must first be discovered by science'.[14]

In a letter to Kugelmann, Marx goes so far as to maintain that such relations are the entire subject matter of science.[15] This extreme view is staked out again in *Capital* III: 'all science would be superfluous if the outward appearance and the essence of things directly coincided'.[16] If fundamental relationships could be understood for the looking, we would not have to ferret them out. Afterwards, it is often found that the truth about an entity runs counter to appearances: 'It is paradox that the earth moves around the sun, and that water consists of two highly inflammable gases.' For Marx, 'Scientific truth is always paradox, if judged by everyday experience of things.'[17] The job of the scientist, then, is to learn the relevant information and piece it together so as to reconstruct in his mind the intricate relations, most of them not directly observable, that exist in reality.[18]

Marx's comments should indicate why most discussions on the theme 'Is Marxism a Science?' are carried on at cross purposes. On Marx's definition, Marxism's claim to be a science is clearly justified, and he would not have been interested to debate the question using any other definition; nor, with my purpose of getting at what he is saying, am I. It is also worth noting in this connection that the German term *Wissenschaft* has never been so closely identified with the physical sciences – and hence with the criteria operating in the physical sciences – as its English equivalent. Marx's use of 'science' and our own use of this term to refer to his ideas must also be understood with this in mind.

II

If the dialectic as inquiry is the search for internal relations within and between abstracted units, the dialectic as exposition is Marx's means of expounding these relations to his readers. We will recall that Marx specifically condemns explanations in economics and theology which attempt to go back to first causes, and claims that they assume what still has to be accounted for, namely, the relations existing in the first cause.[19] Explanation for Marx always has to do with clarifying relationships; it is helping others to discover the 'hidden substratum' which one has discovered through science. But how does one report on relations when what one sees is not relations between things but things as Relations? Marx's solution is to try to present his readers with a 'mirrored' version of reality. He says success in exposition is achieved "if the life of the subject-matter is ideally reflected as in a mirror'. When this occurs, "it may appear as if we had before us a mere *a priori* construction'.[20]

Marx's self-acclaimed goal, then, is to produce works whose parts are so interlocked they seem to belong to a deductive system. This is also the sense in which he asserts that all his theoretical writings are an 'artistic whole'.[21] But, as Lafargue tells us, Marx was constantly dissatisfied with his efforts 'to disclose the whole of that world in its manifold and continually varying action and reaction'.[22] He felt that he was never able to say just what he wanted. Marx's correspondence during the time he was writing *Capital* is full of allusions to his efforts at perfecting his exposition. The approach adopted in the *Grundrisse* (1858) was soon left behind. Just months before *Capital* I was published, he once more altered his exposition, in this instance to meet his friend Kugelmann's request for a more didactic account. The second German edition was again significantly revised, and so too the French edition which followed a few years later. And at the time of Marx's death in 1883, Engels tells us that Marx was again planning to revise his major work.[23] It appears, therefore, that this mirrored presentation of reality maintained a goal which Marx was forever approaching, but on the basis of his own evidence never actually attained.

The means at Marx's disposal for creating a reflection of the reality he uncovered were the organization of his material and his choice of terms. Marx presents his subject matter both historically, laying stress on factors he considers most important, and dialectically, which for him meant elucidating their internal relations in the period under examination. *Capital* offers many examples of material organized along each of these lines: capital, labor and interest, for example, are examined in terms of origin, and also as component parts of each other and of still other factors. In their correspondence, Marx and Engels frequently discuss the problems involved in harmonizing these two types of organization.[24]

What appears here as a clear dichotomy, however, like all such 'polar opposites' in Marxism, is really not one. Engels tells us that the dialectical method 'is nothing else but the historical method only divested of its historical form and disturbing fortuities'.[25] We have already seen that for Marx any factor is a product of historical development. The dialectical tie which binds value, labor, capital and interest in *Capital* only holds good for a single period in world history. Thus, by uncovering the connection between these and other social factors Marx is also displaying their real historical relations. And, conversely, in writing history all developments are conceived of as the temporal relations of the factors concerned.

The two outstanding features of Marx's use of the dialectic for presentation are, first, that each subject is dealt with from many different vantage points, and second, that each subject is followed out of and into the particular forms it assumes at different times. Engels notes the presence of this first feature in his Preface to *Capital* III, where he lists some of the difficulties he encountered in editing the unfinished volumes of *Capital*.[26] This tactic of presentation led Marx to treat production, for example, when he was really dealing with consumption (how does production affect consumption and vice versa), or distribution (the same) or exchange (the same).[27] Again, the capitalist acquires his full character in Marx's writings only through being discussed in studies on factory work, the role of the state, the demands of the market, and so on, aside from examinations in which he is the principal. And whenever the capitalist is the principal, we are certain to find insights on the proletariat, the state, the market, etc., viewed now from this angle. One result is that Marx's works often appear very repetitious.

As for tracing things through their development into various forms, the outstanding example of this in Marxism is the metamorphoses of value from labor, where it originates, to capital, interest, rent and money. This is a neat, no doubt too neat, outline of *Capital*, where each of these factors is treated as another form of what is essentially the same thing (see Chapter 27 below). In both presenting the same thing from different angles and apparently disparate ones as 'identical', Marx is trying to mirror a reality where entities are connected as essential elements in each other's Relations.

Not able to unfold all the relations in a factor immediately, Marx was forced to deal with any problem in stages, using what Paul Sweezy calls the method of 'successive approximations'.[28] In any one place and even, as Sweezy rightly points out, in any one book, Marx treats his material in a very partial manner. His conclusions, therefore, are generally of a provisional nature, since the introduction of new developments later often yields the necessary qualifications.[29]

Consequently, Marx assumes the greater part of what he conceives in a Relation in order to get on with his task, and in so doing subsumes what is unexpressed in the part expressed, which means too in the terms he uses. When Marx says, 'no equation can be solved unless the elements of its solution are involved in its terms', this has a literal application to Marxism.[30] A common experience people have as they continue to study Marx's writings is that terms they think they know take on new and broader meanings. In fact this may be taken as one of the surest signs that one is making progress in understanding Marx.

Besides forcing him to make assumptions in order to treat a Relation one-sidedly, Marx's conception of reality requires some shorthand method to point out the connections he sees without having to go into them in detail. The specialized vocabulary which serves this purpose for Marx has been the bane of critics from his time to our own. Some of its main terms and expressions are as follows: 'reflection' (*Spiegelbild*), 'corresponding case' (*Entsprechung*), 'manifestation' (*Ausserung*), 'confirmation' (*Bestatigung*), 'another expression' (*andrer Ausdruk*), 'in the same measure' (*in dem selben Grade*), 'in one of its aspects' (*nach der einen Seite*) and 'another form' (*andrer Art*). Clearly, these expressions do not all mean the same thing, but they perform the common function for Marx of drawing attention to the internal relations he sees between unlike entities; in every case, the elements referred to are held to be aspects of one another.

This is the only way to understand such otherwise confusing claims as 'Value in general is a form of social labor', or when Marx calls money 'the commodity in its continually exchangeable form' or private property 'the material summary expression of alienated labor'; and this list, of what are not peripheral but central theses in Marxism, could be extended much further.[31] Lacking the relational framework to make sense of such 'equations', critics generally misinterpret them along causal lines, setting apart horse and cart where Marx meant each conception to convey both.[32]

Perhaps the most difficult of these shorthand usages to comprehend is the term 'identical'. When Marx says 'division of labor and private property are . . . identical expressions', he is not offering an empty tautology but directing us to the internal ties he sees between these two in real life. This assertion is followed by the explanation that 'in the one the same thing is affirmed with reference to activity as is affirmed in the other with reference to the product of activity.'[33] One should not expect to grasp the specific nature of the connection Marx sees between the division of labor and property at this stage (that will come in Chapter 24 below), only that each is said to be a necessary condition of the other, conceived of as part of the other.

F. H. Bradley, who also subscribes to a philosophy of internal relations, distinguishes between 'identity' and 'similarity' by stating that the latter can only apply to objects which 'remain at least partly undistinguished and unspecified'. And whenever such objects are fully analysed, that is, when their internal relations to each other are uncovered, they are seen to be identical.[34] Identity, for Marx as for Bradley, is the relation between entities whose role as necessary elements in one another is appreciated for what it is. Consequently, a full account of any one requires an account of the other (or others).[35]

Two corollaries of Marx's unusual view of identity, which have already been briefly alluded to, are that he feels he can use the same word to refer to heterogeneous entities and a wide assortment of words to refer to what we would take to be the same one. The different things expressed by a single term are the varied aspects of the relationships bound up in it. In wanting to exhibit connections which cross into separate fields, Marx sometimes feels constrained to borrow terms from their common sense homes and apply them elsewhere. In so doing, he is merely tracing out their component relations further than he usually does. Sometimes he goes as far as to use the same expression for all as well as each of the main elements in the reality it depicts. His much misunderstood use of 'man's essential powers' and 'society' are examples of this.[36]

Using more than one word to convey the same thing is again a way of emphasizing a particular tie. In this case, the entity viewed from diverse angles is given names corresponding to how it functions or appears from each. This allows me in the next section to make use of 'animal functions', 'natural powers and 'physical needs' as if they were equivalent expressions. The whole of Marxism supplies us with examples of these two practises, although they are more noticeable in the early works.

SUMMARY

Before proceeding to Marx's conception of human nature and his theory of alienation, it was necessary to clarify the character of Marxism itself. In this section, I examined the view of the world on which Marxism is based and the use of language which this view necessitates. We saw that for Marx the basic unit of reality is not a thing but a Relation. It is this conception which allows him to attribute a truth value to concepts, to manipulate their meanings and to use such terms as 'identity', 'form', 'expression' and the others noted, in the otherwise inexplicable ways he does. It is this same conception that permits him to bridge the fact–value, cause–effect, and nature–society distinctions which characterize the common sense view of reality. The better known dialectic embodies this conception and is as well Marx's means for inquiring into a world viewed in this way and for expounding what he finds there.

Marx's relational conception of reality and corresponding use of language to convey relations makes it necessary for any large scale examination of his work to proceed by piecing together what he is saying while simultaneously reconstructing the concepts with which he is saying it. To pursue these dual aims with regard to his conception of human nature is the task of the following section.

PART II

Marx's conception of human nature

7. Powers and needs

Of Bentham, Marx declared, 'he that would criticize all human acts, movements, relations, etc., by the principle of utility, must first deal with human nature in general, and then with human nature as modified in each historical epoch'.[1] Instead, Bentham devotes little attention to human nature, taking the English shop-keeper as his all-purpose model. For him, 'what is useful to this normal man and his world is absolutely useful. This yard-measure ... he applied to past, present, and future.'[2] But Marx too has such a yard-measure in his conception of man, and he too applied it to all periods. Therefore, if Marx is right about Bentham, before we can comprehend Marx's own explanation and criticism of 'all human acts, movements, relations, etc.', of capitalism, its history and progress into communism, we must first learn how he deals with 'human nature in general, and then with human nature as modified in each historical epoch'.

Marx's views on man have not been neglected by writers on Marxism, particularly in recent years. In answering whether Marx has an ethic I had occasion to mention several works which contain important accounts of these views. Nevertheless, human nature is most often treated as a cipher in Marx's system or described with a few simple adjectives. In those instances where it is taken as a sig-nificant variable, it has never been sufficiently integrated with Marx's other theories. The latter fault is particularly evident in Vernon Venable's 'classic', *Human Nature: the Marxian View,* in which the important *1844 Manuscripts* does not appear to have been used at all, though it was available to the author in the *Gesamtausgabe.*[3] With the growing popularity of this early work of Marx, some writers have sought to abstract his remarks on human nature from the rest of his theories in order to present him as a humanist. Erich Fromm's *Marx's Concept of Man*, which has its own justification as an attempt to make Marxism 'respectable' to a hostile American public, is the outstanding example of this approach.[4]

Catholic writers have been especially attentive to Marx's views on man. From Victor Cathrein's *Socialism,* published at the end of the nineteenth century, to J. Y. Calvez's recent work *la Pensée de Karl Marx* which devotes over 400 pages to the theory of alienation, Marx's materialist conception of human nature has been the main target of Catholic criticism.[5] None of these authors, however, nor any of their peers, treats this conception as itself the canvas on which are inscribed Marx's other major theories, as a theory with internal relations to the rest of Marxism (and hence coextensive with the sum of his other views). Whereas it is the avowed aim of the present study to expound Marxism in a full account of Marx's conception of human nature, the capitalist version of which is his theory of alienation.

The place to begin this account, judging from Marx's own comments on Bentham, is with his views on what is common to all men at all times. Contrary to a widely accepted opinion, Marx has such a conception of man 'outside of history'. 'Power' (*Kraft*) and 'need' (*Bedürfnis*), the terms most frequently employed in expressing this view, are also the keys for opening up what might be labelled Marx's conception of 'human nature in general'. Marx believes that every man simply because he is a man possesses certain powers and needs, some of which he calls 'natural' and other 'species'.[6] Man's natural powers and needs are those he shares with every living entity. Species powers and needs, on the other hand, are those man alone possesses. They are what make him unique in nature, what set him apart as a 'species being' (an expression Marx took over from Feuerbach) from the rest of the animal world. This distinction between natural and species man is the generally unrecognized foundation on which Marx erects his entire conception of human nature.[7]

Before examining the character Marx ascribes to natural and species man respectively, we must try to clarify his use of the two terms 'power' and 'need' which are central to his exposition. Though Marx would have frowned upon such 'dictionary' procedure, I believe it essential that readers grasp from the start some of the broader implications of these terms. The nearest ordinary language equivalents of 'power', as used by Marx, are 'faculty', 'ability', 'function' and 'capacity', and whenever Marx refers to man's powers some measure of comprehension can be achieved by substituting one or more of these words.

Once this is admitted, however, a major theme in Marx's use of 'power' still eludes us. For 'power' also suggests potential, the possibility – particularly in changed conditions – of becoming more of whatever it already is. As elements in Marx's conception of reality, powers are related to their own future forms as well as to other entities in the present. As with everything else, Marx sees them in the process of change and, through a study of their organic law, knows in a general way what they are changing into. At each stage their progress can be charted by the evidence of the individual's skills and achievements. The standard from which judgements are made is Marx's conception of what constitutes proper fulfillment for these powers, which is that state when the ends he takes to be inherent in them have been attained.

If Marx's 'powers' are 'queer things', which stretch our understanding, Marx's 'needs' are relatively simple, at least when viewed apart from their relationship to 'powers'. For Marx, 'need' refers to the desire one feels for something, usually something which is not immediately available. The subject is man and the object his objects. Animals, objects and situations are also spoken of on occasion as having 'needs'. However, the area of 'need' usage is not really so broad, since animals can be said to feel their needs in much the same way as man, and most cases of object and situation needs can legitimately be translated into human terms. For example, when Marx says that the 1789 revolution satisfied the 'needs of the world of that day', this can be translated as meaning the needs of the people then living.[8] The remaining cases of object and situation needs can be viewed simply as what is required by these objects and situations if they are to develop in the way Marx believes they will. Actually, the statement just quoted on the 'needs of the world' may also be interpreted in this way. In which case it passes beyond my present interest – which is with man's needs, what they are, where they come from and how they develop.

As we have seen, for Marx, man not only has needs but feels them. They exist in him as felt drives, as wants. The link between objective state and the subjective recognition of it, which is fixed in Marx's use of 'need', makes 'drive' and 'want' practically synonyms for 'need' in Marxism.[9] The fact of having needs is never lost, although people seldom realize all their implications and learning how to satisfy them most efficiently requires intellectual effort.

Marx believes further that men are more or less conscious of their proper objects, that they want the things they need. In the post-Freudian world, where the 'unconscious' is a household expression, this use of 'need' will appear too narrow. People have unconscious needs for which they do not feel wants or for which the wants they feel are misdirected, that is, fixed on objects that will not satisfy the underlying need.

Yet, what appears to denote less than our ordinary use of 'need' from one angle is seen to denote more from another. For Marx also uses 'need' to refer to what was discussed earlier under 'power', viewed from the vantage point of the feeling individual. 'Need' is always attached to 'power' in Marx's writings as the means through which man becomes aware of the latter's existence. Each power is coupled in man with a distinctive need for the objects necessary for its realization, to make itself known and allow for its development as a power. Likewise, a power is whatever is used that 'fulfills' a need. To know any power is therefore to know its corresponding need and vice versa. It is in this sense that I will later speak of needs and powers reflecting one another.[10]

The tie between powers and needs is further complicated when we leave the a-historical setting in which we have been operating for actual societies 'inside of history'. According to Marx, each stage in history creates its own distinctive needs in man, and with the passing to the next stage these needs disappear, along with their owners, to be replaced by new people and new needs.[11] In primitive society, man's needs were poor, few in number and only capable of meager satisfaction.[12] Communism provides the other extreme, where man is said to be rich because he needs 'the totality of human life activities'.[13] This alteration in man's needs simply bespeaks a development which has occurred in his powers. Throughout history, the changes which take place in either can be read into the other.[14]

8. Natural man

The powers most frequently associated with natural man, with human beings as living parts of nature, are labor, eating and sex. Marx never drew up a full list of man's natural powers; nor is he concerned to remove the verbal cloak which hides some from public inspection. What he labels a 'natural power' in one place is referred to as an 'animal function' or a 'physical need' in another. These expressions are not exact equivalents, but they are so closely related that we may take the examples Marx offers for any one as examples for the other two. Animal functions are the processes that living creatures undergo and the actions they undertake in order to stay alive; while physical needs are the desires they feel for the objects and actions required to keep them alive and functioning. With certain qualifications drawn from our earlier discussion, we could say that natural powers are similar to animal functions and the relation between both of them and physical needs is similar to the relation between power and need. When Marx refers, therefore, to drinking and procreation as animal functions, we are justified in adding them – assuming we want to distinguish between procreation and sex – to our list of man's natural powers.[1]

Marx's reference to the needs of animals and savages can be viewed in the same light as his reference to physical needs; both reflect natural powers. In Marx's claim that savages and animals have 'the need of companionship', there is suggested the power of sympathetic relationship with other beings of the same species.[2] He also speaks of savages and animals having a 'need to hunt, to roam'.[3] The power reflected here must be something like the power to play or seek out variety. When Marx points out much later that uniform work disturbs 'the intensity and flow of man's animal spirits, which find recreation and delight in mere change of activity', I understand him as alluding to this power.[4]

Man's natural powers are said to have two outstanding characteristics: first, that they exist in him as 'tendencies and abilities – as impulses' (*Anlagen und Fähigkeiten, als Triebe*); and second, that they seek their fulfillment in objects outside his own body.[5] Marx's

77

choice of words to describe man's natural powers, particularly 'tendency' and 'impulse', indicates some of the meaning he gives to 'power' over and above its common sense one. The best way to grasp the first part of this description is to take the pieces in the opposite order to that in which they appear. For each natural power that he possesses man feels 'impulses' (needs) to realize or actualize it; he has 'abilities' which enable him to realize it; and he carries 'tendencies' which direct this realization towards particular goals. Taking eating as a natural power, man's impulses which drive him to eat are clear enough: he is hungry. The abilities which enable him to eat include all that he does when eating. The tendencies which direct him toward satisfactory objects are his taste and his general knowledge as to what is edible and what is not. For more obscure powers, such as playing and relating oneself to others, the characteristic impulses, abilities and tendencies are less clear, and we shall just have to take Marx's word that they exist.

The second main characteristic of natural powers, that they seek fulfillment in objects outside man, is where the relation of powers to needs is most apparent. According to Marx, 'the objects of his impulses exist outside him, as objects of his need – essential objects, indispensable to the manifestation and confirmation of his essential powers'.[6] Marx uses 'object' in the sense of 'the object of a subject' (real or potential), rather than in the sense of 'material object', though all of the latter are included in the former and it is material objects which are usually being referred to. Thus, anything with which man comes into contact in any way is an object for Marx. Plants, animals, stones, air and light are objects which are named explicitly, but, as we have seen, this list is far from complete.[7] If man's powers can only manifest themselves in and through objects, he needs these objects to express his powers. Hunger is an example of such a need for objects. Marx says that hunger 'needs a nature outside itself, an object outside itself . . . to be stilled. Hunger is an acknowledged need of my body for an object existing outside it indispensable to its integration and the expression of its essential being.'[8]

This object needing characteristic of man's natural powers is made to depend on the fact that man is a 'corporeal, living, real, sensuous, objective being'.[9] That is to say, man's body is a living material object possessing both senses and the potential for engaging in a variety of activities. Not only do his powers inhabit one object, himself, but they are only realizable in other objects, nature.[10] 'Realization' in Marxism always carries this double sense of fulfillment of the powers involved and their objectification in nature, though it is the latter that he generally wants to stress. Here too, we can see the double edged meaning conveyed by Marx's expression 'objective being'. The power of eating, for example, only exists through the human objects utilized in eating, such as the mouth, the stomach, etc., and the objects eaten, food.

By declaring man 'sensuous' Marx wants us to treat what we generally take to be human senses in the same manner. We only know of them through what they come into contact with and where they reside. Thus, Marx can say that man 'is established by objects', and that objects 'reside in the very nature of his being'.[11] Between the two there exists an internal relation. This is the point of all Marx's comments which place the one (or some part of it) within the other.[12] Realization or the objectification of man's powers in nature is the transfer of elements (now suitably altered) within an organic whole.

'Human nature' emerges from this discussion as an expression which includes all that is of nature as well as what is of man; the appearance and realization of man's powers in objects bind these two spheres inextricably together practically and conceptually. When Marx asserts, therefore, that 'all history is nothing but a continual transformation of human nature', this is a claim about both man and his objects.[13]

One part of man's relationship to nature is the bond between each particular individual and his fellows. As an objective and sensuous being, as I have described these qualities, man has his object and sense content outside himself. If this is the relationship of one individual to all of nature, since man is a part of nature – since he too is an object – this must also be the relationship of each man to all other men. That is, each person is himself object and sense content for other people, just as they, being equally parts of nature, serve in this capacity for him.[14] It is this sense of 'object' that Marx uses when he says in *Capital,* 'man, himself, viewed as the impersonation of labor power, is a natural object, a thing, although a living conscious thing'.[15] The reciprocal character of man's relations with his kind is said to be most evident in the sexual tie between man and woman where 'man's relationship to nature is immediately his relation to man, just as his relation to man is immediately his relation to nature'.[16]

Marx sums up his account of man as a natural being, as an objective and sensuous creature, by referring to him as 'suffering, limited, and conditioned'. Man suffers because of what he undergoes. To be sensuous, according to Marx, is necessarily to suffer.[17] Man cannot obtain everything he needs to realize his natural powers, since, in one way or another, it is the whole world that is required. There will always be a woman (or man), food, etc. which is unavailable, if only for a moment, and whatever is denied him causes suffering. It should be clear that the term 'suffering' is used here to embrace everything from the slightest discomfort to the most intense pain. Because he feels what he undergoes, because to undergo is to suffer, man is said to be a passionate being. Passion is the quality which animates the individual's effort to obtain his objects.[18] Viewed from the vantage point of the feeling subject, it is this effort itself.

Finally, man is said to be a limited being because of the restrictions which surround his desires and activities on all sides. These restrictions are those placed on any part of nature by the whole. The availability of objects in nature and their particular qualities control man in all he attempts to do; they regulate when and how his powers can be used. An individual cannot do more with nature than can be done with it, given its existing state. It is in this sense that nature determines all that man is and can become.

The easiest way to grasp Marx's conception of man as a natural being is to abstract this figure from all that we consider peculiar to the species, to view him as *not yet* a man but still an animal. As a natural being, Marx claims, man is like an animal in being 'identical with his activity'.[19] At this level, man is as he does, because he is unable to distinguish himself in his imagination from what he is doing. He is a 'person' without intellectual abilities or self-awareness. His faculties operate only to secure his physical needs, only to realize what have been called his natural powers. As such, he produces only his physical self, adding to his weight, stature and offspring and improves his health; but, according to Marx, he cannot reproduce nature or create things of beauty.[20] His actions are 'spontaneous' rather than 'voluntary', which is a way of stating that man is completely controlled by natural forces rather than the reverse.[21]

Labor, which was mentioned earlier as one of man's natural powers, appears in this context like the efforts of a silkworm which spins in order to continue its existence as a caterpillar.[22] Such labor is mere energy expended to satisfy immediate physical needs and has little in common with human productive activity. All animals engage in it, but, as we shall soon learn, only man is capable of genuinely creative work.[23]

9. *Species man*

Alongside natural man, the other half of Marx's dichotomy is species man. As a species being man can be distinguished from other living things, for he now possesses qualities which are uniquely his own. In Marx's words, man 'is a being for himself (*fuer sich*). Therefore, he is a species being, and has to confirm and manifest himself as such both in his being and knowing.'[1] By describing man as a being 'for himself', Marx is referring to man's self-consciousness, to his awareness of himself as an individual active in pursuing his own ends. This is how he confirms himself through knowing.

Mutual recognition, the act of seeing oneself in others, extends each individual's awareness to cover the whole human race; he realizes that the actions of others have aims similar to and even connected to his own. Man is also conscious of having a past, which is the record of his successes and failures in attaining these aims, and of the possibilities which constitute his future. He does not know, of course, what the future will be like but merely *that* it will be. In short, man is a species being because he knows what only man can know, namely that he is the species being, man.

Man confirms and manifests himself in his 'being' in two ways: firstly, by looking, sounding, smelling, feeling and, we may suppose, even tasting like a man. His peculiar physical make up and characteristics are those of a man. Secondly, and more important for Marx, man manifests himself as a species being through activity of a kind, quality and pace, that could only be done by human beings.

As a member of the human species, each individual is said to have a number of distinguishing powers and needs. In one list, Marx offers the following as species powers: 'seeing, hearing, smelling, tasting, feeling, thinking, being aware (*Anschauen*), sensing (*Empfinden*), wanting, acting (*Tatigkeit*), loving'.[2] 'Acting' is meant here in the sense of 'acting as' and 'practising', and is not the same thing as 'activity' which has a much broader meaning. On the basis of other statements by Marx, we can also view willing, procreating, sex, knowing and judging as species powers.[3] One must try to overcome the initial shock of seeing such a strange mixture of actions, functions and conditions brought under the same rubric, and to withhold judgement until I have had an opportunity to explain.

The species powers Marx attributes to man are also spoken of as 'senses', and these are sometimes separated into 'physical and mental senses', the former being what we normally mean in speaking of man's senses.[4] Further complications are that what Marx calls the 'mental senses' in some places are labelled the 'practical senses' elsewhere; and 'mental senses' and 'physical senses' together are also referred to as 'human sense', or man's 'human relations to the world'.[5] These are the main guises worn by man's species powers.

Like man's natural powers, his species powers have to do with establishing particular relationships between himself and nature, including other men as parts of nature; and as with natural powers, they 'can find their objective realization in natural objects only'.[6] Seeing must see objects; feeling must feel objects; even thinking must think about objects – recalling the broad sense Marx gives to 'object'.

The distinction between natural and species powers stands out clearly if we try to conceive of one without the other. This is easy to do for natural powers – we see them every day in all animals. Natural powers are the processes of life devoid of human attributes. It is inconceivable, however, how species powers could exist without natural powers, without the qualities man shares with all living things. Man's species powers of seeing, feeling, thinking, loving, etc., are only possible because man labors, eats, drinks and is sexually active, because he manages to stay alive and healthy. Man without any relations to nature is a relationless void; without any specifically human relations to nature, he is an animal; and without his animal relations to nature, he is a dead human being – assuming of course that these relations once existed, or else he would have never been alive to die. If natural powers can be viewed as establishing the framework in which life itself goes on, then man's species powers express the kind of life which man, as distinct from all other beings, carries on inside this framework.

Having made these two types of powers as clear and separate

from one another as Marx's account allows, they must now be conflated. For at the same time that natural powers serve as a basis for species powers they also retain the possibility of becoming species powers themselves. Sex is a natural power but it is also a species power. Women are regarded and treated in a wide variety of ways the world over. Marx believes that when women are accepted as equals, possessing the same rights and deserving the same thoughtfulness as males, then man's sexual activity is no longer that of an animal; sexuality will have been raised to the level of things peculiarly human.[7]

Similarly, any natural power which man exercises in a way markedly different from that of the animals can become a species power.[8] Of course, the natural power which has become a species power keeps its special significance for the life and health of the individual, but now it is also a means by which he expresses himself as a human being. Marx includes all five senses as species powers even though animals also possess them, because man uses his senses in a human fashion. The intimacy of the total relationship Marx posits between natural and species powers can be observed in such phrases as 'man's essential powers' and the 'essence of man', which are generally used to refer to both groups. And in keeping with Marx's use of 'essence' to emphasize relationships, the objects through which these powers are realized are also conveyable, if not always conveyed, by these expressions.[9]

10. *Relating man to objects:*
orientation, perception

The previous chapters dealt with man in the abstract, as an entity possessing powers and needs. It should be clear, however, that this abstract entity has no separate existence for Marx who always sets the individual inside a world of particulars, of other men, institutions, ideas, etc., and sees every one of his powers and needs binding him inextricably to his period. The tie between each individual and the world was proffered in terms of his needing those objects which are necessary for the realization of his powers. Yet, to say that powers are 'realized', 'actualized', 'manifested' or 'confirmed' in objects is to say very little in a concrete way about what actually occurs. How exactly do powers, that strange mixture of senses, functions and conditions which Marx attributes to each human being, get realized in objects? And what are the signs of this realization both in man and in nature which serve Marx as evidence, and allow him to claim these objects as part of human nature? Attention will now be directed to these questions.

The relations established between man's powers and the world in Marx's system are the work of three interconnected processes, perception, orientation and appropriation. I call them processes, but I could just as easily refer to them as events or aspects of the same process or event, since they most often occur simultaneously. However, their separate functions require that some division between them be maintained. Perception is the immediate contact with nature man achieves through his senses. But, as we have seen, what Marx calls 'senses' are also man's species powers. Their 'identity' is that of two overlapping Relations, two different points of emphasis in a single whole which may go by either name.[1] Sense is power in its coming into contact with nature; whereas power is sense in its interaction with nature and its movement toward inherent goals.

Orientation (*Verhalten*), on the other hand, has to do with how we perceive things, and particularly what we understand of their purposes. It establishes patterns, assigns places and worth, and, consequently, involves setting up an entire framework for our action *vis à vis* the rest of the world.

Appropriation, the third process mentioned, is the interaction between man's senses and nature, in which the powers involved use the nature they come into contact with for their own ends. 'Appropriation', in Marx's writings, always refers to the realization of some or other of man's powers.

To be able to distinguish between these processes, I have broken a unity which really cannot be broken in this way, for each process is included in the operations of the other two. Perception leads immediately and necessarily to orientation, and orientation provides the meaning and structure, as well as the future goals of perception. From the very moment that man perceives something, the objects perceived have a certain order and worth. Furthermore, orientation is present before perception, pre-choosing the objects one will try to see and those one will consider irrelevant.

And as man perceives nature, as he orients himself to it, so does he appropriate it.[2] Perception itself is an act of appropriation in the mere exercise of the power involved. The same is true of orientation which sets limits to the exercise of any power, determining, in this way, its possible achievements. And, conversely, appropriation can only occur through and after perception and orientation. Finally, appropriation can even be said to affect future perception and orientation through the changes it brings about in man and his objects. Of these three processes, appropriation occupies the most prominent place, and in Marx's later works, perception and orientation are wholly subsumed under it.

Marx says that 'Sense perception . . . must be the basis of all science,' and we may assume that this includes the science of Marxism.[3] Be this as it may, Marx showed little concern to develop his own views on this matter. He realized, of course, that there are differences between the five senses and man's other powers, which he also referred to as 'senses'. We observed how he divides senses into 'physical' and 'mental' (or 'practical'), and he sometimes speaks specifically of the 'five senses'.[4] Yet, he never bothers to explain how some of the senses that come into his discussion are necessarily based on others, or in what else they differ. The questions which are ordinarily answered by a theory of perception are never asked.

Consequently, I am inclined to say that Marx does not have a theory of sense perception at all but has in its stead a broader theory of man's relationship to nature, which embraces, along with much else, the five senses and their contents. Marx goes so far on one occasion as to equate personal powers and Relations: 'The transformation . . . of personal powers (Relations)' (*persönlichen Mächte* (*Verhältnisse*)).[5] According to this interpretation, what are regarded as senses or powers are seen as equal means by which man learns about nature and interacts with it. Seeing, hearing, smelling, tasting, touching, knowing, judging, making love, thinking, sensing, being aware, wanting, procreating, loving and willing each makes us aware of certain aspects of entities that would have remained unknown to us if we had never seen, heard, etc. something in connection with them. They are all 'vehicles' carrying a mutual effect between the individual and his object (joined together in an internal relation), altering both to a greater or lesser degree.

Though centering upon the five senses, Marx's concept 'perception' may be said to cover all the individual's contacts with nature. To characterize such perception in terms of the reflection of the real world in men's minds (Lenin) or man's becoming conscious of the world (Sartre) is equally correct (or incorrect), depending on the degree to which each characterization permits the other. That is to say, taken as means of emphasizing different aspects of an interaction, both are right. Whereas, taken as the whole account, neither is.[6]

The discussion of Marx's views on science in the previous section revealed that there are important limitations on what one can learn through perception. For Marx, man's senses only bring him into contact with appearances; the essence of any thing, the major relations out of which it is composed, can only be learned through lengthy investigation and study. Here, controlled experiments (where possible), reductionism, imaginative reconstruction of broken links and the like make use of the results of immediate perception to uncover the 'hidden substratum'.[7]

As with his perception of nature outside the species, man's perception of other men teaches him appearances rather than essences. Perception alone can never probe into the essence of man. According to Marx, man first establishes his identity as a man by comparing himself with other individuals who represent the type *homo sapiens* for him.[8] His attention is wholly taken by their surface features. But the forms actually assumed by man's powers and their objects have as many possibilities as there are ages and classes in human history. Nevertheless, Marx notes, the appearance of the person under scrutiny strikes the viewer not only as all there is to say about the other but as his own true essence as well.[9] Human potentiality, what man can become at other times and in other circumstances, is completely neglected in such comparisons. It is in this way that our perception misleads us. The limitation on our perception is the world as it appears and, for Marx, this is a grave limitation affecting both thought and action, because the world is a great deal more than it appears.

11. *Appropriation*

Appropriation, together with perception and orientation, is the third process which occurs when man relates to nature. In its most general sense, 'appropriation' means to utilize constructively, to build by incorporating; the subject, whether stated or implied, is man's essential powers. For Marx, the individual appropriates the nature he perceives and has become oriented to by making it in some way a part of himself with whatever effect this has on his senses and future orientation. To 'capture' a sunset, it is not necessary to paint, write or sing about it. It becomes ours in the experiencing of it. The forms and colors we see, the sense of awakening to beauty that we feel and the growth in sensitivity which accompanies such an event are all indications of our new appropriation. To paint the sunset, or to write or sing about it, if joined by genuine emotions, would achieve an even higher degree of appropriation, would make this event even more a part of us.

If the appropriation is a significant one, it may increase our appreciation for beauty to such an extent that we now regard the whole of nature in a new way. Nuances of color, light and shape, which were formerly missed, have become striking objects of attention. Orientation, too, is affected as some things assume new or broader meanings depending on which of our fires has been kindled. Our thought and activity in regard to the appropriated entity will also vary accordingly. Though it is an extreme example to which most of our everyday experience can only approximate, it is on this model of appropriating a sunset that 'appropriation' in Marxism can best be understood.[1]

The example of appropriating a sunset was drawn from the species power of seeing. In Marxism, each power, as a separate sense with its own unique possibilities for contacting nature, has a distinctive mode of appropriation. Of man's appropriation of objects, Marx says,

The manner in which they become his depends on the nature of the objects and on the nature of the essential power corresponding to it; for it is precisely the determinateness (*Bestimmtheit*) of this relationship which shapes the particular, real mode of affirmation. To the eye an object is another object than the object of the ear.[2]

Marx refers to Hegel's insight into the meaning of alienation as his 'appropriation'.[3] As queer as this may sound, it appears that insights are among the entities that can be appropriated by what Marx calls the power of thinking. Viewed from inside Marx's system, Hegel's power of thinking appropriates, 'constructs' an insight from the elements about which he is thinking. Other powers find their objectification in other kinds of objects.

The characteristic mode in which any object exists for a power is the characteristic mode through which this power achieves its gratification.[4] Thus, if only church music exists, the power of hearing can only be gratified as to music in church; or if one lives in a society overpopulated with nuns and prostitutes, fornication in brothels becomes a characteristic mode of gratification for the power of sex.

Each of man's essential powers has as many possible realizations, and hence, too, objects of appropriation, as it does potential forms in its development through history. Marx says, 'It is obvious that the human eye gratifies itself in a way different from the crude non-human eye; the human ear different from the crude ear, etc.'[5] Seeing only monetary value in jewels is appropriation of another order than seeing their intrinsic beauty. Again, grasping at food like a hungry animal achieves a far different satisfaction than eating with a knife and fork and taking the time to taste each morsel. The close correspondence Marx sees between the form and level of appropriation and the state of the object concerned is made explicit in his claim that

The most beautiful music has no sense for the unmusical ear – is no object for it, because my object can only be the confirmation of one of my essential powers and can therefore only be so for me as my essential power is present for itself as a subjective capacity, because the sense of an object for me goes only so far as my senses go.[6]

In offering concrete examples of the operation of man's powers, I have had to treat them separately. However, in life, because of their interconnection, they tend to function in groups and sometimes all together. Man is bound to each of the objects he comes into contact with by many cords. For example, the sunset which was said to be related to the individual through his power of seeing may also be related to him through his powers of feeling, thinking and loving (he feels it, he thinks about it, he loves it). Consequently, this sunset will affect all these powers.

Furthermore, one power frequently reacts on another making new achievements by the latter possible. To love a woman means that one will see and hear her and everything associated with her differently from before, just as seeing the rich variety of colors in a sunset can increase one's ability to feel and be aware of the world generally. The number and complexity of the relations Marx posits between man and nature insure that no power grows to its full stature while others stagnate. As a rule, all a person's abilities for appropriation move 'forward' together. Thus, too, for any given individual, his natural powers are likely to have developed up to par with his species power. Does not the eating of a cultured person reveal his culture as much as his seeing does? By the time of communism this interdependence of man's powers has proceeded so far that Marx can claim, 'Man appropriates his total essence in a total manner, that is to say, as a whole man.'[7]

The degree to which man's appropriation has moved toward the ends inherent in his powers is said to be 'entirely dependent on the stage of development which production and human intercourse has reached'.[8] In primitive society, man appropriated the naturally existing means of production in producing boats, knives and shelters out of wood and stones, and in using them for his life purposes. Since relatively few articles were appropriated, however, and these inefficiently, the powers involved in this activity can be said to have achieved only a low level of fulfillment. This in turn is reflected by primitive man's having minimal needs.[9] With the appearance of new and radically different objects, however, such as occurs wherever the production process is forging ahead, man's powers realize themselves in ways which were not before possible. And powers which are presented with 'unusual' objects become transformed as powers. This is Marx's meaning when he says, 'The forming of the five senses is a labor of the entire history of the world down to the present'.[10]

In Marx's day, and we may assume he would stretch this period to cover our time, appropriation is supposed to have lost its creative character. Instead of leading to the enrichment of man's powers, capitalist appropriation has become, in Marx's words, 'direct, one-sided gratification – merely in the sense of possessing, of having'.[11]

The human condition reflected in such appropriation is given in Marx's claims that 'man has no human needs' and that money is the only 'true need' produced in capitalism.[12] People no longer feel drives to see, hear, love and think, but only to have, to own what is seen, heard, loved and thought about. Ownership, with all it entails in the way of greed, status, rights to use and abuse, has become the only adequate expression of man's powers at this stage in their development. For Marx, the desire to own is not a characteristic of human nature but of historically conditioned human nature, and the desire to own everything with which one comes into contact is the peculiar product of capitalism. It should not be necessary to point out that there are exceptions, individuals and sometimes certain powers within individuals where the shoe does not fit; but, generally speaking, Marx's description of man's powers in terms of their lowest common denominator, the power of 'having', applies more or less – with the necessary reservations made for differences of class – to all the people of the capitalist era.[13]

Just as capitalism is the 'low point' of appropriation by man's powers, communism is its 'high point'. Comparing the role that money plays in capitalist society with a situation where money does not exist, Marx states:

Assume man to be man and his relationship to the world to be a human one: then you can exchange love only for love, trust for trust, etc. If you want to enjoy art, you must be an artistically cultivated person; if you want to exercise influence over people you must be a person with a stimulating and encouraging effect on other people. Every one of your relations to man and to nature must be a specific expression corresponding to the object of your will, of your real individual life.[14]

This state of affairs, which only exists in communism, is referred to by Marx as 'the real appropriation of the human essence (*menschlichen Wesens*) by and for man' – 'real' because it occurs in life and involves objects, and 'human' because it represents the ultimate achievement of man's potentialities.[15] In Marx's talk of 'human objects', 'human activities', 'human essence', etc., the temporal reference is almost always to communist society.

Communism emerges as an era when man 'brings his species powers out of himself'.[16] The vast storehouse of his potentialities is at last emptied. Until then the greater part of these powers lie hidden inside him, which is to say that they are only partially and improperly fulfilled. Only in communism, Marx claims, is 'the richness of subjective human sensibility (a musical ear, an eye for beauty of form – in short, senses capable of human gratification, senses confirming themselves as essential powers of man) either cultivated or brought into being'.[17] Communism is the time of full, personal appropriation.

12. *Nature as evidence*

It is not only the powers involved in appropriation but also the objects appropriated that are said to become human in communism. Until now, our chief concern has been with man, the subject, and his powers. Equal attention must be given to man's objects as the necessary manifestations of these powers. According to Marx, 'Communism is the complete emancipation of all human senses and attributes; but it is this emancipation precisely because these senses and attributes have become, subjectively and objectively, human.'[1] They have become 'subjectively' human in that man's powers and needs have attained their full potential, and 'objectively' so in the sense that his objects are indicative of this achievement. Such objects constitute the 'human essence' that Marx says will be appropriated in communism.[2] In his words, 'The eye has become a human eye just as its object has become a social, human object – an object emanating from man for man.'[3]

Because his powers are so extensive, communist man requires the whole of nature brought up to the level of his appropriation to satisfy him. Thus, in this period, the entire world is spoken of as 'the world of man's essential powers – human reality . . . all objects become for him the objectification of himself, become objects which confirm and realize his individuality'.[4]

Man's powers can be observed in their objects not only in communism but throughout history. In each era, these objects bear the tell-tale 'mark', the sign of what he has become, before appropriation as well as afterwards. We have already heard Marx say that the characteristic mode in which an object exists for any power is the mode in which this power generally realizes itself; man can only appropriate an object in ways the latter will allow, with each of its qualities serving as a limiting condition. Human beings cannot see Impressionist art in the highly stylized paintings of the fourteenth century, nor truly love in a society of nuns and prostitutes, nor think about calculus when it has yet to be invented. At each level in the development of man's powers, the objects through which they seek expression will also be given. From these objects themselves, therefore, we can deduce the state of man's powers together with the level of their appropriation.

More indicative still of the quality of appropriation of each generation and class are the actual results, the changes in form, shape, number, etc., that are achieved. For only man, being what he is at this time and place, would have done these things, with these objects, in this way. Most powers bring something new to nature in their realization, forming or transforming the myriad of objects with which the individual comes into contact in a manner that expresses the then state of his powers. The stylized religious paintings of the fourteenth century offer us striking evidence of man's capacities in this period in the same instant that they help set the boundaries to his further development. Some powers, such as eating and drinking, abolish a part of nature in their realization, but even here the very hole left says something about the quality of the powers involved.

Every sphere of life provides both occasions and materials for the objectification of man's essential powers. Production, religion, politics, art, literature, family, state, law, morality and science are each to be regarded in this light. In all their observable forms they embody the interaction between man's powers at the level to which they have matured and the then existing objects of nature. Man is always surrounded by factories, currency, implements, clothing, types of shelter, foods, gods, prayers, moral codes, rulers, laws, statues, art, literature, philosophical ideas, scientific hypotheses and forms of family life suited to what he has become, and he is constantly trying to fit them better to what he is becoming. In each historical period, we are presented throughout nature with the evidence of what man wants, what he is capable of and what satisfies him.

Material production, because of the necessary character of this task and the amount of time devoted to it, is the area of life where the individual's powers are most evident. According to Marx, 'The object of labor is . . . the objectification of man's species life: for he duplicates himself not only, as in consciousness, intellectually, but also actively, in reality'.[5] Man's species life, which is the operation of his essential powers, is said to become visible in production through the various modes adopted and products produced. Both are referred to, in Marx's peculiar terminology, as man's 'duplication' of himself in the real world. What is duplicated here is not man's appearance (his phenomenal self) but his powers (his essential self). How and what man produces are taken as certain indications of 'who' he is and 'what' he has come to. In this way, Marx calls industry, by which he means man's products as well as his implements, 'the exoteric revelation of man's essential powers', and the history of industry, 'the open book of man's essential powers, the exposure to the senses of human psychology'.[6] Again, such remarks are not meant to indicate a close relation but an internal one.

With industry and man's powers viewed as two sides of the same Relation, changes in one invariably reflect changes in the other. And, according to Marx, the history of the productive forces, that is, of industry, is also 'the history of the development of the powers of the individuals themselves'.[7] They have the same history, because they are, as Marx would have it, 'identical'; the concepts which describe one convey likewise the sense of the other. So it is that Marx can claim of the coming socialist take-over of capitalist industry, 'The appropriation of these forces is itself nothing more than the development of the individual capacities corresponding to the material instruments of production.'[8]

For Marx, the means of production in advanced capitalism, though the result of capitalist appropriation, are objects with which humanity can begin its climb into communism. Socialist appropriation of these means of production, however, involves much more than transferring titles of ownership; primarily, it involves controlling, using and regarding them in a manner and on a scale that expresses powers in the process of becoming fully human. And since appropriation in communism concerns the whole personality, Marx maintains, 'The appropriation of a totality of instruments of production is for this reason the development of a totality of capacities in the individuals themselves.'[9] The developments which occur in nature are met here as always by a corresponding transformation in the character of man.

13. *Activity, work, creativity*

Activity is the chief means by which man appropriates objects. We saw earlier that perception is the individual's immediate contact with nature; orientation how he understands this contact; and appropriation – roughly – the use he makes of it. Most kinds of appropriation, however, require some 'mediation' to bring man's powers and nature together. Relatively few acts of appropriation are as motionless as seeing a sunset, which was the model offered. Appropriation generally demands a more active role from man himself. Activity, for Marx, *is* this role; it is man interacting with nature with his body as well as his mind. As such, activity is the actual movement of man's powers in the real world, the living process of objectifying these powers in nature.

The static account presented so far comes alive in man's activity. With the actors, the setting and most of the plot before us, the acting was until now missing. Change and development are now occurring, as well as provided for. It is activity which establishes man in all the areas of his life; and, for Marx, the form of this activity in any period, as with industry and appropriation itself, is indicative of the state of man's essential powers.

Just as industry predominates over all other objects in nature, so too Marx gives precedence to activity in industry over other types of activity, and for the same reasons. He says,

The work-process resolved as above into its simple elementary factors, is human action with a view to the production of use-values, appropriation of natural substances to human requirements; it is the necessary condition for effecting exchanges of matter between man and nature; it is the everlasting nature-imposed condition of human existence, and therefore is independent of every social phase of that existence, or rather common to every such phase.[1]

Activity devoted to obtaining the material demands of life is more necessary, arduous and time consuming than activity in any other sphere. In his later writings, where Marx directs most of his attention to the productive life, 'activity' is replaced by the specialized term 'work'.

In two notes to the English edition of *Capital* i, Engels singles out 'work' as the term which most clearly expresses Marx's intended meaning of conscious, purposive activity in the productive process. Engels says, 'The labor which creates use-value, and counts qualitatively, is *Work,* as distinguished from Labor; that which creates value and counts quantitatively, is *Labor* as distinguished from Work.'² (In German, the term *Arbeit* covers both meanings.) I am only concerned here with 'work', or what it is that Engels says creates 'use-values' (and not with 'labor' which is said to create 'value'). The use-value of any product is essentially its ability to serve the purpose for which it was made.³ In this sense, use-values can be found in all areas of life, wherever in fact man has molded objects to suit his purposes. Constitutions, religious dogmas and filial obedience are as much use-values as are shoes. Consequently, Marx can claim, 'Religion, family, state, law, morality, science, art, etc., are only particular modes of production.'⁴ As components of an organic whole, religion, family, state etc., can be called by a name usually reserved for material production when they function in a way generally associated with it, that is, to produce use-values. The activity in any area of life which produces use-values is 'work' in the broadest sense, but 'work' in this sense is also 'activity'.

Productive activity, or work, which creates use-values of material objects, is seen as related to man's essential powers in three ways. First, it is the leading example of action by man's combined powers. Whatever man does several of his powers are likely to be involved and in a given relationship to nature. In a walk around the block for example, our eyes, ears and nose are each, in their own manner, making contact with various objects. During productive activity, however, all man's powers are engaged to a greater or lesser extent. According to Marx, the 'working up of objects' to satisfy man's material life purposes requires planning, skillful effort and concentration. We must have some notion of what we want beforehand, know how to make it, and be able to concentrate on its production. No other activity demands as much.*

As the outstanding example of action by man's combined powers, Marx calls productive activity 'the life of the species'; it is

---

* A more detailed description of work will be found below, in Chapter 15.

man's 'life-activity'.[5] It is chiefly in this sense that Marx speaks of work as a need, adding elsewhere that even in communism there will be a need for a 'normal portion of work'.[6] It is the need of all man's powers for the most direct means to their combined fulfillment, and it is common to people in all societies.

Productive activity is further related to the individual's powers in establishing new possibilities, in extending the boundaries in nature, for their fulfillment. Work must occur in nature; it is only the external world 'in which it is active, from which and by means of which it produces'.[7] As we saw, the world of objects as it exists at any one time constitutes the real limits for the realization of man's powers. If this world were to remain unaltered, these powers would always achieve the same type and degree of fulfillment. It is only because reality undergoes constant transformation that we can speak of fulfillment in terms of 'levels' and 'modes'. That our world does change is due, Marx says, to the activity of man which never ceases to change it.[8]

The direction this productive activity takes, its immediate and basic aims, can be traced to the demands that nature makes on the individual, given his own peculiar make up. According to Marx, 'Neither nature objectively nor nature subjectively is directly given in a form adequate to the human being.'[9] In creating a nature which is adequate, in producing food which he can eat, clothes he can wear and a house he can live in, man is forever remolding nature, and with each alteration enabling his powers to achieve new kinds and degrees of fulfillment. Industry exists in order to satisfy human needs, but industry in turn creates conditions of life which generate new needs. These make necessary a new advance in industry and a diversification of products. It is such a development Marx is describing when he declares, 'the needs of people are themselves the ultimate grounds (*letzten Gründe*) for their satisfaction'.[10]

What would happen if nature were given in a form which man found adequate? In *Capital* I, Marx mentions the tropics where nature is too lavish, where it is 'adequate', and as a result keeps man in the condition of a child. Instead of growth there is stagnation. In this instance, nature

does not impose upon him any necessity to develop himself. It is not the tropics with their luxuriant vegetation, but the temperate zone, that is the mother-country of capital. It is not the mere fertility of the soil, but the differentiation of the soil, the variety of its natural products, the changes of the seasons, which form the physical basis for the social division of labor, and which, by changes in the natural surroundings, spur man on to the multiplication of his wants, his capabilities, his means and modes of labor.[11]

Thus, it is not nature as such but variations in nature which force and lure the individual and, in the last analysis, enable him to develop his powers.[12] With nature viewed as an incentive as well as a limitation on activity, the natural features of each locale assume a special significance.

The link between work which maintains life and merely reproduces existing conditions (tropical societies) and work which goes further and alters these conditions is the social division of labor. Specialization among individual workers results from man's attempt to satisfy his basic life needs in an 'inadequate' nature, but it brings in its train an increase in society's overall efficiency for transforming nature. More can be done; more is done; new needs are generated – the march of progress has got under way. With the division of labor, man's productive activity acquires a logic which will bring him eventually to the portals of the communist society.*

Besides serving as the main vehicle for the expression of man's combined powers and as the principal means by which the nature imposed limitations on his fulfillment are lifted, productive activity is also the chief influence on the development of these powers *qua* powers. 'How could work', Marx asks, 'ever be anything but a "development of human capacities"?'[13] The growth of man's capabilities toward the ends inherent in them, in each individual as in history itself, is primarily the result of his productive activity. Referring to such activity, Marx claims, 'By thus acting on the external world and changing it, he at the same time changes his own nature. He develops his slumbering powers and compels them to act in obedience to his sway.'[14] Man's 'nature' in this statement is meant to include both his powers and the objects through which they manifest themselves.

As with appropriation, whose history has already been outlined, the precise character of man's productive activity is different in each period. In one place, Marx points out that productive activity

---

* The division of labor is discussed again in the following chapter, but receives its fullest treatment in Chapter 24 below.

both expends man's powers and develops them.[15] Work always involves the consumption of powers, but it does not always alter them for the better. Whether an individual's ability to fulfill himself is actually increased or not will depend on the particular activity – what it is and how it is carried on – along with all the surrounding circumstances. The productive activity of the proletariat in a capitalist system is the outstanding instance of what might be called the 'retrogression' (to use my own term) of essential powers.

Productive activity develops powers capable of their ultimate fulfillments only in communism, and in communism only such activity exists. Marx says that in the communist society all work is 'self-activity', that is, activity which realizes the genuinely human powers that constitute the 'self' in this period.[16] Looking back over time from the vantage point of the future, Marx declares, 'for the socialist man the entire so-called history of the world is nothing but the begetting of man through human work, nothing but the coming to be (*Werden*) of nature for man'.[17] All transformations in man and his objects through all time will be viewed, from the perspective of communism, as having been determined by the character of human productive activity.

This brief sketch of the history of work is likewise an account of the changing meaning of 'work', each new development making the notion so much richer. Through its internal relations, in the first instance, with distribution, exchange and consumption, and beyond this with whatever other factors in and through which it takes place, work expresses the full character of a period. In the broadest sense, it is this period viewed from what Marx considers its most enlightening vantage point. Given the internal relation he posits between language and reality, all this is captured (if only occasionally conveyed) in the covering concept.[18]

It must also be noted that there is no clear distinction in Marx's writings between 'activity', 'work' and 'creativity'. In interacting with nature, each man deposits part of his personality, the distinctive contribution of his powers, in all he does. The modifications made are a reflection of the person acting, embodying some of his own qualities in a more or less recognizable form. This describes equally activity, work and creativity. Thus, all work in any area of life which produces use-values may also be viewed as creativity.

Marx even speaks of a 'worker's productive activity' as his 'creative power'.[19] Rather than a belittling of 'creativity', its equation with 'activity' and 'work' represents an unusual extension of these other concepts. Marx is not downgrading Milton's creative powers when he says, 'Milton produced *Paradise Lost* for the same reason that a silk worm produces silk. It was an activity of his nature.'[20] The activity of Milton's nature was such creative acts as writing *Paradise Lost*. Nor is Marx disputing the creativity which is involved in singing when he speaks of it as 'work' and 'activity'.[21]

'Creativity' is a term much used by the early Marx, the zenith of its use being reached even before 1844. Many of the poems, for example, that Marx wrote while still a student are songs of praise for man's creative drives and cries of defiance against whatever would fetter him. As far back as 1835, just before Marx left high school, he wrote an extremely revealing essay called 'Reflections of a Youth on Choosing a Calling', in which creativity and fulfillment are central themes.[22] 'Creativity' never leaves Marx's vocabulary but it is effectively replaced there, first by 'activity' and then by 'work'. 'Activity' is the term which figures most prominently in Marx's philosophical writings, especially the *Economic and Philosophic Manuscripts of 1844*. In his later economic writings, of course, 'work' has become the pivotal expression.[23]

The difference between 'activity', 'work' and 'creativity', however, is more than one of periods in Marx's life; it is also a matter of emphasis. Each term excels in bringing out certain aspects of what is essentially the same interaction between man and nature. 'Activity' stresses the separate motions involved and its totality as purposeful endeavor; 'work' points to material production as the prime area of activity and the production throughout life of use-values; and 'creativity' focuses on the uniqueness of the product, its source in man, the most advanced of nature's creatures, and the effect of this activity on his progress toward communism.

What begins as a difference in emphasis is seen at the limits of these concepts as independent meanings, for 'activity', 'work' and 'creativity' do not completely overlap. Not all activity is work; nor is all activity, nor all work, creativity. The activity of running around in circles, for instance, is not work for no use-values are produced, nor can such activity be considered creative. Likewise, work in a capitalist factory where, according to Marx, man has been reduced to 'a cog in the machine' also cannot be called 'creative', since like running in circles such work does not aid man's powers to mature. A given case of activity and work is also one of creativity when it involves human powers or helps man's powers to develop positively. In communism, as far as possible, all activity and work is creative. Even outside communism, each term weighs heavily on the meanings of the others, and, on most occasions, where one is used the other two could be substituted with only a change in emphasis resulting.

14. *Man's social nature*

Marx's conception of man's powers and of what is required for their realization provides the basis for his claim that man's activity (work, creativity) must be done with and for others, and, consequently, that he is a social being. Marx says that by 'social' he means 'the cooperation of several individuals, no matter under what conditions, in what manner, and to what end'.[1] This cooperation may be active, conscious and purposeful, as in production, or it may be passive, unconscious and without apparent purpose, as in using a language which other people understand. 'Cooperation', then, covers all the forms in and through which man relates to his fellows; but Marx also uses it in a narrow sense where it refers to joint activity aimed at achieving mutually accepted ends.

'Society', the last in Marx's trio of all-group expressions, is defined as 'the sum of the relations in which . . . individuals stand to one another'.[2] These relations are sometimes treated as existing externally to man, as when Marx calls society (the actual forms taken by cooperation) 'the product of man's reciprocal activities'; and sometimes as lying within man himself, as when he says, 'Society itself, that is man himself in his social relations'.[3] And as people are seen related to each other not only directly but through their objects, the term 'society' at the limits of its definition covers both man and the world he inhabits.

According to Marx, people are invariably in a close relationship with one another because 'their needs – therefore their nature – and the manner of satisfying them creates between them reciprocal links (sexual relations, exchange, division of labor)'.[4] So much is this the case, he maintains, that 'the history of an individual in particular cannot be separated from the history of preceding or contemporary individuals'.[5] It is man's need for other men and what they can do to aid him in the realization of his powers, whatever their condition, that holds civil society together in all periods. This glue binding man to man is also referred to by Marx as natural 'necessity' (*Naturnotwendigkeit*) and 'interest'.[6]

Production is the area of life where man's social character

emerges most clearly and it generally serves Marx as his prime example of human cooperation. In opposition to the atomistic views of many of his contemporaries, Marx holds that

Man is in the most literal sense of the word a *zoon politikon*, not only a social animal, but an animal which can develop into an individual only in society. Production by isolated individuals outside of society – something which might happen as an exception to a civilized man who by accident got into the wilderness and already dynamically possessed within himself the forces of society – is as great an absurdity as the idea of the development of language without individuals living together and talking to one another.[7]

Producing with, for or through others, and on the basis of what others have requested, supplied or taught are the obvious social ties to be found in production. Beyond this, we must recall what was said about Marx's conception of production being 'identical' with consumption, distribution and exchange, whereby each process is viewed as an integral facet of the others, in order to appreciate the full range of cooperation that Marx finds in production.[8]

If productive activity outside tropical lands is to succeed in satisfying man's most basic needs, it must involve a division of labor. Instead of one person doing all the tasks necessary to maintain his life, he specializes in a particular line of work knowing that other people are doing likewise. A man must be certain that others are producing food for him in order to concentrate on making shoes, and he must know that he will be able to exchange his shoes for food whenever he wants. Soon he will produce only one part of the shoe while his co-workers produce the remainder. With his job technically diminished, his dependence on the efforts of others for finished product and, thus, the necessity for cooperation with them augments proportionally.

Through the social division of labor, too, the conditions of life of one person are found to cover many, with the result that what were individual needs have become social needs: whole groups are conscious of desiring the same ends. Social needs reflect a situation where the powers of many men have developed up to the same level, which results, in turn, from their having similar experiences at home and at work. Such needs are likewise reflected in social wants (feelings), social demand (stated feelings or actions) and social utility (the use to which articles are put).

The individual cannot escape his dependence on society even when he acts on his own. A scientist who spends his lifetime in a laboratory may delude himself that he is a modern version of Robinson Crusoe, but the material of his activity and the apparatus and skills with which he operates are social products. They are inerasable signs of the cooperation which binds men together. The very language in which a scientist thinks has been learned in a particular society. Social context also determines the career and other life goals that an individual adopts, how he tries to carry out his choices and whether or not he succeeds. No one becomes a scientist or even wants to become one in a society which does not have any. In short, man's consciousness of himself and of his relations with others and with nature are that of a social being, since the manner in which he conceives of anything is a function of his society.[9]

The individual, then, is always social; yet, Marx thinks of him as being more so in communism, where competition as we know it has given way to cooperation as we have still to learn about it. The resulting social functions of the communist man are described as 'so many modes of giving free scope to his natural and acquired powers'.[10] Knowledge may be superficial and one-sided or deep and many-sided. Just so man's relations with his fellows, and it is only in communism that the potential within these relations is fully realized. Marx even equates the expression 'social being' with 'human being', where the latter means man living at the high tide of his accomplishments.[11] This is but another example of a concept meaning what Marx is using it to describe, the sense of 'social' keeping pace with changes in the real world. In communism, 'society' and 'social being' come to mean all that is distinctive in this period of man's social relationships, and are often used by Marx with this broad reference in mind.

All man's efforts, products, thoughts and emotions relate him to others and, in communism, besides the strengthening of such ties, now suitably transformed, the objects at both ends of each person's relations are appropriated by everyone; or as Marx puts it, 'The senses and enjoyment of other men have become my own appropriation.'[12] We saw earlier that each man, as a unit of nature, is an object for everyone else and therefore part of everyone else through their appropriation. For Marx, people are appropriating one another in all their contacts. And like the other objects in nature, the individual in his role as object must be up to the level at which he is being appropriated; otherwise others will not be able to fully realize their powers in him. Hence, only communist men are 'fitting' human objects of appropriation by other communist men, who require such ideal friends, neighbors and co-workers to manifest the full range of qualities that Marx attributes to them. 'All history', Marx says, 'is the preparation of "man" to become the object of sensuous consciousness, and for the needs of "man as man" to become (natural, sensuous) needs.'[13] This latter aim has been treated in my description of what the individual will be able to do in communism, but it is also a question of 'what he can be done to'. As communist objects, human beings possess those necessary attributes which enable others to achieve complete fulfillment through them.[14]

With each man only able to appropriate other communist men, their fulfillment concerns him as much as his own. His stake in their accomplishments and happiness could not be more personal; yet the result is his coming to view all of nature in terms of humanity. Objects that any individual needs are seen as objects that society needs, since everyone's fulfillment requires the satisfaction of this individual. Hence, Marx can claim that in communism, 'Need or enjoyment have consequently lost their egotistical nature'.[15] A person can no longer satisfy his own need by depriving others, since the effect of their disappointment would punish him along with everyone else. Essential to grasp is that man at this time believes that whatever others appropriate, whether in production or consumption, belongs equally to him, and whatever he does equally to them.

In harness with this belief, both affecting it and being affected by it, is communist man's conception of others and their necessary objects as extensions of himself. The extraordinary cooperation which exists brings a revolution in the way each individual conceptualizes his relations with what we take to be the 'outer' world. For Marx, as we have seen, all such relations are internal to each of the factors involved, but it is only in communism that this way of viewing reality acquires general acceptance and that its consequences become part of people's daily lives. Through this conceptual revolution, the individual has, in effect, supplied himself with a new subject, the community, for all but his most personal activities. There are few developments in communism which are as difficult to grasp or as far reaching in their implications as the substitution in people's minds of man the species for the separate and independent individuals each of us takes himself to be. With this change, the integration, both practical and theoretical (in life and in outlook), of the individual into the group is completed. The age-old conflict between man and society has been resolved.[16]

The path which we have trodden brings us to the conclusion expressed in Marx's claim that in communism, 'nature becomes man'.[17] In this period, the variety and intensity of the individual's activity has brought him directly, or as a unit of society, into contact with all of nature. Former tenuous relations are strengthened and objects once untouched by his powers become involved in the work of their fulfillment. For the first time, objects and the desires they generate are uniting people rather than making them compete.[18] With society viewed as the sum of interpersonal ties, including people's relations with each other's objects, Marx concludes that communist society 'is the consummate oneness in substance (*vollendete Weseneinheit*) of man and nature – the true resurrection of nature – the naturalism of man and the humanism of nature both brought to fulfillment'.[19] Like the conflict between man and society, the conflict between man and nature is also resolved. In communism, the Relations expressed by 'nature', 'man' and 'society' have converged into one another; people both recognize and treat what are referred to by these concepts as 'identical'.

15. The character of the species

While attacking Grün's interpretation of Fourier's psychology, Marx claims that no single attribute of real individuals can indicate the whole man: 'What manner of man can possibly be deduced from the lobe of his own ear, or from such other feature which distinguishes him from the beasts? Such a man is contained in himself, like his own pimple.'[1] Yet, Marx attempts such a summary of his conception of 'human nature in general' when he says 'The whole character of a species . . . is contained in the character of its life activity; and free, conscious activity is man's species character.'[2] In a sense, any of the major categories in which Marx offers his views, given the web of connections between them, could serve this function. Marx chooses man's 'life activity', which refers to all activities that distinguish the human species, because he considers it the most favourable vantage point from which to observe man's other relations.

At the core of 'life activity' is productive work; for Marx, 'productive life is the life of the species. It is life engendering life'.[3] And elsewhere he asserts, 'As individuals express their lives, so they are. What they are, therefore, coincides with their production, both with what they produce and with how they produce.'[4] We have already explored the human relations involved in 'what they produce', where industry was found to be the 'exoteric revelation of man's powers', but not yet in 'how they produce'. Though we have seen the part work plays in expressing man's powers, how it transforms his nature imposed limitations, and what it does to develop his capacities, the actual qualities exhibited while producing remain to be described. Because of the prime importance of work, Marx believes these qualities, with certain minor exceptions, will also be found in the individual's other life activities.

Even accepting Marx's assertion that man's species character is best summarized in the character of his life activity, I find the specific content he gives to this latter category doubly misleading: first, though it appears to apply to the species through its development, it does not – it only applies to man's activity in communism; secondly, as a description of man's activity in communism, it is woefully lacking in detail as we can see from Marx's other comments on this subject. Marx's summation of man's species character as free and conscious activity occurs in a discussion of alienation under capitalism, in which his main aim is to show that alienated activity is not free.[5] If we want to obtain man's species character for capitalism as well as for other societies, however, it is necessary to seek out a kind of lowest common denominator, or those qualities which all men past, present and future share just because they are men. Marx occasionally attempts such an exercise, though he never draws any conclusion in terms of man's species character; if he had, it would be different from the one stated above.

Man's species activity, in the sense of a lowest common denominator, emerges when one contrasts it with his natural activity, or that activity he has in common with other living creatures. This is the same method I applied to distinguish between natural and species powers. Marx says:

The animal is immediately identifiable with his life-activity. It does not distinguish itself from it. It is its life-activity. Man makes his life-activity itself the object of his will and of his consciousness. He has conscious life-activity. It is not a determination with which he directly merges. Conscious life-activity directly distinguishes man from animal life-activity.[6]

Man's activity is said to differ from that of animals in that he is able to set himself off mentally from whatever it is he is doing, while animals just do. They have no awareness of themselves as acting entities. Conscious of a distinction between his acts and himself as actor (knowing himself as someone who acts to attain his ends), it is the individual's choice on any given occasion to act or to rest tranquil. Such conscious and willed activity is unique to man among all living creatures.*

Another unique feature of human activity, according to Marx, is that it is planned beforehand; it is purposive.

---

* Marx's meaning is more than what is commonly meant by 'self-consciousness', taking in what some existentialists and present day psychoanalysts refer to as establishing the independence of the 'I', or creating the feeling of 'ego identity'. In Marx's case, however, man always possesses this quality.

A spider conducts operations that resemble those of a weaver, and a bee puts to shame many an architect in the construction of her cells. But what distinguishes the worst architect from the best of bees is this, that the architect raises his structure in the imagination of the laborer at its commencement. He not only effects a change of form in the material on which he works, but he also realizes a purpose of his own that gives the law to his *modus operandi,* and to which he must subordinate his will.[7]

Whatever material changes are achieved through the productive process are seen by Marx as 'designed from the commencement'.[8] The use-value created by work symbolizes its purposive character, since it is in order to obtain use-values that these tasks are undertaken.

Marx's view of purposive action raises a wide variety of objections, central of which is that the activity of the architect is not a prototype of all human work. Very few of a person's productive activities are intended in this way, and there are many of which it is difficult to say they are intended at all. For Marx, these are 'fine points' irrelevant to his chosen function of highlighting interrelations, and consequently for which he shows little concern. In Marx's defense, it must be added that the terms 'purpose' and 'plan' ('design') are generally used in their weak senses. What he seems to have had in mind is simply that man knows *what* it is he is going to produce, and which actions and implements will produce it. It is questionable, however, whether even this limited degree of purposiveness has such wide application.

Physical and mental flexibility are other characteristics that Marx ascribes to man's life activity. 'An animal forms things in accordance with the standard and the need of the species to which it belongs, whilst man knows how to produce in accordance with the standard of every species, and knows how to apply everywhere the inherent standard to the object.'[9] Man's physical and mental flexibility is his skill in adapting his activity, which is aimed at satisfying needs, to the requirements of different objects. Land, wood and iron all require special treatment if they are to be transformed into what they are potentially, that is, farms, tables, spoons, etc. The individual's ability to use tools to aid him in his work is an indication of how far his flexibility extends.

Marx also points out that man alone of all creatures is capable of giving close attention to what he is doing over any length of time; only man can concentrate. The subordination achieved in work, he claims, 'is no mere momentary act. Besides the exertion of the bodily organs, the process demands that, during the whole operation, the workman's will be steadily in consonance with his purpose. This means close attention.'[10]

Finally, from what was said about man as a social being, one further quality emerges: the individual's activity is always social. Even when it is not done with or for other men, production is social because it is based on the assumptions and language of a particular society.

If life activity, in its most general sense, is life itself, the energy, movement, change of pace and rhythm devoted to satisfying natural needs, then species life activity stands out as its conscious, willed, purposive, flexible, concentrated and social facets which enable man to pursue the unique demands of his species.

All the qualities Marx attributes to species life activity fit rather neatly into a category which Marx never used for this purpose. What have I said but that Marx views work as 'rational', in the sense that man grasps the nature of what he wants to transform and is able to direct his movements accordingly? In ordinary language, 'to act rationally' means to understand the 'why' and 'wherefore' of what one is doing and to proceed in the most efficient way when doing it. Consciousness, which was described as man's ability to distinguish himself from his activity, is obviously a constituent relation of reason in this sense. Before man can weigh the advantages of alternative courses, he must be aware of his distinction as chooser from what is to be chosen. The act of choosing itself shows will to be another building block in reason. However, it is in Marx's portrayal of man's life activity as purposive that its rationality is most evident. What is setting a plan and following it but to act rationally? Hegel had even referred to reason, on one occasion, as 'purposive activity'.[11] Though one may speak of purposes which are 'irrational' and, more strainedly, of rational activity that has 'no apparent purpose', such usages are not at all typical.

Man's mental flexibility is yet another aspect of his rationality, for it presumes the ability to understand objects, particularly in relation to their own future states. As for physical flexibility this is a prerequisite for follow-up activity that attains the stated goal in the most efficient manner. Concentration too can be brought under the same rubric by viewing it as a considered response to the requirements of the plan. The social nature of life activity is another element in its rationality, for do not all forms of cooperation aid man in his work? In bringing together Marx's scattered descriptions of human production under the single term 'rational' I have been more concerned with completeness than with avoiding overlapping. Thus, all the parts fit, though some of them find their way into my use of 'rational' two and three times over.

Though easily the best term by which to distinguish man's life activity from that of animals, Marx refrained from using 'rational' because it is alien to his system (he does use it, however, to describe man's activity in communism). The image that 'rational' usually presents us of a man choosing between numerous possibilities, with neither material pressures nor disturbing emotions acting upon him, is completely foreign to Marx's thinking. Still, the mental process that goes on when the individual feels particular needs and tries to satisfy them in the most efficient manner he knows may justly be labelled 'reasoning'. Such reasoning, of course, is carried on within carefully prescribed boundaries determined by the state of his powers and of nature. It is severely limited in the kind of problems it considers, the way it deals with them and, too, the type of solution it arrives at. Nevertheless, I find it useful to bring together the various aspects of Marx's conception of life activity under this term, because they are all more or less associated with it in the common mind. The explanatory value of 'rational' in this instance justifies infringing on my fundamental rule of remaining within Marx's categories.

16. *Freedom as essence*

In issuing a declaration of man's species character, Marx was drawn to portray life activity in communism, because only then does the individual develop into a complete species being, only then do the differences between man and the animal world become all that they can be. According to Marx, 'The real active orientation of man to himself as a species being, or his manifestation as a real species being (i.e., as a human being), is only possible by his really bringing out of himself all the powers that are his as the species man.'[1] Elsewhere, he states explicitly that the individual living under capitalism is not a real species being and, again, that the work of this individual 'has lost all semblance of life activity'.[2] The fact is that by 'species man' Marx can refer to all men always as well as to communist men alone, but he most often uses this expression to refer to the latter. In this case, species life activity is what people are moving toward rather than what the people of all periods actually engage in.

On this interpretation, Marx's description of species life activity must be considered very incomplete. Besides being 'free' and 'conscious', this activity will also be willed, purposive, physically and mentally flexible, concentrated and social. However, as we have seen, man's social activity in communism is quite different from what goes by the same name in all earlier societies. This applies likewise to each of the traits that distinguishes man's life activity from that of animals. Man's conscious activity in a capitalist factory, for example, can mean little more than being awake and knowing that one is pulling a lever rather than turning a handle. In communism, consciousness entails alertness, and the individual is aware of the complexities of what he is doing, including its manifold relations to himself and to other people and things. Man's activities are always purposive, but in communism the plan setting is more conscious, more creatively enjoyable, and the plan itself grander than ever before. Furthermore, the communist man will be able to concentrate harder, if not longer, than any of his predecessors.

Marx believes too that the physical and mental flexibility of the

114

communist man will far surpass anything our world has seen. The requirements of objects are many and can be met in various ways; communist man will know and be good alone or in coordination with his fellows in satisfying all of them. Man has always been able to manipulate some parts of his environment, but it is only in communism that his physical and mental flexibility takes in all of nature; and it is only then that this flexibility covers the most useful as well as the most beautiful forms of each thing.

To achieve this degree of success at transforming nature, communist man must be extraordinarily good at whatever he undertakes. All physical and mental work is done with the ease of an expert. Thus, the activity of this Jack-of-all-trades, who is also master of them all, is always skillful. This new found ascendancy over objects may also be attributed to man's heightened rationality in this period. In his knowledge, he has at last gotten beneath appearances to essences. Marx says that in communism, we find men 'rationally regulating their exchange with nature', attaining their human purposes 'with the least expenditure of energy and under conditions most worthy of their human nature'.[3] Such activity is rational in that it is based on a firm grasp of natural laws, with each movement carried out so as to make the most effective use of these laws.

Marx also says that man's species activity is free, which is additional evidence that he generally locates it in the time of communism. In his most explicit statement on this subject, Marx calls man's freedom 'the positive power to assert his true individuality'.[4] This 'true individuality' is man at the height of his powers and needs, thoroughly and intensively cooperating with his fellows, and appropriating all of nature. Free activity is activity that fulfills such powers, and freedom, therefore, is the condition of man whose human powers are thus fulfilled; it passes beyond the absence of restraint to the active unfolding of all his potentialities.[5]

In a sense, freedom of some sort (and therefore in some sense of the term) must have always existed. Leaving our ordinary linguistic practise aside, this conclusion is required by Marx's view that the history of man's development is likewise the history of the developing meanings of his concepts. This would also seem to follow from his occasional use of 'freedom' to refer (roughly) to being able to do what one wants, whatever that happens to be – as when he says,

'No man fights against freedom; at most he fights against the freedom of others.'[6] Yet, Marx is usually so concerned to link freedom with the full development of man's powers that I am inclined to say that this concept, in its 'Marxist' sense, only has application in communism.

The same conclusion follows from Marx's claim that, 'Only in community with others has each individual the means of cultivating his gifts in all directions; only in community, therefore, is personal freedom possible.'[7] By 'community' Marx has in mind a sincere and multi-faceted relationship binding each individual to everyone else in his society. Such a bond can only come into existence after all artificial barriers to the mutual involvement of people have been torn down. Its first prerequisite is the abolition of classes. Only then can all man's social functions register as free activity; only then, in Marx's words, 'is personal freedom possible'. Engels goes as far as to maintain that it is impossible even to speak of freedom while classes and the state exist.[8]

Central to man's free activity in communism is free work. Though exhibiting all the characteristics that have been ascribed to free activity, work at this time is something more and less than activity outside production. In *Capital* III, Marx divides all communist life into the 'realm of necessity' and the 'realm of Freedom'.[9] In so far as material production is necessary to maintain life, it remains in all societies, communism included, a 'realm of necessity'. Even if the individual wants to work and enjoys it, which is the case in communism, there is still a sense in which he has to do it if he is to stay alive. In this field, man has to cooperate with others and apply himself, or there would be hunger and chaos. The fact that he wants to do this is due to his unusual character and the equally unusual conditions of this period, but that he must whether he wants to or not is an indication that we are still operating in the 'realm of necessity'.

In communism, however, even inside the 'realm of necessity', man's activity is free in the sense that it both develops and fulfills his human powers. In the same pages where Marx distinguishes between these two realms, he makes it abundantly clear that man is not coerced to work, that he plays an important role in helping to determine his work conditions, that in this work he joins together with his fellows to rationally regulate nature, and that he controls and uses natural forces for his own purposes. A similar description of free work occurs in the *Grundrisse,* where emphasis is laid on overcoming obstacles. Marx speaks of work here as the 'activity of real freedom', and adds that it will not be play, as Fourier suggests, but the most earnest and intense effort.[10] Marx believes that efforts which are truly creative tax the entire personality. Hence, production will always require great exertion; only, in communism, this exertion, rather than being unpleasant and draining the individual of his capacities, is joyful, satisfying and fulfilling.

The 'realm of freedom' is said to begin 'only where labor which is determined by necessity and mundane considerations ceases', and Marx characterizes it as 'that development of human energy which is an end in itself'. He maintains, however, that such perfection can 'blossom forth only with the realm of necessity as its basis'.[11] Art, music and love can only be engaged in after man has provided himself with food, clothing and shelter. Where there is nothing that must be done, the last boundary to the exercise of man's human powers has been removed. Doing what he wants is no longer based on the condition of choosing correctly or perishing. The characteristics of work and non-work activity in communism are the same; only this condition differs.

It should be possible to extract all the qualities of man's life activity in communist society from our discussion of free work. Yet, 'freedom' is sometimes used to refer to a single element in this package, as when Engels claims, 'Freedom is control over ourselves and over external nature which is founded on knowledge of natural necessity'.[12] The view stated here is frequently held to be the whole of Marx's conception of freedom.[13] Apart from Engels' comment, this misinterpretation springs from the dangerous practise of making analogies with other thinkers. In this case, Hegel, who equates freedom, in its this-worldly sense, with recognizing necessity and willing one's actions to be in accord with it, is said to be expressing Marx's views as well as his own. But though this meaning is contained in Marx's broad conception of freedom, it is freedom as seen from one angle only. If left in this lopsided condition and out of context, even this partial reference cannot be comprehended. To be adequately defined, 'freedom', in the Marxist sense, must be presented as a union of its constituent relations – the whole web of interconnections must be apparent – and it is such a definition which I have tried to put together in this chapter. To be grasped correctly, Engels' comment must be viewed as an instance of the whole being subsumed in the part. 'Freedom' is controlling and knowing only when these qualities are conceived of in their relations with the rest of man's powers and with the necessary means for their fulfillment.

To borrow Marx's own categories, one may say that the 'essence' of man's life activity in communism is 'freedom'; this aptly characterizes the connection between the parts out of which Marx's conception of communist man has been constructed. The 'appearance', or phenomenal form, of this activity is well covered by all the adjectives that have gone before. To the observer, activity in communism will appear 'conscious', 'purposive', 'concentrated', 'physically and mentally flexible', 'social', 'skillful' and 'rational' (in the developed senses Marx accords these expressions when treating this period). Given their internal relations to life activity in communism, the same description will apply to creativity, full appropriation, the satisfaction of human needs and the fulfillment of human powers.

Lest these comments on communist man be misunderstood, I should like to stress that my account of communism has been part of an attempt to explain Marx's conception of human nature and in particular the conceptual framework in which he examines the interaction between man, society and nature. With alienation in capitalism as my main subject, the future has been introduced only where necessary to help explain the present. The reconstruction of communism found in this section, therefore, is neither full (given Marx's many comments on this subject) nor adequate. Of these shortcomings, I am most sensitive to the lack of any sense of evolution such as finds expression in Marx's presentation of communism in two stages, a first stage, also called the 'dictatorship of the proletariat', and a second called 'full communism' or simply 'communism'. This first stage, the main characteristics of which are described in *The Communist Manifesto, The Critique of the Gotha Program* and *The Civil War in France,* is an absolutely essential transition period of indefinite length, during which the technological, social and human foundations of communist life are laid down. The achievements of this period follow directly from the unfulfilled potential of capitalism and, as opposed to the more extreme developments of full communism, stand out clearly in any serious analysis of capitalist society. The latter, in turn, represents the realization of a potential inherent in the first stage of communism and can only be grasped as a real possibility from the perspective of the first stage. One cannot hope, in other words, to fully understand or fairly judge Marx's vision of communism outside of an historical account that roots the distinctive human and social attributes of each period in the unfulfilled potential of the previous one. To offer such an account is one of the main tasks of Marx's materialist conception of history, but it is not one of my tasks in this book to present this theory.

17. *Man, classes, people*

What have been stressed so far in this study are those qualities which all men have in common, while the qualities which distinguish different classes of men and bring them into conflict with one another have been underplayed. Before recounting the alienation (both common and unique) of workers and capitalists, the basis for such differences as exist between them must be clarified. Furthermore, the status of exceptions in Marxism, of men who do not share or only minimally share the fate of their class, requires attention before this fate itself is examined. Otherwise the theory of alienation is open to the facile refutation of pointing to instances where it does not apply.

According to Marx, social conditions determine character, both directly, through their effect on the individual's powers and needs, and indirectly, through the creation of interests which he then strives to satisfy; and the conditions under which capitalists and workers live differ significantly. As for the first, every person experiences with the social group to which he belongs how his particular tie to the mode of production and the familial, educational and religious training which that occasions, blocks certain personality developments and allows for and even spurs on others. These conditions fix the state of one's powers and needs, just as they determine the degree to which such needs will find satisfaction. The visible result is a psychological and ideological superstructure which is practically the same for all men caught up in a given set of material relations. This is what permits Marx to generalize about people of different classes and to treat most of the individuals who come into his work as instances of a kind.

Those same conditions which determine a group's character establish their boundaries as a class. Based on the social division of labor, the most important of these are their relation to the prevailing mode of production, similar economic conditions and interests, a consciousness of these interests, cultural affinity and a common political activity. This is, for example, what makes the capitalists a class, and as a class have the qualities of capitalists. A thread which runs through all of these criteria is the hostility a class displays for its opponent classes. Whether in work, politics or culture, an essential defining characteristic of each class is its antagonism in this same sphere to others. For the capitalists, this can be seen in their hostile relations to the workers and the landowners at the point of production, in their political struggle to promote their interests at the expense of these classes, and in the cultural sideswipes they are forever directing against them. Of the bourgeoise, Marx says, 'The separate individuals form a class in so far as they have to carry on a common battle against another class: otherwise they are on hostile terms with each other as competitors.'[1] This common battle is fought on as many fronts as there are criteria for constituting a class. On each front, it is the fact of battle itself which earns each side its label. Hence, Marx calls a society where only one class exists, such as occurs after the proletarian revolution, a classless society. Without an enemy, the antagonistic nature of the proletariat disappears and with it the designation 'class'.

Only in advanced capitalism is it possible for a group to qualify as a class on all the criteria listed here. It is in this sense that Marx's refers to class as a 'product of the bourgeoisie'.[2] To take just one instance, the absence of effective communication in earlier periods inhibits the exchange of information and contacts which is essential for class formation. An awareness of common interests as well as coordinated action to promote them are impossibilities for people living in scattered communities. But we also know that Marx speaks of all history as the history of class struggle and often refers to social groups in pre-capitalist societies as 'classes'.[3] Rather than a contradiction, this is but another example of Marx applying a concept when only a few of its many components are present. Which these are varies somewhat with his purpose in making the particular classification. Whether it was proper of Marx to apply the label 'class' on the basis of only a few of the relevant criteria may be disputed, but that he could not wait for all of them to be satisfied is clear. Otherwise, he would have defined himself out of the running, for even the capitalists and the proletariat are sometimes seen to be without some of the requisite attributes. Marx was well aware that for most of the period during which he was writing the proletariat lacked both a clear consciousness of its interests and a class-wide political organization.[4] In such cases, it is not only the definition of a 'class' that has fewer aspects but – as I indicated earlier – the conditions which determine the character of its members are likewise fewer in number.[5]

Because of the amount of time spent working and its crucial importance for maintaining and advancing life, the conditions surrounding this activity – which includes the manner in which one prepares for it in early life – are held to be the single greatest influence in molding character.[6] Work also reveals what people are to such an extent that Marx feels justified in referring to them, on occasion, as embodiments of the social and economic relations involved. In this manner, capitalists and wage-laborers are spoken of as 'mere embodiments, personifications of capital and wage-labor'.[7]

Some readers have taken such statements to mean that Marx is not dealing with real people at all in his writings but with ideal types. This interpretation falls down, however, when confronted with statements of a directly opposite kind. Earlier we saw Marx label industry 'the exposure to the senses of human psychology', and when treating alienation we will learn that the worker's product is 'alien, hostile, powerful, and independent of him' because 'someone is master of this object, someone who is alien, hostile, powerful, and independent of him'.[8] Whereas above, the capitalist was treated as an aspect of capital, capital appears in the latter quotation as an aspect of the capitalist whose bidding it does. What we have here, of course, are two sides of the same social Relation which may go by either name. Though Marx believed that the nature of the investigation he undertook in *Capital* required that he generally treat people as part of their economic product or activity, this does not detract from his conception of them as real living people.

As indicated, the influence of productive activity on class character also operates indirectly through the creation of interests which the individual then strives to satisfy, remaking himself in the process to more effectively attain his ends. For Marx, 'interest' refers to what it makes sense for people to want and do, given their overall situation, the most important element of which is their relation to the mode of production. It is not everything people want but – as Brian Barry has pointed out – those generalized means which increase their ability to get what they want that is generally covered by the term 'interest'.[9] This same distinction applies to Marx's use of the term, where money, power, ease and structural reform or its absence are in the forefront of his mind whenever he speaks of any group's interests. The higher wages, improved working conditions, job security and inexpensive consumer goods, for example, that most workers say they want are only to be had through such mediation.

Still more is involved. For the interest of any class is not only what will enable them to get what they now want but as well what they will want when they get it. Hence, the aptness of C. Wright Mills' description of Marxian interests as 'long run, general, and rational interests'.[10] These two stages are never separated in Marx's use of this concept because – and this is based on his relational outlook – the future of any person, including what he comes to want, is conceived of as an integral part of what he is.

Marx also departs from our ordinary notion in believing that interests are 'objective'. Coming out of an individual's life situation, interests are construed as a necessary element in this situation, capable of being found there by all who seriously look. Upon study, one can learn what is required to get people what they want (or will want upon the getting), and whether they can get it within the existing system or only through its transformation. And finally, what satisfies the interests of one group in class divided society is invariably taken, more or less forcibly, from other groups, so that Marx's notion of 'interest' should also be understood as 'interests hostile to those of other groups'.[11]

Though all members of a group share the same interests, the connection with their group personality is neither immediate nor direct. Individuals may possess characteristics, the product of direct conditioning, which actually fly in the face of their interests. The submissiveness before authority of many workers is one such instance. Interests have a really substantial effect on personality only when they are recognized, but, even prior to this, seeking for what is as yet imprecisely felt carries its own characterological rewards. Interests, through the needs they service, constitute an ever present appeal to man to open his eyes and fashion himself according to what he sees; and, as a result, are constantly encouraging qualities which make people more efficient in obtaining class ends. Over a period of time, Marx believes pressure coming from a group's interests will transform most of its members. Relying on the cumulative effect of rational decisions, interests supply Marx with the 'attractive' force which eventually brings people's character and action into line with their objective situation.

II

The relegation of people to social units, particularly classes, did not preclude Marx from recognizing the unique character of each individual and of something called the 'personal life'.[12] He felt it necessary to defend his concentration on groups by saying, 'We do not mean to be understood . . . that, for example, the rentier, the capitalist, etc., cease to be persons; but their personality is conditioned and determined by quite definite class relationships'.[13] What can be so conditioned is never clearly distinguished from what cannot, so we are never quite sure how far the 'personal life' extends in any given case.[14]

Marx's writings contain several arresting examples of people who grow up in the conditions of one group but who do not partake of that group's characteristic sentiments or illusions. The English factory inspectors and doctors whose testimonies appear in *Capital* are recognized as an impartial body of men, despite their middle class backgrounds.[15] Marx admits, too, the existence of something similar, now called 'scientific impartiality' and a 'love of truth', which he ascribes to the capitalist economist, Ricardo.[16] More important exceptions, which could not have eluded Marx, were Engels and himself. Both founders of Marxism had bourgeois upbringings; yet, somehow they managed to surmount the training of their early years. Marx never mentions himself and Engels as exceptions, but he does explicitly state that it is possible for some individuals among the bourgeoisie to lay aside their class characteristics and adopt a communist consciousness, that is, the way of thinking of the most advanced section of the proletariat.[17] Likewise, on the side of the proletariat, it is recognized that individuals may stand against the trend.

Whether these practical exceptions are compatible with Marx's general scheme has long been debated. If people are the products of their material life conditions, how is it possible for them, any of them, to exhibit contrary and even opposing characteristics? Is

Marx's own life as a socialist, as some writers have suggested, an all consuming criticism of his political theory? Marx would have two replies to offer to such queries. First, he would undoubtedly claim that we are viewing 'condition' in too narrow a sense. Everything that the individual comes into contact with from the time of birth onwards are the conditions of his life. In so far as a relation to the mode of production is shared by many men, the tendency is for the same personality traits to develop in all. But each man is bounded by innumerable factors and is heir to as many experiences even when engaged in work which is his alone. It is a matter of family, friends and one's very place on the earth each moment of the day. The what, when and how of every action differs from man to man, because no one walks inside our skin with us. This is the area of human existence which Marx stakes out, without too much precision, as the 'personal life'. On occasion, the conditions operating in this area are sufficient to overturn the results that naturally flow from one's activity in the mode of production and the class relations based upon it.

By separating out the 'personal life' in the above manner, neither Marx nor this writer, in discussing Marx, is suggesting that there is an area of human existence which is unaffected by the individual's economic function. On the contrary, the 'personal life' of all workers will differ drastically from the 'personal life' of all capitalists just because of their contrasting relations to the prevailing mode of production. However, in the 'personal life' of each individual worker and capitalist enough other special and incidental factors are operating, all of them influenced in some way by 'economics', to enable occasional crisscrossing of class lines in politics as in other matters.

So far human beings have been treated solely as creatures of their environment. Marx's second reply to the question raised earlier would probably be that this is not the whole story. Heredity may be played down and insufficiently integrated into Marx's system, but it is never dismissed. That it is present in his thinking can be inferred from such a statement as, 'differences of brain, of intellectual capacity, do not imply any differences whatever in the nature of the stomach and of physical needs'.[18] It would also appear that Marx saw certain racial characteristics as transmissible through heredity.[19] What precisely can be inherited we never learn; nor, consequently, are we ever instructed as to the kind of interplay that exists between heredity and environment.[20] All we can be certain of is that heredity is one of the loopholes through which Marx would pass in trying to account for exceptions to his general theory. No doubt this and the other loophole of 'extended' conditions can be made bigger than Marx would have liked, making a shambles or, worse, a truism of his views. This is a danger Marx avoided, rather too successfully, by exaggerating in his general remarks, as Engels tell us, the determining role of economic factors.[21]

Given the possibility of exceptions, it remains the case that most of the qualities Marx ascribes to any group apply to practically all its members, their personal peculiarities notwithstanding. What is perhaps more significant for the present study is the qualification Marx tacks on to whatever admission he does make regarding exceptions. He says, though 'particular individuals are not always influenced in their attitude by the class to which they belong . . . this has as little effect upon the class struggle as the secession of a few nobles to the *tiers état* had on the French Revolution.'[22] Whatever we may think of this example, it clearly illustrates Marx's belief that history is the product of mass movements, and this is the perspective in which the human element in his writings must always be viewed. Though individuals who fall out with their class provide the markers that tell us where a theory ends, these are not the people it is most essential to know about in order to comprehend Marxism. Marx might have said of psychology what he declared of economics: 'The reasonable and necessary in nature asserts itself only as a blindly working average'.[23] Exceptions are admitted when treating both people and prices, but Marx does not allow them to disturb his general rules.

SUMMARY

In Part II, we have learned that what all men have in common, according to Marx, is the ability to appropriate nature at the same time that they objectify themselves in it, developing themselves and altering nature simultaneously. The chief means for making the world a part of oneself and oneself a part of the world is the individual's productive activity. Marx conceives of this activity as a series of dynamic relationships between each man, or his particular powers and needs, and the real objects in the world, including other men. It is the concrete forms taken by man's powers and their objects, reflecting the level of their development, that determine the character of this interaction. All the major concepts used to treat this interaction – such as 'power', 'need', 'appropriation', 'objectification', 'realization', 'work', 'creativity', 'freedom' – convey from their own special vantage points the full sense of what occurs. In reconstituting man's basic relations with nature therefore, in exhibiting their internal unity, I have also constructed a set of interlocking definitions, providing the terms in which Marx speaks of man with their only proper dictionary.

In the final chapter, a transition was made from 'man' to classes and real living people. The unique conditions in which each class lives and works produce the different characteristics of capitalists and workers, both directly by molding their powers and needs, and indirectly by creating interests which they then try to satisfy. While an unusual personal life and/or heredity are responsible for individuals who do not share the special traits of their class, the importance of such exceptions should not be exaggerated as Marx's concern is with most people most of the time, and it is they who are the subject matter of the following section.

PART III

The theory of alienation

18. *The theory of alienation*

The theory of alienation is the intellectual construct in which Marx displays the devastating effect of capitalist production on human beings, on their physical and mental states and on the social processes of which they are a part. Centered on the acting individual, it is Marx's way of seeing his contemporaries and their conditions (a set of forms for comprehending their interaction) as well as what he sees there (the content poured into these forms). Brought under the same rubric are the links between one man, his activity and products, his fellows, inanimate nature and the species. Hence, as a grand summing up, as Marx's conception of man in capitalist society, the theory of alienation could only be set out after its constituent elements had been accounted for.

For purposes of discussing alienation, the following points, made early in Part I and illustrated in subsequent chapters, will serve as my philosophical charter: Marx's subject matter comprises an organic whole; the various factors he treats are facets of this whole; internal relations exist between all such factors; reciprocal effect predominates and has logical priority over causality; laws are concerned with patterns of reciprocal effect; the concepts Marx uses to refer to factors convey their internal relations; this makes it possible to speak of each factor as an 'expression' of the whole (or some large part of it) or as a 'form' of some other factor; finally, Marx's view that factors are internally related, together with his practise of incorporating such relations as part of the meanings of the covering concepts, allows him to transfer qualities which are associated in the popular mind with one factor to another to register some significant alteration in their reciprocal effect. In attempting to construct a coherent account of Marx's theory of alienation within this framework, this framework itself will be put to test.

Perhaps the most significant form into which the theory of alienation is cast – most significant because it chiefly determines the theory's application – is the internal relation it underscores between the present and the future. Alienation can only be grasped as the absence of unalienation, each state serving as a point of reference for the other. And, for Marx, unalienation is the life man leads in communism. Without some knowledge of the future millennium, alienation remains a reproach that can never be clarified. An approach to grasping the 'logical geography' involved may be made by contrasting the expressions 'health' and 'disease': we only know what it is to have a particular disease because we know what it is not to. If we did not have a conception of health, the situation covered by the symptoms would appear 'normal'.[1] Furthermore, when we declare that someone is ill we consider this a statement of 'fact' and not an evaluation based on an outside standard. This is because we ordinarily conceive of health and disease as internally related, the absence of one being a necessary element in the meaning of the other. Similarly, it is because Marx posits an internal relation between the states of alienation and unalienation that we cannot regard his remarks as evaluations. There is no 'outside' standard from which to judge.

'Alienation', then, is used by Marx to refer to any state of human existence which is 'away from' or 'less than' unalienation, though, admittedly, he generally reserves this reproach for the more extreme instances.[2] It is in this sense and on this scale, however, that Marx refers to alienation as 'a mistake, a defect, which ought not to be'.[3] Both the individual and his way of life can be spoken of as 'alienated', and in the latter case the tag 'realm of estrangement' is applied to the most infected areas.[4]*

Moreover, it follows from the acceptance of communism as the relevant measure that all classes are considered alienated in the ways and to the degree that their members fall short of the communist ideal. Accordingly, Marx claims that one of the manifestations of alienation is that 'all is under the sway of inhuman power', and adds, 'this applies also to the capitalist'.[5] The forms of alienation differ for each class because their position and style of life differ, and, as expected, the proletariat's affliction is the most severe. Marx dwells far more, too, on the fate of the producers, and usually has them in mind when he makes general statements about 'man's alienation'. In such cases, other classes are included in the

---

* For most purposes, 'alienation' (*Entäusserung*) and 'estrangement' (*Entfremdung*) may be taken as synonymous. The difference in emphasis which is sometimes suggested by these terms will only become clear in the course of the following discussion.

reference in so far as they share with the proletariat the qualities or conditions which are being commented on. I have adopted the same practise in relating Marx's views. By adding a special chapter on the peculiar alienation of capitalists, I hope to dispel whatever confusion this may cause.

The theory of alienation, however, is more than a mere summary of what has already been said regarding Marx's conception of man. It is also a new focal point from which to view human beings and hence to speak of them, one which stresses the fact of segmentation or practical breakdown of the interconnected elements in their definition. All those traits, grasped by Marx as relations, which mark man out from other living creatures have altered, have become something else.[6] In one statement of his task, Marx declares:

What requires explanation is not the *unity* of living and active human beings with the natural, inorganic conditions of their metabolism, with nature, and therefore their appropriation of nature; nor is this the result of a historical process. What we must explain is the *separation* of these inorganic conditions of human existence from this active existence, a separation which is only fully completed in the relation between wage-labor and capital.[7] (Marx's emphasis.)

Given the particular unity between man and nature with Marx – abetted by his conception of internal relations – grasps as human nature, any significant alteration in these relations which diminishes the individual's role as initiator is seen as rendering them apart. From evident expressions of his distinctive character, the relations between man and the external world have become means to dissimulate this character behind each of the various elements over which he has lost control. The theory of alienation focuses on the presumed independence of these elements.

The distortion in what Marx takes to be human nature is generally referred to in language which suggests that an essential tie has been cut in the middle. Man is spoken of as being separated from his work (he plays no part in deciding what to do or how to do it) – a break between the individual and his life activity. Man is said to be separated from his own products (he has no control over what he makes or what becomes of it afterwards) – a break between the individual and the material world. He is also said to be separated from his fellow men (competition and class hostility has rendered most forms of cooperation impossible) – a break between man and man. In each instance, a relation that distinguishes the human species has disappeared and its constituent elements have been reorganized to appear as something else.

What is left of the individual after all these cleavages have occurred is a mere rump, a lowest common denominator attained by lopping off all those qualities on which is based his claim to recognition as a man. Thus denuded, the alienated person has become an 'abstraction'. As we saw, this is a broader term Marx uses to refer to any factor which appears isolated from the social whole. It is in this sense that estranged labor and capital are spoken of as 'abstractions'.[8] At its simplest, 'abstraction' refers to the type of purity that is achieved in emptiness. Its opposite is a set of meaningful particulars by which people know something to be one of a kind. Given that these particulars involve internal relations with other factors, any factor is recognized as one of kind to the degree that the social whole finds expression in it. It is because we do not grasp the ways in which the social whole is present in any factor (which is to say, the full range of its particular qualities in their internal relations) that this factor seems to be independent of the social whole, that it becomes an 'abstraction'. As an abstraction, what is unique about it (which – again – is the particular ways in which it is linked to others, conceived as part of what it is) is lost sight of behind its superficial similarities with other abstractions. And it is on the basis of these similarities, generalized as classes of one sort or another, that alienated men set out to understand their world. In this manner is intelligence misdirected into classification.

Alienated man is an abstraction because he has lost touch with all human specificity. He has been reduced to performing undifferentiated work on humanly indistinguishable objects among people deprived of their human variety and compassion. There is little that remains of his relations to his activity, product and fellows which enables us to grasp the peculiar qualities of his species. Consequently, Marx feels he can speak of this life as 'the abstract existence of man as a mere workman who may therefore fall from his filled void into the absolute void'.[9] Though Marx clearly overstates his case in calling alienated man a hole in the air, it is in such an extreme notion that the term 'abstraction' is rooted.

At the same time that the individual is degenerating into an abstraction, those parts of his being which have been split off (which are no longer under his control) are undergoing their own transformation. Three end products of this development are property, industry and religion, which Marx calls man's 'alienated life elements'.[10] (This list is by no means complete, but the point does not require further examples.) In each instance, the other half of a severed relation, carried by a social dynamic of its own, progresses through a series of forms in a direction away from its beginning in man. Eventually, it attains an independent life, that is, takes on 'needs' which the individual is then forced to satisfy, and the original connection is all but obliterated. It is this process which largely accounts for the power that money has in capitalist societies, the buying of objects which could never have been sold had they remained integral components of their producer.

What occurs in the real world is reflected in people's minds: essential elements of what it means to be a man are grasped as independent and, in some cases, all powerful entities, whose links with him appear other than what they really are.[11] The ideas which encompass this reality share all its shortcomings.[12] The whole has broken up into numerous parts whose interrelation in whole can no longer be ascertained. This is the essence of alienation, whether the part under examination is man, his activity, his product or his ideas. The same separation and distortion is evident in each.

If alienation is the splintering of human nature into a number of misbegotten parts, we would expect communism to be presented as a kind of reunification. And this is just what we find. On one occasion, Marx asserts that communism is 'the complete return of man to himself as a social (i.e. human) being – a return become conscious, and accomplished with the entire wealth of previous development'. It is 'the positive transcendence of all estrangement – that is to say, the return of man from religion, family, state, etc., to his human, i.e. social mode of existence'.[13] In communism the breach is healed, and all the elements which constitute a human being for Marx are reunited. Many of the characteristics ascribed to full communism, such as the end of the division of labor (each person is engaged in a variety of tasks) and the erasure of social classes, are clear instances of this unification process at work. In the remainder of this study, I will be mainly concerned to show the evidence of segmentation that required such a remedy.[14]

19. Man's relation to his productive activity

In his only organized treatment of the subject, Marx presents alienation as partaking of four broad relations which are so distributed as to cover the whole of human existence. These are man's relations to his productive activity, his product, other men and the species.[1] Productive activity in capitalism is spoken of as 'active alienation, the alienation of activity, the activity of alienation'.[2] Asking 'What, then, constitutes the alienation of labor?', Marx offers the following reply:

First, the fact that labor is external to the worker, i.e., it does not belong to his essential being; that in his work, therefore, he does not affirm himself but denies himself, does not feel content but unhappy, does not develop freely his physical and mental energy but mortifies his body and ruins his mind. The worker therefore only feels himself outside his work, and in his work feels outside himself. He is at home when he is not working, and when he is working he is not at home. His labor is therefore not voluntary, but coerced; it's forced labor. It is therefore not the satisfaction of a need; it is merely a means to satisfy needs external to it.[3]

In claiming that labor does not belong to man's essential being, that in it he denies rather than affirms himself and that it is not a satisfaction of a need but merely satisfies needs external to it, Marx's point of reference is species man. In asserting that labor in capitalism mortifies man's body and ruins his mind and that in it he is uncomfortable and unhappy, Marx is alluding to the actual appearance of the proletariat. Alienated labor marks the convergence of these two strands of thought.

Before trying to explain Marx's comments on labor from the standpoint of species man, a brief review of what was said about activity in the previous Part is in order. Marx attributes to man certain powers, which he divides into natural and species, and maintains that each of these powers is reflected in one's consciousness by a corresponding need: the individual feels needs for whatever is necessary to realize his powers. The objects of nature, including other men, provide the matter through which these powers are realized and, consequently, for which needs are felt. Realization occurs through the appropriation of objects which accord in kind and level of development with these powers themselves. 'Appropriation' is Marx's most general expression for the fact that man incorporates the nature he comes into contact with into himself. Activity enters this account as the chief means by which man appropriates objects and becomes, therefore, the effective medium between the individual and the outer world. Marx sees such activity in three special relationships to man's powers: first, it is the foremost example of their combined operation; second, it establishes new possibilities for their fulfillment by transforming nature and, hence, all nature imposed limitations; and third, it is the main means by which their own potential, as powers, is developed.

In asserting that labor in capitalism does not belong to man's essential being, that he denies himself in this labor and that he only satisfies needs external to it, Marx is describing a state where the relations between activity and man's powers exist at a very low level of achievement. As we saw earlier, the terms 'essence' and 'essential' are used by Marx to refer to the whole thread of real and potential ties that link man and nature. Capitalist labor does not belong to man's essential being in the sense that it leaves most of the relations that constitute a human being for Marx unaffected. With the development of the division of labor and the highly repetitive character of each productive task, productive activity no longer affords a good example of the operation of all man's powers, or does so only in so far as these powers have become fewer and narrower in their application. As regards the second relationship, by producing slums, wastelands, dirty factories, etc., such labor does as much or more to decrease the possibilities in nature for the fulfillment of man's powers than it does to increase them.

However, it is the third relationship between activity and powers that capitalism almost completely reverses. Instead of developing the potential inherent in man's powers, capitalist labor consumes these powers without replenishing them, burns them up as if they were a fuel, and leaves the individual worker that much poorer. The qualities that mark him as a human being become progressively diminished. I referred to this process on another occasion as the 'retrogression' of man's powers. It is in this sense that Marx refers to labor as 'man lost to himself'.[4] Communist society supplies the proper contrast. Here, man's productive activity engages

all his powers and creates ever widening opportunities for their fulfillment. In this manner, work in communism is an affirmation of
human nature, while capitalist labor is its denial, withholding from
man what in Marx's view belongs to him as a human being.

Marx also conceives of alienated labor, in part, as the actual
appearance of people who engage in such activity. What has capitalist labor done to workers on a level where everyone can observe
the results? Marx's answer is that it 'mortifies his body and ruins
his mind'. *Capital* I is, in at least one very important respect, an
attempt to document this thesis. Among the physical distortions
described in this work are stunted size, bent backs, overdeveloped
and underdeveloped muscles, gnarled fingers, enlarged lungs and
death pale complexions. Some of these distortions – Marx singles
out the overdevelopment of certain muscles and bone curvatures –
may even add to the worker's efficiency in performing his limited
and one-sided task, and become in this way an advantage to his
employer.[5] Such physical traits are matched by as many industrial
diseases. In Marx's words, the worker is a 'mere fragment of his
own body', 'a living appendage of the machine', and he looks the
part.[6]

The worker's mind, too, has been ruined by the nature of his
task and the conditions in which he does it. His delusions, decaying
will power, mental inflexibility and particularly his ignorance are all
of monumental proportions. Capitalist industry produces in its
laborers, according to Marx, 'idiocy' and 'cretinism'.[7] The total
contrast between this condition of man and his condition under
communism is too obvious to require comment, and, as before, it is
the connection Marx presumes between them which allows him to
register the one as alienation.

The worker's subjective feelings of being 'at home when he is
not working' and 'not at home' when he is working is still another
indication of the alienated character of his labor. Marx's concern
about workers being discontented and uncomfortable is incomprehensible if we adopt the view that people will always dislike their
work, that work is by its very nature an activity that people cannot
wait to finish with. Given what he foresaw in communism, Marx
did not and could not share this view.

With capitalist labor variously described as a 'torment', a 'sacrifice of life' and 'activity as suffering', it is not to be wondered at
that no one in capitalism works unless he is forced.[8] Only circum-

stances which require that one labor in order to eat drives workers to make such an extraordinary sacrifice. Whenever compulsion disappears, 'labor is shunned like the plague'.[9]

Two other aspects of alienated labor dealt with by Marx are that this labor is the private property of non-workers and that it results in a reversal of man's human and animal functions. As regards the former, Marx says, 'the external character of labor for the worker appears in the fact that it is not his own, but someone else's, that it does not belong to him, that in it he belongs, not to himself, but to another'.[10] If labor is forced, even if its effectiveness lies in the worker's impoverished circumstances, someone must be doing the forcing. According to Marx, 'If his own activity is to him an unfree activity, then he is treating it as activity performed in the service, under the domination, the coercion and the yoke of another man'.[11] This overlord, of course, is the capitalist. And so complete is his control that he determines the form of labor, its intensity, duration, the kind and number of its products, surrounding conditions and – most important of all – whether or not it will even take place. The worker engages in his productive activity only on the sufferance of the capitalist, and when the latter decides he has had enough, that is, that further production will not yield a profit, this activity comes to a halt.

What we called a 'reversal of man's human and animal functions' refers to a state in which the activities man shares with animals appear more human than those activities which mark him out as a man. Marx claims that as a result of his productive activity,

man (the worker) no longer feels himself to be freely active in any but his animal functions – eating, drinking, procreating, or at most in his dwelling and in dressing-up, etc.; and in his human functions he no longer feels himself to be anything but an animal. What is animal becomes human and what is human becomes animal. Certainly eating, drinking, procreating, etc., are also genuine human functions. But in the abstraction which separates them from the sphere of all other human activity and turns them into sole and ultimate ends, they are animal.[12]

An abstraction, as we saw, is a break in connections, a link in the chain which has set itself off as an independent piece. Eating, drinking and procreating are occasions when all man's powers may be fulfilled together; yet, in capitalism, they only serve their direct and most obvious functions as do their equivalents in the animal kingdom. Despite their depraved state, however, the individual exercises more choice in these activities than he does in those others, work in particular, which distinguish him as a human being. As unsatisfactory as eating and drinking are from a human point of view, the worker feels at least he is doing something he wants to do. The same cannot be said of his productive activity.

All the components of alienated labor are best understood as particular relations which converge to form the Relation, alienated labor. Stated as accurately as possible, the relations of capitalist productive activity to man's species self, to his body and mind, to his subjective feelings when doing labor, to his will to engage in labor, to the capitalist, to his own human and animal functions and to what productive activity will be like under communism equal alienated labor.[13]

It should be apparent that these particular relations are constantly finding their way into one another, but Marx never meant them to be distinct. His practise of seeing the whole in the part links all particular relations together as aspects in the full unfolding of any one of them. Overlapping explanations, therefore, cannot be avoided. This coin has another side: just because a full explanation of each of these relations results in the conception of alienated labor, it does not follow that the latter contains only these parts. In reconstructing alienated labor I have limited myself to the largest and most obvious building blocks given in the few pages devoted to this subject in the *1844 Manuscripts*. Many other relations enter into its structure, and we are about to learn that at least one of them, which has been bypassed to facilitate exposition, is of crucial importance.

20. *Man's relation to his product*

The second of the four broad relations into which Marx divides alienation is the individual's relation to his product. This is, in Marx's words, 'the relation of the worker to the product of labor as an alien object exercising power over him'.[1] Between activity and product the link is clear and direct; man is alienated from his product because the activity which produced it was alienated. According to Marx, 'the product is . . . but the summary of the activity, of production . . . In the estrangement of the object of labor is merely summarized the estrangement, the alienation, in the activity of labor itself.'[2] He asks, 'How would the worker come to face the product of his activity as a stranger, were it not that in the very act of production he was estranging himself from himself?'[3]

Man's alienation in his product can be viewed as one of the particular relations which constitute alienated activity or as a coequal general relation. If taken in the context of alienated activity, product alienation appears as a result alongside the ruination of the worker's own body and mind. However Marx, by treating product alienation on a par with alienated activity, wishes to stress its significance, some might claim its primary significance, for understanding the worker's overall alienation.

The account of product alienation is scattered through Marx's writings. Nevertheless, the pieces can be collected without too much difficulty under the three particular relations that appear in the following statement: 'The alienation of the worker in his product means not only that his labor becomes an object, an external existence, but that it exists outside him, independently, as something alien to him, and that it becomes a power on its own confronting him.'[4] The first relation is brought out more clearly in Marx's claim that 'The product of labor is labor which has been congealed in an object, which has become material: it is the objectification of labor. Labor's realization is its objectification.'[5] As the chief means of expressing the life of the species, productive activity is often referred to as life itself. So it is more than a turn of phrase when Marx says, 'The worker puts his life into the object.'[6]

We can only grasp the full sense of this claim by returning once again to Marx's conception of human nature. Here, man's relation to nature was declared to be intimate, because his powers exist in one real object, himself, and can only be expressed in others equally real. Accordingly, Marx says of man, that 'he is nature', and of objects, that they 'reside in the very nature of his being'.[7] The relation between the two is an internal one. As the chief means by which man's powers interact with nature, productive activity is also the medium through which they become objectified. These powers exist in their products as the amount and type of change which their exercise has brought about.[8] The degree of change is always proportionate to the expenditure of powers, just as its quality is always indicative of their state. Marx, we will recall, refers to industry, by which he means the forces of production as well as its products, as 'the exoteric revelation of man's essential powers'.[9] By transforming the real world to satisfy his needs, man's productive activity leaves its mark, the mark of his species powers at this level of their development, on all he touches. It is in this manner that he 'puts his life' into his objects, the latter expressing in what they are the character of the organic whole to which both they and the living person who made them belong.

Man's productive activity, however, is objectified in his products in all societies. What distinguishes such objectification in capitalism is the presence of two further relations which have their roots in alienated labor. These are that man's product 'exists outside him, independently, as something alien to him, and that it becomes a power on its own confronting him'. What Marx means by the objectification of products that are alien to the worker is elaborated upon when, speaking of alienated labor, he says,

The worker can create nothing without nature, without the sensuous external world. It is the material on which his labor is manifested, in which it is active, from which and by means of which it produces. But just as nature provides labor with the means of life in the sense that labor cannot live without objects on which to operate, on the other hand, it also provides the means of life in the more restricted sense – i.e., the means for the physical subsistence of the worker himself. Thus the more the worker by his labor appropriates the external world, sensuous nature, the more he deprives himself of the means of life in the double respect: first, that the sensuous external world more and more ceases to be an object belonging to his labor – to be his labor's means of life: and secondly, that it more and more ceases to be means of life in the immediate sense, means for the physical subsistence of the worker.[10]

The worker's products are alien to him in that he cannot use them to keep alive or to engage in further productive activity.[11] Marx claims, 'So much does the labor's realization appear as loss of reality that the worker loses reality to the point of starving to death', and elsewhere that 'the more the worker produces, the less he has to consume'.[12] The worker's needs, no matter how desperate, do not give him a license to lay hands on what these same hands have produced, for all his products are the property of another.

Not only can he not use them, but he does not recognize them as his. It follows, of course, that he has no control over what becomes of his products, nor does he even know what becomes of them. Only indirectly, through spending the wage he receives for his labor, can the worker take possession of part of what this same labor has created.

Like the products the worker requires to live, the products he needs for his work are also beyond his control: 'So much does objectification appear as loss of the object that the worker is robbed of the objects most necessary not only for his life but for his work.'[13] Thus, the forces of production, which are products of yesterday's labor, 'appear as a world for themselves, quite independent of and divorced from the individuals, alongside the individuals'.[14] Although man's species powers can only be fulfilled through his use of the means of production, the means of production which come into existence in capitalism are decidedly hostile to his fulfillment.[15] By transforming nature through alienated labor, man has deprived himself of all that he has transformed. The individual's helplessness before his products must be contrasted with the ready accessibility of nature in communism to grasp the full measure of his alienation in this area.

What remains of the worker after subtracting the products he needs to live and to carry on his work – both internal components of human nature according to Marx – is an abstraction, the 'abstract individual'. Earlier, work in capitalism was labelled 'abstract activity' because of an equally drastic paring down of relationships. This abstract individual is humanly impoverished; he has lost his life in proportion to his having lived it and as much of nature as he has worked upon. His productive potential has been drained off into his product without giving him any return. According to Marx,

the more the worker spends himself, the more powerful the alien objective world becomes which he creates over-against himself, the poorer he himself – his inner world – becomes, the less belongs to him as his own . . . The worker puts his life into the object; but now his life no longer belongs to him but to the object. Hence, the greater this activity, the greater is the worker's lack of objects. Whatever the product of his labor is, he is not. Therefore the greater is this product, the less is he himself.[16]

The interaction which occurs in all productive activity between man's species powers and their object results, in capitalism, in a one-sided enrichment of the object. The product gains in power the more the worker spends his own and, Marx maintains, even acquires qualities (now suitably altered) that the worker loses. As the embodiment of powers the workers no longer have, products may be spoken of, Marx believes, in ways otherwise reserved for the people who produce them. Essential here is that these products have the ability to enter into certain relationships with one another and with man himself as a result of their production under conditions of capitalism, which ability the workers have lost, likewise as a result of such production.

This displacement of certain relations from the worker to his product is responsible for the illusion that the inanimate object is a living organism with powers and needs of its own: 'In bourgeois society capital is independent and has individuality, while the living person is dependent and has no individuality.'[17] For the most part, the life of the workers' products in capitalist society is the course of events which befall them in the process of exchange, which includes their production for purposes of exchange. People follow the progress of these products in the market place as if they were watching a play enacted by real flesh and blood creatures. In this drama, the part played by individuals 'is that of owners of commodities only. Their mutual relations are those of their commodities.'[18] With men taking themselves and others as appendages of their products, their own social relations will appear in the first instance as relations between things. Thus, an exchange of shoes for cloth, an exchange in which given amounts of these articles are seen to be equivalent, merely masks a relationship between the people involved in their production. In terms of the attention Marx gave it, particularly in *Capital,* this aspect of alienation constitutes one of the major themes in his writings.*

The third relation in product alienation has to do with the worker being subservient to what he has lost. His product has become 'a power on its own confronting him'. 'So much', Marx claims, 'does the appropriation of the object appear as estrangement, that the more objects the worker produces the fewer can he possess and the more he falls under the dominion of his product, capital.'[19] For Marx, those things with which the individual is closely related but which he does not control are, in fact, controlling him. He requires his products for consumption and further production, but he has no power to make them available. The worker, further, has no part in deciding what form these needed products will take. Instead, in every situation, he can merely respond to what already exists. His products face him as something given, both as to amount and form. The resulting interaction between the worker and his product, therefore, becomes one of total adjustment on the part of the former to the requirements (and hence the demands) of the latter. It is chiefly in this sense that the products of capitalism control their producers. This is probably the outstanding example of what was referred to above as a 'displaced relation'; whereas man, being a man, has the power to control nature, through exercising this power, his product is now in a position to control him.[20]

This exchange of roles between the worker and his product is equally evident in production and consumption. The former, in particular, is emphasized, as where Marx says:

It is no longer the laborer that employs the means of production, but the means of production that employ the laborer. Instead of being consumed by him as material elements of his productive activity, they consume him as the ferment necessary to their own life-process . . . Furnaces and workshops that stand idle by night, and absorb no living labor, are 'a mere loss' to the capitalist. Hence, furnaces and workshops constitute lawful claims upon the night-labor of the workpeople. The

---

* This theme will be explored in greater detail in the chapters on Marx's economics and again in the chapters on class, politics and religion.

simple transformation of money into the material factors of the process of production, into means of production transforms the latter into a title and right to the labor and surplus-labor of others.

Marx adds that 'this complete inversion of the relation between dead and living labor' is a 'sophistication, peculiar to and characteristic of capitalist production'.[21]

Articles of consumption, on the other hand, have power over their producers by virtue of the desires which they create. Marx understood how a product could precede the need that people feel for it, how it could actually create this need. Consumption, we are told, 'is furthered by its objects as a moving spring. The want of it which consumption experiences is created by its appreciation of the product. The object of art, as well as any other product, creates an artistic and beauty-enjoying public.'[22] What can we expect, therefore, where consumers have no say in the production of things which they must consume? In this situation, the very character of man is at the mercy of his products, of what they make him want and become in order to get what he wants. These products are responsive to forces outside his control, serving purposes other than his own, generally the greed of some capitalist. Hence, Marx's claim that 'every new product represents a new potency of mutual swindling and mutual plundering'.[23]

Besides manipulating people's needs, the form given to articles of consumption helps determine the prevailing mode of consumption. Every product carries with it a whole set of accepted usages. Taken together they constitute the greater part of what is meant by the way of life of a people. In capitalism, the worker's way of life has degenerated into one drawn out response to the requirements of his own products. Herein lies the inhuman power of man-made matter over man.

21. *Man's relation to his fellow men*

The third broad relation in which Marx exhibits the worker's alienation is his tie with other men. This social alienation is fitted on to
activity and product alienation in the following manner:

> If the product of labor does not belong to the worker, if it confronts
> him as an alien power, this can only be because it belongs to some
> other man than the worker . . . man's relation to himself only becomes
> objective and real for him through his relation to other men. Thus, if
> the product of his labor, his labor objectified, is for him an alien, hos-
> tile, powerful object independent of him, then his position towards it is
> such that someone else is master of this object, someone who is alien,
> hostile, powerful, and independent of him . . . Every self-estrangement
> of man from himself and from nature appears in the relation in which
> he places himself and nature to men other than and differentiated from
> himself.[1]

The hostility of the worker's product is due to the fact that it is
owned by a capitalist, whose interests are directly opposed to those
of the worker. The product serves Marx as both the mask and the
instrument of the capitalist's power.

If, when describing capitalists, Marx states they are but personal
embodiments of capital, he is equally able to assert, when dealing
with capital as a product, that it is an expression of the real power
of the capitalist. One claim must not be read as being more 'ultimate' than the other, or else we shall forever be turning in circles
as Marx's writings abound with claims of both sorts. On the basis
of the internal relations Marx posits between the worker, his product and the man who controls it, these otherwise incompatible
remarks become complementary characterizations of the same
whole. When proceeding from the vantage point of the product,
Marx wants to show ways in which the product of alienated labor
exercises power over people (including, as we shall see, the capitalist). And when proceeding from the vantage point of the capitalist,
he wants to show ways in which this man controls the product. It is
with this latter relation that the present chapter deals.

The worker's dwelling provides an excellent example of how his
relation to his product is bound up with his relation to the man

who owns it. Marx refers to the worker's home as a 'cave' which he occupies 'only precariously, it being for him an alien habitation which can be withdrawn from him any day – a place from which, if he does not pay, he can be thrown out'. Comparing capitalism with primitive society, Marx adds:

The savage in his cave – a natural element which freely offers itself for his use and protection – feels himself no more a stranger, or rather feels himself to be just as much at home as a fish in water. But the cellar-dwelling of the poor man is a hostile dwelling, 'an alien, restraining power which only gives itself up to him so far as he gives up to it his blood and sweat' – a dwelling which he cannot look upon as his own home where he might at last exclaim, 'here I am at home', but where instead he finds himself in someone else's house, in the house of a stranger who daily lies in wait for him and throws him out if he does not pay his rent.[2]

As elsewhere in capitalism, the worker's need carries no title to use what his own labor has produced. In his dwelling, man should feel himself 'at home as much as a fish in water'. This really expresses the degree of acceptance and trust in the possession of nature that all men will feel in communism. Under capitalism, however, the worker's relation to his home is one of uncertainty which he manifests through his fear of the landlord.

As with the worker's relation to his product, his alienated relation to the man who owns his product is a necessary result of his productive activity being what it is. Marx maintains:

through alienated labor man not only engenders his relationship to the object and to the act of production as powers that are alien and hostile to him; he also engenders the relationship in which other men stand to his production and to his product, and the relationship in which he stands to these other men. Just as he begets his own product as a loss, as a product not belonging to him; so he begets the dominion of the one who does not produce over production and over the product. Just as he estranges himself from his own activity, so he confers to the stranger activity which is not his own . . . a man alien to labor and standing outside it . . . the capitalist, or whatever one chooses to call the master of labor.[3]

Each capitalist only retains his pedestal through the repeated acts of workers. Without capitalist production in which the creative force is alienated labor there would be no capitalists. By engaging in totally unfulfilling labor, labor which destroys his mind and body, labor which is forced upon him by his drive to live, labor in which all choice is left to someone else who also controls the finished articles, that is, capitalist labor, the worker is said to produce the degrading social relations that distinguish this period.

Marx is capable, as we know, of approaching the same relation from the other side. He says, for example:

> The estrangement of man, and in fact every relationship in which man stands to himself, is first realized and expressed in the relationship in which a man stands to other men. Hence within the relationship of estranged labor each man views the other in accordance with the standard and the position in which he finds himself as a worker.[4]

By separating out social relations and treating them as primary, Marx has in mind the fact that the worker–capitalist relation is already established when the worker asks for a job. On the other hand, this relation is the product of previous labor, and is reproduced for tomorow by labor today.

In making the transition from man's relation to his product to his relation to the owner of this product, Marx allows, we will recall, the adjectives applied to the former to stand also for the latter. He claims that 'if the product of his labor . . . is for him an alien, hostile, powerful object independent of him, then his position towards it is such that someone else is master of this object, someone who is alien, hostile, and independent of him'.[5] The worker faces the capitalist with the very same attitudes, but whereas his employer is able to act toward him with the callous and reckless abandon of the strong, the worker shows his weakness only too clearly through sullen and hateful acquiescence. Their social alienation is a two-way street. Pulling in opposite directions, at the command of competing interests, their relations are necessarily antagonistic.*

---

* This account of the worker's alienated relation to the capitalist is only a partial account of social alienation, which includes mutual hostility within a class as well as between classes. A fuller treatment of this subject is given in Chapter 29.

22. Man's relation to his species

The last of the four broad relations Marx uses to reconstruct man's alienation in capitalist society is the tie between the individual and his species. Species, as we saw, is the category of the possible, denoting in particular those potentialities which mark man off from other living creatures. In so far as the conditions of communism allow an individual to develop and express all that he is capable of as a human being, communist man and species man are identical. When, therefore, Marx claims that 'estranged human labor estranges the species from man', he is saying that the unique configuration of relations which distinguishes the individual as a human being has been transformed into something quite different by the performance of capitalist labor.[1]

Man's relation to his species differs qualitatively from the other relations that were examined. His relations to his work, product and other men are tangible, both ends of which exist in the present, while the relation between man and his species is removed, in which living people are measured by the standard of what it means to be a man. Perhaps this facet of alienation can be more clearly grasped if we consider it a reformulation of man's alienation in his work, product and other men, viewed now from the angle of the individual's membership in the species. As Marx says:

In tearing away from man the object of his production . . . estranged labor tears from him his species life, his real species objectivity, and transforms his advantage over animals into the disadvantage that his inorganic body, nature, is taken from him. Similarly, in degrading spontaneous activity, free activity, to a means, estranged labor makes man's species life a means to his physical existence.[2]

The connection between species alienation and social alienation is made explicit elsewhere: 'The proposition that man's species nature is estranged from him means that one man is estranged from the other, as each of them is from man's essential nature.'[3]

Marx makes several comparisons between man and animals in his attempts to clarify what is lost through species alienation. When the capitalist appropriates the product of the worker's labor, Marx declares that the latter's 'advantage over animals' is transformed 'into the disadvantage that his inorganic body, nature, is taken from him'.[4] All living creatures have numerous relationships to the natural objects about them. As a result of his powers and needs being more extensive than any animal's, man enjoys the advantage of having the most complex ties of all. This shows in production where he is able to create things which are not objects of immediate need, a greater range of things, more beautiful things; he can also reproduce the objects he finds in nature.[5]

All man's advantages over animals become disadvantages when the natural objects to which he is related become the property of other men. While animals in the forest take whatever they need from their immediate surroundings, man is restricted in his use of objects to what their owners will allow, which is invariably less than his powers require. If, as Marx says, 'The object of work is . . . the objectification of man's species life,' with the removal of these objects from his control, the human species is deprived of its reality, of what it requires to manifest itself as the human species.[6]

We must be careful here as elsewhere not to substitute our concept of the processes and events which come into the discussion for Marx's own. Thus, though we may consider that people realize their human potential in conditions of private property, Marx does not. And his conception of this potential and of individual control over any part of nature is such that each necessarily excludes the other. This conclusion in no way affects the historical role that Marx attributes to the institution of private property in helping to prepare a time when man – through the abolition of such property – will be able to fully manifest his species powers. Until then, however, the distinctive character of man's complex relationship to nature is lost below the horizon of the animal world through the confiscation of this entire nature by another.

In treating species alienation, Marx gives a favored place, as we might expect, to man's relation to his activity. For Marx, 'the productive life is the life of the species'.[7] Such activity is the chief means through which the individual expresses and develops his powers, and is distinguished from animal activity by its range, adaptability, skill and intensity. In capitalism, however, the worker's labor 'turns for him the life of the species into a means of individual life'.[8] Work has become a means to stay alive rather than life being an opportunity to do work. Living, mere existence, has always been a necessary pre-condition for engaging in productive activity, but in capitalism it becomes the operative motive.

The worker's departure from what it means to be a man is also found in the world of thought. Marx says, 'The consciousness which man has of his species is thus transformed by estrangement in such a way that the species life becomes for him a means.'[9] As a conscious being, the individual is aware of what he is doing and possesses the faculty of being able to choose and to plan. He can also make provisions to acquire the skills and knowledge necessary for his fulfillment. This degree of foresight belongs to him as a member of the human species. In estranged labor, however, 'it is just because man is a conscious being that he makes his life activity, his essential being, a mere means to his existence'.[10] The greater part of man's consciousness in capitalism is used to direct his efforts at staying alive, for he recognizes that such concentration is necessary if he is to be successful.

What is left after the most distinctive qualities which set man apart from other living creatures are erased by the processes of capitalist society? For Marx, the 'rump' of human nature which remains is neither man nor animal, nor is it simply matter. It is, in his terminology, an 'abstraction'. Thus, when he says estranged labor 'makes individual life in its abstract form the purpose of the life of the species, likewise in its abstract form', he is asserting that man's existence, denuded of all human characteristics, has become the purpose of work, likewise denuded of all human characteristics.[11] In this comment, the reversal of his species relations to activity, product and other men has gone the full distance, and man has succeeded in becoming all that he is not.

23. *The capitalist's alienation*

Alienation has been discussed up till now as if it were primarily a working class phenomenon. Yet, if alienation is taken to be a set of relations between people and nature, both animate and inanimate, then many of the traits observable in the proletariat can be found, only slightly altered, in other classes. The connection Marx sees between proletarian alienation and that of the rest of mankind is expressed in his claim that 'the whole of human servitude is involved in the relation of the worker to production, and every relation of servitude is but a modification and consequence of this relation'.[1] By producing alienated material objects and, in the process, themselves as an alienated class, the proletariat can be said to produce the alienation of people with whom they and their products have relations. Consequently, we should not be surprised that 'the emancipation of the workers contains universal human emancipation'.[2]

We have already heard Marx declare that capitalists as well as workers are alienated.[3] However, only once did he attempt to present his views on this subject in an organized fashion. What follows are his comments on this occasion:

First it has to be noticed that everything which appears in the worker as an activity of alienation, of estrangement, appears in the non-worker as a state of alienation, of estrangement. Secondly, that the worker's real, practical attitude in production and the product (as a state of mind) appears in the non-worker confronting him as a theoretical attitude. Thirdly, the non-worker does everything against the worker which the worker does against himself; but he does not do against himself what he does against the worker.[4]

With the analysis just begun, the manuscript which contains these distinctions comes to an abrupt end. However, on the basis of what Marx says of capitalists in this and latter works their peculiar alienation may still be pieced together.

Compared to the worker who supplies in his activity the dynamic for his own self-destruction, the capitalist's role in his own alienation is a passive one. He rides a wave another has created.

153

Yet, living in the 'realm of alienation', the capitalist must be in a 'state of alienation'. Because workers cannot have human relations with him, he cannot have human relations with them; a knot is the same whether one looks at it from up or down. The capitalist's state of alienation shows up most clearly, perhaps, in his tie to the activity of the worker as its owner, as the one who permits it and determines its form and duration. Rather than contributing something of his own in a joint effort, he merely accepts the work of another, trying only to extend it. Notwithstanding his predatory function, the capitalist's relation to labor is essentially that of 'passive' exploiter.

The capitalist's relation to the product of the proletariat's labor likewise places him in a state of alienation. For him, the object of another man's life activity is only something to sell, something to make a profit with. He is as indifferent to what it is actually used for and who will eventually use it as he is to the process by which it came into being.

As a producer, in so far as this label applies, the capitalist is not dominated by products in the same way as the worker; nonetheless, he is dominated by the social conditions in which they are produced and exchanged, by competition, which in Marx's scheme is a component relation of the product itself. The requirements of competition take as great a toll of his initiative as that of workers. He is forced to do with his product what the market demands – making it more, less or different, selling it here or there, for this price or that, and so on. Hence, he is in some respects as much under the control of his product (of what trying to make it and sell it get him to do), as it is in other respects under his control.

As a consumer, the capitalist, like the worker, is limited in satisfying his needs to what he can buy, the only difference being that he can buy more. However, driven as he is by the desire to amass profits, the capitalist does not take full advantage of his wealth. In short, his relations with the product as well as with the activity of workers is a far cry from the relations that each man will have with the activity and products of others in communism.

Marx's second claim that non-workers have a 'theoretical attitude', as compared to the worker's 'real, practical attitude', refers to the contrasting mental pictures each group has of the productive process. This in turn is merely a reflection of whether they work or not. The proletariat's attitude is alienated because the 'real, practical' activity it reflects is alienated; the capitalist's attitude is alienated because it does not reflect any 'real, practical' activity, because it reflects its absence. His inactivity in this sphere gives the capitalist odd notions of work and, hence, of the worker and product as well. For Marx, a direct working relationship to production is essential for human fulfillment. Therefore, the capitalist's one-sided development, whether registered on mind or body, is part of his peculiar alienation. Hence, Marx can speak of the capitalist as well as of the worker as a 'spiritually and physically dehumanized being'.[5]

The third aspect of the capitalist's alienation is that he 'does everything against the worker which the worker does against himself; but he does not do against himself what he does against the worker'. The capitalist's favored position saves him from the humiliation of actively alienating himself at the factory bench. However, his treatment of workers as objects of exploitation produces deformity in himself as well as in them.

The outstanding qualities which Marx observes in capitalists are greed, cruelty and hypocrisy. Greed is seen as the motive of most capitalist actions, cruelty as its all too willing handmaiden, and hypocrisy as the mask capitalists wear to hide their motives and means from others. Greed, the trait which takes up most space in this portrait, actually expresses the state of the capitalist's needs molded as they have been by his life situation. The relation which Marx posits between needs and powers insures that the condition of a person's needs invariably reflects the state of his powers. We saw earlier that man's varied powers have contracted in capitalist society into what Marx calls the single power of 'having', for which the apposite object of need is money. Because they lack human powers (are 'dehumanized'), the only way capitalists can use objects is by buying them. Consequently, they are greedy for the money which enables them to buy things. If the only aim of buying things, however, is to have them, retaining the ability to buy them, simply amassing money, will serve the same end. Marx regards greed, therefore, as the subjective means through which capitalists appropriate nature as well as an omniscient and unruly passion.

The capitalist's greed, cruelty and hypocrisy emerge from his dealings with competitors and customers as well as with workers.[6]

And in each instance, one has only to compare how capitalists treat their fellow men with human relations in communist society to see the degree to which capitalists are socially alienated.

The capitalist's alienation, therefore, like the worker's, stands out not only in all he is but in all he is not. Communist fulfillment is equally unavailable to both classes. Thus, when Marx comments that the capitalists achieve some of their personal aims, that they enjoy some 'freedom' as against the workers' none, this must be viewed in the context of a totally alienated society.[7] The capitalists' advantages over the proletariat are relative rather than absolute; they concern registering a higher score on a scale which itself must be condemned.

The *Rights of Man,* according to Marx, 'do not . . . free man from religion, but give him freedom of religion; . . . they do not free him from property, but procure for him the freedom of property; they do not free him from the filth of gain, but give him freedom of choice of a livelihood'.[8] Clearly, those people who can make use of the freedoms mentioned in the *Rights of Man* are in a better position than those who cannot. But, it is apparent that Marx does not consider the aims themselves worthwhile. Until religion, property and gain disappear from social life, everyone who comes into contact with them in any way suffers from alienation.*

---

* These aspects of alienation along with others, such as class and state, which also affect all members of society, will be discussed in greater detail in the succeeding chapters.

24. The division of labor and private property

From the worker's fourfold alienation in the means of production our investigation branches off in two directions. The first takes us further into economics proper, to the division of labor, private property and, eventually, to Marx's treatment of the economic components of the capitalist system in *Capital*. The second takes us to other areas of man's life, social intercourse, politics and religion being the most important of these.

Our journey of inquiry will begin with Marx's economics, but, in the present chapter, evidence from *Capital* will not be used. The *Economic and Philosophic Manuscripts of 1844* and other of Marx's early writings contain a great deal of economics which has been clearly fashioned as part of the broader theory of alienation. *Capital* exhibits the same connections, but they are not made explicit as often as they are in these early works.[1] My aim in this chapter is to lay bare the ties between man's alienation, as described thus far, and the whole sphere of economics. Afterwards, when I come to Marx's chief contribution to economic thought, the labor theory of value, my main source will be *Capital*.

Engels declares 'economics deals not with things but with relations between persons, and, in the last resort, between classes; these relations are, however, always attached to things and appear as things'.[2] On this definition, it is man's alienated relations to his activity, products and other men, as expressed in the overt relations between things, that is the subject matter of Marx's economics. The immediate links between these relations of alienation and the rest of what is commonly understood by 'economics' are the division of labor and private property.

According to Marx:

The division of labor is the expression in political economy of the social character of labor within the estrangement. Or, since labor is only an expression of human activity with alienation, of the living of life as the alienating of life, the division of labor, too, is therefore nothing else but the estranged, alienated positing of human activity as a real activity of the species or as activity of man as a species being.[3]

The division of labor whereby people do only one kind of work and rely upon others to do whatever else is necessary to keep them alive is a more inclusive social expression of man's alienated productive activity. With its core notion in the kind of cooperation that occurs in production it allows us to see as well all its surrounding conditions and results, that is, the real organic whole of which it partakes. In short, it is the whole of the last five chapters viewed from the angle of social labor.

Private property, for Marx, is of a similar nature. He refers to it as 'the material summary expression of alienated labor'; and elsewhere says that it is

the sensuous expression of the fact that man becomes objective for himself and at the same time becomes to himself a strange and inhuman object; just as it expresses the fact that the assertion of his life is the alienation of his life, that his realization is the loss of reality, is an alien reality.[4]

As such, 'private property' is Marx's most general term for the objects produced by alienated labor, and encompasses all the products that come out of capitalist society. It *is* alienation viewed from the angle of the social product.

We are now in a position to make sense of Marx's claim that

Division of labor and private property are . . . identical expressions: in the one the same thing is affirmed with reference to activity as is affirmed in the other with reference to the product of the activity.[5]

They are 'identical' in that both affirm alienation, a state which encompasses his activity as well as his product and makes of each a necessary condition and result of the other. They are 'identical' in being facets of the same whole which can be deduced from a full exposition of either.

The account offered of the division of labor in Marx's early writings is sketchy but coherent. Cast in many roles its essence easily eludes us. The division of labor serves Marx historically as the exit by which men leave primitive communism, sociologically as the root cause of the division of society into classes, economically as the fount of private property and psychologically as the means of anchoring their distinguishing characteristics in the people of different classes. Marx's treatment of the division of labor, therefore, is both analytic and synthetic, if one can call the imaginative reconstruction of pre-history 'synthetic'.

Of the origins of the division of labor, Marx says it was at the start

nothing but the division of labor in the sexual act, then that division of labor which develops spontaneously or 'naturally' by virtue of natural predisposition (e.g. physical strength), needs, accidents, etc., etc. Division of labor only becomes truly such from the moment when a division of material and mental labor appears.[6]

This is the point in history when some men become predominantly workers, farmers, hunters, shepherds and the like, and others become predominantly rulers, priests and overseers. It is connected with the rise of towns and the division of the population into town-dwellers and country-dwellers.[7] Primitive communism, the clan dominated society with which Marx begins his account of man's life on earth, has reached the end of the line.

The new developments which bring on the division of labor are 'increased productivity, the increase of needs, and, what is fundamental to both of these, the increase of population'.[8] The spark is ignited in production – more is produced than is required for the maintenance of life; the natural elasticity of human needs allows demand to rise to the level of supply and, once in motion, to exceed it; the increase in the means of subsistence also enables the population to grow, sending up the level of both production and the amount of goods needed to maintain life. A surplus is created only to create conditions that require a greater surplus. The former makes the division of labor possible just as the latter makes it necessary, and, caught in this vise, every success of the division of labor leads to its extension.[9]

For my purposes, it is not necessary to go into detail on the historical genesis of the division of labor, even assuming that Marx had provided sufficient information to do so. What is of concern is that the division of labor occurs and that it brings alienation in its wake. The further it develops, that is the smaller the task assigned to each individual, the more alienation approximates the full blown form it assumes in capitalism. Even at its origins, however, Marx could speak of the division of labor affording us the first example in history of how 'man's own deed becomes an alien power opposed to him, which enslaves him instead of being controlled by him'.[10] For Marx, alienation exists in all societies where the division of labor is the operative principle of economic organization:

For as soon as labor is distributed, each man has a particular, exclusive sphere of activity, which is forced upon him and from which he cannot escape. He is a hunter, a fisherman, a shepherd, or a critical critic, and must remain so if he does not want to lose his means of a livelihood.[11]

As the means by which his productive life is organized, a disinterested means outside his control, the division of labor towers over each individual as an inhuman master. Unless he chooses to starve, man cannot escape from the single occupation in which he is caught. Only the constant repetition of his productive task earns for him from others who are similarly bound the products he needs to live. Those of his powers which require other activities for their realization become atrophied. And even the single activity which is his preserve does not fulfill all the powers that are engaged, and cannot, because it is owned by someone else.

Marx sees the division of labor arising in society as part of a complex which includes private property, exchange and class divisions, so that to speak of an individual doing only one kind of work is already to assume a society where man's activity and its product are not his own. All this can be read out of the concept itself. Marx maintains that

The division of labor implies from the outset the division of the conditions of labor, of tools and materials, and thus the splitting up of accumulated capital among different owners, and thus, also, the division between capital and labor, and different forms of property itself.[12]

II

Private property, according to Marx, is the 'summary material expression' of alienated labor, just as the division of labor is the summary expression for the real activity which occurs. Therefore, the relationship between these two is the same as that between alienated labor and its product; a change in scope and emphasis are the only distinctions. Practically speaking, the objects which come under private property are most noteworthy for the individual's attitude toward them as 'prolongations of his body'.[13] On one occasion, Marx defines 'property' as a man's 'relation to the natural prerequisites of his production as his own'.[14] It is the attitude that one has the right to use and abuse the conditions of existence over which one has effective control, which entails the right to deny their use to others, no matter how much they may want and need them.

As with the division of labor, private property is approached synthetically as well as analytically: Marx relates the story of its appearance and also extracts it from the concept of alienated labor. Of the origins of private property, Marx says:

> With the division of labor . . . is given simultaneously the distribution, and indeed the unequal distribution (both quantitative and qualitative), of labor and its produce, hence private property: the nucleus, the first form of which lies in the family, where wife and children are the slaves of the husband.[15]

The examples given of private property show that, for Marx, this Relation may be extended far beyond food, clothing, shelter and tools, though its core notion lies in material objects. Man's productive activity has a direct or indirect effect on everything with which he comes into contact. In so far as the transformation of his work through the division of labor results in equally startling changes in these things, they all may be viewed as his products. In the instance quoted, the persons in the relation of wife and children to the individual have become his private property. He can do with them as he will, or practically so; the family has become an object of his manipulation, reflecting the character of his own alienated labor.

Marx does not attempt to offer any details on how the first transfer of common to private property took place. No doubt this was considered too much like guess work. For Marx, the corner into the new era is turned when production provides a greater amount of goods than that needed for the bare maintenance of life. He only goes so far as to say that 'Private property . . . evolves out of the necessity of accumulation.'[16] In *The Origin of the Family, Private Property, and the State,* Engels confesses 'How and when the herds and flocks were converted from common property of the tribe or gens into the property of the individual heads of families we do not know to this day'.[17] Marx's thesis seems to be that when there was just enough wealth for people to exist, property was held in common. When a little more was produced, those individuals who were able to take it for themselves did so and defended it with every means at their disposal, which included devising a claim to private ownership.

Forms taken by private property alter with developments in the division of labor. Early on it still has what Marx calls 'the forms of the community', but as time passes 'it approaches more and more the modern form of private property'.[18] In much of the ancient world, a man had to use his land in order to claim ownership over it. In the Middle Ages, pasture land was frequently owned in common by all the people of a village. In the modern era, such 'quaint customs' have passed on.

Marx, as I have indicated, also arrives at the notion of private property from an analysis of alienated labor:

Private property is thus the product, the result, the necessary consequence, of alienated labor, of the external relation of the worker to nature and to himself. Private property thus results by analysis from the concept of alienated labor – i.e., of alienated man, of estranged labor, of estranged life, of estranged man. True, it is as a result of the movement of private property that we have obtained the concept of alienated labor (of alienated life) from political economy. But on analysis of this concept it becomes clear that though private property appears to be the source, the cause of alienated labor, it is really its consequence, just as the gods in the beginning are not the cause but the effect of man's intellectual confusion. Later this relationship becomes reciprocal.[19]

Marx is claiming here that though it is the 'movement of private property', that is its real history, which leads us to the concept of 'alienated labor', now that we have this concept we can deduce the character of private property. In so doing, that is in viewing the internal relation between alienated labor and its necessary product from the vantage point of the former, we see that private property could only result from alienated labor. Approaching the same tie from the other side, as was done earlier, leads to the conclusion that alienated labor could only arise because some people were already treating the conditions of their existence as private property.

This 'reciprocal effect' between private property and alienated labor is given the distinction of being called the 'secret' of private property, where Marx says, 'on the one hand it is the product of alienated labor, and . . . secondly it is the means by which labor alienated itself, the realization of this alienation'.[20] The logical tie which Marx posits between the two makes it impossible for one to appear without the other, and makes any attempt to establish historical primacy a fruitless task.

In so far as Marx sometimes speaks as if the division of labor or private property came first (we can find examples of both in his writings), this must be viewed as an attempt to emphasize one facet of their total relationship for a special purpose. This is facilitated by his practise of manipulating the meanings of one or both concepts (in accordance with his relational conception), so that what is said to come first is grasped in a more limited sense. Thus, for example, the division of labor which is offered as preceding private property is less advanced than the division between mental and bodily labor which is what Marx usually understands by this concept. So, too, whenever he makes it appear that private property has come first, it is because he treats it as the act of considering a condition of existence as one's own, which is only part of what he ordinarily means by 'private property'.

Perhaps the major service performed by Marx's conception of private property is as a meeting place for various strands in his thinking, that is as a broad Relation which avowedly contains many others. Though all of Marx's important concepts are capable of expressing the whole of Marxism by virtue of their interrelations, they are almost always used with more restricted meanings in mind. However, Marx occasionally uses 'private property' to the full range of its possibilities, for example when he says private property 'is not a simple Relation, or even an abstract concept, a principle, but consists in the totality of middle class production relations'.[21]

The 'totality of middle class production relations', given Marx's extended sense of production and his view of all factors related to it as cause and/or effect, subsumes all of capitalism. And, as his understanding of capitalism includes how this society came into existence and what it is in the process of becoming, one can see how Marx could instill the whole of Marxism into the concept of 'private property'. Though the rods of meaning are seldom stretched so far, it is only by grasping the extremities that we can make sense out of the exceptions, as when Marx refers to the proletariat as 'self-satisfied private property'.[22] The relations of a group of men to their activity, their product and the owner of both, that is, capitalist production relations, are all facets of private property. That 'private property' owes its first loyalty to material objects does not keep Marx, on occasion, from applying the name elsewhere.

In his treatment of private property in the *Economic and Philosophic Manuscripts of 1844,* Marx provides us with an outline of what was to become his life's work:

From the relationship of estranged labor to private property it . . . follows that the emancipation of society from private property, etc., from servitude, is expressed in the political form as the emancipation of the workers; not that their emancipation alone was at stake but because the emancipation of the workers contains universal human emancipation – and it contains this, because the whole of human servitude is involved in the relation of the worker to production, and every relation of servitude is but a modification and consequence of this relation.[23]

Emancipating the proletariat is said to be the 'political form' of abolishing private property because the two are internally related facets of the same whole. By accomplishing either we get rid of an entire way of life that includes both. In the relationship of private property to alienated labor, which may also be given as the relation of private property to itself, Marx sees not only what capitalism is but the lever with which it can be overturned.[24]

Marx's writings in economics 'proper' also follow a plan which he set out in all its essentials in 1844. What else is it but a preview of what is later to appear in *Capital* when Marx says,

Just as we have found the concept of private property from the concept of estranged, alienated labor by analysis, in the same way every category of political economy can be evolved with the help of these two factors; and we shall find again in each category, e.g., trade, competition, capital, money, only a definite and developed expression of the first foundations.[25]

Just as private property itself is an expression of alienated labor, one of the forms this labor takes, all capitalist economic categories express some development that has occurred in private property. These specific forms, and Marx has supplied us with only a partial list here, can all be deduced from the concept of private property.[26] *Capital* stands forth as a work of unravelling. In this monumental treatise, Marx follows private property, and hence alienated labor, into and through the host of forms it assumes in capitalist society, uncovering relationships the great majority of which were already clear to him as early as 1844.

We are also led directly to *Capital* by Marx's comments in the *Manuscripts* on the economic writings of the time:

Political economy proceeds from the fact of private property, but it does not explain it to us. It expresses in general abstract formulae the material process through which private property actually passes, and these formulae it then takes for laws. It does not comprehend these laws – i.e., it does not demonstrate how they arise from the very nature of private property.[27]

Caught in a net which contains the whole of society, economists have proceeded to describe the intricacies of the net. Their laws are inadequate as explanations of economic life, because they are merely inductive generalizations based on experience in an arbitrarily limited section of society. Such laws are said to be 'abstract' because they ignore (with or without assumptions) the ties between the incidents studied and the rest of the social body. Thus, they may instruct us as to what has happened and even as to what might happen, but never as to why. Marx's laws, as we saw, are concerned with the character of their subject matter and it is just these ties between the momentary subject and everything it affects and is affected by, past, present and future, that they cover. Dismissing such a broader inquiry, Marx maintains, 'political economy has merely formulated the laws of estranged labor'.[28]

Marx's own version of what is required to understand economics is never in doubt: 'only when labor is grasped as the essence of private property, can the economic process as such be penetrated in its actual concreteness'.[29] The labor referred to is alienated labor which, in the process of alienation, gets transformed into capital, wages, money, etc. Since private property is the broader Relation most frequently used to convey these specific entities, the laws governing the latter are said to 'arise from the very nature of private property'. In short, 'private property' means what capitalism does. It now remains to relate, in the language preferred by an older Marx, 'what capitalism does'.

25. *The labor theory of value: labor-power*

All Marx's economic theories are attempts to mirror the relations he sees in the real world, and for him this world underwent no basic changes in the period 1844–67. Hence, his theoretical activity between the *Economic and Philosophic Manuscripts of 1844* and *Capital* (1867) is devoted to following out the more obscure relationships, refining his organization and language, and, above all, to collecting supporting material.

Yet, Marx's efforts at obtaining clarity have generally failed, because most of his readers remain ignorant of the 'deeper' meanings of his terms, of how they function in his overall system. 'Capital', as he reminds us over and again, is a social production relation, and cannot be given an ostensive definition. The same applies to 'labor', 'value', 'profit', 'interest', 'money' and every other tool of Marx's economic analysis. By treating these entities as things rather than relations, followers as well as critics have cut themselves off from what Marx is saying, and no amount of scholarship can heal the breach. It is as if they sought to put together a puzzle after systematically twisting all its pieces out of shape.

Most of the present work, including the preceding chapters of this section, can be viewed as my attempt to determine what these pieces are; I am now ready to fit them together. Earlier, Marx's economics was examined from the standpoint of the theory of alienation; the theory of alienation will now be allowed to emerge from the economic theories put forward in *Capital*. Where I have heretofore been tied to the language of the *Manuscripts,* I shall now accept Marx's vocabulary in *Capital* as given.

At the core of Marx's economics, it is generally conceded, is the labor theory of value and the adjoining theory of surplus-value. Marx offers what is probably the most concise statement of his theory of value where he says:

That which determines the magnitude of the value of any article is the amount of labor socially necessary, or the labor-time socially necessary, for its production. Each individual commodity in this connection is to

be considered as an average sample of its class. Commodities, therefore, in which equal quantities of labor are embodied, or which can be
produced in the same time, have the same value. The value of one
commodity is to the value of any other, as the labor-time necessary for
the production of the one is to that necessary for the production of the
other. As values all commodities are only definite masses of congealed
labor-time.[1]

The theory of surplus-value is best seen as an appendage to the
theory of value; for, according to Marx:

If we now compare the two processes of producing value and of creating surplus-value, we see that the latter is nothing but a continuation of
the former beyond a definite point. If on the one hand, the process be
not carried beyond the point where the value paid by the capitalist for
the labor-power is replaced by an exact equivalent, it is simply a process of producing value; if, on the other hand, it be continued beyond
that point, it becomes a process of creating surplus-value.[2]

Before trying to explain what Marx is saying here, we must
know what *kind* of thing is being said. What, in other words, is the
labor theory of value about? It is most often viewed as a theory of
price determination, holding that the cost of any article is determined by the amount of labor-time given to its production. More
sophisticated critics see it as a theory which explains existing
exchange relationships, price being but a handy indication of what
these generally are. A variation on this theme has Marx's labor
theory of value expressing a view as to what ought to determine
exchange relationships rather than what actually does. The theory
of surplus-value is usually seen as a theory dealing with profits and,
sometimes, simply as a way of highlighting capitalist exploitation.
(This list of interpretations is not means to be exhaustive.)

Marx's theories are criticized or defended differently, of course,
depending on which interpretation is adopted. In my opinion, there
is a degree of truth in each of them – Marx's theories of value and
surplus-value have some application in all these areas – but the
purpose for which these theories were constructed lies elsewhere.
Sweezy has underlined what should be obvious but unfortunately is
not, that the problems great economists have directed their attention to are not the same. He gives as examples:

'the nature and causes of the wealth of nations' (Adam Smith); 'the
laws which regulate the distribution of the produce of the earth'
(Ricardo); 'man's actions in the ordinary business of life' (Marshall);

'price and its causes and its corollaries' (Davenport); 'human behavior as a relationship between ends and scarce means which have alternative uses' (Robbins).[3]

Marx's preoccupation was different still. In every case we can only comprehend the person's theories after clearly grasping the problems he set out to answer, what he wants his theories to do. Yet, this preliminary task, particularly – it seems to me – as regards Marx's writings, is frequently shirked. The result is that much of the comment on Marxism is simply beside the point, beside, that is, the point Marx was trying to make.

Marx's declared aim in *Capital* is 'to lay bare the economic law of motion of modern society'.[4] His is an attempt to establish how capitalism works. There is no other economist who has undertaken a similar task. Viewing society as an organic whole made up of internally linked parts, Marx is concerned with men's relations to all their activities, products and others, and not only with those found in the economic sphere. For him, all human relations in capitalism are part of the necessary conditions and results of what occurs in production and exchange, and, hence, a proper extension of their subject matter. It is often forgotten that *Capital* was originally intended as the opening salvo in a broader study of capitalist society that was to include works on law, morals, politics and still other sectors of social life.[5] The ways in which factors throughout society are mutually dependent on one another, both for what they are and are becoming, is 'the economic law of motion' that Marx sought to reveal.

Capital I approaches this problem from the vantage point of economic life, narrowly understood, and makes use of the categories which are generally applied to this subject. The labor theory of value emerges as Marx's conceptualization of capitalist economic life, in which are included the ties he sees to its necessary conditions and results, and in particular to the totally alienated people who inhabit this period. It was to describe, explain and condemn their situation that this theory was given birth. In the labor theory of value Marx welds together the main economic categories of capitalism, their links with each other and with categories far distant from economics proper, his conceptualization of the sum of these relations as alienation, and his belief that a truly human society is the next stage in man's development. What is today called the fact-value distinction is bridged by the same extending of relationships which we found elsewhere in Marx's writings. The very terms 'labor' and 'value', as I hope to show, are only applicable to the kind of society Marx believes capitalism to be both 'factually' and 'morally'. With words such as these, Marx is saying in effect, 'This is how capitalism works, and this is the workings of an alienated society soon to be supplanted by communism.'

The theory of alienation offers the ideal perspective from which to treat the labor theory of value, since it is the actual line of thinking on which its components are strung. The way Marx presents his central economic theory, the patterns in which value forms are set out, can also be traced to the broader theory of alienation. Thus, the foregoing account of alienation has put me in a position to explain four of the most prominent as well as most puzzling features of Marx's economics: labor-power, value, the metamorphosis of value and the fetishism of commodities.

II

Labor is the center piece of the theory which bears its name. We have already gotten considerable insight into what Marx meant by 'labor' from the analysis of his earlier writings. This meaning remains basically the same in *Capital*. For Marx, labor is always alienated productive activity with all that this entails regarding the individual's relations to his activity, product, other men and the species. Thus, for example, we find Marx stating in *Capital* that before entering the process of production the laborer's 'own labor has already been alienated from himself by the sale of his labor-power, has been appropriated by the capitalist and incorporated with capital'. As a consequence, 'it must, during the process, be realized in a product that does not belong to him'.[6]

Nor does Marx ever waver over the physical and mental effects of such activity on the worker himself. Consequently, wherever the term 'labor' appears in Marx's economic writings what is conveyed is something more than and different from what this same term conveys in the works of bourgeois economists.[7] We will recall that, for Marx, concepts are 'forms' or 'manifestations' of their own subject matter, that they come into existence as part of the conditions to which they apply, that their meanings alter with changes in these conditions, and that, as a result, they invariably express more of this structured whole than is evident in their core notions. Capitalist economists, who are unaware of such facts, use concepts with but a limited sense in mind. Marx, on the other hand, purposefully intends his concepts to convey a large part of what, on his view, they express. The widespread misconception that in his later life Marx left the theory of alienation behind him bears most of the responsibility for the equally widespread misunderstanding of his term 'labor'. Grasping 'labor' whenever it appears in his writings as 'alienated labor' in its full multi-dimensional sense is the key to understanding Marx's economic theories.

In *Capital,* Marx separates out the potential for engaging in labor from the term 'labor' and refers to it apart as 'labor-power'. This conceptual bifurcation, it must be stressed, does not affect the character of the productive activity involved; 'labor-power' is the potential for doing that kind of work which the worker in capitalism can do, that is, alienated labor. Thus when Marx says, 'By labor-power or capacity for labor is to be understood the aggregate of those mental and physical capabilities existing in a human being, which he exercises whenever he produces a use-value of any description,' he has in mind the capabilities of alienated men.[8] 'Use-value', as we shall soon learn, means far more than that which people value because someone wishes to use it. For the present, it is only necessary to declare that the use-value of labor-power (potential productive activity) is labor (actual productive activity). This innovation was introduced because, as Marx states, 'Labor itself in its immediate being, in its living existence, cannot be directly conceived as a commodity, but only labor-power, of which labor itself is the transient manifestation'.[9] Labor disappears, is used up as soon as it appears and, hence, is not available for trading; labor-power, which is more stable, can be traded.

Therefore, it is the potential for work which the worker sells and the capitalist buys. In this transaction, 'The former receives the value of his commodity, whose use-value – labor – is thereby alienated to the buyer.'[10] 'Alienate' here means essentially to give up the use-value of one's productive activity; the most important of all human functions is put under the control of another. The worker sells his labor-power in order to acquire the means of subsistence to live. To keep from dying the worker sells his life. While the capitalist buys the worker's labor-power in order to make a profit. Labor-power is unique among all commodities in having a use-value which creates a greater amount of exchange-value than its own exchange-value. That is, labor, the use-value of labor-power, creates a store of commodities, shoes, steel, etc. which exchange for a greater value than that which hired the labor-power expended in their production.

The human result of the worker alienating the use-value of his labor is the alienated worker.[11] Both his person and mind exhibit its effects. And, as always for Marx, the mountain is capped when the individual himself misconstrues appearance for essence. 'The capitalist epoch is, therefore, characterized by this, that labor-power takes in the eyes of the laborer himself the form of a commodity which is his property; his labor consequently becomes wage-labor.'[12] 'Wage-labor' is society's label for productive activity that has become alienated, really and ideally, from the producers.

But if the worker's alienation follows from the sale of his labor-power, it also precedes it. This emerges clearly from Marx's frequent claim that the labor-power involved in the aforementioned sale is 'abstract' and 'general'. For him, wage-labor is always 'indifferent to the specific character of its labor and must submit to being transformed in accordance with the requirements of capital and to being transformed from one sphere of production to another'.[13] It is only such productive potential not tied to any particular activity that the term 'labor-power' conveys. Hence, Marx's criticism of Ricardo that, by using 'labor' instead of 'labor-power', Ricardo 'forgets the qualitative characteristic that the individual labor, through its alienation, must present itself as abstract, general, social labor'.[14] No other labor could do and be done to in this manner.[15] Marx is also indicating his belief here that the undifferentiated character of labor is more evident in the concept 'labor-power', with its emphasis on open ended potential, than in the concept 'labor', where its abstract quality is partly hidden in the small differences which do exist between real tasks. This would appear to be another reason why Marx substituted 'labor-power' for 'labor' in his later works.

Marx has frequently been criticized for treating labor as an abstraction, as productive activity in general, not taking into account where and how it is exercised. However, it should be clear that this particular innovation is not Marx's alone but belongs to the whole school of political economy which began with Adam Smith. Marx's contribution to the discussion was to exhibit the ties between this use of 'labor' and the particular social conditions it is meant to describe and out of which it arose. The question is not how could Marx treat labor as an abstraction, but how could society do so. It is in virtue of his response to this question (and others like it) that Marx can describe *Capital* as 'a critique of economic categories or, if you like, the system of bourgeois economy exposed in a critical manner'.[16] Marx's critique is equally one of capitalism and of the accepted ways of understanding capitalism.

By introducing 'labor in general' into economic discourse, Adam Smith is said to have found an expression for the special character of productive activity in capitalism, where people pass easily from one kind of work to another and are generally indifferent to what they do. This, in turn, presupposes a situation where there there are a great many highly developed productive tasks, none of which is clearly dominant. Thus, though 'labor' also expresses productive activity in the simple, uncomplicated sense in which it must go on in all societies, the concept 'labor' (meaning abstract productive activity) could only be formulated at a time when the common quality of all such activity had become evident, and conveys for Marx the full set of conditions that make it so. Accordingly, 'labor' is declared to be 'a product of historical conditions' and only 'fully applicable to and under those conditions'.[17]

Marx's conception of labor as alienated productive activity also lies behind his claim that labor has 'socially a two-fold character': it can satisfy a definite social want, and all its particular forms are on a par with one another, that is, are measured for worth on the same scale. The former characteristic derives from the nature of productive activity as invariably purposive, and the latter from its abstract quality under capitalism, where all labor is directed toward producing wealth in general rather than particular objects.

To the individual worker, however, these distinctive features of his productive activity appear

only under those forms which are impressed upon that labor in everyday practise by the exchange of products. In this way, the character that his own labor possesses of being socially useful takes the form of the condition, that the product must be not only useful but useful to others, and the social character that his particular labor has of being the equal of all other particular kinds of labor, takes the form that all the physically different articles that are the products of labor, have one common quality, viz., that of having value.[18]

Hence, the qualitative aspect of labor may be said to create use-value and its quantitative aspect to create exchange-value, the two-fold character that Marx sees in labor being responsible for the two-fold character he attributes to value.[19] Labor becomes use- and exchange-value when its product is treated and understood as such, and that this does occur is a function of labor's quality of alienation. But, before focusing attention on the different aspects of value, the total relation between labor and value must be clarified.

26. *Value as alienated labor*

If alienated labor is at the center of Marx's economics, value is not
one whit closer to the perimeter – for the two are 'identical', different facets of the same whole, contrasting expressions for the
same social relations. According to Marx, 'Value is labor'; it is
'materialized labor in its general social form'.[1] Or again, he claims,
'Value as such has no other "material" than labor itself'.[2] There
are other such forthright statements of the equation of labor and
value, but they seem equally to have missed their mark.[3] For most
readers of *Capital*, 'value' remains an economic expression synonymous with 'worth', a judgement strictly measurable in monetary
terms. Its tie with labor is believed to be capable of conclusive
empirical demonstration; this applies to most defenders of the
labor theory of value as well as its critics.[4] However, Marx's conception of value is of an altogether different nature. Its unity with
labor is assumed, and the rich assortment of facts brought forward
on this subject are for purposes of illustration and not proof. For
Marx, value, or as he sometimes says, 'value in general', is trans-
figured labor, and no manner of evidence could serve him as a
counter argument.

Thus, while Marx frequently declaims what value is, he never
sets out to discover it, nor is he interested in proving it. Indeed, he
treats the 'necessity of proving the concept of value' as 'nonsense'.[5]
In *Capital*, Marx tries to measure value, to chart out where it goes,
and to detail the forms it takes, but he devotes little time to uncovering its basic character. His chief concern is with a question other
political economists have never asked: 'Why is labor represented
by the value of its product and labor-time by the magnitude of
that value?'[6] Rather than presenting the case that value is labor, he
is attempting to explain why in our era labor is expressed as value.

Marx's is an investigation into socio-economic praxis rather than
economics proper, and he brings the whole of his social theory to
bear in providing the answer. It has only proved necessary to affirm
the 'identity' of labor and value, because Marx's assumption, albeit
a stated assumption, has been generally overlooked. What Marx

could take for granted, with some justification, in a period where labor theories of value dominated economic thinking must be made fully explicit now that these views have been generally discarded.

In a sense, all the labor theory of value economists accepted in practise the equation of value and labor, so it was not necessary for Marx to stress this point. Since, however, the political economists also equated value with price, the relation they saw between value and labor was open to empirical rebuttal. For them the concept of value arose from price every bit as much as from labor, and any one of the three was readily quantifiable in terms of the others. In effect, theirs was an empirical generalization that products tended to exchange in proportion to the average amount of labor needed to produce them. Marx, who would not have denied this claim, arrived at his concept of value from what he took to be the relations bound up in alienated labor. The connection of value with price, therefore – as we shall see – is of an altogether different order.

Besides Marx's few direct statements that labor is value, the 'identity' of the two also emerges from his treatment of what are widely held to be exceptions to his value theory. For example, though land may have a price, not being a product of labor it can have no value. Consequently, Marx claims that rent is irrational.[7] His critics frequently confuse value with price, but Marx is adamant that there are items which have prices but no values, 'i.e., are not the products of labor'. In such cases, prices are said to be determined by 'fortuitous combinations'. Land, antiques and works of art are offered as instances of this.[8]

Also indicative of the equation of labor and value is Marx's claim that machines add to the value of their product only what they lose in exchange-value. The exchange-value of any machine is the amount of labor-power, as measured by labor-time, which went into its production. With each increase in the value of the product for which it is held responsible attributed to a decrease in its own exchange-value and, hence, indirectly to the efforts of those who made these machines, the equation of labor with value is left intact. Whatever other benefits these machines confer, such as shortening that part of the day the laborer works to produce his own means of subsistence, is viewed in the same light as a gratuitous gift of nature.[9]

But simply to assert *that* labor is value is not to tell *how* it could be so. What is the essential character of value which allows Marx to equate it with the labor that goes into its production? The answer is pointed to when Marx calls value 'the most abstract form of bourgeois wealth'.[10] Value is the abstract product of abstract labor. Recalling the definition of 'abstract' as the absence of specificity, value could only be the form of the product where it is nothing in particular but, instead, everything which all the products of capitalism have in common. Marx maintains, 'the value form of the product of labor is not only the most abstract, but is also the most universal form, taken by the product in bourgeois production'.[11]

However, robbed of all specificity, these products have nothing in common besides the fact that they were produced by alienated labor. Hence, *value is the relations of alienated labor, transmitted by such labor, as they appear in the product.* It may also be viewed as a power, the power to do and be done to in ways which characterize all the products of capitalist production, ways which themselves express the relations of alienations out of which they arose. This is the meaning of Marx's declaration that capital 'produces value as the power, alienated from labor, of labor's own material conditions over labor, only as one of the forms of wage-labor itself; as a condition of wage-labor'.[12]

Though labor creates value, value – as the relations embodied in labor transferred to its products – constitutes the most general conditions in and through which future labor must be exercised. In this manner, value may also be said to create labor, that is, to transform man's potential for productive activity into alienated labor. Thus, we saw in the citation given above that value is not only a product of capital but serves as well as 'a condition of wage-labor'.

It should be clear from the foregoing that Marx's concept 'value' like 'labor' itself is especially tailored to fit capitalist society. Marx says that 'to stamp an object of utility as a value is just as much a social product as language'.[13] Value, in its strict sense, could only be produced in capitalism; and capitalism had to issue in the production of value.[14] Granted that some elements of the capitalist mode of production, such as wage-labor for example, have existed from time to time on the fringes of older societies, value, as I have described it, could not have resulted. If Marx uses the term 'value' in such cases, it is to express but a part of the relations this term generally conveys in order to indicate resemblance, just as 'labor' when applied to pre-capitalist societies refers to but the universal element of what is meant by 'labor' in capitalism.

For, in Marx's eyes, the existence of value 'presupposes: the dissolution of (1) primitive communism (India, etc.); (2) of all undeveloped pre-bourgeois modes of production not completely dominated by exchange'. He says of value: 'Although an abstraction this is an historical abstraction which could only be adopted on the basis of a particular economic development of society.'[15] It is simply that the most general expression for capitalist production relations could not exist before capitalist production relations.

Likewise, it is only in late capitalism, the stage of society in which Marx believed he was living, that the equation of 'labor' and 'value' became apparent. According to Marx, 'The secret expression of value, namely, that all kinds of labor are equal and equivalent, because, and so far as they are human labor in general, cannot be deciphered, until the notion of human equality has already acquired the fixity of a popular prejudice.'[16] Where slavery or feudalism exist, the productive activity of different people appears manifestly unequal, and the notion of human equality, which is the basis for understanding value, can hardly arise.

II

So far I have only been concerned with 'value in general'. What of its better known facets, exchange-value and use-value? Exchange-value, which Marx oftimes rather misleadingly calls 'value', is the 'ideal' ratio at which a product exchanges for others, that is, its trading power or ability to relate to other products on the basis of embodied labor-time. Exchange-value, which corresponds to the quantitative aspect of labor referred to earlier, is said to have the qualitative characteristic 'that the individual labor, through its alienation, must present itself as abstract, general, social labor'.[17] As the labor in all products is the same alienated labor, value can be measured by the amount of labor-time expended in production. Commodities would not be sufficiently alike to be measured by one standard if the labor in them were not the same abstract, general labor (alienated labor) that Marx sees constituting the soul of value. Thus, it is the theory of alienation, with its insight into the worker's relations to his activity and product, which provides Marx with the answer to his question, 'Why is labor represented by the value of its product and labor-time by the magnitude of that value?'[18]

The external events of trading, that is, price ratios, correspond so closely to the results of Marx's *a priori* arithmetic, because the items exchanged, coming from the same source, are qualitatively the same. They are all abstract wealth, the only possible product of alienated labor, and are exchanged as such. Their individual concrete forms determine, of course, who buys what, but don't count for purposes of exchange ratios. The 'fluctuations' in price that occur in the market place, which result from some commodities exchanging at more or less than the amount dictated by embodied labor-time, is explained chiefly by competition, whether of buyers or sellers. Given this fluctuation, however, Marx mantains that the price will be determined primarily by the amount of labor-time necessary to produce it.[19] From this, it follows that when supply and demand cancel each other out a commodity tends to sell at its market value (or average value of commodities in that sphere of production).[20] Marx states further that over the long run, where for any given commodity this does occur, price will generally equal value.[21]

These conclusions, which indicate a tendency for price to move toward value, are qualified by a directly opposite tendency that results from the equal rate of profit capitalist competition brings to spheres having different rates of surplus-value (due to different organic compositions of capital).[22] Given this equal rate of profit and the different proportions of constant (fixed) and variable (worker) capital in each sphere, price would seem forever out of the reach of value. Yet, in so far as Marx concerned himself with prices, it was the first tendency (modified by competition) that he stressed. This is partly due, no doubt, to the fact that the organic composition of capital in the industrial sector, the sector of the economy with which Marx was chiefly concerned, does not vary very much in any given period from sphere to sphere. Probably more important is the fact that embodied labor-time is far and away the main factor in determining exchange ratios, and therefore too changes in exchange ratios. Marx never satisfactorily integrated these opposing tendencies into a single theory of price; his explanation of exchange as an historical process rooted in specific social conditions did not require that he do so.

In ascribing a major role to competition in effecting actual prices, Marx is taking account of the realities of the market place which so many of his critics have accused him of dismissing.[23] However, competition, for Marx, always has a point of reference from which it takes its start. This is the exchange-value, or 'ideal' trading power of the commodity. When supply is equal to demand, it is what makes the price of one pair of shoes equal to the price of one pair of trousers, and not more and not less. It is the median around which the actual price of shoes and trousers, swayed by various market factors including the competition of capitalists who extract different rates of surplus-value, will always gravitate. The exchange-values themselves can only be altered by tehnical advances which affect the amount of labor-time required to produce one or the other commodity. Hence, a new invention which enables workers to produce twice as many shoes in the same amount of time will reduce the exchange-value of a pair of shoes to one half that of a pair of trousers. The prices of these two commodities may not immediately reflect this drastic alteration in their exchange-value ratios, but, according to Marx, over the long run they will.

Exchange-value, however, is more than the ratio at which the products of alienated labor exchange; along with value itself, it is a definite social expression for the underlying relations of alienation. The need to work and to distribute the social product exists in every society; only the forms differ. And Marx claims that 'the form in which this proportional division of labour operates in a state of society where the interconnection of social labor is manifested in the private exchange of the individual products of labor is precisely the exchange-value of these products'.[24]

Thus, exchange-value is a 'form' taken by the division of labor in societies where there is 'private exchange of the individual products of labor'. It is not only that which facilitates such exchange but is an expression of the conditions in which it occurs. 'It can', as Marx says elsewhere, 'have no other existence except as an abstract one-sided Relation of an already concrete and living aggregate.'[25] As such, it is – in his speech – a 'form' of each of the other main elements in the situation. We have already seen Marx refer to 'value in general' as a 'form of social labor', and we shall shortly discover that capital, money and commodities are also presented as 'forms' of one another, or of value, or labor. Only by conceding that these factors are internally related, such that each is actually part of the others, can Marx's practise be adequately accounted for. With such an outlook, it is *logically* impossible for any of the factors which distinguish capitalist production to appear without the others.

It pays to examine, in this connection, what seems to be a major exception to this rule. In an isolated comment in volume III of *Capital,* which Engels later develops at some length, Marx declares:

it is quite appropriate to regard the values of commodities as not only theoretically but also historically *prius* to the prices of production. This applies to conditions in which the laborer owns his means of production, and this is the condition of the landowning farmer living off his own labor and the craftsman, in the ancient as well as in the modern world.[26]

In other words, some products were traded at their exchange-value before the modern era, and it is only under conditions of capitalist competition that all prices have strayed as far from exchange-value as is now the case. To understand Marx's position here it is essential to distinguish what he is talking about from the way he talks about it. Certainly, exchange in some sense has existed from earliest times. So, too, Marx is probably right that labor-time was the operating measure by which people who owned their own means of production exchanged their products (it is important to note that the qualification of owning that with which they produced leaves out more classes than it includes).

Given this was the case, the question which remains to be asked is – 'In what sense can we speak of the existence in pre-capitalist times of "exchange-value"?' And Marx's answer, it appears to me, is that exchange-value may be said to exist only in a very limited sense, where its concept conveys but a small part of what it conveys when applied to capitalist society. This is the same thing we saw earlier in regard to the concept 'labor'. In so far as products in any period exchange in proportion to the labor-time that goes into their production, we may expect to find – suitably altered for the occasion – alienated relations between the worker and his activity, product and other men. Alienation, as Marx affirms, is not peculiar to capitalist society. It is in the modern era, however, that it has become so thoroughgoing and evident that concepts have been formulated to mark its more prominent features. Such is 'labor' (meaning labor in general) and such is 'exchange-value'. In focusing attention on particular facets of man's alienated life situation in capitalism, such concepts also instruct us regarding the undeveloped character of these same facets in earlier times. In Marx's words, what 'had formerly been intimated has now developed to complete significance' in the categories of bourgeois society. It is in this sense too that he declares that 'The bourgeois economy furnishes a key to ancient economy', and that 'the categories of bourgeois economy contain what is true of all other forms of society' (though they contain this truth in a much modified form, that is, by incorporating in their meanings the developments which have occurred since).[27]

Thus, although exchange on the basis of exchange-value took place in pre-capitalist times, 'exchange-value' is a modern concept, arising out of modern conditions and conveying – in virtue of Marx's relational conception – the whole state of affairs which made its appearance both possible and necessary. It conveys, in effect, the situation where exchange-value is the *dominant* principle governing the exchange of products. In slave owning and feudal societies (leaving aside the people who owned their means of production), products coming out of the division of labor changed hands on the basis of force or right; while in communism products will be secured by everyone on the basis of need. Only in the modern period, where production relations are completely alienated, has exchange-value become the dominant principle governing the exchange of all man's products. Thus, exchange-value in its full sense (which is how Marx generally understands it) does not exist in pre-capitalist societies, and cannot because of all that is meant by its concept.

The conclusion that the major 'forms' of capitalist society logically entail one another still holds. Exchange-value can no more appear independently of labor, capital, commodities, interest, etc., than they of it, each factor expressing – as part of what it is – the full conditions which make it that and nothing else. In the instance cited, however, we see that this does not preclude Marx from using 'value' (in the sense of exchange-value) to refer to an element in its full definition in order to mark some feature which different stages of social evolution have in common. Earlier, we saw how such manipulation of language was possible. Only by allowing that Marx meant much more by 'value' than is suggested when he uses it to refer to pre-capitalist societies can we reconcile this practise with his repeated assertions that value is a special product of capitalism. The fact that Marx devoted so little attention to recounting what occurred in periods when some goods actually traded at their exchange-values, and so much to unravelling the relations expressed by 'exchange-value' as a category of modern political economy (at a time when all prices fluctuated from it) demonstrates clearly what he considered to be the priority task.

III

As already indicated, besides exchange-value, another facet of value is use-value. A commodity is a use-value because it has the power to satisfy some human need. It receives this quality from the workers who have produced it, who have engaged in purposive productive activity, and in so doing have transferred something of what they are to their product. One one occasion, Marx defines 'use-values' as *'the reproduction of the individual* in certain definite relationships to his community' (Marx's emphasis).[28] A use-value, therefore, is not simply that for which an article is used, but a specific relation between the worker and his activity, product and other men.

The worker in capitalism, being who he is, creates what he does; and what he does – including many of the physical characteristics of his produce – indicates clearly who he is, being in fact the extension of his person in society. Given Marx's relational conception of reality, his view of the internal tie between man and nature and his belief in the worker's alienation, the attempt by workers to produce useful objects must, of necessity, result in objects whose very usefulness bespeaks the alienated relations of the workers involved in their production. Even the notion of utility, we saw Marx declare, is a definite social product. Thus, whereas exchange-value corresponds to what was referred to as the 'quantitative aspect' of labor, use-value corresponds to its qualitive aspect, to what kind of labor it is.[29]

How does use-value bespeak the alienated labor that goes into its production? In capitalism, no commodity is a use-value for the workers who make it. A worker does not produce what he wants, but what will earn him sufficient money to buy what he wants. He produces use-value for others, and only further degradation for himself, the price he must pay for his extraordinary generosity. Thus, his product becomes a use-value only after it is exchanged, and must contain such abstract and general labor as qualifies it for exchange.[30] According to Marx, 'To become use-values commodities must be universally alienated; they must enter the sphere of exchange . . . Hence, in order to be realized as use-values, they must be realized as exchange-values.'[31] Putting the use of one's own products under the control of others, producing them with this aim in mind, lies at the core not only of use-value but of alienation itself. The production of use-values in capitalism is the production of articles from which the workers who made them are alienated; it could only proceed from alienated workers and is the selfsame action which perpetuates their condition.

The alienated character of use-value also stands out in many of the physical traits of the products produced by alienated labor. Production is said to 'put the finishing touch on consumption' because its 'object is not simply an object in general, but a definite object, which is consumed in a certain definite manner prescribed in its turn by production'.[32] In producing for sale to people who lead alienated lives, what kind of articles does the worker produce? He produces, first of all (and on instigation of the capitalist), articles whose qualities are intended to attract customers rather than to give satisfaction. Hence, we find in all capitalist societies a great emphasis on design and little attention paid to durability. The worker will also produce some articles which are only suitable for alienated societies; such are locks of all sorts, guns, most advertisements, stock market ticker tape and churches. Finally, many products which have their equivalent in a non-alienated society are made here in a way that indicates the alienated social relations in which they are found. Thus, houses are made in family units; washing machines, automatic dish washers and most other household durables are generally quite small and can service only a few people; automobiles are mass produced in preference to mini-buses, and so on. In all these ways, the alienated character of capitalism can be read from the real physical characteristics of the goods produced, from their use-values, from seeing how they are made to be used.

Though use-value, as we have said, is predicated on production for exchange, exchange-value is also predicated on production for use and use by others: 'Thus, while a commodity can become a use-value only after it has been realized as an exchange-value, it can on the other hand, be realized as an exchange-value only if it proves to be a use-value in the process of alienation.'[33] The two facets of value presuppose one another, and really cannot be conceived of apart. Like exchange-value, therefore, use-value expresses capitalist production relations.

Still, on occasion, Marx uses the concept 'use-value' to refer to only the universal part of its component relations, and this can be misleading. For example, he states:

So far as work is a creator of use-value, is useful work, it is a necessary condition independent of all forms of society for the existence of the human race; it is an eternal nature imposed necessity, without which there can be no material exchanges between man and nature, and therefore no life.[34]

In this case, use-value enters the theory of alienation when it becomes the 'material depository of exchange-value'.[35] The explanation for this practise has already been given as it applied to 'exchange-value'. It remains the case that Marx almost always uses 'use-value' to refer to a situation where what is useful has already been given over to another and is in fact being produced with this end in mind, that is, as a component relation of capitalist production. Consequently, neither use-value nor exchange-value ever come into Marx's descriptions of communism, where each individual, as a conscious and fully cooperating member of the community, produces what he wants and consumes what he needs.

IV

At the beginning of this discussion of the labor theory of value, I spoke also of the adjoining theory of surplus-value. The latter is indeed an extension of the former but only now can we judge their common substance. Like so many of his expressions, 'surplus-value' has a long history, but the sense that Marx gives it is unique.[36] For him, surplus-value is the amount of the abstract product of alienated labor which is not returned to the worker in the form of wages. It constitutes that part of the use- and exchange-values created in capitalist production which goes to everyone other than the workers. Marx considers it one of his original contributions to political economy that he works with the general form of surplus-value rather than any of its specific forms such as profit or rent.[37] But Marx could only regard surplus-value in its pure form because 'value' meant something more to him than what is usually understood by 'exchange-value'. Without a conception of value as the abstract product, he could not treat surplus-value as the surplus abstract product. Without this conception, Smith, Ricardo and the other labor theory of value economists writing before Marx, could only treat surplus-value in its concrete, exchange-value forms.[38]

Marx seems to believe that the mistake of his predecessors in not dealing with surplus-value in its pure form is less excusable than my own account of this matter would suggest. For in order to operate with the pure form of surplus-value, Smith and Ricardo would have had to grasp value as the abstract product, and this, in turn, would have required an understanding of alienated labor. In believing all this was within the range of the classical economists, Marx seems to have thought that the real world, and especially the plight of the proletariat, could exercise the same effect on other honest men seeking for the truth that it did on him. One is well aware of his great respect for Ricardo. Furthermore, though the political economists had no conception of labor as alienated productive activity and its division, as such, into use-value and exchange-value, this distinction, according to Marx, 'is practically made, since this school treats labor, at one time under its quantitative aspect, at another under its qualitative aspect'.[39] Could the intellectual realization of what they were being forced to do in practise really be so long in forthcoming?

My own conclusion on this subject is more severe. I would consider the theory of value exposed here a closed book for anyone who has not mastered, at least in broad outline, the theory of alienation of which it is part and the philosophy of internal relations which serves it as a necessary frame. Marx's revolution in economics consists in providing a full answer to a question only he asked, and stating it with concepts which partake of the originality of his analysis. Immersed as they are in capitalist assumptions, whose import is only indifferently grasped, no one is less qualified to understand the unique contribution of Marxian economics than the economists.

Joan Robinson expresses the frustration of even the best intentioned economists on reading *Capital,* when she complains, 'What business has Hegel putting his nose between me and Ricardo?'[40] Similarly, Joseph Schumpeter remarks that if 'value' means more than exchange-value a lot of what Marx says might make sense, but he cannot see what more it can mean.[41] This is not to say that all misconceptions regarding Marx's economic theories result from ignorance of the theory of alienation and its philosophical underpinnings. A careful study of *Capital* would have spared generations of readers most of the critical works that have appeared on this subject. In so far as such study would have enabled critics to grasp the capitalism Marx was describing, however, they would be seeing reality, whether they knew it or not, through the prism of the alienation theory. For, in the last analysis, *Capital* is sufficient to understand *Capital,* as Lukács in *Geschichte und Klassenbewusstsein* (1923), well before Marx's early works became available, most notably demonstrated. Unfortunately, most critics have been unable to get as far as the last volume of *Capital,* where Marx makes over and over again the distinctions between value and price, and between surplus-value and profit, and where he puts into place the till then dismissed element of competition. Critics who disregard these pages (and one is tempted to put Böhm-Bawerk among them) cannot be let off so lightly with the excuse that they were not aware of Marx's theory of alienation. Yet it may also be the case that not knowing this theory, no amount of repetition by Marx that value *is* labor and that surplus-value *is not* profit could register as anything but inconsistency.

27. *The metamorphosis of value*

Having presented labor-power as potential for alienated productive activity and the equation of labor and value, I am now in a position to explain the metamorphosis of value and the fetishism of commodities. Labor, as we saw, is embodied in all its products. Hence, as its equivalent in capitalism, the same applies to value. The worker produces an article which contains his labor in the form of use and exchange-value. Then, according to Marx:

> The actual process of production, as a unity of the direct production process and the circulation process gives rise to new formations, in which the vein of *internal connections* is increasingly lost, the production relations are rendered independent of one another, and the component values become ossified into forms independent of one another (my emphasis).[1]

The guises assumed by value in its merry-go-round journey through the economy include capital, commodity, landed property, profit, interest, rent, wages and money. Marx would maintain that these are 'more concrete economic determinations from which value is abstracted and which from another point of view, can therefore also be regarded as a further development of it'.[2] All derive from the worker's alienated productive activity, and each expresses the full set of conditions in which it exists. As components of value they are facets of the same organic whole, capitalist society. On this view, too much of orthodox economics has been devoted to trying to explain how such apparently distinct entities are related. For Marx, the reverse was the problem: he sought to show how such essentially identical entities differ, or what is each value form's peculiar function in the economy. Their 'identity' is assumed; where as the distinctiveness of each form, which includes the unique ways in which it is related to others, is the subject of his empirical research.

No doubt the most important of these concrete economic determinations is capital, which lends its very name to the period. Marx declares that capital is 'value that sucks up the value-creating power'.[3] It is that part of surplus-value which re-engages labor for the production of further value. A more complete account is given where Marx says:

> capital is not a thing but rather a definite social production relation, belonging to a definite historical formation of society, which is manifested in a thing and lends this thing a specific social character. Capital is not the sum of the material and produced means of production. Capital is rather the means of production transformed into capital, which in themselves are no more capital than gold or silver in itself is money. It is the means of production monopolized by a certain section of society, confronting living labor-power as products and working conditions rendered independent of this very labor-power, which are personified through this antithesis in capital. It is not merely the products of laborers turned into independent powers, products as rulers and buyers of their producers, but rather also the social forces of their labor and socialized form of this labor, which confront the laborers as properties of their products.[4]

Capital, in short, expresses the major economic relations of capitalism from the standpoint of the products of former labor which now constitute the means of production. It is the use of such means to produce value, and presupposes all those conditions necessary for it to operate in this way, subsumes these conditions as component relations. Hence, as we saw, Marx speaks of the alienated worker as 'variable capital' and says the capitalist himself 'is contained in the concept of capital'.[5] So too, money, commodities and interest are all spoken of on occasion as capital.[6] In so far as each expresses the alienated relations bound up in labor, each is a 'form' of value; but in so far as each functions in a way associated with the core notion of capital, that is, contributes to the production of value, each is also a 'form' of capital. Thus money, for example, may be viewed as value, capital, commodity, etc., depending on which of its potential functions Marx takes it to be fulfilling, which depends in turn on the problem he is then considering.

So it is that the title *Capital* is capable of conveying the whole story of capitalism told in the rest of the work. It is a story which begins logically with alienated labor and proceeds through the creation of value to various concrete economic determinations of which capital is the outstanding example. Hence, stretched to their full meanings, 'capital', 'capitalist mode of production' and 'capitalism' are equivalent expressions. 'Capitalism', as Marx ordinarily uses this term, simply follows these relations further into people's daily lives, but it does not introduce elements which are not already present in 'capital' conceptualized as a unity of its necessary conditions and results.

'Capital' is given the further distinction of being called the 'dominant category' of the capitalist era, 'its determining production relation'.[7] 'Determining' is to be understood here in the sense of 'most important'. For Marx, the use of the means of production to produce wealth in general is the most striking of the many unique features of capitalism, the most influential in the interaction between its various parts, and the Relation the unfolding of which offers the clearest insight into the whole. The latter claim requires qualification in light of Marx's decision to begin *Capital* with an explanation of 'commodity' and 'value', though the outline of this work found in the *Grundrisse* starts with 'capital'.[8]

Taking 'capital' (or 'commodity' and 'value' as he did in *Capital*, or 'money' as he did in *Critique of Political Economy*) as his central concept permits Marx to enter the economic debate with the fewest preliminary qualifications. To have chosen 'alienated labor' would have required at least as extensive an investigation into philosophy and anthropology as appeared in the *1844 Manuscripts*. Without such qualifications, however, it is all too easy to mistake key categories, such as 'capital', 'commodity' and 'value', for their equivalents in the works of other economists. If we view Marx as treating his subject on two interrelated levels, that of economics proper, as reflected in the writings of Smith and Ricardo, and that of alienation, then it has proven the bane of Marxism that by transferring commonly accepted meanings to his terms enough sense could be made of what Marx was saying on this first level that most people deferred trying to make sense of what was being said on the second. However, given their interrelated character – even the idea of two levels is misleading – the result has been widespread misunderstanding of the whole corpus of Marx's economics.

II

The discussion of private property and product alienation has prepared us to grasp how value could be embodied in such concrete products as capital, or in commodity and landed property, for that matter; but in what sense is value embodied in money, whether cash or in one of the guises in which it is distributed to the population – profit, interest, rent and wages? Marx would maintain that money contains value in the same sense that capital does: both result from alienated labor and both, therefore, possess a use-value as well as an exchange-value. In the case of money, its use-value is its facility in being exchanged; whereas its exchange-value, as with capital, is the amount of value it exchanges for.

As a product of alienated productive activity entering into exchange, money, like capital itself, is a commodity. Money differs essentially from other commodities, first, in being the form in which all the rest 'appear as exchange-values to each other'; or as Marx says elsewhere, it is 'the commodity in its continually exchangeable form'.[9] According to him:

> The particular commodity which thus appears as the specifically adopted expression of the exchange-value of all other commodities, or the exchange-value of commodities as a particular exclusive commodity, is money. Money is a crystallization of the exchange-value of commodities which they themselves form in the process of exchange. Thus, while commodities become use-values to each other in the process of exchange by casting off all definite shape, they must assume a new form, viz., proceed to the formation of money in order to appear as exchange-values to each other.[10]

To facilitate the comparison of commodities on the basis of a single standard, value, money is evolved. According to Marx, it is a form of commodities themselves, that in which they exchange for one another, and it expresses the same alienated conditions which make the exchange of equivalents both possible and necessary.

As the substance in which their relative worths are reckoned, money replaces over a period of time all other commodities as the object of practical effort. This is a second distinguishing feature of money as a commodity: people work to make money. As the necessary mediator between man and his wants, money has come to be what he wants.[11] Furthermore, by possessing the power to buy everything, money puts the individual into relations with other commodities and people that he could not enter into on the basis of his own needs and personal characteristics. Money enables him to buy the food which his hunger cannot secure, to occupy the hearth to which his numb limbs give him no right or to possess the woman whom his personal traits cannot win.

It is the same alienated labor which makes it impossible for workers to appropriate the world of objects that enables money to do so. The ability of money is man's own, man's potential for entering into relations with nature, including other men, which has been taken from him in labor and incorporated in his products. The power of money to buy is a function of people's necessity to sell what they have (labor-power, products, virtue); this is a function of their inability to acquire what they need as human beings by simply manifesting their needs; and this, in turn, is a function of a situation in which those who control what is needed have interests other than and hostile to the interests of the persons in need. By producing a product which he gives over to the control of another the worker begins a chain reaction that culminates (on this scale at least) in the particular role that money plays in capitalist society.

What money is able to buy, therefore, is no more than what people potentially can do but actually cannot. For if they were doing it, then money could not buy it; and if they could never do it, then there would be nothing for money to buy. It is in this sense that Marx declares that 'money is the *alienated ability of mankind*' (Marx's emphasis).[12] Without alienation there would be no money; people would not offer a sterile metal for what they want and would refuse to accept it for what they have. In describing the dictatorship of the proletariat, where the worker's alienated relations to his activity, product, and other men have already been seriously modified, Marx dispenses with the concept of 'money' and speaks instead of 'labor vouchers'. In communism, of course, even these have disappeared.[13]

III

The metamorphosis of value from one form to another occurs through the alienation in exchange of use-value. To alienate the use-value of labor-power, capital, money, etc., means in every instance to give up all control over it to another. This presupposes, of course, that individuals have such control over the value forms in their possession, and accept that others do as well. According to Marx, exchange becomes possible whenever 'men, by a tacit understanding . . . treat each other as private owners of those alienable objects, and by implication as independent individuals'.[14] All acts of exchange, then, are characterized by the mutual transfer of the power to use-value forms. Afterwards, both the buyer and the seller 'have the same value they had before the transactions'; only the form of value is different, as each has acquired what the other had.[15]

In answer to his question, 'What is alienated in an ordinary sale?', Marx replies, 'Not the value of the sold commodity, for this merely changes its form . . . What is really alienated by the seller, and, therefore passes into the individual or productive consumption of the buyer, is the use-value of the commodity – the commodity as a use-value.'[16] Value cannot be alienated in a sale, for all capitalist products continue to express, both before and after their sale, the relations which underlie their production. However, the form of value changes in the sense that the object of value performs a different function for the buyer than it did for the seller, and, as we saw, changes in function betoken changes in the concept which applies. Hence, the value form of a machine in the hands of a merchant is commodity; he uses it to make money. In the sale, the merchant gives up its use-value to a capitalist, who uses it to employ workers to produce value. The machine owned by the capitalist remains a value (it continues to express the alienated relations involved in its production), but its value form has changed to capital with the new function that it serves. According to Marx, each form of value has a unique mode of alienating its use-value: 'A special sort of commodity, capital has its own peculiar mode of alienation,' which is transferring the value that went into its production to its products.[17] And elsewhere, lending is given as the mode in which the banker alienates the use-value of his money to the capitalist.[18]

The whole process of transferring use-value has its start when the worker alienates his labor-power to the capitalist in order to earn enough money to buy means of subsistence. Labor-power, we will recall, is the only commodity whose use-value, labor, is capable of creating a greater exchange-value than its own. The capitalist sells the workers' products, i.e., alienates their use-value to buyers, for money, i.e., to obtain the use-value of their money. He then alienates the use-value of part of the money he receives to a landlord in the form of rent, and of another part to a banker in the form of interest. This is really the exchange, though in this instance not an equitable one, of a new for an old value, the product of previous workers whose use-values were initially alienated to the capitalist by the landlord and the banker. In this way the surplus-value is distributed. What the capitalist retains for himself is his profit, part of which he will undoubtedly alienate to workers to obtain more labor-power.

From the foregoing discussion it may appear that the sense of 'alienate' has shifted somewhat from what it was when we began. To give up all control over use-value does not seem to be the same thing as what was treated above under this concept. It is from such evidence that some critics, who note the appearance of 'alienation' in *Capital,* have concluded that Marx intends something quite different than he did in his earlier writings. Aside from the fact that this concept is frequently used, particularly in the *Grundrisse* (1857-8), to convey exactly the same information that it does in the *1844 Manuscripts,* the discussion of use-value should make it clear that the difference which does exist is more apparent than real.[19]

When, in *Capital,* Marx speaks of 'alienating' any commodity, he does not simply mean the act of selling it; he means giving up all control over its use-value. And as I have shown, this transaction could only take place because the workers, who create all value, engage in alienated activity on a product from which they are alienated and on behalf of a capitalist from whom they are alienated. To transfer use-values is one facet of alienation and is fully integrated into and dependent on its other facets. By referring to such a sale as 'alienation', Marx is using this concept, as he does so many others, to express but part of the structured information that comes under it in order to meet some immediate purpose. In this instance, the practise of giving up the right to use what one has for a price is called 'alienation', first, because the act itself is an alienated one and, second, in order to draw attention to the source of such exchange (and, hence, the entire metamorphosis of value which evolves from it) in the alienated labor of workers.[20]

IV

Capital is a treatise on the law of value, and as such could only be a work about alienation. Earlier, in labeling it a work of unravelling, private property was said to be the subject matter. This was true but not wholly accurate since it is value, the most abstract form of private property (the form in which all traces of specificity have been lost), which is Marx's proper subject. Like all other laws in Marxism, the law of value has to do with the necessary development of an entity through the temporal relations Marx sees bound up in it. It concerns not only what happens but what must happen to value given its 'essential nature'. The transformation of value into capital, wages, rent or money, as well as its transformation into prices of production and eventually into market prices all come under this law. In following value in and through the various forms it takes in capitalist circulation, Marx is charting the law of its development. He is uncovering what is referred to at different times as the 'inner relations', 'hidden substratum', 'physiology', 'organic coherence' and 'life process' of capitalism. It is this which makes Marx's work – on his own understanding of the term – a 'science': 'The science', we have seen him declare, 'consists precisely in working out how the law of value operates.'[21]

Marx's labor theory of value, therefore, unlike Smith's and Ricardo's, is *not* the claim that labor produces value, but the whole panorama of faces exposed in the metamorphosis of value, in which the equation of labor with value is the underlying assumption.

28. *The fetishism of commodities*

The 'fetishism of commodities' refers to people's misconception of
the products of labor once they enter exchange, a misconception
which accords these forms of value leading roles in what is still a
human drama.[1] The metamorphosis of value is a tale about man,
his productive activity and products, and what happens to them all
in capitalist society. Misreading this story as one about the activities of inanimate objects, attributing to them qualities which only
human beings could possess, positing living relations for what is
dead, is what Marx calls the 'fetishism of commodities'.[2]

According to Marx, 'This fetishism of commodities has its origins . . . in the peculiar social character of the labor that produces
them.'[3] This character, as we saw, is reproduced in the product,
value. As the abstract product of alienated labor, value expresses
the relations of the individuals engaged in such labor. However,
though value contains human relations, it actually conveys them as
relations between their products. Hence, the remark, 'When, therefore, Galiani says: Value is a relation between persons . . . he
ought to have added: a relation between persons expressed as a
relation between things'.[4]

For Marx, it is through the monetary expression of exchange-
value that the ties between people at work have remained so carefully hidden. He maintains that it is

this ultimate money-form of the world of commodities that actually
conceals, instead of disclosing the social character of private labor, and
the social relations between the individual producers. When I state that
coats or boots stand in a relation to linen, because it is the universal
incarnation of abstract human labor, the absurdity of the statement is
self-evident. Nevertheless, when the producers of coats and boots compare these articles with linen, or, what is the same thing, with gold or
silver, as the universal equivalent, they express the relation between
their own private labor and the collective labor of society in the same
absurd form.[5]

With the relations between people so artfully disguised as relations between things, we should not be surprised that this is how

they are grasped. In the fetishism of commodities the appearance of the metamorphosis of value is mistaken for its essence. By treating value solely as the ratio at which their products exchange, people attribute to these products the personal ties which make such an exchange of equivalents possible. Accordingly, Marx declares that a commodity is a 'mysterious thing, simply because in it the social character of men's labor appears to them as an objective character stamped upon the product of that labor'.[6]

In this manner, a commodity is seen to have a 'natural price', a relation to money and other commodities independent of the human factors involved. This price, which – as an indication of exchange-value based on the alienation of use-value – simply expresses relations between people in production, is taken as a non-social quality of the commodity on a par with its physical character. Shoes have openings for the feet, and cost five dollars a pair. So it is with other forms of value, where this same phenomenon is better described as 'reification'. Capital, for example is seen to 'earn' a profit; this is taken as its proper, natural, and, therefore, deserved product.[7] Admittedly, this way of speaking is sometimes no more than a shorthand for presenting a complex situation, but Marx believes that it usually is not, that most people who speak of capital earning a profit actually grasp the relation between the two in terms of cause and effect.

Capital is also reified in its relations with workers. For Marx, capital exploits workers as an instrument of the capitalists. Dead matter dominates living labor because it is in the hands of men whose interests are diametrically opposed to those of the producers. Though Marx speaks of the capitalist's actions as a 'mere function of capital', it is the capitalist and not capital who is endowed with a conscience and a will.[8] Only because machines, factories, etc., are used for the purpose they are does alienation result. However, in the course of experiencing exploitation, workers are prone to confuse the means with the people who direct them, and to attribute to inanimate objects the social character of an exploiting agency. In this way, machines are seen to need workers, and factories blamed for making the life of the proletariat intolerable.

Reification also occurs with landed property, which is invested with the natural ability to produce rent.[9] According to Marx, 'One of the objective conditions of labor alienated from labor, and therefore confronting it as the property of others' is land, which in our era takes the form of 'monopolized land, or landed property'.[10] Life profit, rent is a social relation, in this case, that part of value which is siphoned off to landlords. Marx maintains, 'Just as products confront the producer as an independent force in capital and capitalists who actually are but the personification of capital – so land becomes personified in the landlord and likewise gets on its hind legs to demand, as an independent force, its share of the product created with its help'.[11] As in the case of capital, the domination of landed property over men is misconstrued as deriving from the land itself, rather than from its owners.

The reification that Marx uncovers is not limited to the concrete products of labor but applies equally to all the forms touched upon by the metamorphosis of value. We saw earlier all that money was able to do in capitalism, but, instead of seeing this as the expression of man's relation to his products being turned on its head, money is taken to possess these colossal powers as natural attributes. People's attitude toward money is, undoubtedly, the outstanding instance of capitalist fetishism, reaching its height in interest bearing capital (money lent at interest). Here, people think they see 'money creating more money, self-expanding value'.[12] When money 'grows' in this way, Marx says, 'The result of the entire process of reproduction appears as a property inherent in the thing itself.'[13] Workers, machines, raw materials – all the factors of production – are downgraded to mere aids, and money itself is made the producer of wealth.

Finally, the labor relation itself is reified, made into a 'ghost', wage-labor, an abstraction divested of its unique character. People in capitalism see labor, their distinctive alienated labor which produces value, as the productive activity of all men at all time and as an activity which is responsible for only the part of value that is returned to them as wages. Hence, labor is thought of as having a 'natural price', a conception Marx considers 'as irrational as a yellow logarithm'.[14]

In treating the social production relations, capital, landed property and labor, as things, their integral unity is lost, and the society in which they exist united hopelessly distorted. According to Marx:

In capital-profit, or still better capital-interest, land-rent, labor-wages, in this economic trinity represented as the connection between the component parts of value and wealth in general and its sources, we have the complete mystification of the capitalist mode of production, the conversion of social relations into things, the direct coalescence of the material production relations with their historical and social determination. It is an enchanted, perverted, topsy-turvy world, in which *Monsieur le Capital* and *Madame la Terre* do their ghost-walking as social characters and at the same time directly as things.[15]

What could only have been expected once the different forms of value are reified, the very connections between them, the time sequences on which they are hung, are also given lives of their own. In this case, where production relations appear to people as things, their

interrelations due to the world market, its conjecture, movements of market prices, periods of credit, industrial and commercial cycles, alternations of prosperity and crisis appears to them as overwhelming natural laws that irresistibly enforce their will over them, and confront them as blind necessity.[16]

People tend to view these recurring economic events, which they dignify with the label 'law', as natural attributes of nature. But neither god nor nature demands their occurrence. What appears as 'blind necessity' is but the unchecked development of the social production relations of capitalism.

The practical effect of all such fetishism, of course, is the blanket ignorance it imposes on anyone trying to understand the capitalist economic system. With its origins, real mechanisms and future possibilities so well hidden, criticism is misdirected and action that would alter the situation rendered ineffective. As Marcuse rightly points out:

If wages . . . express the value of labor, exploitation is at best a subjective and personal judgment. If capital were nothing other than an aggregate of wealth employed in commodity production, then capital would appear to be the cumulative result of productive skill and diligence. If the creation of profits were the peculiar quality of utilized capital, such profits might represent a reward for the work of the entrepreneur.[17]

By dismissing the essential human relations, the basic relations of alienation which underly capitalist production, its surface relations become everything.

II

So far, I have been proceeding as if reification had necessarily to be based on faulty evidence. However, by attributing an independent life to the various forms of value, people succeed in transferring to them certain powers for regulating their own existence. In a situation where all entities are related to each other as both cause and effect, to be viewed as an initiating force is to become one in fact. To conceive of machines as needing workers is to accord machines the power to need workers. Likewise, to conceive of money as having the power to buy everything is indeed to have money which has the power to buy everything. The laws of capitalism operate as eternal necessity in the same manner. They become necessary in virtue of everyone thinking and acting as if they are. For all practical purposes, that is for purposes of life in capitalism, reification brings about the very mistake it embodies.[18]

The difficulty in grasping this notion comes from the impossibility on what I have called the common sense view of treating man's objects as 'subjects' without falling into the error of personifying the inanimate. Man, it is said, uses, needs and has power over his products; he may misuse them, be ignorant or ineffective, but these products cannot actually use, need or have power over him. Yet, as we have seen, these are claims that Marx often makes. By holding that the relation between man and nature is an internal one, Marx is able to transfer qualities usually associated with one to the other to mark some special feature. The power man has to affect his relations with nature, for example, is a quality he has as a facet of the whole, which includes nature; hence it is also a quality of the whole (what applies to any of its parts applies to the whole); and so, too, of other facets (what applies to the whole applies to all its parts – assuming internal relations between them). Thus, as explained in Chapter 2 above, the qualities of one factor are applicable to another (whether offered as part of the meaning of its concept or ascribed in separate adjectives) whenever the latter functions in ways associated with the core meaning of the former.

Through his alienated productive activity in capitalism, the worker has established relations between himself and his products (both parts of human nature for Marx) which enable each to function in some respects like what is generally meant by the other's concept. The worker has needs for objects to fulfill his powers as a human being but cannot acquire these objects. Instead, he passes his days producing value, satisfying the profit needs of his employer, behaving in short as 'variable capital'. His product, which is meant to satisfy human needs, serves instead to re-order the lives of the people who come into contact with it, getting them to act in ways that affirm its character as a capitalist product. The worker has no claim to a machine when he is unemployed, while the machine has a claim to the worker when it is unemployed. Hence, a machine (as capital) is said to need the night labor of workers; the relation between the two is such that what the product is determines what the worker does rather than the reverse.

All forms of the worker's product are, on occasion, spoken of in terms that we ordinarily reserve for men, but it is money which is most frequently characterized in this way. Money, as we saw, is the mediator between man and all his objects in capitalism; he can get nothing he needs without paying for it. Cast in this role, money is said to have 'changed into a true god, for *the intermediary reigns in real power over the thing it mediates for me. Its cult becomes an end in itself.'*[19] The notion that the mediator between man and his object (the means which enable him to make use of it) is something that exercises 'real power' over him comes up again – as we shall see – in Marx's discussion of religion and the state.

Thus, for Marx, the relations between men are not only reified in their products, but these reified products interact with men so as to make what appeared false true. Rather a contradiction, this is perhaps the most important example in Marxism of reciprocal effect: people acquire their conception of reality from what they experience (they reify the forms of value because of what occurs in the metamorphosis of value), and their conception of reality helps determine what they experience (the metamorphosis of value only occurs through the reification of the forms of value). The power of capital, or of any of the worker's products, over the worker always reflects the power of the people who dominate it and use it as an instrument. However, through reification and inside the context of capitalism, capital itself may exercise certain powers. Marx is not guilty of the fetishism he discovers in capitalist society, because the powers he ascribes to products are never considered theirs as natural qualities.

To exclude either side of this internal relation between man and his products (such that each may be seen to dominate the other) is to arrive at a dead end, in one instance of 'vulgar determinism' and in the other of equally vulgar 'free will'. To admit only one of these perspectives is to treat *Capital* as a work on fetishism or a fetishized work. Though Marx, here, as in his historical essays, emphasizes the effect until then neglected proceeding from material factors, the full cloth, Marxism, is the product of the dialectical interweaving of the two.

29. *Class as a value Relation*

Alienation is not solely an economic phenomenon. As already indicated, the worker's fourfold alienation in the means of production finds expression in all areas of his life. In one listing, 'religion, family, state, law, morality science, art, etc.' are said to be the 'particular modes of production' which come under the law of private property.[1] A mode of production, according to Marx:

> must not be considered simply as being the reproduction of the physical existence of the individuals. Rather it is a definite form of activity of these individuals, a definite form of expressing their life, a definite mode of life on their part.[2]

Under capitalism, all such expressions of life are facets of man's alienation by virtue of their internal relation to private property, or world of alienated objects, and fall under its law as the necessary steps to its full working out.

The life activity of the alienated individual is qualitatively of a kind. His actions in religion, family affairs, politics and so on, are as distorted and brutalized as his productive activity. The man taking part in these different activities, after all, is the same; his powers and needs stand at a particular level of their development, restricting all intercourse with nature within certain bounds. Nature, too, the world of objects through which man must realize himself, has developed apace with these powers and dictates from its side what is possible. There is no sphere of human activity that lies outside these prison walls; hence escape, one-sided development, can only be peripheral and temporary.

With all man's activity of a kind, so too must be its products. Alienated activity in any sphere results in objects from which the individual involved is alienated. Accordingly, Marx refers to politics, art and literature as examples of 'the objectified essential powers of man in the form of estrangement, displayed in ordinary material industry'.[3] When Marx says, therefore, that industry and its products are the 'open book of man's essential powers', the same applies to his products in other spheres of life as well.[4]

What holds true for man's relations to his various activities and products also applies to relations with his own kind. The indifference and outright hostility which characterizes relations between workers and capitalists have their counterparts throughout society. No one recognizes the needs of others, or the role that others must play in helping to satisfy his own needs. In Marx's words, the egoistic individual who lives in capitalism has inflated 'himself to the size of an atom, i.e., to an unrelated, self-sufficient, wantless, absolutely full, blessed being'.[5] Judging by its results, alienation is what is left of a nut after it has been opened by a sledge hammer. The pieces of what it means to be a man, in terms of activities, products and necessary human interchange, have been everywhere disassembled and their common unity lost beyond recognition.

If alienated activity is differentiated according to the sphere in which it takes place, its product must also be set apart as value, class, state, religion and so on. However, the very attempt to compartmentalize alienation in this manner is itself a symptom of the 'disease' I am describing, for alienation is 'essentially' the same wherever it occurs. Thus, too, the products of alienated activity, as equal elements in the world of private property, share certain basic similarities, and can be characterized as 'value', no matter what their particular form. Do not all the achievements of capitalist man express the same underlying relations? So it is that money, the carrying form of economic value, is able to buy not only the products of industry but all products resulting from alienated activity. Everything in capitalism has its price.[6] Furthermore, of the worker's role in production, Marx states explicitly that 'every relation of servitude is but a modification and a consequence of this relation'.[7] Thus, class, state, religion, etc., in the form in which they appear, are not only the fruits of capitalist production; they are as well part of what is meant (or can be meant) by 'capitalist relations of production'.

Besides expressing the same fundamental relations conveyed by the products of labor and, like them, possessing exchange-values which become apparent in price, these products of alienated nonproductive activity also have use-values. Based, like the products already examined, on the assumption of alienability, such use-values express the aims for which these articles were created; and again, as with the products of industry, such use-values are clearly indicative of the alienated relations out of which they arose.

Likewise, the metamorphosis of value described above can be extended to cover all the products of alienated activity. Having accepted that in capitalism money is able to buy everything, we can see how the same value, which is the essence of money, is as well the essence of all those products money can buy. In lobbying a legislature to pass a law or in purchasing outright a religious office there has been, as in the market place itself, an exchange of value equivalents. The alienated relations expressed in the one are, on Marx's organic conception, basically the same as the alienated relations expressed in the other. If this were not so the exchange of one for the other would not be possible.

Finally, the fetishism of commodities also applies to all spheres of alienated activity. The same misconceptions of the place and role of man's creations that we observed in economics are apparent everywhere though, admittedly, some spheres and some products lend themselves more easily to this treatment than others. In all these respects, therefore, class, state, religion, family, ethics, science, art and literature are aspects of value or, as I prefer to label them, 'value Relations'.[8]

II

As a value Relation, class is the abstracted common element in the social relations of alienated people. The ties between people in capitalist labor and in its necessary and resulting conditions exhibit a set of similarities and, indeed, an overall pattern to which Marx assigns a separate indentity. Of central importance is the fact that throughout society the relations between men have taken on an independent existence. Marx declares, 'The social character of activity appears here as an alien object in relation to the individuals . . . their mutual relationship appears to the individuals themselves as something alien and autonomous, as an object'.[9] It is chiefly this quality, drawn from the various sectors in which it is found, which Marx conceptualizes as 'class' for purposes of treating alienation.

For class to be grasped as an object, of course, the social relations which give rise to it must be conceived of as an activity, and, given the elasticity of Marx's dialectic, such a conception is legitimate. As a product, then, of people's activity of getting on with their fellows, class is as indicative of their character and lot as are the products of their material production. Class and commodity are brothers under the skin.

What is the relationship between class as a product of alienated activity and class as an agglomeration of people who share certain qualities? Earlier I used 'class' to refer to social units based on people's relationship to the mode of production, similar economic conditions and interests, a consciousness of these interests, the existence of a group-wide political organization, cultural affinity and a common antagonism for opposing groups. In maintaining now that 'class' also refers to a particular kind of social tie, the criteria for delimiting classes become component relations for the classes so delimited. Thus, people's interaction at work is not only based on their contrasting relations to the mode of production, but one facet of this interaction is this contrasting relationship, which for Marx is a dynamic fact that is constantly being reaffirmed through fresh appropriations. Likewise, bourgeois culture not only helps create a capitalist class in distinction to the proletariat, but is as well part of their active response to one another. In particular, the antagonism which one exhibits toward people in other similarly constituted groups is not just an indication of class but its very substance.

What were treated as standards by which to constitute and distinguish groups are viewed here as so many facets of the interpersonal relations involved. As such, that is as activities, broadly understood, they produce a typical product. This product is class, in the sense of reified social relations. Conversely, it is clear to Marx that people are able to interact in the stated manner only because their social relations have already taken on for them the character of an independent entity.

In each sphere of life, real material practise corresponds with mental practise; the class form of social relations in life becomes the form 'class' in man's understanding. The alien and hostile treatment that each person receives and metes out as a member of a class occurs while he is regarding all his fellows, their needs and interests, through the prism of class. This does not mean that one grasps social interaction in terms of classes – this is one of the byproducts of class consciousness, a late development. Instead, the only qualities which are noticed in any interchange are those which accrue to men through their class position. People react to one another as one of a kind; therefore, they react to the kind and only indirectly to the individual as a reflection of it. It is the mock independence of their kind whence real living people derive the qualities and claims with which their fellows interact. The uniqueness of each separate individual is never found for it is never sought. It is this more than anything else which enables a person, when pressing claims on his fellows, to think only of himself.

The character of the ensuing struggle is well brought out in Marx's definition of 'competition', its all-purpose label' as 'avarice and war among the avaricious'.[10] Competition may thus be viewed as the activity which produces class. Throughout society, calculator meets calculator in the never ending battle of who can get the most out of whom. 'Mutual exploitation' is the rule.[11] Other people are mere objects of use; their wishes and feelings are never considered, cannot be on pain of extinction. A lapse into kindness for those who have their own knives poised can prove fatal. In this situation, hearts are opened only to absolute losers; charity becomes the only form of giving.[12]

The class battle between workers and capitalists for the surplus-value of the former is one to the death, the slow, timeless death of the workers. Given the capitalists' superior position in society and their control over the most powerful weapon in this struggle, money, their indifference to the needs of workers issues in far more painful results than the parallel indifference of workers to the needs of their employers.

With such hostility ingrained in the way of life and outlook of everyone, it is not surprising that the competition between members of each class for a greater portion of the fruits which go to them as a class is no less intense. For the social relations bound up in class include ties between people living in the same conditions as well as between those in contrasting conditions. Here, too, people react to one another as one of a kind rather than as real living individuals. Again it is chiefly this conception which enables them to scramble for their own personal success while being indifferent to the plight of others. Thus, among capitalists, individual fortunes are raised on the buried hopes, and, sometimes, bodies of competitors. The only criterion of good business is success. And, in business as in war, victory generally goes to the side with the more ruthless disposition.

Among the proletariat, competition first rears its head at the factory gate where some are allowed in and others not. Inside the factory, workers continue to compete with each other for such favors as their employer has it in him to bestow, especially for the easier and better-paying jobs. After work, with too little money to spend, workers are again at each other's throats for the inadequate food, clothing and shelter available to them. It is such competition at all levels, with its accompanying attitudes, which makes organizing the proletariat such a difficult task.[13] Also, without a conception of his identity in the group, an ideal which only arrives with class consciousness, the individual worker is incapable of appreciating the essential links between his own labor and that of his co-workers. So it is that both his social activity and product are viewed as alien powers.[14]

The forms taken by class as a product of competition range from those metal constructs which enable men to respond to others as class individuals to such real world expressions of our mutual antagonism as political parties. It is with the latter group of forms, where the independent entity that has arisen from our social relations is institutionalized, that the operation of class as a value Relation is most evident. For Marx, all social institutions, organizations and the like which promote directly or indirectly the interests of any class are particular expressions of this antagonism. And since, in a society dominated by private property, neutrality and communality in respect to any social aim is ruled out, all organizations and institutions in capitalism are class organizations and institutions, or forms of class. Besides political parties, other obvious examples are the state, unions, employer federations, the media of communication, cultural societies and schools.

As value Relations, all forms of the product class express men's alienated activity in getting on with each other. Their exchange-values are evidenced by the role that money plays in all these organizations; what office, what rule, what practise does not have its price? They also have use-values indicative of the alienated ends for which they were created. The metamorphosis of value can be seen, not only from their saleability, but also from their interchangeability: pressure groups become political parties which, in turn, become governments. Lastly, reification takes place in attributing to these expressions of men's alienated relations the human qualities of purpose and power. People's respect, amounting to reverence, for their own creations is what allows the latter to dominate their lives.

III

Individuals never could have descended to such depths if their practical isolation from each other were less complete. Acquiring an identity in the part, in class, with each class in opposition to all others, required that an individual's identity in the whole, in society, be lost from view. Men do not know themselves and others as social beings whose needs demand mutual cooperation but as private and competing entities, an anarchistic galaxy of selfish worlds. Without a universal cooperative community which unites everyone, people are siphoned off into partial communities based on shared antagonisms. The less people grasp of their social nature the more this nature becomes distorted into classes. Hence, the growth of what Marx calls the 'personal life' – of those areas of existence where the individual believes he affects no one and is affected by no one, of a conception of himself set apart from the social ties established at his place of labor – registers the full development of class relations.[15] Man is most completely a class determined being when he least believes himself to be one.

In its full blown form, this feigned independence from class relations is a distinctive feature of capitalism. Marx says in feudalism 'a nobleman always remains a nobleman, a commoner always a commoner, apart from his other relationships, a quality inseparable from his individuality'.[16] People in that period were never able to conceive of themselves or others without their social ties; the links which establish privileges and duties were never forgotten. Marx's explanation for this is that in feudal times

There still exists the semblance of a more intimate connection between the proprietor and the land than that of mere material wealth. The estate is individualized with its lord: it has his rank . . . his privileges, his jurisdictions, his political position. . . . Similarly, the rule of landed property does not appear directly as the rule of mere capital. For those belonging to it, the estate is more like their fatherland. It is a constricted sort of nationality . . . Similarly, those working on the estate have not the position of day-laborers; but they are in part themselves his [the lord's] property, as are the serfs.[17]

With the threads of their private property so carefully inter-
woven with their individuality, neither lord nor serfs could separate
themselves, as individuals, from it.[18]

With the development of private property into the abstraction,
value, it is no longer possible to conflate a man's individuality with
his private property. Distinctive private property, as something containing unique personalizing characteristics, has come to an end.
No one is attached to the form of value he possesses in the way
that feudal lords and serfs were attached to their particular private
property. The duties, sentiments, special loyalties, etc., which followed upon the older arrangement have likewise disappeared, and
it is impossible to take any social relations outside of production
for granted. In capitalism, the worker believes himself a 'free' man
outside the factory, an independent being without social needs or
obligations. For him, his character as producer ceases with the
daily completion of his task in production. It is the same with the
capitalist. Once these two have concluded their exchange of equivalents, neither feels bonded to the other in any way. As the social
relations formed in a context where people believe none to exist,
class may be spoken of as the special product of capitalism.[19]

Yet, it is just this independence of individuals, which appears to
them to be the greatest freedom, that is 'precisely the slavery of
civil society'.[20] Marx maintains that

Free industry and free trade abolish privileged exclusivity and thereby
the struggle between the privileged exclusivities. In its place they set
man free from privileges – which isolates from the social whole but at
the same time joins in a narrower exclusivity – man, no longer bound
to other men even by the semblance of common ties. Thus, they produce the universal struggle of man against man, individual against
individual.[21]

Social ties in feudalism, degraded as they were, provided each
person with help in time of need and gave a meaning to his existence that extended beyond the desire to stay alive. In capitalism,
these ties have been obliterated and nothing has been put in their
place. The resulting 'equality' between men is a spurious one,
an equality in abstraction, in being without the links that were cut
asunder; their new freedom is but the necessity to struggle, their
right to live but a duty to try to stay alive.

A person's independence from his fellows is never more than a dream, but in so dreaming and attempting to act upon it he puts himself 'at the mercy of chance'.[22] Struggling, cajoling, begging, conniving, stealing, lying and pushing others out of line may succeed in obtaining for one the necessities of life, but, in a society where everyone is acting like this and goods are scarce, the results cannot be counted on. Hence, Marx's claim that 'in imagination, individuals seem freer under the dominance of the bourgeoisie than before, because their conditions of life seem accidental; in reality, of course, they are less free, because they are more subjected to the violence of things'.[23] People are more likely to be deprived of what they desperately need in capitalism, where responsibility and control over such matters is diffused, than under feudalism, with its institutionalized concern over the fate of others. The same chance which holds sway over the products of labor holds sway over the act of labor itself. Workers are forced under threat of starvation to accept any job they are offered, but their conditions make it uncertain that they will be offered a job. In capitalism, men are all prisoners of conditions which have marked out some of them – they do not know whom – for defeat. Hence, the crude, chance ridden 'violence of things'.

If we now step back for a moment to regard the Marxist system as a whole, we find that class occupies a position in it akin to labor and value. Whereas labor (earlier, the division of labor) is the preferred Relation for encompassing alienated productive activity and value (earlier, private property) the products of such activity, class is the preferred Relation for encompassing the interpersonal ties which are established in this activity and through its products. Class, labor and value stand directly beneath the capitalist mode of production itself in the hierarchy of Relations with which Marx makes Marxist sense of his society.

Though differentiated, these expressions of man's alienation in capitalism are as interdependent as people, activity and products, and the causal tie operates in all directions between them. Furthermore, given the elasticity of Marx's units, the Relation, class, is also a component of the Relations, labor and value, and they of it: how can we explain social ties, for example, without bringing in the activity and products in and through which they are expressed? Thus, the best known descriptions of communism – a 'classless society', a time when 'the division of labor has come to an end' and when 'private property has been abolished' – are full alternatives and not merely complementary. In each expression the same whole is depicted from a different vantage point. Properly understood, therefore, 'class' – like 'labor' and 'value' – may be taken to convey the whole story of capitalism.

30. *State as a value Relation*

If 'class' expresses the relations of each atomized individual to all others who share his socio-economic conditions of life, and the relations between him as a member of this group to other similarly constituted groups, then 'state' expresses the relations of each such individual to society as a whole. Since the interaction of atomized individuals of the same and opposed classes subsumes their relations to society, state is really a facet of the class Relation; nevertheless, the distinction drawn above will prove practically useful. Whenever people relate to one another as members of the general community, that is as citizens – no matter what they do or want – they can be said to be engaging in politics.

For Marx, man's life as a citizen in capitalism is severely cramping. His private life offers an inadequate outlet for qualities whose full exercise demands a public stage. For example, though it is in his nature to legislate for himself what he will do, he is reduced to deciding narrow personal matters and having everything which has a bearing on his standing in the community decided by others. And though it is in his nature to administer whatever touches him, he is reduced to administering his own personal affairs and being wholly administered by others publicly. Also, though it is in his nature to judge himself and those people with whom he comes into contact directly, he is reduced to judging none but himself and having all matters involving his interpersonal relations judged by others. In his life as a citizen, all peculiarities of ability and need are disregarded, and the individual both acts and is acted upon with all the equality of a statistic. To appreciate this degradation for what it is, we must compare this situation with the one Marx foresees in communism, where the very division between caring for oneself and for others has disappeared with the return of the individual from the state to 'his human, that is, social mode of existence'.[1]

In capitalism, the state is an abstraction in political life on the same plane that value is in economic life; the one is the abstract product of alienated political activity, just as the other is the abstract product of alienated productive activity. And just as value becomes a power over man when realized in the concrete forms of commodity, capital, money and so on, the state exercises power over him when expressed in the real institutions of government – in legislatures, executive agencies, courts, political parties, constitutions and laws. As creations of men intended to serve them in their communal relations, all forms of the state, like other intermediaries we have examined, take on the very powers they were meant to mediate. Marx claims that the state is the intermediary to which man confides 'all his human freedom'.[2] It is both man's activity in disposing of his freedom and its necessary results which allow Marx to refer to the state as a 'mode of production' that falls under the law of private property, and as a power 'which has won an existence independent of the individuals'.[3]

Like value, the state expresses the alienated relations of capitalist society. It has a use-value expressing the aims its various forms are meant to serve, and an exchange-value evidenced by the role money plays in influencing these forms. Like value, too, the state is based on a spurious equality of man, in this instance, his common citizenship. The workers' treatment of their material products as foreign entities also has a parallel here, where people do not recognize the concrete products of their political activity as their own. As with commodities, man's political products, through their appropriation under conditions of alienation, have acquired a life and movement of their own, a metamorphosis which carries them into and out of various forms independent of man's will. In this way, simple voting, for example, contributes to the maintenance of a parliament. Meanwhile, parliaments, laws and the rest have assumed the guise of quasi-supreme beings to which their own creators are asked to pay obeisance. The same fetishism we observed in economics is as widespread and at least as successful in politics. Regard how constitutions manipulate the very people who drafted them, to say nothing of those who looked on, because they treat these rules as holy writ.

The comparison between value and state can be carried further: as with the products of capitalist industry, the power of any objects over man resides primarily in the relationship of control over these objects by persons who are alien and hostile to him. The tie between workers and their capitalist boss in the factory is duplicated with citizens and the men who run the machinery of govern-

ment. Both are value and class relations, and, in each case, alienation occurs through the transfer of use-values. Just as workers give
up the use-value of their labor-power, labor, and with it all its
products, people, as citizens, give up the use-value of their political
activity – of legislating, administering and judging for all – and
with it the use-value of the products created by the ensuing political
interaction. Such means enable the capitalists to dispose of the
use-value of capital, landed property, etc., and rulers to dispose of
the use-value of legislatures, courts, etc. For Marx, despite the
facade of democratic processes, those who dominate capitalist
political institutions and through them the public life of all citizens
are beyond popular control. No matter what the vagaries of voting,
government is for as well as by the bourgeoisie, a change of parties
being invariably a change of bourgeois parties.

Another aspect of political alienation in capitalism is that the
centralization of governmental institutions together with burgeoning
population has gone so far as to rule out all meaningful face to face
contact between governed and governors. As a result, the rulers
remain vague insubstantial beings, barely possible to believe in, let
alone order. Also as a result, people can no longer identify themselves with their rulers even to the degree that this was possible in
feudalism where, beside the proprietory nature of the political
bond, the units of government were smaller and hence closer to
their subjects. The interaction between the state and its citizens
then, because it was more personal, was altogether more human,
even when on occasion the actual results were more harsh.[4]

The absolute inhumanity of political relations in capitalism is
aptly summed up in the notion of patriotism. Though Marx never
says so explicitly, what we ordinarily understand by 'patriotism'
best expresses the detached impersonal kind of belonging that is
associated with the state. To be patriotic is to recognize one's
duties not to real living people, but to the abstract community, to
the very links of alienation which bind the social whole after the
human ties have been cut. It is to reify all the products of such
political activity from the uncomfortable hat it puts on someone's
head to the piece of colored cloth it runs up a flag pole. Other
human beings are recognizable only as fellow patriots, only as
beings which share the same degrading relations to scraps of paper,
a hat, a piece of cloth, a song, a mace. These relations are degrad-

ing because they do not exist for the satisfaction of human needs but for the satisfaction of the community which arises out of the destruction of such needs.

I I

Whence the state? For Marx, the state has its origins in the same segmentation of human relations which gave birth to classes.[5] This, in turn, as we saw, arose as part of the early interaction between the division of labor and private property. All individuals who service one another through the division of labor share a communal interest by virtue of their interdependence. This is reflected in the conditions of their cooperation, and finds expression in the maxim that each continue to do what he is doing for the good of all.

However, the same divison of labor which establishes the communal interest also creates a host of particular interests in the specialized tasks which fall to different parties. The two exist alongside one another; they arise as facets of the same situation. Now, it happens that in pursuing their particular interests individuals lose sight of the communal one. They cannot look over their shoulders at the effect their activity has on others when its uncertain effect on their own life and happiness requires full concentration. The result is, though it is a creature of their cooperation, individuals are only conscious of the community when they come into conflict with it, when they are restricted in their attempt to satisfy personal interests. Or in Marx's words, people have always belonged to the community 'only as average individuals, only in so far as they lived within the condtions of their class'.[6]

With the communal interest lost behind a host of competing particular interests, society becomes a battleground. People experience others only by struggling against them. In this situation, the conditions of cooperation which were established by the division of labor win 'an independent existence over against the separate individuals' and become a 'bond alien to them'.[7] People who do not know that they are cooperating cannot have a proper estimate of the means by which they are cooperating, nor can they control them. These means will seem something apart, but yet – because they cannot escape their mutual dependence – something to which they owe a strange, compelling allegiance. Just as social relations take on an independent existence in class, political relations (defined as the interaction between individuals and the community as such – as one facet of their social relations) take on an independent existence in the state.

According to Marx:

The Social power, i.e., the multiplied productive force, which arises through the cooperation of different individuals as it is determined within the division of labor, appears to these individuals, since their cooperation is not voluntary but natural, not as their own united power but as an alien force existing outside them, of the origin and end of which they are ignorant, which they thus cannot control, which on the contrary passes through a peculiar series of phases and stages independent of the will and the action of man, nay even being the prime governor of these.[8]

In this manner, the state is born as the expression of a situation where interdependence is universal but nowhere fully appreciated, as the version of the community appropriate to class ridden societies. The state Relation is a facet of the broader class Relation; the two emerge together, are dependent on one another, and in communism are destined to disappear together.[9]

The actual institutions of the state exercise a hostile domination over the individual, as we have said, because they are themselves dominated by a class of men who are alien and hostile to him. Again, it is simply because the communal interest is not recognized for what it is that one class is able to disguise its special interest as the 'general good' and to promote it through the organs of the state Marx maintains that

Just because individuals seek only their particular interest, i.e., that not coinciding with their communal interest (for the 'general good' is the illusory form of communal life), the latter will be imposed on them as an interest 'alien' to them, and 'independent' of them, as in its turn a particular, peculiar 'general interest'; or they must meet face to face in this antagonism in democracy.[10]

All classes, including the proletariat, strive for political power in order to represent their special interests as the 'general good'. Democracy allows this competition, as with competition in other fields, to come to the surface only to muffle it, for every manifestation of the class struggle is damaging to the interests that have come out on top. In Marx's words, 'the practical struggle of these

particular interests, which constantly really run counter to the communal and illusory communal interests, make practical intervention
and control necessary through the illusory "general interest" in the
form of the state'.[11] The state is an illusory community because it
represents the domination of one class over another, in which all
political forms are fetters (some well, some badly disguised) on the
subjugated peoples.[12] It represents an 'illusory "general interest" '
because it invariably resolves threats to the real communal interest
by acting in accord with the particular interest of its ruling class.
Both its composition and the specific ends it serves lead Marx to
assert, 'The executive committee of the modern state is but a committee for managing the common affairs of the whole bourgeoisie'.[13]

It is not inconsistent with this general conclusion to hold that
unusual circumstances may bring a government into power for a
short period which does not *directly* represent the ruling economic
class. This is how Marx viewed the reign of Napoleon III in
France. While continuing to protect basic capitalist interests, he
actually ruled over all classes.[14] As with individual character and
the prices of commodities, Marx was always willing to make room
for exceptions due to unusual circumstances, simply because the
real world contained such exceptions. I do not consider that this
admission requires any important modifications in what was said
concerning the place of the state in the theory of alienation.

Marx was more interested in the character of the forms he was
examining than in who controlled them, though an understanding
of the one generally allows him to make conclusions in regard to
the other – just as the evidence of who actually controls the institutions of the state entered into any decision about their character.
The state is an illusory community as well as the instrument of rule
in class ridden societies: this best expresses its essential
character.[15] As such, the state is almost invariably in the hands of
the strongest economic class. When class relations are replaced by
human ones, as occurs in communism, the state must of necessity
disappear.

III

To prevent possible misunderstanding, I want to stress that I
have not tried to explain Marx's entire theory of the state but only

to describe how the state appears and functions as part of his theory of alienation. Though extremely helpful in shedding light on such problems as legitimacy, patriotism, participation and the relations between economic and political forms generally, the conception of the state as the alienated social power (or illusory community) is partial and the analysis derived from it one-sided. Aspects of the state Relation which are necessarily underplayed and distorted, though not falsified, in my treatment include the dominant role of the ruling economic class, the structures which maintain the cohesion and equilibrium of the social system, the state's function in the reproduction of value, the institutions of government, political parties, political socialization and the hegemonic political ideology.

Each of these aspects provides a focal point for study as well as a perspective from which to unravel the entire state Relation. For, just as the state is both a part and a version of the social system in which it exists, its various aspects – also conceived of as Relations – can serve as complimentary dimensions for the examination of the state. And as with the study of the state as an aspect of society, the study of any aspect of the state provides privileged access to certain kinds of information (just as it distances us from other things) and results in a weighted and one-sided ordering of the elements in the system as a whole. Thus, for example, the ties between the alienated social power, the ruling economic class, objective social-political structures, etc. will have one appearance and significance when examined from the vantage point of these alienated powers (as part of an extended analysis of alienation) and a somewhat different appearance and significance when the focus of attention is the political domination of the ruling economic class (as part of an extended analysis of this class). The same imbalance is reflected in the meaning of concepts used in analyses made from different perspectives. The concept of 'class', for example, in an analysis of the state made from the vantage point of the ruling economic class, refers mainly to a group's relation to the prevailing mode of production; while in an analysis, such as I have made, which takes off from the illusory community, the main emphasis in the meaning of 'class' is on alienated social relations.

A lot of the confusion over Marx's theory of the state in the writings of both Marxists and non-Marxists is due to a writer's focusing on only one or a couple of aspects of the state Relation and treating his analysis as the full truth about the subject. This was the case in the recent *New Left Review* debate between Ralph Miliband and Nicos Poulantzas where the former analysed the state as the executive committee of the ruling economic class and the latter analysed it as those objective structures which produce social cohesion and reproduce the conditions of existence of the system.[16] Viewed within the perspective that emerges from focusing on any one aspect, the relative importance attributed to the various elements of the state within another perspective will appear objectionable. So it was that neither Miliband nor Poulantzas could really accept the claims made by the other. Given the framework provided above, however, we have no difficulty in giving due weight to the claims that the capitalist state is an instrument of the capitalist class and that the objective structures in which any government operates determine the broad lines of its policies. Rather than contradictory, these are simply complementary insights into the workings of the capitalist state that come from approaching it from different vantage points. Among other examples, we have seen how Marx sometimes speaks of the capitalist as the bearer of capital, and sometimes suggest that capital functions as it does because it is under the control of capitalists.[17] Dialectical truth does not fit together neatly like the pieces of a puzzle but allows for the kind of multiple one-sidedness that is the necessary result of studying a subject within the different perspectives associated with its different aspects.

What is needed, of course, is a mult-dimensional study of the dynamics of the capitalist state which proceeds from all these aspects. Only the beginning of such a study is found in Marx himself. He did leave some rough plans for a systematic work on the state (indicating that he attributed more importance to this approach to the study of capitalism than can be gleaned from his published writings), but like so many of his other projects it was sacrificed to the demands of his political economy. This is doubly unfortunate since, as Marx says in a letter to Kugelmann, the state is the area in which he felt his views would be most difficult to reconstruct in the absence of a systematic analysis.[18] It is with the intention of facilitating such an analysis that I moved from treating the state within the theory of alienation to displaying the broad contours of the theory of the state itself, to showing what such a theory contains and how its major aspects (perspectives when used as take-off points for study) are related.

But the problems involved in developing a Marxist theory of the state today arise not only from people's faulty understanding of the dialectic and the fact that Marx never delivered a systematic statement of his views on this subject, but also from the changes that have taken place in the capitalist state over the last one hundred years. Here, I can do no more than signal that I consider the most important of these to be the growing importance of international and regional levels of state activity, the burgeoning role of the state in directing the economy (capitalist planning) and, as a byproduct of the latter, increased political activity to legitimate the social-economic relations that were formerly legitimated by the unimpeded operations of the market. The revisions in the Marxist theory of the state required by these new developments involve, first, an upgrading in the importance of certain aspects of the state – most notably its function in the reproduction of value and political socialization – as vantage points for analysing the whole state Relation; and, second, a redistribution in favor of the political of the relative influence that Marxists have traditionally apportioned to political and economic processes.

This is also a way of saying that a systematic exposition of the Marxist theory of the state is more essential now than ever. If the analysis of the relations between the state and the capitalist economy from the vantage point of such economic Relations as commodity, capital, labor and value (as found in *Capital*) was only mildly distorting of real complexity when the state exercised minimal control over the economy, at present – with the state's role so enlarged – an understanding of the state-economy relationship (and therefore of capitalism) within these limited dimensions is seriously deficient. Marx's political economy must be not only brought up to date but supplemented by what might be called a Marxist 'economic polity', or dialectical analyses of the same subject matter made from the different political vantage points mentioned above.[19]

31. *Religion as a value Relation*

Still awaiting discussion as value Relations are religion, ethics, science, family, literature and art. Wherever one travels in the realm of estrangement the story is the same. The fourfold relations of man to his activity, product, fellow men and species in each sphere are the misshapen midgets of what comes into existence in communism. Religion is the only other sphere, however, in which these relations are brought out in any detail. For Marx, 'Religious estrangement as such occurs in the realm of consciousness, or man's inner life.' This is contrasted with economic estrangement, 'that of real life'.¹ Whereas the latter concerns those distortions which are produced by man's efforts to stay alive, the former focuses on the distortions which result from his trying to comprehend this life. The connection Marx sees between the two halves of this dichotomy is expressed in his claim that 'The religious world is but the reflex of the real world.'² The same disintegration that characterizes material existence characterizes the life of the mind.³

As the 'spontaneous activity of the human imagination, of the human brain and human heart', religion can be no more advanced than man's powers, together with their real achievements.⁴ What Marx says of the abstract thinker can be applied equally to all religious people: 'his intuition of nature is only the act of confirming his abstraction from the intuition of nature – is only the conscious repetition by him of the process of begetting his abstraction'.⁵ In his quest to make cosmic sense of hostile and overpowering surroundings, the alienated individual can only mimic those processes which have brought on his affliction. Marx declares that for a commodity based society, where men 'reduce their individual private labor to the standard of homogeneous human labor', Christianity (particularly Protestantism), with its belief in man's abstract equality before god, is the most suitable religion.⁶ Equality before god is the religious counterpart of those acts of levelling which preceded alienation in the other areas discussed.

All religious activity is premised on a belief in the 'unnatural' character of nature. Trees, clouds, cows, bread and finally man

221

himself are not to be taken for granted, accepted for what they are or even *that* they are. For the religious person, these are all 'gifts' of god, mysterious entities whose essential qualities are beyond human understanding. The proper response to nature, therefore, is one of awe and reverence, and to the being who rules over nature of praise and thanks for services rendered. To serve god completely, without reservations derived from competing principles and without the distraction of bodily needs, is the aim of a truly religious life. As a result, religious activity directed against oneself is the inhibition of all those qualities which mark one out a human being: reason is replaced by faith, real love by love of god, and real will power by 'will in Christ'.[7] All striving after happiness in the here and now ceases, for only happiness in heaven counts. Man must die entirely to this world in order to prepare himself for the next.

Whereas religious activity directed toward the self is suicidal, directed toward the other, toward god or his 'agents' on earth, it is sacrificial. Prayer is a superstition which renders one helpless, and obeisance is total submission before the knife. Through unthinking worship, the repetition of empty symbols, the only god served is self-contempt. To bend the knee is the kind of trick one teaches a dog; to mumble words is better suited to a parrot; to accept the punishment of a hard life without flinching is the lot of an ox. Man is meant for better things. Though the chief function of religion is to aid human beings to make sense out of their lives, for Marx, the life of religion is the destruction of all sense except the non-sense it itself creates.

As we saw on other occasions, the same activity which receives its character from its product is responsible for it. Thus, although religious activity is premised on the existence of god, god (really, the idea of god) is its own creation. The product of activity directed toward something non-existent could only be a non-existent something worthy of such activity. Marx says thinkers estranged from nature and their fellow man could only construct 'fixed mental shapes or ghosts dwelling outside nature and man'.[8] Once in existence, these 'productions of the human brain appear as independent beings endowed with life, and enter into relations both with one another and the human race'.[9]

As with man's other products, god derives his peculiar character from what the individual himself gives up in the process of creation. Consequently, Marx maintains, 'The more man puts into God, the less he retains in himself. The worker puts his life into the objects; but now his life no longer belongs to him but to the object . . . Whatever the product of his labor is, he is not. Therefore, the greater this product, the less is he himself.'[10] What qualities the individual gives up to god may be seen from an examination of his religious activity. Man makes god omniscient by the gift of a reasoning faculty he refuses to exercise to question religious dogmas. God's omnipotence results from the restriction man puts on his own efforts by his faith that god will help. God's splendour comes from a gift of man's self-respect in creating a creature he considers so much more splendid than himself; and so on.

Rather than qualities he is actually and fully using, the individual's gift to god consists, for the most part, of his potential for achievement, a potential whose full realization requires communist social relationships. God emerges from all this as the estranged power of a socialized humanity, or the most advanced statement of what it means to be a man, a social being who, in cooperation with his fellows, rules over nature. It is in this sense that Marx declares, 'Christ is the intermediary to whom man attributes all his own divinity.'[11] Again, that which mediates between man and his real life is seen to dominate both. Through religious activity, the individual's potential for controlling nature is transferred to god, which, in turn, reduces the actual control he is able to exercise. Thereafter, it is god who is seen related to nature in ways that human beings, through their alienation, are no longer capable of. God, then, represents not only what man can become, but as well what he cannot become as long as he continues to reify his potential as god. It is likely that such religious fetishism, which had already been decribed in the writings of Feuerbach, served Marx as a kind of model in constructing the fetishism of commodities.

II

A parallel development to the metamorphosis of value can also be observed in religion. The god-objects toward which religious activity is directed undergo a transformation from god to Christ, to Mother Mary, to Holy Ghost, to Saints, to Church, to Pope, to

Cross, to Bible and to a wide assortment of relics, symbols and holy places. Like the value product of labor, god, the immediate product of religious activity, becomes metamorphosed into a number of subspecies, all of which enjoy the same basic relations with their creator, man. But this process as it occurs in religion is not simply akin to the metamorphosis of value; it is the same process, the working out of the same relations of alienated activity in different areas of the individual's life. So it is that Marx could extend 'mode of production' and 'industry', as we saw, to cover religion. How else could money buy so much, including, in the capitalist period, most god-objects of religion? If every purchase is an exchange of equivalents, money, the exchange form of value, could only buy objects which also express value, that is, which arise like money from alienated activity.

In every area, the object that has been given its life through the exertion of man's own confronts him not only as an independent being, but as one which is 'hostile and alien'.[12] In the case of religion, the power he has placed in the keeping of the divinity has turned against him. His distinctive qualities, such as reason and human sexuality, are disapproved of and their exercise labelled 'crimes against god'. In god, man has created a mortal enemy, and one to whom he has already admitted defeat. The only response that remains to him is a plea for mercy, but as 'divine wisdom' is too subtle for mere mortals to fathom, he never knows if his plea has been heeded. Thus, his total submission must also be permanent. The relation of a religious person to god is that of a frightened ant to an oncoming steamroller. That the steamroller is purely a figment of his imagination makes it no less frightening to the ant who sees it.

As with other products of man's alienated activity, his subservience to god is reflected in his relations to those who control god. According to Marx:

Every self-estrangement of man from himself and from nature appears in the relation in which he places himself and nature to men other than and differentiated from himself. For this reason religious self-estrangement necessarily appears in the relations of the layman to the priest, or again, to a mediator, since we are here dealing with the intellectual world.[13]

The use-value of man's religious product has been given up to the priest. Claiming to speak in god's name, he controls the deity every bit as much as the capitalist controls commodities and rulers the organs of government. In this instance, the priest uses the qualities transferred to god by the believers themselves to overawe and threaten them.

Since the deity is constructed out of 'human' poverty, it is the self-appointed task of the priest to make people poor, to exact a pound of flesh for each one offered, and to insure that everything human is offered. Hence, Marx's claim that 'every imperfection in man, is a bond with heaven – an avenue giving the priest access to the heart'.[14] The priest utilizes every possible tack and technique of intellectual impoverishment: sin, prayer, absolution, indexes, inquisition, heaven, hell and guilt, especially guilt. He has a potion to take advantage of every weakness. With them, he 'saves', 'consoles' or 'condemns', while deluding people into believing that what he does to them is owed to god. The result is that the same inhuman reverence and submission that man shows to god is duplicated with the priest, who accepts it as his due tribute.

This travesty of human relations brings in its wake a mockery of human love. Men are asked to love each other because they are made in god's image, or because god loves them. Rather than affection based on an appreciation of the other's real personality, Christian love is the ethereal love of god in which individuals can partake. It rests on man's love of god, itself the denial of his humanity. It is the bounding back in a more distorted form than ever of the human attributes man has cast skyward, but another relation with which he has adorned his heavenly phantom that has returned to earth to plague him.

For Marx, religion will continue to exist as long as it satisfies a need in the life of alienated man. In his words, 'The religious reflex of the real world can . . only then vanish when the practical relations of every-day life offer to man none but perfectly intelligible and reasonable relations with regard to his fellow men and to nature'.[15] This degree of true consciousness is possible only in communism. As Marx says, 'The abstract enmity between sense and spirit is necessary so long as the human feeling for nature, the human sense of nature, and therefore also the natural sense of man, are not yet produced by man's own work'.[16] Until man consciously creates himself in nature, nature will seem to create him. His placing a being above himself and nature can only occur because of the split between the two, only because the individual's appropriation is partial, still leaving secrets to be guessed at.

Marx is careful to point out that total social appropriation in communism will not result in atheism, the denial of god, for there is nothing to deny.[17] Instead, it is as if the bottom had dropped out of the debate; the problems which lead people either to affirm or deny the existence of god never arise; all questions are answered or, at least, recognized as answerable. The needs which religion satisfies for the alienated man, as with the needs satisfied by his economic, social and political activity in this period, vanish with his alienation. The qualities whch mark his alienation have ceased to be necessary at the same time that they are no longer possible. And – as I have had occasion to remark in regard to other spheres – religious alienation only becomes impossible when all of man's alienated relations to his activity, product and other men have been transformed. As a disease of the entire social body, alienation anywhere demands a total social cure.[18]

32. *Marx's critique of bourgeois ideology*

The discussion of religious alienation in the previous chapter clearly illustrates the main characteristic Marx finds in ideology, and particularly in bourgeois ideology, which is its back to front picture of how things actually happen. In religion, this is seen in the belief that god creates man rather than the reverse. In ethics, people are said to derive judgements from an absolute moral principle of some sort, whereas it is their judgements, reflecting their class conditions and interests, that have constructed over time (and through generations) this principle. In politics, we found the belief that the state grants its citizens certain rights, whereas it is really the people who have abnegated their social power to the state. Also in this sphere, there is the apparently contradictory but really complementary view that the government is elected by the people, whereas people are manipulated in their electoral choices by their rulers.

In history, there is the belief that 'great men' and ideas decide the course of events, whereas events, together with their underlying conditions, establish the limitations and opportunities which determine in broad outline who shall be 'great men' and which ideas will triumph. In economics, people think they decide where they work and what they buy, but in actuality the jobs and commodities available determine both. Also in economics, there is the belief that capitalists serve the community by investing in the production of goods and jobs, whereas it is really the community which serves the capitalists by giving them the lion's share of what is produced, including the right to decide on questions of further investment into goods and jobs. Referring to Luther's description of the Roman mythological figure, Cacus, who steals oxen by dragging them backwards into his den so that the footprints make it appear they have gone out from there, Marx comments, 'an excellent picture, it fits the capitalist in general, who pretends that what he has taken from others and brought into his den emanates from him, and by causing it to go backwards he gives it the semblance of having come from his den.'[1]

What stands out clearly from this example of Cacus and his

oxen is that ideology does not so much falsify the details as misinterpret them so as to reverse what actually occurs: the footprints are there for all to see, our 'great men' do make such important decisions as whether to go to war, capitalists do offer jobs, people do choose what they want to buy, and so on. In what is politically perhaps the most pernicious piece of bourgeois ideology, workers who believe they are paid for all their labor have before them the fact that they get paid by the hour and that their wages represent payment for all the hours they have worked. In every case misinterpretation results from focusing too narrowly on facts which are directly observable and from abstracting these appearances from the surrounding conditions and results which alone give them their correct meaning, a meaning that often runs counter to the obvious one. We have already seen Marx declare that 'scientific truth is always a paradox if judged by the everyday appearance of things.'[2] Cut off from the processes out of which they emerge and their own potential for change and development, the apparent features of events lose their historical specificity and take on the guise of natural phenomena. According to Marx, the contradictions of capitalist life 'seem the more self-evident the more their internal relations are concealed from it'.[3] When – as in the operations of the market – what is apparent are the relations (prices) between things, abstracting away underlying social relations results in the fetishisms of capital, commodities, money and landed property that were the subjects of earlier discussions. The mystification is completed when these appearances are given concepts which link them to whatever they superficially resemble in other places and times. Well suited for the work of classification and the search for analogies, these concepts do not and cannot permit an adequate comprehension of their subject matter.

As unfamiliar as 'surplus-value', 'relations of production', 'alienation', 'exploitation' and 'class struggle' are to most people, it is these concepts of Marx's which correctly depict capitalist reality. And as familiar as 'wage labor', 'fair price', 'supply and demand', 'justice' and 'freedom' are, it is they which hide and distort this reality. But they hide it by focusing on what is immediately observable. Thus, one might say that bourgeois ideology is composed of half truths which result from an exclusive emphasis on appearances. They become distortions of the whole truth and particularly of the dynamic factors in the situation whenever their limitations go unrecognized.

Capitalism differs from all other oppressive systems in the amount and insidious character of its mystification, in the thoroughness with which it is integrated into all its life processes, and in the degree to which it requires mystification in order to survive (all other oppressive systems relying far more on direct force). The importance of bourgeois ideology is reflected in the attention given it in Marx's writings which are, throughout, criticisms of capitalist practises and of the ways these practises are ordinarily understood. In this space, I can only indicate in a general way what this critique of ideology contains. Marx is concerned, first, with how the various ideas and concepts that constitute bourgeois ideology arise (as a result of what activities, at what juncture in the class struggle, within which groups, in what connection to other ideas and events, etc.) , and, second, with how they help to reproduce existing conditions of existence.

As the reflection in men's minds of a segmented, alienated reality, bourgeois ideology is both a necessary premise and an equally necessary result of all activity in capitalist society. It is also, however, an important component of alienated activity itself, of how it is conducted, and particularly of alienated labor. In production, as we saw earlier, men appropriate nature (make it part of themselves) in a manner determined by the character of their objects and the level of development of their powers. With human powers reduced to the power of 'having' and surrounded by alien objects, workers view everything they come into contact with as private property, as things to have which can be disposed of at the will of their owner.[4] It is this understanding of their own qualities, including their ability to do labor, as private property that C. B. MacPherson describes as 'possessive individualism'.[5] For workers to be able to sell what they have (especially their labor-power) and offer money for what they want, all social ties that might inhibit such transactions must be abolished, in thought as well as in practise. In order to permit their labor-power and products to enter exchange, in order to produce them with this in mind, workers cannot grasp themselves as part of their work, nor their work as part of the product, nor their product as part of themselves.

For Marx, work always involves consciousness: people are

aware of and can communicate what they do, when and how they do it and its general purpose. Within the capitalist division of labor, however, work goes on as if it were independent of the rest of a worker's life and the work and lives of other people. The notion of work in bourgeois ideology is limited to what one is doing (like the notion of people is limited to their persons, and the notion of product to material objects). Understanding work in a broader sense, which means grasping its internal relations with workers and their products, would make it clear that the existing conditions of work are a social rather than a natural phenomenon, and detract from one's effectiveness on the job as well as one's willingness to accept capitalist terms of work in the first place.

Marx believed it is relatively easy to show how religion reflects real life, but much more difficult to demonstrate how real life gives rise to this particular religion.[6] The same is true of all kinds and forms of ideology. Mainly, this is a consequence of ideology's being both a reflection of a real situation and a product of conscious efforts to manipulate people's understanding. In the case of capitalism, the same conditions which are reflected in bourgeois ideology give rise – however confusingly and haltingly – to a correct understanding of capitalist processes. The fact is that while bourgeois ideology is systematic, it is also unfinished, inconsistent, contradictory and constantly fighting for its life against a science of society whose most complete expression is Marxism. A formidable system of interlocking and mutually supporting distortions, bourgeois ideology offers explanations that are sufficiently in touch with the real world to permit life to go on and indeed for real progress to be made in some sectors. Though neither clear nor definitive, there are limits, however, to what it can explain and what people will accept. These limits are set by its own deficiencies, unintended events and alternative systems of explanation, all of which have their own patterns of development and peculiar effects on the success of bourgeois ideology. In the most recent period, the expanded economic role of the state – as I indicated in the last chapter – which was made necessary by the increasingly serious disruptions of the market undercuts people's belief in the market as a natural phenomenon and with it their acceptance of their place and rewards in life as facts of nature. The conscious production of ideology becomes, as a consequence, all the more essential for the survival of capitalism, and our era has seen the flourishing of a 'consciousness industry' that was virtually unknown in Marx's time.

As for reproducing the conditions of existence, it should be clear that bourgeois ideology serves capitalist interests not only when it provides pro-capitalist solutions to pressing social problems but also when it confuses people, or makes them overly pessimistic and resigned, or makes it difficult for them to formulate criticisms or imagine alternative systems. For the most part, these are the practical effects of the class biased distortions of reality that are themselves produced by capitalist processes of abstraction. All thought and study of the whole (Marxism included) begins by breaking it down into manageable parts. Marx's criticism, therefore, is not based on the fact of abstraction, but on the character of the parts abstracted and, more especially, on the view of them as absolute, natural and finished, rather than – as in the case of Marx's abstractions – relative, historically specific and incomplete. Given the philosophy of internal relations, the first step in studying reality – for Marx or anyone else – is to decide on the units in and of which knowledge is possible. In bourgeois ideology, it is here, at this fundamental level, that abstractions occur – generally unconsciously – which do not permit the adequate comprehension of their real subject matter. With a narrow focus on appearance and an uncritical acceptance of traditional constructions in which old appearances live on after their real lives have ended, the average citizen of capitalism is simply without the mental means, the conceptual tools to understand the dynamics of his society.

Two examples must suffice. Probably the most distorting and least recognized of all such abstractions are the basic dichotomies, such as fact-value, cause-effect, freedom-necessity, nature-society, and reason-feeling, in which most people organize their everyday thoughts and experiences. With each half grasped as independent and the direct opposite of the other, things are taken to be either one or the other – nothing is ever both. Yet, as we saw, perhaps most clearly in the chapter on Marx's reputed ethics, these differences are neither absolute nor permanent. Given internal relations, things are both. To be sure, these dichotomies are themselves abstracted from the conditions and activities of real people. As modes of thought, they clearly reflect lives that are artificially broken up into times for thinking and times for feeling, into a place for working and a place for living, into ways of knowing and ways of judging, and so on. They are based, in other words, on appearances. But by rendering dialectical knowledge 'unthinkable' they play an essential role in reproducing this segmented existence. John Mepham rightly remarks, 'Ideological language does not just distract attention away from real social relations, nor does it explain them away, nor does it ever directly deny them. It structurally excludes them from thought.'[7]

The breakdown of knowledge into competing disciplines, each with its own subject matter, goals and even methods, is another outstanding instance of abstractions distorting reality in the service of capitalist interests. Again, this parcellation in the study of man and society reflects the real differences observed in and between the reified activities and products of our alienated society, but it helps in turn to confirm and rigidify these differences. Once discipline boundaries become established, the same problems are judged by different and often contradictory criteria. Knowledge that ordinarily leads to positive activity is rendered impotent, because any activity suggested by one analysis appears unwarranted or irrational or inefficient on the basis of analyses done in other disciplines. We have already seen Marx point out how bourgeois ethics and economics use different yardsticks: if one indicates it is important to feed hungry people, the other is likely to show that this would unduly interfere with the price of food. Limiting research to a single discipline in the manner of most of our economists, political scientists, psychologists and so on also hides the full implications of any problem and, consequently, what might be the need for a comprehensive (read: revolutionary) solution. Finally, by accepting disciplinary boundaries as given, all thinking about social life as a whole is left to amateur philosophers and those who do not know much about a single discipline – or else, it is strongly suggested, they would recognize the futility of such an effort. The very organization of thought in each discipline leads to rejecting comprehensive thinking as unscientific. Operating out of this model, reality has simply become too 'complex' for us to be able to think how to change it.

Bourgeois ideology takes many other forms, but it is always partial, it is always unscientific (limited to appearances), it is always class biased, it always loses sight of the real history and actual potential of its subject and it always confuses – generally turning in an opposite sense – the real relations between its elements. Arising from the abstractions made in alienated labor and in confrontation with its alienated products, bourgeois ideology is the way of thinking most appropriate to the alienated men of capitalist society. It is the general form of their alienation in the realm of thought.[8]

SUMMARY

Part III on the theory of alienation is the culmination of this entire work, the task for which all previous chapters may be seen as preparation. Without the discussion of Marx's relational view of reality and his corresponding use of terms, and without the presentation of his conceptual framework for treating human nature, the reconstruction achieved here would not have been possible. Paradoxically, though it is concerned with segmentation, the theory of alienation is the agency with which Marx most carefully interweaves his disparate theories of man and society. I have tried, in this section, to demonstrate this unity by sketching how the alienated relations he took to exist between man and his activity, product, fellows and species operate in the fields of economics, social relations, politics and religion. For all its complexity, the theory of alienation states no more than what Marx uncovered in capitalism, conceptualized in accordance with his relational scheme and organized around patterns found in his conception of human nature. It is Marxism viewed from the vantage point of the acting individual.

PART IV

Conclusion

33. *A critical evaluation*

I

Marxism, as it emerges from this study, is like a magnificently rich tapestry with a multitude of colors and patterns superimposed on one another. To see them all we must begin by seeing them singly, to grasp one and then start on the outlines of another and so on, until every pattern is grasped along with the interconnections between them, as these interconnections too are part of the overall design. Yet, even as our attention is directed to the first pattern, we cannot help noticing sections of others, for each piece functions in more than one. Marx's theories are not interrelated, as this is ordinarily understood, but rather include one another. Thus, no matter with which one we begin, to draw out all its relations is to present Marxism, though it is the whole observed from a particular angle and expressed in a one-sided way.

The necessary distortion of Marxism introduced by this account of the theory of alienation can only be righted by equally detailed accounts of the same material as part of other major theories, and of the materialist conception of history in particular. Only then would Marxism be revealed with anything like the thoroughness with which Marx sought to reveal society. The chief justification for my own one-sided study lies in its dealing with the side that has received least serious attention. So much has been done in presenting Marxism, and so much remains to do. Consideration must now be given to an evaluation of the theory of alienation and its underpinnings in the philosophy of internal relations and in Marx's conception of human nature.

II

For purposes of evaluation, Marxism can conveniently be divided into three parts; that for which there is evidence, that for which there is none, and that for which there could be none. Whereas the events of the last hundred years, for example, offer some kind of evidence for the inadequacy of Marx's projections on the immediate future of capitalism, there is no similar evidence which applies one way or another for his views on communist man. Since the conditions which Marx required for the degree of human development he foresaw have never existed, to agree or disagree with him on this matter is equally baseless. For it is not a question of people being influenced by special conditions, but of such conditions, over a period of time, creating new people. And nothing in the past history of mankind permits us to state with any degree of certainty what manner of men would emerge from conditions as extraordinary as those Marx envisioned.

It is equally no use to say (though people continue to say it) that the kind of society which Marx predicts has never existed. The communist society is the ultimate achievement of a long series of developments which begin with the socialist appropriation of the capitalist mode of production. Its distinctive characteristics evolve gradually out of the programmes adopted in the dictatorship of the proletariat (the transition period from capitalism to full communism) and the new relationships and possibilities established. These characteristics cannot exist – and one should not expect to find them – before this context itself has developed in ways that the world has yet to experience. If the extraordinary qualities Marx ascribes to the people of communism could never exist outside the unique conditions of this period, it is also true that, given these conditions, the development of other qualities – certainly of opposing qualities – simply makes no sense. One can only state the unproven assumptions on which this expected flowering of human nature rests. These are: that the individual's potential is so varied and so great; that he possesses an inner drive to realize all this potential; that the whole range of powers in each person can be fully realized together; and that the overall fulfillment of each individual is compatible with that of all others. In Marx's defense it should be added that with the development and/or discovery of each new social form our view of what is humanly possible has had to be extended. Consequently, those critics who declare Marx an impossible visionary strike me as vainly dogmatic as those of his followers who promise that this vision will come true.

There remains but one way to evaluate Marx's vision of communism and that is to examine his analysis of capitalism to see if the communist society is indeed present within it as an unrealized potentiality. If Marx sought, as he tells us, 'to find the new world through the criticism of the old', then any judgement of his views on communism rests in the last analysis on the validity of his critique of capitalism.[1] This is not the place for the extensive examination that is required, but I would like to offer three guidelines to those who would undertake it: (1) capitalism must be conceptualized in terms of social Relations, Marx's way of incorporating the actual past and future possibilities of his subject into his study of its present forms; (2) a Marxist analysis of today's capitalism should be integrated into the study of Marx's analysis of late nineteenth-century capitalism (the social Relations from which projections are made must be brought up to date); and (3) one should not try to show that communism is inevitable, only that it is possible, that it is based on conditions inherent in the further development of our present ones (Marx, whose excessive optimism is often mistaken for crude determinism, would not deny, for example, that in present conditions 'barbarism' and world destruction are real alternatives to communism). After all, communism is seldom if ever opposed because one holds other values, but because it is said to be an unrealizable ideal. In these circumstances, making a case for communism as a *possible* successor to capitalism is often enough to convince people that they must help to bring it about.

The main theories dealt with in this work – Marx's philosophy of internal relations, his conception of human nature and the theory of alienation – are for the most part not amenable to the evidence of experience, whether actual or potential. Evidence can be used to help solve any problem except how this same evidence should be viewed: hence the difference between theory as interpretation and theory as hypothesis. Like all philosophy which concerns itself with organizing reality, with interpretation, the value of these theories must be measured by utility rather than truth (unless, of course, the two are equated). It is in this sense that philosophical systems are never exploded, but instead, like styles of clothing, simply go out of fashion, usually because other interpretations are found more useful or because the group whose interests these ideas serve itself disappears.

Essentially what is at stake here is asking whether organizing qualities in this way, emphasizing these aspects, making these connections, starting out from this angle, etc., helps make sense of our chaotic experience. With society as complex as it is, where is the theory that allows for much control in any but insignificant matters? And in the social world, even when predictions are fulfilled, it is difficult to say exactly why they were, just as it is easy with practically any theory to find excuses for why predictions have faulted. Naturally, there is information which fits more snugly into some interpretations than others, some theories which offer a more comprehensive account of phenomena, some which appear more coherent, some which are more productive of testable hypotheses, some which are more complimentary to our egos or do less violence to our emotions, some which make it easier to get along in existing society (a mixed blessing), and even some which are slightly more effective in controlling and predicting events. To be sure, if events go counter to what is expected too often, the modified explanation may become very cumbersome, calling for its replacement by a simpler one. However, in the last analysis, all these virtues simply go into helping us decide whether an interpretation meets the admittedly inconclusive test of making us feel we understand. Such understanding must itself be judged in the long run on whether it enables us to shape reality to our purposes, both as individuals and as members of a class, but as regards Marx's interpretive theories this is not a test that at present offers clear results.

For me, then, Marx's relational view of reality (which means too, his dialectic), his conceptual framework for dealing with human nature and his theory of alienation, one part of which is the labor theory of value, are extremely useful aids for understanding nature, man and society. To view reality, with Marx, as being whole and in flux and composed of internally related parts is to rely on no more information than is available to everyone. It is merely to structure this information differently, which, in this instance, is chiefly to remove the intervening structures that the 'common sense' view has placed in the world. What requires explaining on this view – change, movement, interaction, progress (because they are not conceived as part of what things are) – is taken for granted in Marx's and my own. They belong to the world as its natural qualities, and are incorporated into the sense of its factor parts.

The utility of the relational view is chiefly that it predisposes us to look for why things have stopped (really, why they seem to have stopped) rather than why they have started, why they appear separate rather than why they come together. Moreover, by treating change and interaction as necessary rather than contingent, we can concentrate on how these processes occur and never get bogged down in trying to decide whether they can occur or not. One is never faced by such questions as 'How does a cause produce its effect?', 'How can we know?', 'Can we trust our senses?' and 'How can values be derived from facts?' Most western non-Hegelian philosophy is simply bypassed by the refusal to state these problems in this way, by a denial that the parts that need to be related exist outside these same relations.

Reality, being whole and in flux, cannot be grasped in bits and pieces. What concerns me, however, and what does not seem to have bothered Marx (or Hegel either for that matter) is whether such 'distortions' are not due, at least in part, to limitations inherent in man's senses and even in his mental powers. Are we not naturally drawn to lines, beginnings and ends, partly because of the simple fact of contrast and partly because our needs, which exercise the predominant influence on our thinking, are limited and so too all their satisfactions? Do not all our senses tend to treat what they perceive as something – and, therefore, a thing – apart from what they are not perceiving? Our glance, for example, draws a boundary where it stops. May it not be, in other words, that the aspect of alienation which has man dissect reality into separate and easily separable units is due to certain 'weaknesses' of the species as well as to social influences, that people proceed part by part because to do so is in the nature of human conception?

The same kind of query may be raised from the vantage point of the reality perceived. If, as Dietzgen says, we generalize qualities into things on the basis of their real similarity, may it not be that the similarities which incline us to individuate the same things also incline us to conceive of them as logically independent? This position must be distinguished from that of Peter Strawson who believes that material objects enjoy a pre-conceptual existence as things (see Appendix I). I am only suggesting that there may be a relation between the individuation of qualities into things (based on preconceptual similarities) and the belief in their logically separate existences. It is sufficient to ask these questions – I do not profess to know the answers.

It may be, of course, that these doubts themselves are simply an expression of my own alienation, of a strictly personal failure to perceive and think relationally due to my upbringing in capitalist society. Or it may be that the nature of man is really inadequate for coming to grips with the nature of the world. If the latter, mankind is doomed to misconceive reality, at least to some degree, in all societies. In this situation, though we may believe that entities are the sum of their relations and that change is what is real, we can only approximate these beliefs in our understanding of actual phenomena. Rather than an all encompassing vision of the world, the relational view becomes a working hypothesis, a basic assumption about the nature of reality, which teaches us how we should try to look at everything rather than describing how we do or ever will.

Even if accepted however, the doubts raised here do not force me to modify the analysis I have made of Marx's theories, or the analysis that I take him to have made of society. All that is required is that we understand the term 'conceive' in a strong and a weak sense, the first being what we actually and immediately do and the second what we try to do through an intellectual decision (until now, both senses have been fused in my own use of the term). Hence, we may actually conceive of fatherhood as a Relation; whereas we only choose to conceive of a material object as such. Why we should choose to do this has already been explained earlier in this chapter where I gave the advantages of this outlook.

The social factors which come into Marx's analysis contain elements which we can conceive of relationally in both the strong and the weak senses. As regards capital, for example, we can actually conceive of its quality of exploitation relationally but must – I think – choose to see its physical basis in this manner. The end result, capital, remains a Relation with all the properties with which Marx endowed it. Because of its abstract character and more obvious interdependence, the subject matter of the social sciences is far easier to conceive of in terms of relations than are material objects. For purposes of treating society and Marx's views on society, therefore, it should be possible to actually grasp relationally most of the relations which are there.

The problems raised by Marx's relational view of the world are of three types: Is this what the world is really like? Can we actually conceive of reality in this way? Can we communicate what we know relationally to others? My reply to the first question was that in so far as Marx's view is eminently useful in making sense of our experiences and helps us to shape reality to our purposes, then this is what the world is like. To the second question, I answered that even though it may not be possible to conceive of everything in relational terms (in the strong sense of 'conceive') it is possible to do so for most of the subject with which we have been concerned. Attention must now be given to the problem of communicability.

With his relational view, the content or meaning Marx gave to concepts varied somewhat with the particular facet of the Relation he was trying to convey. In Appendix I, Stuart Hampshire, without any thought to criticize Marx, declares that simple communicability requires a class of terms which refers to more or less distinct objects. Marx had no such terms, and one result has been a frequent breakdown in communication between him and his readers, though it has not been so complete as Hampshire's fears would suggest.

Like virtually all thinkers who subscribe to a philosophy of internal relations, Marx was insufficiently concerned with language and the problems posed by the communicability of his views. For categories, like philosophies, are neither right nor wrong, but useful, in this case in so far as they convey the meaning with which one instills them. By this criterion, it must be admitted that Marx's vocabulary does not acquit itself very well, and the techniques used for organizing his material were not enough to overcome this handicap. If Marx is given highest marks for creating Marxism, he can only be given a mediocre rating for his skills as a communicator. Yet, if he had been more aware of the difficulties others had in coming to grips with his relational view, a lot more could have been done to help them. The dire consequences Hampshire outlines could have been avoided better than they have been.

For one thing, Marx could have given more short definitions, repeating them in his different works. Though necessarily partial, because of the relational character of his terms, these definitions would have disposed of the most blatant guesswork regarding his meanings. Then, when he was expanding or otherwise altering the meaning of an expression which was already a part of the discussion, this should have been made explicit. In *Capital*, his major work, he could have adopted a more systematic means for showing the interrelations between his main terms. For example, it is possible to extract a few points from a relational system, define them in terms of each other, and to use this restricted framework as markers in establishing the meanings of other expressions.

It will be noticed that these are techniques I have used in this book (particularly in Part II); they are some of the ways I have sought to go beyond Marx in explaining the relations in Marxism. In meeting Engels' request for better dialectical transitions – for this is what I have tried to do – this work has also provided Marx's terms with the only kind of dictionary they could have.[2] Whether I have also succeeded in making Marx's relational views more easily communicable is for others to say.

III

One of the most useful aspects of Marx's system, and probably the least studied, is the conceptual framework in which he presents the interaction that goes on between man and nature. The powers and needs he attributes to man, their objectification and subsequent reflection in nature, their development through appropriation, particularly in production, and the transformation such activity achieves in nature, including the relations between people, offers an excellent framework in which to set human progress. Like the relational view of the world, of which it is an instrumental part, this set of interlocking categories can be neither proven nor disproven. Again, it is a way of viewing information which is available to everyone, bridges built here along a stream rather than there. Besides bypassing all problems connected with man's supposed 'insularity' from nature, its utility lies in focusing our attention on human development itself, on its change signifying and change producing factors. The emphasis on 'powers' in particular, with its strong undertone of potentialities, makes of the present something the individual is always passing through.

On the deficit side, the main weakness in Marx's conception of human nature is that the link between conditions and behavior, for all the attention accorded it, is underdeveloped. Marx is clearly right in believing that the individual is to a remarkably high degree the product of his society, and that by changing his living conditions we change him, but there are at least two questions which remain to be answered: Are the changes which occur in character always rational, that is, in keeping with new interests which are created? And, how long does it take for new conditions to produce new people?

Marx believed that the effect of conditions on character is invariably rational and relatively quick acting. These views have their roots in his conceptual framework, in the automatic tie between powers and needs, and – more especially – between needs and wants, in his conception of productive activity as purposive, of interests as objective as well as subjective and of consciousness as a reflection of one's surroundings. Though such links may initially aid our understanding of man and society, to adequately account for the rich variety of experienced behavior they require some modification.

For people often proceed in a very irrational manner – they do not grasp their interests, or if they do, they have more difficulty than Marx imagined in seeking for the best way to satisfy them. Instead of class conscious proletarians, for example, most workers are either religious, nationalistic or racist trade unionists (or all together) who vote for 'Social Democrats' ; and so they have been, with the exception of a few significant times and places, for the entire capitalist era. Marx himself offered the greater part of the explanation for such irrational behavior in his theory of alienation. People so broken by circumstances cannot be expected to think straight; they cannot respond either emotionally or intellectually in the manner which takes their objective conditions fully into account. Marx was able to believe otherwise because the categories in which he thought of man were not wholly adequate for the task.

It was only because Marx believed that workers wanted (or were on the verge of wanting) what they needed, and that they were conscious (or were on the verge of becoming so) of their real conditions and interests that he remained forever optimistic regarding a socialist revolution. For even if material conditions are exactly as Marx describes, there is no necessity for workers to respond as he says they will unless they bring to their situation such qualities as render this response likely. These are the qualities assembled by Thorstein Veblen as the 'ability to calculate advantages', and Marx believed the proletariat to possess this ability whatever their degree of alienation.[3]

For Marx, rather than inhibiting understanding, the very extremity of the worker's situation, the very extent of his suffering, makes the task of calculating advantages relatively an easy one. All the facts stand out in stark relief, and the conclusion to be drawn from them cannot be missed. His needs, too, urge recognition of the general means for their satisfaction, both those available within the system and those requiring the system's transformation. For capitalist conditions alone cannot secure for workers, even extremely alienated workers, what they want. In this way, the worker's entire life is his education in becoming class conscious, of learning to accept the interests of his class as conscious goals.

It is important to note that Marx never saw the destruction of human characteristics in the workers as complete but as almost complete: 'the abstraction of all humanity, even the semblance of humanity' is 'practically complete in the full grown proletariat'.[4] Hardly affected is purposive activity, understood as man's ability to grasp the nature of what it is he wants to transform and to direct his energies accordingly. Proletarian class consciousness, when it occurs, is the result of workers using such reasoning powers on themselves and their life conditions. It flows necessarily from what they are, both as rational human beings and as workers caught up in an inhuman situation. Thus, even when Marx recognizes that the weight of evidence is against him, he is handicapped in accounting for the absence of proletarian class consciousness by his operating assumption, encased in his conceptual framework, that it already exists, actually or potentially.[5]

Marx's conceptual distortion is shared by Hegel who, referring to workers, fuses 'abasement' with 'indignation'.[6] But rather than a special gift of Hegel's, the notion of durable rationality in one form or another was part of the intellectual currency of the time. Engels, who as a practising capitalist was thought to have had intimate contact with workers and whose book *The Condition of the Working Class in England* (1844) established him as an expert on this subject, also contributed to Marx's misunderstanding.[7] The kind of contact with ordinary factory workers that might have influenced Marx in the opposite direction was simply lacking.[8] One could argue that men begin by taking the rationality of others for granted, and that what needs to be learned is that they are often (or usually) irrational. On this view, all the major influences operating on Marx conspired against his learning this lesson.

In modifying Marx's conceptual framework to better account for these facts, we must first realize that very little that passes for irrationality here is sheer madness. For the most part it is a matter of too little attention paid to some factors and too much to others, or of the right amount of attention paid too late. Given where his calculations should take him and when, the individual's response to his environment is distorted: he has become fanatical in his devotion to some needs and a cold suitor to others. Some of these excesses and deficiencies may be rectified by redistributing the weights Marx attaches to various powers. But, first, it is useful to distinguish more clearly than Marx did between the five senses and what passes in common parlance for instincts. Though all man's powers may be equal means of relating to nature, when it comes to motivating actions some are more equal than others, and making such distinctions will aid us to discover which these are.

One power in particular which seems to have received less than its due in Marx's writings is the power of sex. Young people are more interested in sex, devote more time to thinking about and trying to satisfy this drive, and are immensely more affected by it (by not having sex even more than by having it) than most adults, even after Freud, would care to admit. If one does not eat one starves to death. But what happens if the sexual drive is not satisfied? One does not die, but how does such abstinence affect the personality? Which characteristics does it reinforce, and which does it weaken? There are no conclusive answers, but it is my impression that the influence of sexual repression on all classes has contributed significantly to their irrationality.[9]

By the right amount of attention paid too late I have in mind the time lag which exists between the appearance of new conditions and resulting changes in character. Though Marx accepted the necessity of some such time lag, he did not make it long enough, nor did he properly estimate the potential for mischief which this delay carried with it. People acquire most of their personal and class characteristics in childhood. It is the conditions operating then, transmitted primarily by the family, which makes them what they are, at least as regards basic responses; and, in most cases, what they are will vary little over their lives. Thus, even where the conditions people have been brought up in change by the time they reach maturity, their characters will still reflect the situation which has passed on. If Marx had studied the family more closely, he would surely have noticed that as a factory for producing character it is invariably a generation or more behind the times, producing people today who, tomorrow, will be able to deal with yesterday's problems.

Even children, whose characters are most affected by existing conditions, do not become all these conditions call for, since the family, which is the chief mechanism through which society bears upon them, is staffed by adults whose outlook reflects the previous state of affairs. If for adults, existing conditions come too late, for the young, who can do little about them in any case, they are reflected through a prism that both modifies and distorts the influence they would otherwise have. As a result, only in extreme cases do new conditions make people behave as they do (and these are generally young people); more often, old conditions do and then, for the reasons given, in an irregular and distorted manner. In a society, such as capitalism, which is changing very rapidly (albeit in its superficial aspects), this means that the character of most people never catches up with their lives. They are destined to be misfits whose responses are forever out of date.

In order to account for the irrationality which comes from this time lag, I would introduce into Marx's conceptual framework the idea of character structure, understood as the internalization of early behavior patterns, as organized habit. Such characterological hardening of the arteries derives whence character derives, but is a product apart, exercising a separate influence on how we will respond to future events and conditions.

The idea of character structure does little violence to Marx's basic framework; the interactions he describes go on as before except that something now stands between conditions and response, between needs and wants, between objective interests and subjective interests and between activity and consciousness, something into and through which the one must be translated to become the other. As such, character structure is both a product of alienation and, with the real conditions of life, a contributing cause of alienated activity. With the introduction of this new factor we can better explain why workers so often find their inclinations in conflict with the demands of the current situation, why they consistently misunderstand and are incapable of responding to it in ways that would promote their interests. We can better explain, too, why people today are driven to act in ways that might have been rational a generation ago, in a war, a depression or a boom which existed then but no longer does.

The idea of character structure also helps account for what has been called the proletariat's 'fear of freedom' and their submissiveness before authority, which are, after all, simply attempts to repeat in the future what has been done in the past.[10] Finally, the notion of character structure helps to explain the irrational sentiments of nation, race and religion by treating them as expressions of internalized early behavior patterns that have acquired a dynamic and power of their own.[11]

Thus, whenever the capitalist system has been in crisis, when it was in the workers' interests to construct new solutions, their character structure has inclined them to go on seeking old nostrums where they can continue to act as they have done and know how to. To be sure, new social and economic conditions did develop with the growth of imperialism, the workers' real lot has improved, inter-class mobility has increased, workers' movements have often been cursed with poor leadership, the white collar component of the working class has grown larger and capitalists have sought to exacerbate national and racial antagonisms – all this, as Marxists rightly maintain, has served to inhibit proletarian class consciousness. What those who accept Marx's analysis have seldom admitted is that the character structure of most workers is also at fault. With the introduction of this concept into Marx's framework, workers must be viewed not only as prisoners of their conditions, but as prisoners of themselves, of their own character structures which are the product of previous conditions.

For the present, the effect of substituting a sense of retarded rationality for one of irrationality on socialist practise can only be suggested. If, as part of their alienation, workers bring to their conditions a character structure that keeps them from reacting to these conditions in a rational manner, no matter how bad they get, all efforts to attain widespread class consciousness are doomed to failure. They are, that is, unless some means can be found of affecting the workers' character structure during its formative years, to make sure that the behavior patterns internalized in character structure never develop or, more to the point, never acquire the degree of durability they now have.

Already in the advanced capitalist countries there are a number of events working to alter the character structure of the working class young. Among these are the Vietnam War, a pause in the Cold War and with it in anti-communist ideology, an increasingly evident racism that goes counter to taught ideals, the hunger and suffering seen daily on T.V., frequent disruption of community services and schools, growing unemployment among the newly trained and among incoming skilled of all sorts, the pill and drugs and the new obscurantist puritanism that has grown up to combat both. In each case, a pattern of behavior in which the older generation grew up and which, through its transformation into character structure, contributed significantly to their passive acceptance of their lot is being transformed into behavior that in one or more respects opposes the young to the existing social and political system. It is this context that the present youth rebellion, particularly as it involves growing numbers of working class youth, permits an alternative vision of the future. This great movement of protest is not itself a revolution, nor is it likely to spark off a socialist revolution, but by helping to change the workers of tomorrow it does – together with coming capitalist crises and the next and succeeding imperialist war – make such a revolution possible.[12]

I V

Besides Marx's relational view of the world and his conceptual framework for dealing with human nature, the third element in Marxism which I have declared positively useful is his theory of alienation. Based upon the kind and number of relations already unearthed in reality, and between man and nature in particular, the theory of alienation goes further to exhibit the precise forms this interaction takes in capitalist society. What Marx's dialectic does for everything, and his conception of human nature for the ties between man and nature, the theory of alienation does for the capitalist version of these ties. The three constitute a pyramid of concerns. To the utility of the first two, therefore, it may now be added that they make the theory of alienation possible; while the utility of the latter lies chiefly in the sense it makes out of capitalist chaos.

The basic relations Marx draws between the laborer and his labor, product, other men (especially the capitalist) and the species have not undergone many significant changes from his time to our own. The only major modification required by the events of the intervening years concerns the improvement which has occurred in the material conditions and lot of the workers, and perhaps, too, the greater civility which marks their relations with capitalists. However, apart from this, labor is still productive activity performed in the service of someone else, a response to external pressures rather than the fulfillment of a need. The product is still one from which the worker is cut off, and whose misunderstood needs he must seek to satisfy. The resulting relations between people in the same class and between classes are still dominated by competition after jobs, goods and money.

Evidence of these alienated relations can be found throughout capitalist society. In every area of life, man remains an object of manipulation by others and by his own products. As a producer, he is told when, where and how to work. As a consumer, he is told what to buy and how to use it. The heady growth of advertising has made the humanity of consumption blatant. People play no greater role in their political life than they did in Marx's time. In the academic world, we have actually witnessed a hardening of the boundaries between disciplines, and the undisputed reign of such alienated principles as the fact–value distinction. In sexual relations, woman is still generally regarded as an object. Socially, class, nation, religion and race remain prisons from which each individual must escape in order to establish truly human relations.

Fetishism runs rampant. People do not recognize their laws, constitutions, queens, gods, customs, moral codes, academic prizes, etc., as their own creations; instead, they offer allegiance and allow themselves to be dominated by them. An individual who sees through this cobweb is little better off, for he remains captive of the relations in which the actions and delusions of others have left him. The ultimate degradation, vicarious living through the royal family, movie stars, football players and assorted Beatles has never been so widespread. To take pleasure through the pleasures of the unreal, paper doll figures cut out by publicity is an abject confession of inner emptiness. Finally, everything in capitalism still has its price, is exchangeable for money, which is indicative of the alienated activity that went into its production. Particularly in America, people more than ever are what they are worth. So long as people, their favors and products can be measured in terms of money, so long will the theory of alienation be useful in explaining why this is so.

To claim that the theory of alienation helps explain these varied aspects of our social existence is not to claim that it offers a full account of any of them or that it explains everything. To judge the role of guilt in religion, for example, one must go elsewhere. Nor am I asserting that the concepts with which Marx depicted capitalism one hundred years ago can be used without alteration to describe the present state of affairs (though, on the relational view, the meanings of these concepts have developed apace with the changes that have occurred in society). Still other ways of carving up the social whole, ways that take better account of recent experiences and new learning without undoing Marx's framework, are called for. A step in this direction was taken in the present study with the introduction of the concept 'character structure'.[13]

Furthermore, emphasizing the place of alienation in capitalism does not mean that other forms of society where some relations of alienation exist cannot be described in similar terms. Marx, as we saw, spoke of alienation in feudalism. As for present day 'communist' countries, there is no question but that many of the qualities associated with alienation are found there. Soviet writers, for example, are simply wrong when they claim that nationalization of the means of production and the abolition of the capitalist class have done away with all forms of alienation. Rather, Marcuse is correct in saying that as long as wealth is measured in terms of labor time, itself a function of the division of labor, alienation will exist.[14]

An important distinction, however, must be made between the existence of alienation, in some form and to some degree, and the applicability of the theory of alienation. As I have explained, Marx does not use the theory of alienation to understand the individual in capitalism but to understand capitalism from the standpoint of the individual. This is achieved by focusing not only on the individual but on those elements of his nature over which he has lost control and which are now controlling him. The whole process is then thoroughly mystified by the operations of the capitalist market, and this mystification too is an integral part of what is meant by 'alienation'. Even if we accept that people in the 'communist' countries are controlled and react psychologically in ways similar to what occurs in the West (an over-simplified assumption in my opinion), it is clear that the agencies and institutions which control them have radically altered. Particularly significant is the substitution of an economic plan for the capitalist market-place. In this new context, the theory of alienation loses a full half of its meaning: from being a theory about man and society, it becomes a theory about man as distinct from his society, for it tells us nothing about the peculiar nature of the 'communist' countries (except, perhaps, by analogy and such lessons are very deceptive). Such a reduction in meaning alters the very character of the theory: from an analytical theory about capitalism, which integrates a description of people with an explanation of how the entire system works, it becomes a psychological theory, simply describing people's subjective reactions to their life conditions, and an ethical theory that finds this situation wanting. And, as the people involved are conceived of apart from their society, the subject of ethical judgements is not real people but abstracted human qualities (man in general as he's found in the 'communist' countries), just as the standard from which judgements are drawn is no longer a potential inherent in a real society but an equally abstract notion of the good, that is an absolute principle of some sort. It is apparent that a theory of alienation so changed has succumbed to the fact–value distinction and is open to all the criticisms aimed at this distinction in Chapter 4 of this book. None of the above is meant to imply that the alienation which is found in 'communist' countries cannot or should not be studied or treated theoretically, but the interaction of these men and these particular societies can only be adequately grasped by a theory which focuses on the decisive role of the plan, the party, the state and the bureaucracy generally. Marx's theory of alienation is not such a theory.

Perhaps the facet of the theory of alienation which is least dated, and hence of most use to us is just the facet whose mistakes are generally considered 'as patent nowadays as the mistakes of Moses'.[15] This is, of course, the labor theory of value. As I have tried to show, most of the critics' fire has been directed at a straw man of their own making. Rather than trying to prove that labor produces value, in the sense of exact selling price, Marx is concerned to explain why in our era work is expressed by the value of its product. I agree with him that this is the major event in capitalism that requires explaining — why does everything that man produces have a price? — and, to my knowledge, Marx is the only social thinker who takes up the challenge. The interlocking relations of alienation, which constitutes his answer, was essentially a way of viewing the economic processes which were then going on. Though modified, they are still going on, and work is still expressed by the value of its product. Only Marx's labor theory of value offers a satisfactory explanation.

The labor theory of value performs the additional service, in my opinion, of placing the burden of justification where it belongs, on the capitalist. Most arguments on behalf of socialism are defensive attempts to answer the question, 'Why socialism?'; they try to show that socialism is more efficient, morally superior, or in some other way better than capitalism. However, if our analysis indicates that value is the most abstract form of alienated labor, that it could only come from such labor, then the obvious question is : 'By what right does the capitalist lay claim to any of it?' The onus of defense is shifted from those who want change to those who oppose it. In short, the labor theory of value forces the capitalist to justify his role and the benefits he receives in a context where no justification is possible. It puts him in a corner from which there is no escape, other than the practical one of keeping the workers from realizing their situation.

Rousseau's argument in *The Social Contract* turned the tables on kings and aristocrats in a similar manner. Instead of defending democracy, he made it seem as if rulers must answer why they should be allowed to rule after having broken the social contract, and in this way performed the same service for liberalism that Marx did later for socialism. One of Marx's aims in the labor theory of value was to get us to see the capitalist as a useless and indeed harmful excrescence upon society, to whom offering compromises made no sense, and in this he succeeded admirably.

It should be clear by now that the theory of alienation, including the labor theory of value, is a useful aid for understanding capitalism only for those people who share with Marx certain basic beliefs. One has to accept, for example, that there are the kind of relations between man, his activity, product and other men which constitute Marx's conception of human nature. Further, one has to agree with the broad outlines at least of his portraits of the capitalists and workers. If one denies, for example, that the capitalists are selfish and claims instead that they really have the workers' 'interests' at heart, a major pillar on which the theory of alienation rests has been removed; the manipulation of some men by others only needs explaining for those who observe it.

More important still, one has to accept Marx's, or something like Marx's, conception of man's potentialities, to view man living today as a small part of what he might be. Without an idea of what is possible in the way of relations between people, their activity and their products, the existing state of affairs will appear 'normal', not requiring a characterization of insufficiency. Unless one shares this general outlook with Marx, the very term 'alienation' will mean something else, that is, convey a different set of relations than it did for him. How could it be otherwise?[16]

However, it should also be apparent that the very organization achieved in the theory of alienation, by drawing out and emphasizing certain relationships and underplaying others, inclines us to go along with Marx's beliefs. Marx's account of capitalism, in other words, brings into focus the relations, real and potential, that we have to acknowledge in order to make this explanation useful. And once we accept Marx's statement of the problem, we have gone the greater part of the distance toward admitting his answer, an answer that transforms all but the most passive observers into agents of revolutionary change. It is in this way that studying Marx serves to make Marxism necessary. Perhaps, every philosopher tries to do as much, but – notwithstanding my earlier qualifications and criticisms – I do not know of any thinker who succeeds in this attempt as well as Karl Marx.

Appendix I. *In defense of the philosophy of internal relations*

In this appendix, I would like briefly to examine some of the major criticisms that have been leveled against the philosophy of internal relations. Perhaps the most frequent objection made, certainly the most telling, concerns the difficulty (some would claim the impossibility) of identifying particulars on this view. How, in other words, do we distinguish – which includes pointing out to others and getting them to accept – that these relations, no more and no other, constitute a chair, a man, or any other particular thing? This is really a version of the problem of individuation mentioned in the text.

Stuart Hampshire, who makes this criticism, admits that there are many possible ways to break up reality, but says that the requirements of communicability necessitate that we always conceive of it as broken up into more or less distinct pieces. According to him, 'we must unavoidably think of reality as consisting of persisting things of different types and kinds', since there must be a 'type of term which enters into utterances having the function "This is a so-and-so" '.[1] For him, there must be a possibility of making an absolute distinction between a thing and its properties. What is taken as the thing serves as a point of reference which remains the same throughout all changes occurring in its properties and in the point of view of the perceiver. The penalty for transgressing this rule, for taking each thing as the sum of its qualities and each quality as potentially a thing, is simply that people will not be able to understand what one is saying.[2]

This argument receives indirect support from Peter Strawson who declares that we only succeed in identifying particular things because these are the forms in which they actually exist. If Hampshire's refusal to countenance the possibility of identifying particulars on the relational view is based on what is required to communicate, Strawson – who does not discount this approach – makes his stand against the same opponent on the basis of a common sense conception of reality. His book, *Individuals* both begins and ends with the assertion that people believe that the world is composed of particular things ('objective particulars'), and that he conceives it his task to find reasons to support this view.[3] It is indicative of the degree to which Strawson is willing to abide by the judgement of common sense regarding the existence of particular things that his work does not contain a single chapter on perception. Essentially, he limits himself to explaining why basic particulars must be material bodies.

If material bodies have, as Strawson believes, a pre-conceptual existence as things how do we identify them? For Strawson, the formal conditions for identifying any thing are satisfied if but a single individuating fact is known of it, something which is true of it and of nothing else.[4] He then admits, however, that every possible individuating fact relates 'the particular concerned . . . to other items in that unified framework of knowledge of particulars of which each of us has a part in his possession'.[5] It is not too much to say that the term which functions for Hampshire as 'this is a so-and-so' is represented here as performing its function by situating the entity in question among other entities, by operating, in short, as a disguised relation. And how could it be otherwise? How could anything be grasped on its own? What would it even mean to say that it was? Shape, color, function, etc. – that is, all qualities by which we know any thing – can only be grasped in their real relations to other similar and contrasting qualities.[6]

The objections raised by Hampshire and Strawson are really of two sorts and require different answers. The latter maintains that identification on the relational view cannot occur because, in actual practice, identification involves the use of particulars. But he then ascribes to these particulars an 'identifiability dependence'. Once it is admitted, however, that what really individuates such a particular is its unique relations with others, there is no longer any 'factual' barrier to viewing its relations as being within the thing itself. It might even be argued that an analysis of conceptualizing activity which satisfactorily accounts for individuation, in the manner of Dietzgen, inclines one to adopt this relational view. In any case, the fact that Strawson (with little or no real empirical study) finds that the people in his culture conceive of reality as divided into basic material bodies is no evidence that this is the only way it can be conceived. Their Oxford colleague, A. J. Ayer, makes a similar complaint when he accuses both Strawson and Hampshire of an '*a priori* anthropology, in assuming that certain fundamental features of our own conceptual system are necessities of language, which is the modern equivalent of thought'.[7]

Once again, what must be stressed is that the philosophy of internal relations is a matter of conception and not of fact. To strike at its factual basis one would have to show that the apparent interdependence of qualities or of what are taken as things is false, and this, of course, no one has attempted to do. The question, then, is – as between the common sense and relational conceptions – which one do we adopt? If the analogy helps – do we view the bottle as half empty or half full? Neither answer is wrong; yet each carries its own implications. The main criterion which counts, or should count, in making this choice is the utility of each conception in solving and/or avoiding problems. After expounding Marx's views on human nature and alienation, my critical evaluation of the relational framework in which they are found will proceed from this standard.

For the moment, I am concerned with the serious problems raised by the philosophy of internal relations such that some modern thinkers have refused to admit that others could even hold such a view (while often attacking them at the same time for holding it). Here, Hampshire's objection occupies a central place, for if it is true that the relational view makes it impossible for a person to communicate the information he has in mind to someone else, then indeed we need go no further. Yet, what is the status of Hampshire's criticism – where does its certainty lie? If it is possible to conceive of things in terms of their relations, the question whether what is conceived in this manner can be communicated or not is an empirical one. And, since one could only deny this possibility at the outset on the basis of an '*a priori* anthropology', Hampshire's judgement requires testing by experience. Thus, whether Marx's relational conception of human nature in general and of capitalist man in particular can be communicated is not for me to say at this time; my purpose is to communicate it. Later, others will tell me if I have succeeded and – only then – if it is possible to succeed.[8]

What has been said requires qualification in one important respect: any attempt to test the viability of the relational view using measures which have come out of another conceptual framework must be satisfied with general results. Once it is granted, for example, that Marx's conceptual scheme is not our own, the criticism that it does not succeed perfectly in conveying facts we have fashioned becomes, as Ayer rightly points out, 'trivial'. According to Ayer, 'the work a language does depends upon its categorical structure; so that no language which differs radically from our own in this respect can be capable of doing exactly the same work'.[9] Thus, the very accusation levelled that Marx is unable to communicate identified particulars, cannot even be expressed on the relational view, where 'particulars', as Hampshire understands them, do not exist, and where 'identity' is often used to register a relation between what we would consider disparate entities (see above, Chapter 6).

Can Marx communicate what he wants to say despite this difference in conception? Ayer claims that a language which is structurally different from our own – and incapable of doing exactly the same work – may still convey 'substantially the same information'.[10] If this is so, it is on such generous criteria that we must judge Marx's success in communication. It is worth noting in this regard that Spinoza, Leibniz and Hegel, who are roundly denounced for their adherence to the philosophy of internal relations, have all managed more or less to communicate their views. How else – taking only the most obvious example – are some modern thinkers able to criticize them for holding just this philosophy?

What qualifies, in Marx's case, as 'substantially the same information' can be divided into two areas: first, do we know when he is speaking about people, work, factories, government, etc.; and second, do we know all that he means in such cases, that is, do we grasp all that he wants his concepts to convey? If despite Marx's relational view we generally know what he is talking about, it is because – as Dietzgen says – people, being what they are, conceptualize the same kinds of things from their shared world of sense impressions. Whether those things are then viewed as particulars or Relations, the basic information (the essential sense impressions) which each individual has an interest in communicating is the same. Thus, the central features, or core relations, of any of Marx's conceptions will correspond more or less to what others who use this term take as the thing proper.

The real problem, as we have seen, is whether Marx succeeds in communicating those additional features which his relational view permits him to append to these core notions. If there is any difficulty in understanding Marx, it is not a matter of knowing when he is talking about capital but grasping all that he makes a part of this conception on each occasion. Thus, we say that 'capital' conveys 'substantially the same information' as Hampshire's and, most likely, the reader's own concept of the same name in virtue of the core notion which all share, but that Marx intends his concept to convey a lot more than this. And again, whether Marx succeeds in making this additional meaning understood can only be judged in the last analysis by whether we succeed in understanding him.

Still another major objection that has been levelled against the philosophy of internal relations concerns what is considered the practical impossibility of conceiving of the whole in each of its parts. Ayer – appearing now for the opposition – simply ridicules Leibniz's notion that a true statement about any particular individual implies the whole of human history.[11] As regards Marx's work, some critics, such as Heinrich Popitz, who have caught a glimpse of Marx's ability to view the whole in a part, treat their revelation as *ipso facto* a criticism.[12] Yet, on the other side, thinkers of the stature of Lukács and Sartre have recognized this aspect of Marx's thought and consider it one of his strengths.[13] Are both sides in this debate speaking of the same thing?

Our common sense conceptions of 'whole' and 'part' are derived from a view of the world in which the whole (any whole) is the sum of its parts, themselves separate and distinct units which have simply been added together (an external relation). The model and often the actual analogy in which we understand the whole is the spacial one of the closed circle. But the claim that the whole is involved in each of its parts does not make use of these ordinary language conceptions, could not at the risk of speaking nonsense. This is really the same problem dealt with above when Hampshire dared those who subscribe to the philosophy internal relations to identify particulars, where neither 'identity' nor 'particular' meant the same thing to them as it did to Hampshire.

In this instance, what is referred to as 'part' is a relational construct, a unit abstracted from reality for some particular end whose interdependence with other similarly constituted units is kept clearly in view; and 'whole' is just this interdependence which, again for a special purpose, may be conceptualized within any of its parts. No exacting knowledge of particulars is required. No conceptual boundaries are violated. The world is not being forced into a gopher hole. It is simply that on the basis of this philosophy concepts of 'part' and 'whole' are acquired which allow one to speak of what is going on in this manner. Clearly, to grasp what is being said, one must first understand the relational view which fashions the concepts for saying it.

The difficulty, it may be argued, still remains; for how is it possible to conceive of even such a whole in one of its parts when the part is known and the whole, which by definition includes the future as well as the past, is not? But, once it is conceded that we are dealing here with different conceptions of whole and part, one should be prepared to concede that the sense in which the former is viewed in the latter may also be unique. Only with a whole that is conceptualized as a sum of separate parts (as a closed circle), that is to say on the common sense view, are we dealing with something whose character appears finished and ultimately knowable in its entirety. However, as the expression of universal interdependence throughout time, the whole, on the relational view is – as odd as this may sound – never completed, and no thinker in the tradition I outlined has pretended to know all the details.

This qualification does not restrict Hegel, Marx, Dietzgen, etc., from viewing what they do know of the whole as relationally contained in whatever parts are treated for the moment as distinct units. What they do know includes not only the particular interactions they have observed but the patterns of change and development to which such phenomena give rise. When projected into the future as possibility, potential, probability or certainty (depending on the writer and the 'facts'), these patterns become elements of the unexperienced whole that are conceived of in the part under examination. It is in this manner, as Marcuse indicated earlier in the text, that the concepts with which Marx treats capitalism already contain his broad notion of communism. Some thinkers who subscribe to a philosophy of internal relations, such as Hegel, give this whole, which necessarily contains elements of which they are ignorant, an independent role to play in their system. Others, like Marx, do not. For all of them, however, the whole is incomplete, and to that extent the part (any part) is also unknown.

In closing, I would like to stress that I am under no illusion that these brief remarks have successfully defended the philosophy of internal relations from its many hostile critics. My aim here, however, has not been to have Marx's relational conception accepted as much as to have it taken seriously. If, in the course of this discussion, I have raised doubts regarding the validity or relevance of criticisms which suggest that this view is unworthy of scholarly attention, I would consider my job done. If it leads further to a more thorough study of this philosophy than I have been able to undertake, I would consider my efforts well rewarded.

Appendix II. *Response to my critics: more on internal relations*

I

Most of the criticisms of the first edition of *Alienation* have centered on my account of Marx's philosophy of internal relations. I would like to take advantage of the appearance of this second edition to develop my defense of this philosophy beyond the brief remarks found in Appendix I.

In ascribing a philosophy of internal relations to Marx, I intended to call attention to the assumption of identity which underlies his analysis of the different processes and institutions of capitalist society. As Relations, these processes are conceived of as aspects of each other and of the whole they come together to compose. Their mutual dependence or reciprocal interaction can be viewed within each Relation in turn, the chief difference being one of focus and perspective on the whole. After examining some of the problems of language posed by this approach, I used it to help explain Marx's conception of human nature and his theory of alienation.

According to many critics, this assumption of identity makes it impossible to register, let alone account for, real differences. If Marx had a philosophy of internal relations, it is asked, how could he distinguish between processes which are closely related, those which are loosely related and those which – for all practical purposes – are unrelated? How can he say that something has different relations at different times, if with the change of relations the thing itself changes? Regarding alienation, if each of the practises and institutions of capitalism reflect the same alienated whole, how could Marx distinguish between degrees and stages of alienation? In the same instances, where everything is necessarily related, how can alienation be represented as a sundering of relations? If – in virtue of the philosophy of internal relations – every society constitutes a totality, how can Marx treat capitalism as an emergent totality and as a more fully integrated social system than any which came before? How, too, can Marx represent the dysfunctions and contradictions in the capitalist system when the functional dependence of its parts is taken as given and necessary?

Finally, and – judging from how often it was mentioned – most problematic, how can any system based on the philosophy of internal relations single out any process or set of processes as 'primary' or 'ultimately determining'? If all the variables which enter into Marx's analysis are equal, in this case possessing an equal identity as expressions of the whole, how can some be more equal than others? And if they cannot be, it is argued, not only does my interpretation fly in the face of Marx's practise of attributing a primacy to the mode of production and economic processes generally but it renders any meaningful explanation of social phenomena impossible.[1]

The form of all these criticisms is very similar; certain distinctions appear in Marx's writings, but the philosophy of internal relations – it is said – would not allow him to make these distinctions or to give them adequate weight. Before responding, I would like only to point out that most of the people who make these criticisms believe my book also contains useful explanations of some of Marx's theories (they differ, of course, on which these are). Surely, no explanation is possible with an interpretive scheme which does not permit one to make distinctions but, if it is admitted that I succeed in recognizing and working with some distinctions (that my approach is responsible for certain creditable insights), how can it be claimed that it is impossible for me *in principle* to make others? Whether in actual fact I make all the distinctions that are called for is something else again. A possible rejoinder, of course, is that I am not entirely consistent in holding to a philosophy of internal relations, that I covertly import external relations in order to invoke distinctions; and it is this rejoinder – the possibility that I am and have to be inconsistent – which keeps the debate from coming to an abrupt halt right here.

In brief, my response to the criticisms mentioned above is, first, that the distinctions indicated there do exist in Marx's writings (I only listed claims with which I am in basic agreement); second, that the philosophy of internal relations does not prohibit Marx (or me in interpreting Marx) from making any of these distinctions; and third, that these distinctions are present in *Alienation* to the extent required by my chosen subject matter.

Although everything in Marx's world is internally related, on the basis of his research, some things are found to be more closely related than others (clearly, there are two senses of 'relation' involved here). The same thing can be treated as having different relations at different times if Marx decides (in order to deal with a particular problem) to abstract such changes from his conception of the thing. Each capitalist practise and institution reflects the alienated relationships of the whole system, but the more distinctive qualities of alienation – separation from and loss of control over one's immediate environment, mistaking human for inhuman agencies, manipulation by indifferent and/or hostile forces, etc. – exhibit differences of degree and form both between classes and through various stages in the development of capitalist society. Admitting the one does not mean that Marx (and I) cannot, on the basis of concrete investigations, recognize the other. Though all manifestations of alienation are internally related, each has its source in the sundering of species relations between the individual and his activity, product and other people (here again 'relation' is used in two different senses). The same applies to the concept 'totality' where all societies are said to be totalities but capitalism is treated as an emergent totality and as one that is somehow more integrated than other societies. Likewise, disequilibrating contradictions can coexist with a necessary functional dependence because two different levels of existence are involved. Lastly, as regards the special place in Marxism of the mode of production, the assumption that everything is internally related in no way keeps Marx (or me) from emphasizing those influences which are found to be more important.

II

But if I can assert (and often develop) what I should not even be able to think, why is it that so many serious readers have believed otherwise? In a not very different situation – though in stronger language that is appropriate for this occasion – Marx declared, 'It is characteristic of the entire crudeness of "common sense", which takes its rise from the "full life" and does not cripple its natural features by philosophy or other studies, that where it succeeds in seeing a distinction it fails to see a unity, and where it sees a unity it fails to see a distinction. If 'common sense' establishes distinction determinations, they immediately petrify surreptitiously and it is considered the most reprehensible sophistry to rub together these conceptual blocks in such a way that they catch fire'.[2] Few of the critics cited see themselves as defenders of 'common sense' (indeed, most would call themselves Marxists), but they all share with this school the either/or approach to identity and difference. Marx, on the other hand, considered any study that treated only one of these relations a distortion of reality. Using this quotation as my basic text, I would like to reformulate my views on Marx's philosophy of internal relations, placing special stress on the dialectical conception of identity.

If Marx takes account equally of identity and difference, their order in his thinking is identity first and then difference. As part of his way of viewing the world, Marx took identity for granted. It is the relation between mutually dependent aspects of a whole before differences are noted. The aspects, as yet unnamed because unspecified, are identical in containing through their internal relations with each other the same whole. There are basically three different notions of the whole in philosophy: (1) the atomistic conception, already present in Descartes and dominant in modern philosophy, that views the whole as the sum of simple facts; (2) the formalist conception, apparent in Schelling, Hegel and most modern structuralists, that attributes an identity to the whole independent of its parts and asserts the absolute predominance of this whole over the parts. The real historical subject in this case are the preexisting, autonomous tendencies and structures of the whole, and research is undertaken mainly to provide illustrations. Facts which don't 'fit' are either ignored or treated as unimportant residue; and (3) the dialectical and materialist conception of Marx (often confused with the formalist notion) that views the whole as the structured interdependence of its relational parts – the interacting events, processes and conditions of the real world – as observed from any major part. Since the ordering of elements and their relative importance varies according to the vantage point adopted, this view admits as many totalities (structured wholes) as there are take-off points for analysis.[3]

Though the dialectical and materialist whole can only be approached from its parts, the actual parts from which the whole is observed and receives its peculiar and complementary structurations are the result of decisions to break up the whole in just this way. In the text, I spoke of this as the problem of individuation – how do the units that are internally related get established in the first place? Dietzgen, whose work in this area received the endorsement of both Marx and Engels, argues – as I indicated – that the possibilities of sorting out and organizing the qualities available to sense experience are endless, and that what is a thing here is but a predicate of some other thing there. The actual decision on where to draw the line, what qualities to include and which to exclude, is made by each individual on the basis of his experience and needs (given the importance of one's relationship to the prevailing mode of production this generally means class experiences and class needs) as well as the broad similarities found in nature itself.

Assuming identity before noting and establishing differences permitted Marx to see identity where he saw differences and vice versa. Whereas taking differences as prior, attributing an ontological status to external relations, restricts the notion of identity to the Aristotelian equation of $A=A$, where both A's refer to the same static, narrowly defined unit, a unit that has already been declared different from everything else. On this conception, identity and difference are mutually exclusive, and the relation between any two units of reality must be one or the other. This is, of course, the either/or approach to identity and difference adopted by most of my critics. As indicated in *Alienation,* however, whenever accepted boundaries are taken as ontologically given, the task of understanding (therefore, too, of analysing and presenting) particular interactions and developments is complicated by the need to show *that* they can occur. The importance of context for any thing appearing and functioning as it does is consistently neglected and undervalued, just as change consistently evokes surprise, because neither is taken as an essential feature of the thing itself. Furthermore, with no ties or changes taken for granted only those found are counted; others are assumed – for all practical purposes – not to exist. Within this view, all pressures operate to reduce reality to appearances, explanations to one-sided causal accounts, and finally knowledge itself to partial and distorted truths controlled by mutually ignoring and ignorant disciplines. No one who conceives of reality in terms of external relations is immune from these pressures, though countervailing forces do exist which can reduce or delay their effect. Only the procedure that moves from the whole to the part, only the prior acceptance of the identity of each part in the whole, permits adequate reflection on the complex changes and interaction that constitute the core qualities of the real world.

Marx does not seem to have had much difficulty in individuating the units which he sets out to investigate and report on. At the beginning, as with everyone else, it was the common experience of the people of his time and place imbibed as parts of the language and culture that mainly determined the character of these units. Very soon, however, Marx's own studies – given the philosophy of internal relations he adopted upon his encounter with Hegel – drove him to extend the boundaries of these units in keeping with the relations he uncovered. It is undoubtedly the case, for example, that the very young Marx grasped 'labor' simply as a synonym for 'productive activity'. With his conversion to the philosophy of internal relations, 'labor' comes to be understood as a social Relation with productive activity as its core notion but including as well the necessary conditions and results of the kind of production which goes on in capitalism. As such, labor becomes a vantage point for viewing (and inquiring into and presenting) the whole complexity of capitalist society. From this structured totality, Marx individuates a notion of labor on each particular occasion that this term appears which is something more than simple productive activity and something less than its full capitalist conditions and results. How many qualities which belong to labor as a social Relation are included and which combination of qualities are stressed are functions of the particular problem under consideration, which is itself – to a large extent – a function of social conditions that make some problems more pressing and/or easier to observe than others. We are often aided in grasping the special sense ascribed to 'labor' by the addition of the words (labor) 'in general', (labor) 'power', 'alienated' (labor), 'abstract' (labor), 'wage' (labor), etc., but just as often no such aid is proffered. What applies to the individuation of labor applies equally to the individuation of the other main elements in Marx's analysis.

The identity, then, of the various elements which come into Marx's analysis is given as part of his ontology, his understanding of what it means for anything to exist, while their real differences (which together with Marx's problem of the moment determine individuation) emerge from his observation and research. But if identity is *always* taken for granted, it is only *sometimes* expressed

That is, Marx refers to some processes as 'identical', others as 'not simply identical', and still others as 'not identical'. In such cases, the term 'identity' is used to refer to one possible relation between already individuated entities which on another level (in their pre-individuated, pre-conceptualized state) are assumed to be identical. To actually refer to two already conceptualized units as identical is a way of emphasizing their mutual dependence and existence as aspects of a common whole which can be viewed (approached and presented) from either side, as part of complementary totalities. On the other hand, when it is something peculiar to the core notion or vantage point of a Relation that Marx wants to stress, this can be done by denying its identity with other Relations. Such a denial does not effect what might be called its first order identity mentioned above. Along with a first order, pre-conceptual identity that belongs to Marx's ontology and never changes, therefore, we must recognize a second order, post-conceptual identity that is part of Marx's strategy of manipulating his subject matter and changes with the problems posed in both inquiry and exposition.

These two notions of identity correspond to the two senses of 'relation' referred to in my response to criticisms earlier in this essay. All the elements in Marx's analysis stand in two kinds of relation to one another: an ontological relation where identity is assumed, and an empirical relation (actual or potential) where the attribution of identity is one means of bringing out certain real connections. Without the prism provided by the former, many of the distinctive features of the latter would go unnoticed.

Returning to the example of labor, we see that as a social Relation it is identical with value: they express the same relations of capitalism from different vantage points (in value it is from the vantage point of the products of labor), and as such each contains the other as a moment or aspect. The assumption of this identity does not inhibit Marx from individuating labor and value as instrumental units (units which change somewhat with time and place) for purposes of uncovering the real relations between capitalist productive activity and its products. Once found, these real relations are sometimes referred to in the language of identity, as when the different aspects of value are said to be 'forms' of social labor, and as often in language that emphasizes the differences of the individuated units.

The labor theory of value, I have argued, is essentially Marx's account of the metamorphosis of value into and through the various forms it assumes as a result of exchange between different functional units in the capitalist economy. Each of these value forms (commodity, capital, interest, profit, rent, wages, money) express in their way and from their vantage point the relations of alienated labor. All 'act' and are acted upon in ways characteristic of and only possible under conditions of such labor. If Marx could not begin to trace the relations between these forms without distinguishing between value and labor, it is equally true that without the assumption of their prior identity the red thread which runs through them is easily missed. By frequently making this identity explicit, Marx calls our attention to the reciprocal effect between all the elements of his value theory and their common function as expressions of a particular historical period, capitalism. Whereas, proceeding to the differences between labor and value directly, taking the fact of difference for granted (which is the method followed by other labor theory of value economists) would incline one to adopt a causal interpretation of their relationship and to treat value a-historically rather than as a product of capitalism. In interpretations of Marxism, this error also leads to replacing the metamorphosis of value with one or another positivistic conception of value at the core of Marx's political economy, and in the process transforming political economy into 'economics'.

Similarly, the identity of mode of production and relations of production, private property and the division of labor, production and consumption, base and superstructure, class and state – to mention only the best known pairings in Marx's writings – constitutes the ontological basis for the investigation of their actual differences. In each instance, the full complexity of their interaction as distinct Relations is charted only after their prior identity has been accepted and their individuation as distinct Relations achieved. And, as in the case of labor/value, some of the real relations Marx uncovers are spoken of in terms of identity and some in language which stresses differences.

III

At the start of his career, Marx said that after writing critiques of political economy, law, ethics, politics, etc., he intended to 'present them again in a connected whole showing the interrelation of the separate parts, and finally . . . make a critique of the speculative elaboration of the material".[4] As we know, Marx never got beyond his presentation of political economy and there are important gaps in his treatment of even this one dimension of capitalist life. While we never get, then, a fully adequate account of capitalism as a 'connected whole showing the interrelation of the separate parts', neither are these connections ever ignored. The *1844 Manuscripts,* in which this remark appears, is especially effective in bringing out this unity through explicit emphasis on the relation of identity. Only the *Grundrisse* (1858), likewise an unpublished work whose main purpose was self-clarification, achieves anything like the same effect – and by using similar means. It would appear, therefore, that the stress on the relation of identity plays a special role in the thought process with which Marx constructs the more finished system (also partial) found in his published works.

Marx's dialectical method, which begins with his epistemology and proceeds through his way of investigating problems and presenting what he finds, requires the individuation of a new moment – let us call it 'intellectual reconstruction' – to mediate between inquiry and presentation.[5] It is the moment when what is learned is incorporated into what is already understood, extending as well as revising and coloring it. Marx understands capitalism before and not always in the same way that he presents it to us. Given the role of internal relations as the organizing principle within Marx's epistemology, it is only natural that the information acquired in inquiry pass into Marx's intellectual reconstruction through the relation of identity, and that this be reflected in the attention given to this relation in works directed to self-clarification. And if certain works stress identity, it should be no surprise to find the same stress in the theories associated with these works. Though – as I have argued – alienation is found throughout Marx's writings, it is undeniable that the *1844 Manuscripts* and the *Grundrisse* contain the fullest treatment of this theory. The theory of alienation was not the form Marx chose to convince people of his analysis and to get them to move on it. For him, the chief importance of this theory, of this organization and conceptualization of the material, lay in integrating the various elements of his understanding in a way that never loses sight of the human subject. Its main function in his thinking is to aid in self-clarification; its locus in his method is the moment of intellectual reconstruction; and its logical scaffolding is the relation of identity.

Earlier in this essay, in admitting the existence of distinctions critics said I could not or did not make, I claimed that they are present in *Alienation* to the extent required by my chosen subject. If the dialectical compatibility of identity and difference permitted me to make all the distinctions mentioned in these criticisms, the particular analysis I was engaged in did not always require them. *Alienation* does not offer a balanced account of Marx's ideas. In the text, I specifically state that this is Marxism viewed from the vantage point of the acting and acted upon individual. As such, it is a version of Marxism, a version whose necessary distortions are the result of where it begins and what it focuses on. Any detailed account of Marx's views in one area is open to the same qualification, and this applies – in my opinion – to Marx's own treatment of capitalist political economy in *Capital*. I do not believe the one-sidedness of *Alienation* is as extreme as that found in most other interpretations of Marx, where it is often coupled with an attempt to separate individual theories from the system. Furthermore, unlike most writers on Marxism, I am conscious of trying to present a complex whole through a single perspective and of the necessary implications and distortions in my approach. At the beginning of the final chapter, I call for studies of other theories, especially of Marx's materialist conception of history, as a way of righting whatever distortions occur from my focus on alienation. Equally important, I believe that in the philosophy of internal relations I have isolated the philosophical framework necessary to understand these distortions and to correct them.

What are the distortions of Marxism to be found in *Alienation?* In light of the criticisms mentioned above, it might have been helpful if I had been more explicit in labelling my stress on identity one of the distortions inherent in an account of alienation. If the philosophy of internal relations permits, as I have argued, the logical coexistence of identity and difference, Marx's theory of alienation – with its chief function of integrating new information into a people-centered intellectual reconstruction – gives disproportionate attention to the moment of identity. From the vantage point of the acting and acted upon individual, *Alienation* treats labor, value, capital, class, state, etc. as forms of each other and as expressions of a common whole, with the main negative result that social transformation (the core subject of Marxist history) is seriously underdeveloped. A possible exception is my account of Marx's concepts, where meanings are shown again and again to evolve with changing conditions. The primacy of the mode of production and the objective facet of social and economic contradictions in particular suffer from this focus on alienation. They are not so much neglected as short-changed, given their overall importance for Marx. Those critics who accuse me of not paying enough attention to capitalism as an emergent system and to the distinctions which press toward a socialist solution are therefore correct, albeit for the wrong reasons. While clarifying the human costs and problems of capitalism and the human potential of a new communist order, the theory of alienation simply offers an inadequate perspective for comprehending the complex dynamic of historical change and consequently, too, for uncovering the real possibilities of human liberation. If Marx (after the pattern of Feuerbach's transformative critique of Hegel) had to put the individual in the center of human history in order to grasp the full dimensions of his problem, both finding the solution and helping to bring it about required other ways of organizing the 'facts'.

The theory which brings into clearest focus those elements in Marxism which have been most distorted in *Alienation* – particularly the mode of production, objective contradictions and class structure – is the materalist conception of history. Unfortunately, most accounts of this theory, by Marxists and non-Marxists alike, play down or dismiss completely the moment of identity in the dialectic and degenerate into one or another versions of economic determinism. If the theory of alienation underplays some of the distinctions that lie at the core of Marx's historical dynamic, the materialist conception of history is equally at fault for underplaying the identity of its varied elements as forms of each other and of a common whole. The philosophy of internal relations provides the corrective to this double distortion by enabling us to grasp Marx's different theories as so many one-sided (in the sense of uni-dimensional and therefore incomplete) versions of the same system and to interpret each theory in a manner that is compatible with the others.

As regards the materialist conception of history, this is perhaps most evident in the place occupied by reciprocal effect. On the basis of the philosophy of internal relations, the mutual dependence of all elements in the world is conceived of in terms of a constant, multi-faceted interaction. This does not rule out causal relationships, where one element or structure or event is primarily responsible for a change in the form or function of others, but simply qualifies them. Whenever a causal claim is made, the interactive context limits the possibilities of what is being asserted and what, apparently, is being denied. In the text, I spoke of Marx's causal claims setting out the most important influence among processes whose reciprocal effect is taken for granted. Since I was only interested in clarifying the logic involved, how and to what degree such influences are decisive was not discussed – except in the formation of alienated character and social relations. The actual working through of the causal role of the mode of production in capitalism as through history, given the assumption of reciprocal effect, is the central concern of the materalist conception of history.

In tracing the special influence Marx attributes to the mode of production, the philosophy of internal relations also puts us on guard against taking the units of his subject matter – including mode of production – as given and unchanging. The subject of Marx's study are the real people, conditions and events of human history, but the actual units in which he investigates and records his views are individuated and vary somewhat, as I have shown, with his purpose and the then state of his knowledge. The concepts which convey these units likewise experience some elasticity in their meanings. Even the unit, history, undergoes significant variations: Marx sometimes has in mind natural history, sometimes human history, sometimes the history of class society, sometimes the history of capitalist society (earlier and later times viewed in terms of the origins and future possibilites of this society), and sometimes the history of developed English (or French, or German, or Dutch, or American) capitalism. The extension of other major units in Marx's analysis vary depending on the boundaries established for 'history'. Thus, man in history, grasped as history of the natural world, can only be a thing of nature or natural being, amenable only to natural laws. In history, conceived of as history of the species, he is abstracted as a human being as distinct from other animals. In history, conceived of as history of classes, man is abstracted as a class being, the real subject of history on this dimension being classes. In history, conceived of as the history of capitalism, as a story which begins in the present and moves backwards, man is abstracted as the typical product of capitalism who serves as the main subject of *Alienation*. In history, conceived of as the history of modern English (or French or American) capitalism, man is abstracted as particular nations, religions and parties as well as factions of classes, and has begun to acquire the distinguishing qualities that justify individual names and domiciles. Only on this level of abstraction of 'history' can we begin to speak about motivation and choice.

What kind of economic processes are and can be determining, and the sense in which they are determining, are also affected by the level of abstraction of 'history' with which one is operating. For example, where capitalism is the accepted framework, the belief in the primacy of economic forces is based mainly on a detailed study of the capitalist political economy and admits to all the alternative developments that Marx found to be there. Moreover, consumption, distribution and exchange share this primacy with production because that is what capitalism is like. Whereas in history, understood as history of the species, economic processes enter into Marx's schema either as part of his conception of human nature (through the relations he posits between productive activity and man's powers, needs and nature itself) or as low level generalizations based on research in a limited number of societies. The more general claims about history organized in this way (really, on this level) – such as that man has to eat before he can engage in politics, culture, etc. – are less open to exceptions than the more specific claims directed to history understood as the history of capitalism.

The ongoing debate over Marx's determinism – a debate in w......... neither side suffers from a lack of quotations — can be largely resolved by concentrating on the character of the abstraction 'history' in each contested claim. Instead of arguing whether Marx is or is not a determinist, the debate will have shifted to uncovering where he is and where he is not, and to accounting for how he can be both. Since Marx often changes levels of abstraction – and the logic of explanation appropriate to each level differs – this approach would enable us to account for apparently contradictory claims regarding freedom and necessity in the same work. An alternative approach to the determinism debate is the one adopted in *Aliena-*

tion, which underscores the elastic meaning of 'cause' and 'determine', but this does not bring out adequately the reasons for such variations. If Marx's materialist conception of history, then, deals with the determining role in history of the mode of production, neither mode of production nor history, nor the sense in which the one is said to determine the other can be correctly interpreted without the aid (explicitly here, or implicitly as in the works of Lukacs, Sartre, Marcuse, Lefebvre, Kosik and a few others) of the philosophy of internal relations. While I am under no illusion of having explained the materialist conception of history in this brief space, I have tried to suggest what an explanation based on the philosophy of internal relations would look like.

Finally, I would like to draw attention to the fact that only a few of those who criticized my presentation of Marxism within a framework of internal relations seem to share my deep concern with the problems posed by Marx's unusual use of language. Without ever denying the assembled evidence or offering definitions of their own, most critics simply assume that the distinctions which I am said to miss or underplay can be clearly and directly stated: 'Marx believed the mode of production is primary', 'For him, the base determines the superstructure', and so on. But it was the problem of finding different and apparently contradictory statements of the same distinction, and of feeling deeply the kind of dilemma voiced by Pareto at the start of this book that precipitated my own inquiry into Marx's epistemology. Marx's words *are* like bats: one *can* see in them both birds and mice. Unless the seriousness of this problem is admitted, the solution which is offered in *Alienation* will seem at the least unnecessary (as it has to some) and probably false and destructive (as it has to others). Perhaps no one who disagrees with Chapter I of my book, where this problem is first set out, should read any further. In the meantime, it is imcumbent upon critics who recognize the difficulties of understanding Marx's language, but reject the philosophy of internal relations, to offer – as none yet have done – another explanation for the same disquieting practises.

Notes to the text

1 Karl Marx, Introduction, *A Contribution to the Critique of Political Economy*, trans. N. I. Stone (Chicago, 1904), p. 294. Though part of the massive manuscript that has recently been published as the *Grundrisse*, this Introduction was originally written for Marx's *Critique of Political Economy*. And though Marx eventually decided not to include this Introduction (indeed, not even to finish it), it has been included in virtually all editions of this work published after 1903. Hence, what many today refer to as the Introduction to the *Grundrisse* is more accurately referred to as the unpublished Introduction to the *Critique of Political Economy*.

2 Karl Marx and Frederick Engels, *The Communist Manifesto*, trans. Samuel Moore (Chicago, 1945), p. 52; see also, Marx and Engels, *The German Ideology*, trans. R. Pascal (London, 1942), pp. 112–13.

3 Marx, *Capital*, trans. Samuel Moore and Edward Aveling, I (Moscow, 1958), 609. Another philosopher who is said to have forged a singular description of man for all times and places is Max Stirner, who takes himself as the ideal. Marx and Engels, *Die Deutsche Ideologie* in Marx and Engels, *Werke*, III (Berlin, 1959), 104–5.

4 Introduction, *Political Economy*, p. 267.

5 *Ibid*. pp. 13–14.

6 Of their common attitude on this matter Engels says, 'we had no wish to propound these new scientific conclusions in ponderous tomes for the edification of professional wiseacres. Quite otherwise. We had both of us entered bag and baggage into the political movement . . . In duty bound, we had to place our outlook upon a firm scientific foundation; but it was no less incumbent upon us to win over the proletariat in particular to our conviction. No sooner had we made the matter clear to ourselves than we set to work.' Engels, *Germany: Revolution and Counter-Revolution* (London, 1933), p. 127. How little concerned Marx was about his works after they had accomplished their purpose is evidenced by the fact that he never kept a collection of his writings. F. Lessner, 'A Worker's Reminiscences of Karl Marx' *Reminiscences of Marx and Engels* (Moscow, no date), p. 169.

7 *Capital*, I, 27.

8 See, for example, Marx, *Grundrisse der Kritik des Politischen Okonomie* (Berlin, 1953), pp. 315, 715–16.

CHAPTER 1: *With words that appear like bats*

1 Vilfredo Pareto, *les Systèmes socialistes*, II (Paris, 1902), 332.

2 Marx, *Capital*, III (Moscow, 1959), 795; Introduction, *Political Economy*, p. 280; Marx, 'Zur Kritik der Hegelschen Rechtsphilosophie. Einleitung', *Werke*, I (Berlin, 1961), 385.

3 *Capital*, I, 4–5.

4 Engels, Preface, *Capital*, III, 13–14.

5 George Bernard Shaw, *Bernard Shaw and Karl Marx,* ed. R. W. Ellis (New York, 1930), p. 171. The articles of which this book is composed were written in 1887. Max Eastman, *Marx and Lenin: the Science of Revolution* (New York, 1922), p. 82. This fault is not exclusively an Anglo-Saxon one, but its rate of incidence is clearly much higher in England and America than on the Continent where 'Hegelianisms' are accepted if not always better understood.

6 *Political Economy,* p. 11.

7 John Plamenatz, *German Marxism and Russian Communism* (London, 1961), p. 83.

8 Georges Gurvitch, *Etudes sur les classes sociales* (Paris, 1966), pp. 54–6.

9 See my article, 'Marx's Use of "Class"', *American Journal of Sociology,* LXXIII (March, 1968), 573–80.

10 *Political Economy,* pp. 11–13.

11 Typical of many is H. B. Acton's complaint that law and morals which are supposed to be part of the superstructure are also treated by Marx as part of the base that is said to determine the superstructure. H. B. Acton, *The Illusion of the Epoch* (London, 1962), p. 164.

12 Aside from Plamnatz, see Karl Popper, *The Open Society and its Enemies,* vol. II (London, 1962); Mandel Bober, *Karl Marx's Interpretation of History* (Cambridge, 1950); R. N. Carew-Hunt, *The Theory and Practice of Communism* (London, 1963); and Acton, *The Illusion of the Epoch.*

13 Marx, *The Poverty of Philosophy* (Moscow, no date), p. 122.

14 Plamenatz, for example, claims that Marx's and Engels' 'own accounts of major social revolutions do not accord with their formulations of the basic pattern of social change'. Plamenatz, *Man and Society,* II (London, 1965), 276.

15 Popper. *The Open Society,* II, 331–2. There is also the approach, offered by A. D. Lindsay among others, which declares that Marx greatly exaggerated what he had to say in order to combat the kind of opponents he faced. A. D. Lindsay, *Karl Marx's 'Capital'* (London, 1925), p. 38.

16 Marx and Engels, *Selected Correspondence,* ed. and trans. Dona Torr (London, 1941), p. 519.

17 *Ibid.* p. 512; see too, *ibid.* pp. 475, 477. Though not wishing to reprieve any of Marx's deterministic followers and critics, it must be admitted that Engels is generally clearer in stating what Marx's and his view of history *is not* than in stating what it is.

18 *Ibid.* p. 480.

19 I am very sympathetic to the stand, taken in several of Rubel's works, that 'Marxism' itself is a caricature foisted on Marx by those who came after. For a fuller discussion of this position, see M. Rubel, 'la Charte de la Première Internationale', *le Mouvement social,* no. 51 (April–June, 1965), pp. 4ff. Nevertheless, I consider 'Marxism' too useful an aid in presenting Marx's views to dispense with it along with the other, more misleading labels by which these views are popularly known.

20 Marx, *Economic and Philosophic Manuscripts of 1844,* trans. Martin Milligan (Moscow, 1959), p. 103.

21 Acton, *The Illusion of the Epoch,* p. 166. In the same vein, Acton

declares that the alternatives to the technological interpretation of Marx's views are 'almost too vague to discuss'. *Ibid.* p. 137.

22 At the start of this chapter, we saw Marx use 'material force', an expression generally reserved for economic factors, to refer to theory. We have also just seen him use 'mode of production', which usually refers to the production of the physical means of life, for such distant sectors as religion, family, state, law, morality, science and art. As for using apparently contrasting expressions to refer to the same thing, an obvious example is his use of 'labor-power' and 'variable capital' to refer to the productive capacity of workers in capitalism. *Capital*, ɪ, 209. Likewise, when he declares the 'division of labor and private property are . . . identical expressions', I take him to mean that essentially the same information is conveyed by each. *The German Ideology*, p. 22. There are many examples of these two practises throughout Marx's writings, early and late.

CHAPTER 2: *Social relations as subject matter*

1 Quite the reverse is the case in France where Maximilien Rubel, Henri Lefebvre and Louis Althusser – to mention only a few of the better known writers – have all made heavy use of this work.
2 Introduction, *Political Economy*, p. 302.
3 *Ibid.* p. 300.
4 *Ibid.* p. 294.
5 *Selected Correspondence*, p. 12. See too, Introduction, *Political Economy*, p. 301 and *The Poverty of Philosophy*, pp. 117–22.
6 *The Communist Manifesto*, p. 33.
7 *Capital, I*, 209.
8 *Grundrisse*, p. 412.
9 *Capital*, ɪɪɪ, 794–5; *Capital*, ɪ, 153; *ibid.* p. 571.
10 Marx also says, 'Capital . . . is nothing without wage–labor, value, money, price, etc.' Introduction, *Political Economy*, p. 292.
11 Marx, *Theories of Surplus-Value*, trans. G. A. Bonner and Emile Burns (London, 1951), p. 302.
12 *The Communist Manifesto*, p. 36.
13 Max Hirsch, *Democracy versus Socialism* (New York, 1901), pp. 80–1.
14 *Capital*, ɪɪɪ, 794; Marx, *Pre-Capitalist Economic Formations*, ed. E. J. Hobsbawm and trans. Jack Cohen (New York, 1965), p. 120; *The Poverty of Philosophy*, p. 137.
15 Though generally translated as 'relation', *Verhältnis* is sometimes rendered as 'condition', 'proportion' or 'reaction', which should indicate something of its special sense. Maximilien Rubel has mentioned to the author that *Verhältnis,* coming incessantly into the discussion, was perhaps the most difficult term he had to deal with in his many translations of Marx's writings into French. As well as using the French equivalents of the words already listed, Rubel also rendered *Verhältnis*, on occasion, as *système, structure* and *problème.* Another complication arises from the fact that *Beziehung,* another standard term in Marx's vocabulary, can also be translated into English as 'relation', though it is generally translated as 'connection'. I intend the concept 'relation' to contain the same complexities which I take to exist in Marx's concept *Verhältnis.*

16 *Grundrisse*, p. 600.
17 Introduction, *Political Economy*, p. 276.
18 *Ibid*. p. 278. Alfred Meyer has ventured close to this formulation by presenting Marxism as among other things a system of 'reciprocally interdependent variables'. A. G. Meyer, *Marxism: The Unity of Theory and Practise* (Ann Arbor, 1963), pp. 24ff. But this still begs all the old questions regarding the quality of their interdependence: if the variables are logically independent, how can they reciprocally affect one another? If they are not, what does this mean? It is my impression that in this manner what is called 'functionalism' is generally either inconsistent or incomprehensible. For too many writers on Marxism, friends and foes alike, talk of 'interdependence' and 'interaction' is simply a matter of papering over the cracks. But once these cracks appear (once we ascribe a logical independence to factors), they cannot be gotten rid of so easily; and if we take the further step and dismiss the notion of logical independence, the entire terrain of what is taken for granted has been radically altered.
19 *Capital*, i, 19.
20 Introduction, *Political Economy*, p. 292.
21 *Ibid*. p. 291. The 'totality' of social life which Marx seeks to explain is, as he tells us on another occasion, 'the reciprocal action of these various sides on one another'. *The German Ideology*, p. 28.
22 Engels, *Dialectics of Nature*, trans. Clement Dutt (Moscow, 1954), pp. 267–8.
2⌃ It is highly significant too that in his political and historical works, as opposed to his more theoretical writings in economics and philosophy, Marx seldom uses *bestimmen* ('determine'), preferring to characterize relations in these areas with more flexible sounding expressions. English translators have tended to reinforce whatever 'determinist' bias is present in Marx's work by generally translating *bedingen* (which can mean 'condition' or 'determine') as 'determine'. Compare, for example, the opening chapter of *The German Ideology* with the German original.
24 Paul Lafargue, 'Reminiscences of Marx', *Reminiscences of Marx and Engels* (Moscow, no date), p. 78. Lafargue was Marx's son-in-law, and the only person to whom Marx ever dictated any work. Consequently, Lafargue was in an excellent position to observe the older man's thinking. Of his subject matter, Lafargue says, Marx 'did not see a thing singly, in itself and for itself, separate from its surroundings: he saw a highly complicated world in continual motion'. Then, quoting Vico who said, 'Thing is a body only for God, who knows everything; for man, who knows only the exterior, it is only the surface', Lafargue claims that Marx grasped things in the manner of Vico's God.
25 *Theories of Surplus-Value*, p. 185. Elsewhere, Marx refers to the 'destination' of man being to develop his powers. *Die Deutsche Ideologie*, *Werke*, iii, 273.
26 Of economic laws and the political economy of his day, Marx says, 'it does not comprehend these laws – that is, it does not demonstrate how they arise from the very nature of private property'. *1844 Manuscripts*, pp. 67–8. The changes occurring in private property (which he inflates here to the size of the economy) are said to be discoverable in its component relations.

27 Quoted in M. Rubel, 'les Premières lectures économiques de Karl Mark (ii),' *Etudes de marxologie*, Cahiers de l'I.S.E.A., Série 5, no. 2 (October 1959), p. 52.
28 *Capital*, i, 8. He also speaks of 'a general rate of surplus-value – viewed as a tendency, like all other laws'. *Capital*, iii, 172.
29 *Capital*, i, 80.
30 *Selected Correspondence*, p. 12.
31 *Ibid.*
32 Herbert Marcuse, *Reason and Revolution* (Boston, 1964), pp. 295–6. Unfortunately, Marcuse does not attempt to explain how such a use of terms is possible, what it presupposes in the way of a conceptual scheme, and the problems of communication it necessarily poses. Without the foundations which I try to supply in Chapters 2 and 3 of this work, such correct insights – of which there are many in the writings of Marcuse, Korsch, Lukács, H. Lefebvre, Goldman, Dunayevskaya, Sartre, Sweezy, Kosik the early Hook and a few others – are left to hang unsupported, and are in the final analysis unconvincing.
33 *1844 Manuscripts*, p. 105.
34 Marx, *Capital*, ii (Moscow, 1957), 226.
35 'Zur Kritik der Hegelschen Rechtsphilosophie', *Werke*, i, 385; *Selected Correspondence*, p. 484. Other striking examples of what most readers must consider a misuse of words are Engels' reference to race as an 'economic factor', and Marx's reference to the community as a 'force of production'. *Ibid.* p. 517; *Pre-Capitalist Economic Formations*, p. 94.
36 *Capital*, i, 209.
37 Engels, Preface, *Capital*, iii, 13. Because the appearance of things is constantly changing, Engels declares, 'the unity of concept and appearance manifests itself as essentially an infinite process'. *Selected Correspondence*, p. 529.
38 Sartre offers an enlightening comparison between Marx, whose concepts evolve with history and his research into it, and modern Marxists, whose concepts remain unaffected by social change: 'The open concepts of Marixsm have closed in.' Jean-Paul Sartre, *The Problem of Method*, trans. Hazel E. Barnes (London, 1963), pp. 26–34. On this subject, see too, Henri Lefebvre, *Logique formelle – logique dialectique* (Paris, 1947), pp. 204–11.
39 Carew-Hunt, *Theory and Practice of Communism*, p. 50.
40 The conception of meaning presented here can also be found in Hegel. Hook is one of the few commentators who recognizes their common and unusual approach to meaning, when, referring to the views of Marx and Hegel, he says, 'Meanings must develop with the objects of which they are the meanings. Otherwise, they cannot be adequate to their subject matter.' Sidney Hook, *From Hegel to Marx* (Ann Arbor, 1962), pp. 65–6.
It is interesting to note that one of the major reasons that has led current linguistic philosophy to make a radical distinction between what a term means and what it refers to (between definitions and descriptions) is the alleged instability of the latter. To equate what a term means with what it refers to is first, to have meanings which change with time and place (sometimes drastically), and second, to get involved with those conditions in the real world which help make what is being directly referred to what it is. In short, this conception

of meaning inclines one *toward* a conception of internal relations. It is from this exposed position that the currently in vogue question, 'Don't ask for the meaning, ask for the use,' marks a total retreat.

41 *Capital*, III, 795.

CHAPTER 3: *The philosophy of internal relations*

1 Introduction, *Political Economy*, p. 270.
2 Outside Marx's peculiar conception of things as Relations, there is nothing so unusual in viewing the whole as bound up in some sense in each of its parts. Writing in 1880, William James says, 'it is a common platitude that a complete acquaintance with any one thing, however small, would require a knowledge of the entire universe. Not a sparrow falls to the ground but some of the remote conditions of his fall are to be found in the milky way, in our federal constitution or in the early history of Europe.' William James, 'Great Men and Their Environment' in *The Will to Believe and Other Essays in Popular Philosophy* (New York, 1956), p. 216. I remain unconvinced, however, that what James calls a 'platitude' ever really was so common, or that if it was it is now, or that if it was and is now that it has ever been more than an unintegrated hypothesis for most of the thinkers concerned. Marx's philosophy of internal relations goes further by conceptualizing these ties in each part and was – as I hope to show – thoroughly integrated in his work.
3 *1844 Manuscripts*, p. 103.
4 'Thesis on Feuerbach', *The German Ideology*, p. 198.
5 *Capital*, I, 202.
6 *Selected Correspondence*, p. 221.
7 *1844 Manuscripts*, p. 74.
8 *Ibid*. p. 156.
9 *Capital*, I, 10; *Pre-Capitalist Economic Formations*, pp. 84–5.
10 Kamenka has noted that Marx sometimes incorporates nature in man, but he treats this as an unfortunate metaphysical departure and an occasion for criticism. Eugene Kamenka, *The Ethical Foundations of Marxism* (London, 1962), pp. 97–9.
11 *1844 Manuscripts*, pp. 68–9.
12 *Ibid*. p. 157.
13 *Ibid*.
14 Engels, whose extensive studies in the physical sciences were well known to Marx, never offers what we ordinarily take to be a causal explanation. Instead, his position is that 'natural science confirms what Hegel has said . . . that reciprocal action is the true *causa finalis* of things. We cannot go back further than to knowledge of this reciprocal action, for the very reason that there is nothing behind to know.' *Dialectics of Nature*, p. 307. And this mutual effect does not occur between conceptually distinct parts, for as Engels tells us, 'What Hegel calls reciprocal action is the organic body'. *Ibid*. p. 406. To explain change in the physical world by referring to the reciprocal action of its parts is said to be the same thing as presenting the world as an organic body.
15 Hook, *From Hegel to Marx*, p. 62.
16 We come across a similar problem within the mode of production itself in trying to grasp the tie Marx posits between the distribution

of the means of production and the distribution of the working population that corresponds to it. Unless the physical means of production are conceived of as internally related to the people who work them, the distribution of the two cannot be part of an organic union, allowing for full reciprocal effect. In this case, there will be a strong temptation to interpret this relation causally, to find that the distribution of the means of production determines the distribution of population. Whereas Marx himself refers to the latter's tie to the former as a 'further determination of the same Relation' (*eine weitere Bestimmung desselben Verhältnisses*). 'Einleitung', *Grundrisse*, p. 17. This has been mistranslated in the English verion as 'what is practically another wording of the same fact'. Introduction, *Political Economy*, p. 286. It is in this manner that the interpretation I am offering is often hidden by translators who do not know quite what sense to make of *Verhältnis*.

17 Sidney Hook, *Marx and the Marxists* (Princeton, 1955), pp. 37, 36.
18 Marx and Engels, *Gesamtausgabe*, ed. V. Adoratsky, I:2 (Berlin, 1932), 99–112.
19 B. Spinoza, *Ethics*, trans. A. Boyle (London, 1925), particularly Parts I and II.
20 G. W. Leibniz, *Nouveaux essais sur l'entendement humain* (Paris, 1966), p. 195. For the clearest statement of Leibniz's views on this subject, see his *Monadologie* (Paris, 1952).
21 G. W. F. Hegel, *The Logic of Hegel*, trans. from *The Encyclopaedia of the Philosophical Sciences* by William Wallace (Oxford, 1965), p. 211. Marx's own use of 'identity' is treated further in Chapter 6.
22 G. W. F. Hegel, *The Phenomenology of Mind*, trans. J. B. Baillie (London, 1964), p. 81.
23 *Ibid.* p. 85. Truth which can only be presented in the form of system can only be evaluated by the criterion of coherence. On one occasion, Hegel goes so far as to equate truth with consistency. *Logic of Hegel*, p. 52. Such an approach to truth sets as the number one problem of logic to 'examine the forms of thought touching their ability to hold truth', that is, roughly, how much of the system which is the whole truth is actually conceptualized (brought to the fore and made an object of consciousness) in each of our concepts. *Ibid.*
24 Typical of statements which indicate this distinction is Marx's claim that "*The Phenomenology* is, therefore, an occult critique . . . but inasmuch as it keeps steadily in view man's estrangement, even though man appears only in the shape of mind, there lie concealed in it *all* the elements of criticism, already *prepared* and *elaborated* in a manner often rising far above the Hegelian standpoint' (Marx's emphasis). *1844 Manuscripts*, p. 150.
25 Introduction, *Political Economy*, p. 293.
26 Of Hegel's philosophy, Feuerbach had said, 'We only have to make of the predicate a subject, and of this subject the object and principle, we only have therefore to invert speculative philosophy in order to have the revealed truth, pure and naked truth.' Ludwig Feuerbach, 'Vorläufige Thesen zur Reformation der Philosophie', *Samtliche Werke*, ed. v. Wilhelm Bolin and Friedrich Jodl, II (Stuttgart, 1959), 224. In the inversion performed by Feuerbach, the notion of internal relations remains unaltered.

27 Marx's critique of Hegel (which includes as well, it must be noted, his favorable remarks) is to be found throughout his writings. The most important discussions of Hegel occur in the *1844 Manuscripts*, pp. 142–71; 'Aus der Kritik der Hegelschen Rechtsphilosophie. Kritik des Hegelschen Staatsrechts', *Werke*, I, 201–336; and 'Zur Kritik des Hegelschen Rechtsphilosophie. Einleitung', *ibid*. pp. 378–91. I would also add, since it is perhaps the clearest treatment of Hegel's central philosophical fault, Marx's attack on the 'Mystery of Speculative Construction' in *The Holy Family*, pp. 78–83. Despite all the pages devoted to Hegel, however, Marx's position is nowhere fully worked out. On the whole, because most of what he wrote on this subject came early in life and was more often than not directed against thinkers who had accepted the worst of Hegel, Marx's attitude appears more negative than it really is. Later on, he often mentioned in letters to friends (Engels, Kugelmann, Dietzgen) that he would like to write something on the positive value of Hegel's method, but he never had the opportunity to do so. My own sketchy and one-sided treatment of the Marx-Hegel link can be supplemented by reading Marcuse's *Reason and Revolution* and Shlomo Avineri's *The Social and Political Thought of Karl Marx* (Cambridge, 1968).

28 The widespread impression that the Young Hegelians were always Critical Critics, an impression due mainly to Marx's attack on them in *The Holy Family* and Hook's popular study, *From Hegel to Marx*, has recently been corrected in David McLellan's *The Young Hegelians and Karl Marx* (London, 1969).

29 V. I. Lenin, *Collected Works*, XXXVIII (Philosophical Notebooks) (Moscow, 1961), 180. It is interesting to speculate what revisions this late enthusiasm for Hegel would have caused in Lenin's major philosophical effort, *Materialism and Empirio-Criticism* (1909), written at a time when – according to Lenin – 'none of the Marxists understood Marx'.

30 In a poem written in 1837, when Marx was only nineteen years old, Kant's and Fichte's preoccupation with the world of thought is contrasted with his own concern for the everyday life of man. *Gesamtausgabe*, I: 2, 42. It is in this context that Marx's oft quoted letter to his father, written in the same year, in which he speaks of moving 'closer' to the Hegelian view of the world, must be understood. Marx, *Frühe Schriften*, I (Stuttgart, 1962), 15.

31 Quoted in Eugene Dietzgen, 'Life of Joseph Dietzgen' in Joseph Dietzgen, *The Positive Outcome of Philosophy*, trans. W. W. Craik (Chicago, 1928), p. 15. Marx's enthusiasm for Dietzgen was not unqualified. To Kugelmann, he writes of a 'certain confusion and . . . too frequent repetition' in a manuscript that Dietzgen had sent him, but makes it clear that despite this the work 'contains much that is excellent'. *Letters to Dr. Kugelmann* (London, 1941), p. 80. Since these comments were directed to the manuscript of Dietzgen's work and forwarded to him, it is not unlikely that they affected the published version.

32 Engels writes, 'And this materialist dialectic, which for years has been our best working tool and our sharpest weapon, was, remarkably enough, discovered not only by us, but also, independently of us and even of Hegel, by Joseph Dietzgen.' Engels, 'Feuerbach and the

End of Classical German Philosophy', in Marx and Engels, *Selected Writings*, II (Moscow, 1951), 350–1. Engels too was not altogether unambiguous in his estimation of Dietzgen, whose work he, like Marx, first saw in manuscript form. Writing to Marx, Engels complains that Dietzgen's use of the dialectic appears 'more in flashes than as a connected whole'. On the other hand, 'the account of the thing-in-itself as a thing made of thought' is scored as 'brilliant'. *Selected Correspondence*, p. 252.

33 Anton Pannekoek, *Lenin as Philosopher*, trans. by the author (New York, 1948), p. 24. This is the nature of their relationship; whether one accepts the claims made by Pannekoek is something else again.

34 Dietzgen, *The Positive Outcome of Philosophy*, p. 96.

35 *Ibid.* p. 110. This approach to truth is accompanied, as in the case of Hegel, by a use of 'identity' to express what I have called 'relational equality'. *Ibid.* p. 111.

36 *Ibid.* p. 103.

37 Dietzgen asks further, 'Is not every *thing* a part, is not *every* part a thing? Is the color of a leaf less of a thing than that leaf itself? . . . Color is only the sum of reactions of the leaf, light, and eye, and so is all the rest of the matter of a leaf an aggregate of different interactions. In the same way in which our faculty of thought deprives a leaf of its color attribute and sets it apart as a "thing itself", may we continue to deprive that leaf of all its other attributes, and so doing we finally take away everything that makes the leaf. Color is according to its quality no less a substance than the leaf, and the leaf is no less an attribute than its color. As the color is an attribute of the leaf, so the leaf is an attribute of the tree, the tree an attribute of the earth, the earth an attribute of the universe. The universe is the substance, substance in general, and all other substances are in relation to it only particular substances of attributes. But by this world-substance is revealed the fact, that the *essence of the thing-in-itself, as distinguished from its manifestations, is only a concept of the mind or mental thing'* (Dietzgen's emphasis). *Ibid.* pp. 103–4. It should be recalled that it is Dietzgen's account of the 'thing-in-itself as a thing made of thought' which Engels said was 'brilliant'.

38 *Ibid.* p. 103.

39 *Ibid.* p. 119.

40 *Ibid.* p. 120. Though Dietzgen makes a determined assault on the empiricist dogma that perception is passive and that our mind merely registers the effect produced upon it by external reality, his account of the conceptualization process remains partial. The link with language is underdeveloped, and the effect of physical needs and of various social and economic structures on conceptualization requires elucidation. Much of the relevant work on these subjects, of course, was unavailable in Dietzgen's time, but what was available – such as Marx's own writings – was not always put to the best use.

41 It is because of the supposed inability of this relational view to house structures that Althusser rejects the conclusion to which so much of his work points. Instead, after clearly demonstrating the impossibility of isolating social factors in Marxism, he argues that Marx instigates a revolution in philosophy by making the 'structure of the whole' (a previously untried concept) ultimately responsible for the character and development of any part. Louis Althusser, 'l'Objet du *Capital*',

Lire le Capital, II, ed. by the author (Paris, 1965), 166ff. On my view, in attempting to reconstruct the whole from each major vantage point, Marx is erecting – if we insist on this expression – as many structures of the whole as there are major units in his analysis. The whole grasped as the interrelated conditions necessary for the existence of capital has a somewhat different structure from this same whole grasped as the interrelated conditions necessary for the alienation of workers, and so on. The difference in where we begin leads to a difference in perspective, in the size and importance of other factors, and in the relevance of the various ties between them. Althusser's fundamental error lies in misusing the concept of structure in much the same way that Hegel misused the concept of idea; that is, a generalization based on examining many particular instances (in this case, various particular structures of the whole) is treated as an independent entity, which is then used to determine the very parts that gave rise to it. Althusser has in fact confused structure with complexity, so that when Marx speaks of the social whole as an 'already given concrete and living aggregate' (*schon gegebnen konkreten, lebendigen Ganzen*), *Grundrisse*, p. 22. Althusser paraphrases this as a 'complex, structured, already given whole' (*un tout complexe structure 'déjà donnée'*). Althusser, *Pour Marx* (Paris, 1966), p. 198. The transition, apparently slight but possessing serious ramifications, from the idea of complexity to that of structure, has no basis in Marx's text.

42 After Dietzgen, the philosophy of internal relations has been largely ignored by Marx's followers and critics alike. Though a number of writers have alluded to relational elements in Marx's thought, I am not aware of a single full-scale study of the philosophy in which they are embedded, with the possible exception of H. Levy's *A Philosophy for a Modern Man* (London, 1938). As a result, it was left to thinkers as far removed from the Marxist tradition as F. H. Bradley and Alfred North Whitehead (to mention only the major figures) to continue wrestling with the problems posed by this relational conception. See, for example, F. H. Bradley, *Appearance and Reality* (London, 1920), pp. 25–34, 572–85, where there is a particularly good discussion of the concept 'relation'. Though burdened with a cumbersome jargon, Whitehead's is (along with Levy's book) the most noteworthy attempt to work out a relational view of physical nature. See especially his *The Concept of Nature* (Ann Arbor, 1957), and *Process and Reality* (London, 1929).

CHAPTER 4: *Is there a Marxian ethic?*

1 *Capital*, I, 80.
2 *Die Deutsche Ideologie*, *Werke*, III, 394–5.
3 Howard Selsam, *Socialism and Ethics* (New York, 1943), p. 52.
4 The best study of the social and economic origins of stock ethical terms is William Ash's *Marxism and Moral Concepts* (New York, 1964).
5 Quoted in M. Rubel, 'Introduction à l'éthique marxienne', *Pages choisies pour une éthique socialiste* (Paris, 1948), p. xl.
6 Lafargue, 'Reminiscences of Marx', *Reminiscences*, p. 70.
7 Charles Taylor, 'Marxism and Empiricism', in *British Analytical Phil-*

losophy, ed. Bernard Williams and Alan Montefiore (London, 1966), p. 244.

8 The fullest statement of Rubel's views on Marx's ethics is found in the 'Introduction' mentioned above (see note 5), though the role of ethics in Marx's thought also constitutes a major theme in his *Karl Marx, essai de biographie intellectuelle* (Paris, 1957).

9 Robert Tucker, *Philosophy and Myth in Karl Marx* (Cambridge, 1964), pp. 21–2. Tucker also tries to make a case that Marxism is structurally a religious system (pp. 22–4), but the parallels which do exist are superficial, and drawing any firm conclusions from them only serves to hamper our understanding of both Marxism and religion.

10 Taylor, who defines 'morality' as 'a doctrine touching the fundamental good and the way to realize it, where "fundamental" good is taken to mean a good which is inescapable and universally the good of man', can treat Marxism as a moral system, for communism does apply to everyone alive at the time and Marx's conception of human fulfillment serves as the guarantee that what occurs in communism is for the best. Taylor, 'Marxism and Empiricism', *British Analytical Philosophy*, pp. 244–5. However, for reasons given in the text, this strikes me as an overly broad definition of morality, and one likely to occasion misunderstanding of the views Taylor is trying to elucidate.

11 *1844 Manuscripts*, p. 121.

12 *The German Ideology*, p. 37.

13 In one form or another, the necessary tie between 'facts' and 'values' in Marx's works has been brought out by many critics. Isaiah Berlin, for example, has commented that 'in opposition to the majority of the democratic theories of his time, Marx believed that values could not be contemplated in isolation from facts but necessarily depended upon the manner in which the facts were viewed'. Isaiah Berlin, *Karl Marx* (London, 1960), p. 6. Once this is recognized, however, what remains to be asked is how could Marx do this and what are its implications for his other views?

14 'Zur Kritik der Hegelschen Rechtsphilosophie', *Werke*, I, 385.

15 *The Communist Manifesto*, pp. 31–2.

16 Althusser rightly criticizes 'humanism' as a concept that does not permit an adequate comprehension of its subject matter. Althusser, *Pour Marx*, p. 256.

17 For helpful summaries of the positions taken by some of the major writers on our subject, see Tucker, *Philosophy and Myth in Karl Marx*, pp. 11ff., and Eugene Kamenka, *The Ethical Foundations of Marxism* (London, 1962), pp. 2ff.

CHAPTER 5: *Dialectic as outlook*

1 See, in particular, *Herr Eugen Dühring's Revolution in Science* [*Anti-Dühring*], trans. Emile Burns (London, n.d.), *Dialectics of Nature*, and 'Feuerbach and the End of German Classical Philosophy', *Selected Writings*, vol. II.

2 *Anti-Dühring*, p. 13.

3 Z. A. Jordan, *The Evolution of Dialectical Materialism* (New York, 1967), pp. 10–11.

4 Marx and Engels, *Briefwechsel,* II (Berlin, 1949), 404–5.

5 *Capital,* I, 309; *Gesamtausgabe,* II, 3, 396.

6 Jordan, *The Evolution of Dialectical Materialism,* pp. 11–12.

7 *The German Ideology,* p. 35.

8 The same kind of response can be given to the question whether the dialectic is in the world or in people's minds thinking about the world. When the logical distinction between the two is rejected, a question which assumes it cannot be asked. In this case, it is important to realize that nature is invariably conceptualized (even as 'nature') and that people's minds are part of nature in reciprocal interaction with its other parts (see the discussion of Dietzgen in Chapter 3). The claim, therefore, that the dialectic exists in nature and the claim that it exists in people's minds are 'identical'.

9 *Anti-Dühring,* pp. 26–7. General statements of this kind on the dialectical outlook appear often in Engels' later works. Another good example is his claim that the dialectic 'grasps things and their images, ideas, essentially in their interconnection, in their sequence, their movement, their birth and death'. *Ibid.* p. 29.

10 *Ibid.* p. 27.

11 *Dialectics of Nature,* p. 353.

12 *Ibid.* pp. 328, 393.

13 *Ibid.* p. 27.

14 *Capital,* I, 309.

15 *Anti-Dühring,* p. 141.

16 Examples of the law of the transformation of quantity to quality which Engels points to in Marx's writings include claims that money must be of a certain amount before it can become capital, and that the cooperation of many people creates 'a "new power", which is essentially different than the sum of individual powers'. *Ibid.* pp. 140–2.

17 *Dialectics of Nature,* pp. 280–2.

18 *Anti-Dühring,* p. 135.

19 *Ibid.* p. 158.

20 The contradiction between workers and capitalists can also be viewed as a contradiction between two separate entities, where the two are treated as major Relations independent of their roles as components of capital. In this case, the contradiction refers to the incompatible development of two entities which are necessarily related (each as a component of the other).

21 *Dialectics of Nature,* p. 376.

22 *Ibid.* p. 91.

23 Engels claims that 'Herr Dühring's total lack of understanding as to the nature of dialectics is shown by the very fact that he regards it as a mere instrument through which things can be proved, as in a more limited way formal logic or elementary mathematics can be regarded.' *Anti-Dühring,* pp. 150–1.

24 *Ibid.* p. 150.

25 On one occasion when Marx does use them, in criticism of Proudhon's attempt to appear Hegelian, his tone suggests more than a degree of skepticism: 'Or, to speak Greek – we have thesis, antithesis, and synthesis.' *The Poverty of Philosophy,* pp. 117–18.

CHAPTER 6: *Dialectic as inquiry and exposition*

1 *Capital*, I, 19. One of the better accounts of the dialectical method, which appeared originally in a Russian review of *Capital*, is given on pp. 17–19 of the Moscow edition.

2 Marx says, 'It is necessary to observe the actual development up to the point when things are completely ripe, and it is only after that that we can "consume productively", that is to say theoretically.' Quoted in M. Rubel, 'La Russie dans l'oeuvre de Marx et Engels: leur correspondance avec Danielson', *la Revue socialiste* (April 1950), p. 5.

3 *Capital*, I, pp. 7–8.

4 Marx sometimes opposes 'abstractions' to 'concretes', where the whole is more apparent. Introduction, *Political Economy*, p. 293. A similar use of these two expressions is to be found in Hegel, who holds that to leave some aspects (for him 'determinations') aside when representing an object is to be 'abstract'; whereas a 'concrete' is said to be the object 'conserved in the plentitude of its determinations'. G. W. F. Hegel, *Samtliche Werke*, ed. Karl Rosenkranz, III (Stuttgart, 1927), 29.

5 Introduction, *Political Economy*, p. 305.

6 *Selected Correspondence*, p. 106.

7 Marx's ability to treat apparently distinct elements as aspects of each in turn is seen when, referring to 'politics, art, literature, etc.', he says industry 'can be conceived as a part of that general movement, just as that movement can be conceived of as a particular part of industry'. *1844 Manuscripts*, p. 110.

8 Engels claims that without Marx the understanding of capitalism would have occurred but more slowly and piecemeal, because 'Marx alone was capable of following all the economic categories in their dialectical motion, to link the phases of their development with the causes determining it, and to reconstruct the edifice of the whole of economics in a monument of science, the individual parts of which mutually supported and determined one another.' Quoted in Lafargue, 'Reminiscences of Engels', *Reminiscences*, p. 91. For a similar appreciation by Lafargue, see *ibid.* p. 78.

9 *1844 Manuscripts*, p. 68. As a statement of Marx's problem, this is a statement already imbued with the solution. By referring to these entities as 'estrangement', Marx shows that the major relations in capitalist society have already been understood; it is his understanding of these relations which is expressed in the term 'estrangement'.

10 The German term *Wesen* has no exact equivalent in the English language. Besides 'essence', it is also translated on occasion by 'nature', 'being' and 'entity'. The fact that *Wesen*, which always suggests certain internal ties, can be rendered by 'entity' may indicate that the relational sense Marx gives to social entities has some basis in the German language which readers of the English version of his work necessarily miss.

11 Marx equates man's 'life-activity' with his 'essential being'. *Ibid.* p. 75; elsewhere, he calls the 'essence of man' the 'ensemble (aggregate) of social relations'. 'Thesis on Feuerbach', *The German Ideology*, p. 198. And of communism Marx says, 'Man appropriates his total essence in a total manner'. *1844 Manuscripts*, p. 106.

12 For an example of the latter error, see Popper's *The Open Society*, II, 107. Together with its synonyms, 'hidden substratum' (*verborgen Hintergrund*), 'inner connections' (*innere Bande*), 'intrinsic movements' (*innerliche Bewegungen*) – the list is not complete – 'essence' bears a large responsibility for charges that Marxism is a metaphysical system.

13 *Dialectics of Nature*, p. 308.

14 *Capital*, I, 542.

15 *Letters to Kugelmann*, p. 74.

16 *Capital*, III, 797. See also *ibid*. p. 307.

17 Marx, 'Wages, Price and Profit', *Selected Writings*, I, 384.

18 Engels takes a slightly different tack, pointing out that our senses give us access to different qualities or types of relations and says, 'to explain these different properties, accessible only to different senses, to bring them into connection with one another, is precisely the task of science'. *Dialectics of Nature*, p. 309.

19 *1844 Manuscripts*, pp. 68–9.

20 *Capital*, I, 19.

21 *Selected Correspondence*, p. 204.

22 Lafargue, 'Reminiscences', *Reminiscences*, p. 78. Marx once compared his condition with that of the hero in Balzac's *Unknown Masterpiece* who, by painting and retouching, tried to reproduce on canvas, what he saw in his mind's eye. Berlin, *Karl Marx*, p. 3.

23 *Capital*, I, 23.

24 *Selected Correspondence*, pp. 108, 110, 220–3.

25 *Selected Writings*, I, 339. See also, *Selected Correspondence*, p. 108.

26 *Capital*, III, 3.

27 Introduction, *Political Economy*, pp. 274ff.

28 Paul Sweezy, *The Theory of Capitalist Development* (New York, 1964), p. 11.

29 *Ibid*. p. 18.

30 *Selected Correspondence*, p. 386.

31 *Theories of Surplus-Value*, p. 52; *Capital*, III, 378; *1844 Manuscripts*, p. 83.

32 Hear Plamenatz, for example: 'We know that, according to Marx, the "relations of production" find "legal expression" in the system of property. Just what is meant by "finding legal expression" I do not pretend to know. Nevertheless, two inferences are, I think, permissible: that the system of property is very closely connected with the "relations of production", and that it is the latter which determines the former and not the other way about.' Plamenatz, *German Marxism and Russian Communism*, p. 30.

33 *The German Ideology*, p. 22.

34 Bradley, *Appearance and Reality*, p. 593. Mao Tse-Tung offers another relevant insight when he says that identity is the relation of two elements in an entity where each finds 'the presuppositions of its existence in the other'. Mao Tse-Tung, *On Contradiction* (Peking, 1952), p. 42.

35 It is in this sense that Marx declares, 'the social reality of nature, and human natural science, or natural science about man, are identical terms'. *1844 Manuscripts*, p. III. Marx sometimes makes the same kind of equation without using the concept 'identity', as when he

says, 'the relation of the productive forces to the form of the intercourse *is* the relation of the form of the intercourse to the occupation
or activity of the individuals' (my emphasis). *The German Ideology*,
p. 71. Another way of doing this is seen in the example, 'bourgeois,
i.e., capital'. *The Communist Manifesto*, p. 21.

36 See Chapters 9 and 14.

CHAPTER 7: *Powers and needs*

1 *Capital*, I, 609.
2 *Ibid.*
3 Vernon Venable, *Human Nature: the Marxian View* (New York,
1945).
4 Erich Fromm, *Marx's Concept of Man* (New York, 1963).
5 Victor Cathrein, *Socialism*, trans. Victor Gettleman (New York,
1962); J. Y. Calvez, *la Pensée de Karl Marx* (Paris, 1956). For
other discussions of Marx's conception of human nature from a pro-
nounced Catholic point of view, see F. J. Sheed's *Communism and
Man* (London, 1938), and Pierre Bigo's *Marxisme et humanisme*
(Paris, 1953). The recent upsurge of interest in Marx in German
Protestant circles has also seen a lot of attention devoted to this
aspect of his thought, particularly in the pages of the *Marxismusstudien*, ed. Iring Fetscher (Tübingen, 1954–69), vols. I–VI. In this
regard, see also Erich Thier's *Das Menschenbild des Jungen Marx*
(Gottingen, 1957). In the post-Stalin era, a number of studies of
Marx's views on man have been done by communists. Among the
most interesting (and readily available) of these are Adam Schaff's *A
Philosophy of Man* (London, 1963), Lucien Sève's *Marxisme et
théorie de la personnalité* (Paris, 1969), and the various essays found
in *Socialist Humanism*, ed. Erich Fromm (New York, 1965).
6 *1844 Manuscripts*, p. 156.
7 Marx makes the distinction between natural and species powers
explicit in criticism of Hegel's belief that the essence of man is self-
consciousness. Though the editor of the *Manuscripts*, following out
the plan indicated by Marx (pp. 17–18), placed the criticism of
Hegel at the end of the long third manuscript, it actually appears at
the start of the third. This practise was followed by all three English
translators of the work. Thus, while Marx makes clear the distinction
between species and natural powers when he has just begun to operate with it, his readers are forced to grapple with the developed
forms of this distinction before they learn what it is about. I can only
suggest that if Marx had prepared the *1844 Manuscripts* for publication, he would have treated this subject very early even if the bulk of
the Hegel critique were left to the end.
8 Marx, 'The Bourgeoisie and the Counter-Revolution', *Selected Writings*, I, 64.
9 *Bedürfnis* can also be translated as 'want', which suggests that this
link may be due, at least in part, to the peculiarities of the German
concept. This suggestion should not be pushed too far.
10 Perhaps the most accurate statement of this relationship is that needs
exist as the subjective aspect of powers. 'Power', being the active,

change signifying concept in Marx's system, properly has 'need' subsumed under itself, rather than the reverse.

11 In a context where man's material life both shapes and is shaped by his needs, Marx says 'the production and satisfaction of these needs is an historical process'. *The German Ideology*, p. 71.

12 Marx, *Grundrisse*, p. 506.

13 *1844 Manuscripts*, pp. 111–12.

14 If Marx treats needs as most often arising 'directly from production or a state of affairs based on production', he does so because these same material forces are chiefly responsible for the development of man's powers. *The Poverty of Philosophy*, p. 45.

CHAPTER 8: *Natural man*

1 *1844 Manuscripts*, p. 73.

2 *Ibid.* p. 117.

3 *Ibid.*

4 *Capital*, I, 341. The same power is represented in Marx's claim that 'the natural laws of life prescribe a social interchange between town and country'. *Capital*, III, 793.

5 *1844 Manuscripts*, p. 156.

6 *Ibid.* Unless otherwise stated, the following information on natural powers is taken from pp. 156–8 of this work.

7 Introduction, *Political Economy*, p. 311.

8 *1844 Manuscripts*, p. 157. 'In effect the need of a thing is the evident, irrefutable proof that the thing belongs to my being, that the existence of this thing for me and its property are the property . . . of my being.' *Gesamtausgabe*, I: 3, 537. See too, *The Holy Family*, pp. 162–3.

9 *1844 Manuscripts*, p. 156.

10 'Nature' is generally used by Marx to refer to the world of objects. On one occasion, we read, 'Nature, including under the latter all objects, hence also society . . .' Introduction, *Political Economy*, p. 311.,

11 *1844 Manuscripts*, p. 156. The same link is brought out in such phrases as 'the humaness of nature', and the 'intimate ties of man to the earth', and when Marx calls the earth the 'true personal property of man', and says 'he is nature'. *Ibid.* pp. 150, 156, 164. For another long statement on this subject, see *ibid.* p. 74.

12 If man, including his mental abilities and activities, and his objects are viewed as internally related, in what sense is Marx a 'materialist' thinker? The French communist Roger Garaudy says the fundamental question of all philosophy is 'where to begin? With things or the conscience we have of them?' Roger Garaudy, *Théorie matérialiste de la connaissance* (Paris, 1953), p. 1. Most 'Marxists' consider this a legitimate question, and do not hesitate to answer it. However, if the two halves of this dichotomy are conceived of as aspects or expressions of the same organic whole, the very question cannot be asked, or if it is, has quite a different sense from the one generally accorded it. In this case, where one chooses to begin is a matter of tactics in inquiry or exposition, and does not have a decisive bearing on the

truth of what is said. Wherever Marx begins in treating a Relation (and it is not always with what Garaudy would consider material factors) his achievement lies in exhibiting the existing interaction. In reconstructing this interaction, I am specifying the sense in which Marx may be said to be a materialist.

13 *The Poverty of Philosophy*, p. 165. Marx's conceptualization of man's manifold objects as aspects of human nature comes from Feuerbach who had said, 'the consciousness of the object is man's consciousness of himself'. Ludwig Feuerbach, *Das Wesen des Christentums*, II (Berlin, 1956), 40.

14 *1844 Manuscripts*, pp. 156–7. 'To be objective, natural, and sensuous, and at the same time to have object, nature, and sense outside oneself, or oneself to be object, nature, and sense for a third party, is one and the same thing.' *Ibid.*

15 *Capital*, I, 202.

16 *1844 Manuscripts*, p. 101. On this subject, see too, *The Holy Family*, p. 32.

17 *1844 Manuscripts*, p. 158. I would like to take issue here with Milligan on his translation of *leidend sein*. In the text he translates it as 'to suffer', but says in a note that this should be understood in the sense of 'to undergo'. Though both senses apply, what is chiefly meant here by *leidend sein* is 'to suffer'.

18 *Ibid.* p. 112: 'The dominion of the objective being in men . . . is emotion.' See too, *ibid.* p. 136.

19 *Ibid.* p. 75.

20 *Ibid.* pp. 75–6.

21 'Natural' has proven one of the most difficult terms for readers of Marx to understand, so much so that the English translator of *The German Ideology* says Marx's use of it is 'not quite consistent' an enormous admission for a communist translator to make in 1938. 'Translator's Notes', *The German Ideology*, p. 201. This failure is the result of not grasping that Marx's sense of 'natural' comes from his use of 'nature' to refer to all objects, man included, and the necessary connections between them. Hence, man's natural state is to be controlled or dominated by surrounding objects. 'Spontaneity', for Marx, is just the response that man, being who he is, must offer – he has no real choice – inside his circumstances, being what they are. Its opposite is 'voluntary action' where the individual is in control of his circumstances or in control of what controls him. This is, obviously, a matter of degree, and it can mean merely that he has some effect on surrounding conditions, as occurs under capitalism where men alter inanimate nature to suit some of their purposes but are stiffly controlled by it in most situations. Activity only becomes fully voluntary in communism where people subordinate the whole of nature to a common plan. Consequently, Marx refers to communism as a time when man's 'natural limitations' are cast off. *Ibid.* p. 68. For Marx's use of 'natural', see *ibid.* pp. 57, 63, 70, 72.

22 'Wage-Labor and Capital', *Selected Writings*, I, 77.

23 As a natural power, labor is often spoken of in terms of 'prime energy' (*Capital*, III, 793); "something flowing' (*Capital*, I, 214); 'the natural force of human beings' (*Capital*, III, 793); 'the normal activity of living beings' (*Capital*, I, 47); 'the worker's own life-activity,

the manifestation of his own life' ('Wage-Labor and Capital', *Selected Writings*, I, 77); and 'energy transferred to a living organism by means of nourishing matter' (*Capital*, I, 215). The emphasis on labor as energy and force suggests something of the greater role Marx gives to this natural power as compared to the others. This role will be examined more closely in Chapter 13.

CHAPTER 9: *Species man*

1 *1844 Manuscripts*, p. 158. The term 'species' is usually reserved for man, but Marx does make clear on at least one occasion that other living beings also belong to species. *Ibid.* p. 74.
2 *Ibid.* p. 106.
3 *Ibid.* pp. 108, 112, 100–1; *Capital*, I, 361.
4 *1844 Manuscripts*, p. 106.
5 *Ibid.* pp. 108, 106. Much later the same powers are referred to as 'a world of productive capabilities [*Anlagen*] and instincts'. *Capital*, I, 360.
6 *1844 Manuscripts*, p. 111.
7 *Ibid.* pp. 101–2. According to Marx, the sexual relationship shows 'how much man as a species being, as man, has come to be himself and to comprehend himself; the relation of man to woman is the most natural relation of human being to human being. It therefore reveals the extent to which man's natural behaviour has become human.' *Ibid.* p. 101.
8 Marx says, 'Certainly eating, drinking, and procreating are also genuinely human functions. But in the abstraction which separates them from the sphere of all other human activity and turns them into sole and ultimate ends, they are animal.' *Ibid.* p. 73.
9 On occasion, 'essential powers' refers to man's natural powers only. This is an expression which, like so many others in his vocabulary, Marx can use to refer to only some of the things that come under it. *Ibid.* pp. 75, 156.

CHAPTER 10: *Relating man to objects: orientation, perception*

1 Marx speaks of 'senses confirming themselves as essential powers of man'. *1844 Manuscripts*, p. 108.
2 Marx declares that man's powers are 'in their orientation to the object, the appropriation of that object'. *Ibid.* p. 106.
3 *Ibid.* p. 111.
4 *Ibid.* p. 108; *Capital*, I, 457. See too, *ibid.* p. 85, where Marx refers to man's 'five and more senses'.
5 *The German Ideology*, p. 74.
6 Marx's willingness to approach perception from the side of the observer as well as from the side of what is observed is evident when he says of the senses under communism, 'They relate themselves to the thing for the sake of the thing, but the thing itself is an objective human relation to itself and to man, and vice versa.' *1844 Manuscripts*, p. 107.
7 The importance of this distinction for Marx's work can be seen from the following: 'Surplus-value and rate of surplus-value are, relatively,

the invisible and unknown essence that wants investigating, while rate of profit and therefore the appearance of surplus-value in the form of profit are revealed on the surface of the phenomenon.' *Capital*, III, 43.

8 *Capital*, I, 52.

9 There is, of course, a distinction which Marx could not help but be aware of between my own 'inside' and the other man's 'outside', between what I deeply and personally want, love, fear and so on, and how I observe the other man to look and act. The discussion earlier of 'reciprocal effect' allows me to say that Marx probably took a person's understanding of his own motives and wishes as his model for understanding the motives and wishes of others; while at the same time their looks and actions, into which his own meanings have been incorporated, serve as the mirror of himself. It is important to realize that Marx's use of 'appearance' is attached to his odd use of 'sense' in order to grasp how the motives and wishes that we attribute to others can be treated as part of their appearance.

CHAPTER 11: *Appropriation*

1 The philosopher Martin Buber offers some examples of this kind of appropriation from the arts: 'the painter is the man who paints with all his senses. His seeing is already a painting, for what he sees is not merely what his physical sight perceives: it is something, two dimensionally intensified, that vision produces. And this producing does not come later, but is present in his seeing. Even his hearing, his smelling, are already painting, for they enrich for him the graphic character of the thing; they give him not only sensations but also stimulations. In the same way the poet creates poetry with all his senses. His perceiving is already a transformation of the thing perceived into the stuff of poetry.' Martin Buber, 'Productivity and Existence', in *Identity and Anxiety*, ed. Maurice R. Stein and others (Glencoe, 1960), p. 631.

2 *1844 Manuscripts*, pp. 107–8.

3 *Ibid.* p. 150.

4 *Ibid.* p. 136. 'Feeling (*Empfindung*), passions (*Leidenschaften*), etc.' stand in for 'powers' in this statement; but it is clear that the discussion which follows can also be taken to apply to man's powers.

5 *Ibid.* p. 107. See too, *ibid.* pp. 108–9.

6 *Ibid.* p. 108.

7 *Ibid.* p. 106. Elsewhere, Marx says, 'It is absurd to suppose . . . that one can satisfy one passion however much separated from the other passions, or that one can satisfy it without satisfying the whole individual.' *Die Deutsche Ideologie, Werke*, III, 245.

8 *The German Ideology*, p. 155.

9 *Grundrisse*, p. 506.

10 *1844 Manuscripts*, p. 108.

11 *Ibid.* pp. 105–6.

12 *Ibid.* p. 117; *ibid.* p. 116.

13 A similar analysis can be applied to what Marx calls the power of envy. Referring to 'crude communism', Marx's designation for the 'soak the rich' schools of socialism that preceded him, he says, 'Gen-

eral envy constituting itself as a power is the disguise in which avarice re-establishes itself and satisfies itself, only in another way.' *Ibid.*
p. 100. Here too, man's powers, or some part of them, have been
reduced to a kind of lowest common denominator.

14 *Ibid.* p. 141.
15 *Ibid.* p. 102.
16 *Ibid.* p. 151.
17 *Ibid.* p. 108.

CHAPTER 12: *Nature as evidence*

1 *1844 Manuscripts*, p. 108.
2 *Ibid.* p. 102.
3 *Ibid.* pp. 106–7.
4 *Ibid.* p. 107.
5 *Ibid.* p. 76.
6 *Ibid.* pp. 110, 109.
7 *The German Ideology*, p. 72. I have substituted 'power' for 'force'
here as the translation of *Kraft* which is more in keeping with my
practise elsewhere in Part II.
8 *Ibid.* p. 66. In this instance, I have translated *Kraft* by 'force' instead
of 'power' in order not to overburden the latter term.
9 *Ibid.*

CHAPTER 13: *Activity, work, creativity*

1 *Capital*, I, 183–4.
2 *Ibid.* pp. 47, 186. The English translators of Marx's writings have not
profited from Engels' distinction. In my own quotations from these
writings, I have tried, particularly in discussing economic matters, to
use 'work' and 'labor' according to Engels' instructions.
3 *Ibid.* p. 42.
4 *1844 Manuscripts*, p. 103.
5 *Ibid.* p. 75.
6 *Ibid.* p. 72; *Grundrisse*, p. 505.
7 *1844 Manuscripts*, p. 70.
8 Marx dismisses non-human forces in nature as being far less important than man in bringing about physical changes in the world. In
many cases where natural forces are given the credit, Marx would
attribute the leading role to man, for example when a flood carries
away rich top soil that would have remained had the land not been
badly farmed. Furthermore, the relatively short time span that Marx
is concerned with removes long term natural calamities, such as the
ice age, from consideration.
9 *1844 Manuscripts*, p. 158.
10 'Zur Kritik der Hegelschen Rechtsphilosophie', *Werke*, I, 381.
11 *Capital*, I, 513–14.
12 Marx believed that their different climates gave the Irish more wants
but less imagination than the Indians. Marx and Engels, *On Colonialism* (Moscow, no date), p. 74. Without knowledge of what in the
Indian climate engenders imagination (Marx offers no details), this
would seem to contradict his view that the more wants a people have

the speedier their development, including the development – it appeared – of their imaginations.

13 *The German Ideology*, p. 117.
14 *Capital*, I, 177.
15 Introduction, *Political Economy*, p. 276.
16 *The German Ideology*, p. 68.
17 *1844 Manuscripts*, p. 68.
18 For a discussion of the changing meaning of 'work', see Introduction, *Political Economy*, pp. 297–302.
19 'Wage-Labor and Capital', *Selected Writings*, I, 85.
20 *Theories of Surplus-Value*, p. 186.
21 *Ibid.* p. 190.
22 Marx, 'Betrachtung eines Junglings bei der Wahl eines Berufes', in Marx and Engels, *Uber Erziehung und Bildung*, ed. P. N. Grusdew (Berlin, 1960), pp. 48–52.
23 For a useful book by book study of Marx's use of *arbeit* and its special place in his system, see Pierre Naville, *le Nouveau léviathan*, vol. I (Paris, 1967).

CHAPTER 14: *Man's social nature*

1 *The German Ideology*, p. 18.
2 *Grundrisse*, p. 176.
3 *Selected Correspondence*, p. 7; *Grundrisse*, p. 600. Another example of the latter appears in his 'Thesis on Feuerbach', where he says, 'the essence of man is no abstraction inherent in each separate individual. In its reality it is the ensemble (aggregate) of social relations.' 'Thesis', *The German Ideology*, p. 198. Marx even speaks of 'productive forces and social relations' as 'different sides of the development of the social individual'. *Grundrisse*, pp. 593–4. It is this conception which permits me to treat Marx's economic views later on as part of his theory of alienation.
4 *Die Deutsche Ideologie, Werke*, III, 423.
5 *Ibid.* p. 267.
6 *The Holy Family*, p. 163.
7 Introduction, *Political Economy*, p. 268.
8 The degree of cooperation Marx saw in production also stands out clearly from what he says about capital, that 'in the last resort, only by the united action of all members of society, can it be set in motion'. *The Communist Manifesto*, p. 33.
9 According to Marx, 'Consciousness is therefore from the very beginning a social product and remains so as long as men exist at all. Consciousness is at first, of course, merely consciousness concerning the immediate sensuous environment and consciousness of the limited connection with other persons and things outside the individual.' *The German Ideology*, p. 19.
10 *Capital*, I, 488. Marx claims too that in this period 'activity in direct association with others, etc., has become an organ for expressing my own life, and a mode of appropriating human life'. *1844 Manuscripts*, p. 107.
11 *Ibid.* p. 102.
12 *Ibid.* p. 107.

13 *Ibid.* p. 111.

14 It is in this sense that Marx refers to poverty in communism as 'the passive bond which causes the human being to experience the need of the greatest wealth – the other human being'. *Ibid.* p. 112.

15 *Ibid.* p. 107. This also is his meaning where he says that in communism practical needs are humanized 'because the conflict of the individual sensual existence with the species existence of man will have been abolished'. 'Zur Judenfrage', *Werke,* I, 377.

15 *1844 Manuscripts,* p. 107.

17 *Ibid.* p. 104.

18 Marx declares that 'human essence', which includes both man's powers and their objects, now all of nature, 'exists only for social man; for only here does nature exist for him as a bond with man – as his existence for the other and the other's existence for him . . . only here does nature exist as the foundation of his own human existence'. *Ibid.* pp. 103–4.

19 *Ibid.* p. 104. See too, *ibid.* p. 102.

CHAPTER 15: *The character of the species*

1 *The German Ideology,* p. 155.

2 *1844 Manuscripts,* p. 75. Activity is given the same prominent role in Marx's claim that the peculiar nature of men can be visualized 'in their activity and in their manner of enjoyment which is conditioned by their activity'. *The German Ideology,* p. 92. See too, *ibid.* p. 155.

3 *1844 Manuscripts,* p. 75.

4 *The German Ideology,* p. 7. Marx adds here that the mode of production 'must not be considered simply as being the reproduction of the physical existence of the individuals. Rather it is a definite form of activity of these individuals, a definite form of expressing their life, a definite mode of life on their part.' *Ibid.*

5 *1844 Manuscripts,* p. 75.

6 *Ibid.*

7 *Capital,* I, 178. This is the attribute of man's productive activity that is mentioned most often in *Capital.* For other examples see *ibid.* pp. 177, 180, 183.

8 *Ibid.* p. 180. Engels extends this view to cover all human actions when he states that 'In the history of society . . . the actors are all endowed with consciousness, are men acting with deliberation or passion, working toward definite goals; nothing happens without a conscious purpose, without an intended aim'. This claim, however, must be understood on the basis of his subsequent qualifications that, because of the conflict of individual wills, most of what is intended does not occur, and when it does, it can have additional results which are neither expected nor desired. Engels, 'Ludwig Feuerbach and the End of Classical German Philosophy', *Selected Writings,* II, 354.

9 *1844 Manuscripts,* p. 76. Other examples given of the differences between man and animals are that 'an animal "produces" only under the dominion of immediate physical need, whilst man produces when he is free of physical need . . . An animal produces only itself, whilst man reproduces the whole of nature. An animal's product belongs immediately to its physical body, whilst man freely confronts his

product.' *Ibid*. pp. 75–6. These examples, however, all deal with reasons for producing (reasons which Marx shows do not always apply), the nature of the products and the relationship of the 'worker' to his product – and not with the character of productive activity as such.

10 *Capital*, I, 178.
11 Hegel, *Phenomenology*, p. 83.

CHAPTER 16: *Freedom as essence*

1 *1844 Manuscripts*, p. 151.
2 'Zur Judenfrage', *Werke*, I, 360; *The German Ideology*, p. 66.
3 *Capital*, III, 800. See too, Marx, 'Uber der Nationalisierung des Grund und Bodens', *Kleine Okonomische Schriften* (Berlin, 1955), p. 322.
4 *The Holy Family*, p. 176.
5 Man's activity is also said to be free because his life has become an object for him, that object being to fulfill his human powers. *1844 Manuscripts*, p. 75.
6 Marx, 'Debatten über die Pressfreiheit', *Werke*, I, 51.
7 *The German Ideology*, p. 74.
8 *Selected Correspondence*, p. 337.
9 *Capital*, III, 799, 800.
10 *Grundrisse*, p. 505. The same point regarding Fourier is made again on p. 599.,
11 *Capital*, III, 799, 800.
12 *Anti-Dühring*, p. 128.
13 See, for example, Isaiah Berlin's *Two Concepts of Liberty* (Oxford, 1958), pp. 25–9.

CHAPTER 17: *Man, classes, people*

1 *German Ideology*, pp. 48–9.
2 *Ibid*. p. 77.
3 *Communist Manifesto*, p. 12. In a footnote, to the 1888 English edition, Engels qualifies this claim to read 'all written history'. He points out that in 1848 Marx and he did not know about primitive communism.
4 *Poverty of Philosophy*, p. 195; *Letters to Dr. Kugelmann*, p. 19.
5 For a fuller discussion of Marx's class division of society, see my article, 'Marx's Use of "Class"', *American Journal of Sociology*, LXXIII (March 1968), 573–80.
6 Of the laborer, Marx says, since he 'passes the greater portion of his life in the process of production, the conditions of the production process are largely the conditions of his active living process, or his living conditions'. *Capital*, III, 86. The same, of course, applies to capitalists and peasants who also spend the greater part of each day 'at work'.
7 *Ibid*. pp. 857–8. Marx also declares the capitalist to be a personification of 'economic categories, embodiments of particular class relations and class interests'. *Capital*, I, 10. See too, *ibid*. pp. 85, 592.
8 *1844 Manuscripts*, p. 109; *ibid*. p. 79.

9 Brian Barry, *Political Argument* (London, 1965), p. 176.
10 C. Wright Mills, *The Marxists* (New York, 1962), p. 115.
11 Are there no common interests then? Marx thinks there are, but that they are extremely limited in modern capitalism. Combatting a plague would be one example. From his claim, 'The common interest is appreciated by each only so long as he gains more by it than without it', we can see his true attitude toward this subject. *Capital*, III, 190. One might also claim that people have common interests as human beings, in the sense that all would truly benefit from life in communism. However, the satisfaction of such interests requires the demise of all existing social groups; whereas it is just these groups and their real and potential conflicts with which Marx is concerned. Hence, interests are almost always tied to the goals he attributes to individuals as members of competing groups.
12 *The German Ideology*, p. 76.
13 *Ibid.*
14 In commenting on a young prostitute in Eugene Sue's novel *Mysteries of Paris*, Marx informs us, 'In spite of her frailty, Fleur de Marie shows great vitality, energy, cheerfulness, elasticity of character – qualities which alone explain her human development in her inhuman situation'. *The Holy Family*, p. 225. It would seem that, on occasion, the influence of an individual's work and its related circumstances on his personality can be very small indeed. When Marx refers to miserliness as an 'ideosyncrasy', this would seem to be another instance of 'the personal life' taking over. *Capital*, I, 592.
15 *Ibid.* p. 9.
16 *Ibid.* p. 438.
17 *The German Ideology*, p. 69. Marx recognizes that 'within a nation itself the individuals, even apart from their pecuniary circumstances, have quite different developments . . . This explains why . . . consciousness can sometimes appear further advanced than the contemporary empirical relationships, so that in the struggle of a later epoch one can refer to earlier thinkers as authorities.' *Ibid.* p. 72.
18 *Ibid.* p. 189.
19 *Capital*, III, 774. For example, Marx speaks of 'inborn racial characteristics'. Elsewhere, he says the starting point of world history is to be found 'in certain facts of nature embodied subjectively and objectively in clans, races, etc.' Introduction, *Political Economy*, p. 309.
20 What evidence there is suggests that Marx believed the forces of environment, if properly marshalled, could remake any and all human qualities transmitted through heredity. Such, it seems, was to occur in communism: Marx says, 'Even the natural diversity of species, as, for example, the differences of race, etc. . . . are and must be checked historically.' *Die Deutsche Ideologie, Werke*, III, 410.
21 *Selected Correspondence*, p. 447.
22 'Die Moralisierende Kritik', *Werke*, IV, 349.
23 *Letters to Kugelmann*, p. 74.

CHAPTER 18: *The theory of alienation*

1 We see the same 'logical geography' in the whole host of 'double-headed' adjectives with which Marx showered his contemporaries.

How can he describe the laborer's plight as 'degradation', 'dehumanization' and 'fragmentation', and the laborer himself as 'stunted', 'thwarted' and 'broken'? Only because he is aware, however imprecisely, of their opposites.

2 That communism is the yardstick by which Marx ascribes alienation in the present emerges clearly from the following: 'the community from which the worker is isolated is a community of quite other dimensions than the political community. The community from which his own labor separates him, is life itself, physical and intellectual life, human morality, human activity, human enjoyment, human essence.' 'Kritische Randglossen', *Werke*, I, 408. 'Human', we will recall, is an adjective that Marx usually reserves for describing communism.

3 *1844 Manuscripts*, p. 170. He states too that 'the existence of religion is the existence of a defect'. 'Zur Judenfrage', *Werke*, I, 352.

4 *1844 Manuscripts*, p. 109. On the broadest possible canvas, and keeping communism clearly in mind, Lichtheim is justified in defining 'alienation' as 'failure to attain this self-realization'. George Lichtheim, *Marxism* (London, 1965), p. 44.

5 *1844 Manuscripts*, p. 126.

6 On one occasion, Marx says, alienation is manifested 'in the fact that everything is in itself something different from itself – that my activity is something else. . . .' *Ibid.*

7 *Pre-Capitalist Economic Formations*, pp. 86–7.

8 *1844 Manuscripts*, p. 75; *ibid.* p. 91.

9 *Ibid.* p. 86. Elsewhere, Marx refers to the proletariat as 'abstract individuals' because the forces of production have been wrested away from them. He claims that, as a result, they have been robbed of 'all real life content'. *The German Ideology*, p. 66.

10 *The Holy Family*, p. 157.

11 *1844 Manuscripts*, pp. 169–70.

12 Marx claims, 'The man estranged from himself is also the thinker estranged from his essence – that is, from the natural and human essence. His thoughts are therefore fixed mental shapes or ghosts dwelling outside nature and man.' *Ibid.* p. 168.

13 *Ibid.* pp. 103–3. See too, 'Zur Judenfrage', *Werke*, I, 370.

14 Of the many recent works dealing with Marx's theory of alienation, three of the most competent are Calvez's *la Pensée de Karl Marx*, Kostas Axelos' *Marx penseur de la technique* (Paris, 1961), and Ivan Mészáros' *Marx's Theory of Alienation* (London, 1970). The latter book contains probably the best discussion of the origins of the concept 'alienation'. In virtually all such works, however, readers are given little help in comprehending Marx's vocabulary, and the theory of alienation is used to help explain communism rather than the reverse. The account which follows is chiefly distinguished by the central role accorded Marx's conception of human nature (as constructed earlier), the use of Marx's vision of communism as an aid to understanding alienation and, most of all, by my emphasis on the internal relations between all components of the theory, including its major concepts.

CHAPTER 19: *Man's relation to his productive activity*

1 The account referred to appears in the *1844 Manuscripts*, pp. 69–80. Most of the material for these chapters on the basic relations of alienation is taken from these pages. As with other relations in Marx's work, the four listed here are aspects of an organic whole. Hence, an explanation of alienation could begin with any one and go naturally on to the others. Marx himself begins with man's alienation in his product, but, for reasons which will soon become apparent, alienated activity offers a better starting point. Also for purposes of facilitating exposition, I have transposed Marx's relations three and four. Thus, what appears in the order – product, activity, species and other men – in Marx's explanation of alienation, appears as – activity product, other men and species – in my own.

2 *1844 Manuscripts*, p. 72. Such labor is also described as 'an activity quite alien to itself, to man and to nature, and therefore to consciousness and the flow of life'. *Ibid.* p. 86. See too, *ibid.* pp. 110, 129, 152.

3 *Ibid.* p. 72. This is also an account of self-estrangement as distinct from estrangement from the thing. *Ibid.* pp. 73–4.

4 *Ibid.* p. 84.

5 *Capital,* I, 349.

6 *Ibid.* p. 360; *ibid.* p. 484.

7 *1844 Manuscripts,* p. 71.

8 *Ibid.* pp. 79, 83, 73.

9 *Ibid.* p. 72.

10 *Ibid.* p. 73.

11 *Ibid.* p. 79.

12 *Ibid.* p. 73.

13 Another similar compilation of the main relations of alienated labor is as follows: 'This relation is the relation of the worker to his own activity as an alien activity not belonging to him; it is activity as suffering, strength as weakness, begetting as emasculating, the worker's own physical and mental energy, his personal life or what is life other than activity – as an activity which is against him, neither depends on nor belongs to him.' *Ibid.*

CHAPTER 20: *Man's relation to his product*

1 *1844 Manuscripts,* p. 73.

2 *Ibid.* p. 72. It is in this sense that Marx declares 'Objectification (*Verausserung*) is the practise of alienation'. 'Zur Judenfrage', *Werke,* I, 376.

3 *1844 Manuscripts,* p. 72.

4 *Ibid.* p. 70.

5 *Ibid.* p. 69.

6 *Ibid.* p. 70. This is another part of what Marx means when he speaks of labor as 'man lost to himself'. *Ibid.* p. 84.

7 *Ibid.* p. 156. Recall too that Marx included among natural objects both animate and inanimate nature as well as such ideational constructs as music and physics.

8 Hence, the claim that 'The object of labor is . . . the objectification of man's species life.' *Ibid.* p. 76.

9 *Ibid.* p. 110.

10 *Ibid.* pp. 70–1.
11 The terms 'outside' (*ausser*) and 'independent' (*unabhangig*) could be substituted for 'alien' (*fremd*) here. The three are practically equivalent expressions for Marx.
12 *1844 Manuscripts,* pp. 69, 71.
13 *Ibid.* p. 69.
14 *The German Ideology,* p. 65. Elsewhere, capital, or the material forces of production in capitalism, is spoken of as 'the alienation of the conditions of social production . . . from the real producers'. *Capital,* III, 259. See too, *Theories of Surplus-Value,* p. 317. In this instance, 'alienation' is being used in a one-sided way (to convey only part of the relations it contains), practically as a synonym for 'alien'.
15 It is in this sense that products in capitalism are said to stand 'in direct opposition . . . to the laborer's own development.' *Capital,* III, 859.
16 *1844 Manuscripts,* p. 70.
17 *The Communist Manifesto,* p. 34.
18 *Political Economy,* p. 41.
19 *1844 Manuscripts,* pp. 69–70.
20 Marx claims, 'This crystallization of social activity, this consolidation of what we ourselves produce into an objective power over us, growing out of our control, thwarting our expectations, bringing to nought our calculations, is one of the chief factors in historical development up till now.' *The German Ideology,* pp. 22–3.
21 *Capital,* I, 310. See too, his claim that workers in capitalism are transferred around according to the 'needs' of their machines. *Ibid.* p. 420.
22 Introduction, *Political Economy,* p. 279.
23 *1844 Manuscripts,* p. 115.

CHAPTER 21: *Man's relation to his fellow men*

1 *1844 Manuscripts,* p. 79. The workers' tie to the capitalist has also been brought forward as a particular relation in alienated labor.
2 *Ibid.* p. 117.
3 *Ibid.* pp. 79–80.
4 *Ibid.* p. 78.
5 *Ibid.* p. 79.

CHAPTER 22: *Man's relation to his species*

1 *1844 Manuscripts,* pp. 74–5.
2 *Ibid.* p. 76.
3 *Ibid.* p. 77.
4 *Ibid.* p. 76.
5 *Ibid.* pp. 75–6.
6 *Ibid.* p. 75.
7 *Ibid.*
8 *Ibid.*
9 *Ibid.* p. 76.
10 *Ibid.* p. 75.
11 *Ibid.*

CHAPTER 23: *The capitalist's alienation*

1 *1844 Manuscripts*, p. 82.
2 *Ibid.*
3 *Ibid.* p. 126.
4 *Ibid.* p. 83.
5 *Ibid.* p. 85.
6 The capitalist's treatment of his customers is strikingly presented in Marx's claim that 'no eunuch flatters his despot more basely or uses more despicable means to stimulate his dulled capacity for pleasure in order to sneak a favor for himself than does the industrial eunuch – the producer – in order to sneak for himself a few pennies – in order to charm the golden bird out of the pockets of his Christianity beloved neighbours. He puts himself at the service of the other's most depraved fancies, plays the pimp between him and his need, excites in him morbid appetites, lies in wait for each of his weaknesses – all so that he can then demand the cash for his services of love.' *Ibid.* p. 116.
7 Marx says too, 'The propertied class and the class of the proletariat present the same human self-alienation. But the former class finds in this self-alienation its confirmation and its good, its own power: it has in it a semblance of human existence.' *The Holy Family*, p. 51.
8 *Ibid.* p. 152.

CHAPTER 24: *The division of labor and private property*

1 It is a popular view that the term 'alienation' disappeared from Marx's later economic writings, but this is not so. The term can be found in *Capital*, I, pp. 87, 168, 570, 584 and 608; in *Capital*, III, pp. 48, 84–6, 226, 259, 297, 324–5, 342–8, 375, 383, 384, 427, 619, 622, 792 and 804; and in *Theories of Surplus-Value*, pp. 122 and 317. This list of citations is not meant to be exhaustive. The *Grundrisse*, which contains Marx's notes for *Capital*, contains literally dozens of references to 'alienation'. One reason that English speaking readers may have thought this term dropped out of Marx's vocabulary is that the much used Moscow edition of *Capital*, I, contains no index, and volume III of the Moscow edition, which does have an index, does not mention 'alienation'. The Eden and Cedar Paul translation of *Capital*, I (1928) has an index, but it, too, leaves out 'alienation'. An exception is the London edition of *Capital*, I (1937), a photographic reprint of the 1887 original that was gone over by Engels, which does give 'alienation' in the index.
   One of the better discussions of the place of alienation in *Capital* can be found in Raya Dunayevskaya's *Marxism and Freedom* (New York, 1958), pp. 103–49.
2 Engels, 'Karl Marx, Critique of Political Economy', *Selected Writings*, I, 339.
3 *1844 Manuscripts*, p. 129. Marx calls the division of labor and exchange 'perceptively alienated expressions of human activity and of essential human power as a species activity and power'. *Ibid.* p. 136.
4 *Ibid.* pp. 83, 105. Private property is also referred to as the material expression of estranged human life'. *Ibid.* p. 102.
5 *The German Ideology*, p. 22.

6 *Ibid.* p. 20. By adding the qualification 'truly such', Marx is indicating the special sense he ordinarily gives 'division of labor'. We saw that on the basis of the philosophy of internal relations Marx could use a concept to refer to only part of the information that comes under it. In this case, 'division of labor' seldom refers to cooperation which does not include the division of mental and bodily labor.

7 Marx claims that 'The antagonism between town and country . . . is the most crass expression of the subjection of the individual under the division of labor, under a definite activity forced upon him – a subjection which makes one man into a restricted town-animal, the other into a restricted country-animal, and daily creates anew the conflict between their interests.' *Ibid.* p. 44.

8 *Ibid.* p. 20.

9 A slightly different account of the origins of the division of labor is to be found in Engels' 'Origins of the Family, Private Property, and the State', *Selected Writings*, II, 278ff. There is nothing here that deprives the division of labor of its central place in the theory of alienation.

10 *The German Ideology*, p. 22.

11 *Ibid.*

12 *Ibid.* p. 65.

13 *Pre-Capitalist Economic Formations*, p. 89.

14 *Ibid.* pp. 87–8.

15 *Th, German Ideology*, p. 21. Engels goes further and hypothesizes that in the primitive family division of labor first existed with the male engaged in productive tasks outside the home and the woman engaged in household chores. Each had control of their own implements and products. When an increase in wealth occurred in the area controlled by the male, which is the only area in which it could occur, a revolution took place in family relationships. Engels, 'Origin of Family, Private Property and the State', *Selected Writings*, II, 281–2.

16 *The German Ideology*, p. 65.

17 Engels, 'Origins of the Family', *Selected Writings*, II, 281.

18 *The German Ideology*, p. 65.

19 *1844 Manuscripts*, p. 80.

20 *Ibid.* p. 81.

21 The range of meaning Marx gives to 'private property' is also indicated by such statements as: 'The relations of private property contain latent within them the relations of private property as labor, the same relations as capital, and the mutual relations of these two to one another.' *1844 Manuscripts*, p. 86. See too, *ibid.* p. 83.

22 *The Holy Family*, p. 51.

23 *1844 Manuscripts*, p. 82.

24 Thus, when Landshut and Mayer declare that for Marx the goal of history is not 'the suppression of private property . . . but the realization of man', they are denying what they are asserting, and vice versa. S. Landshut and J. P. Mayer, *Karl Marx, der Historische Materialismus. Die Frühschriften*, I (Leipzig, 1932), 35.

25 *1844 Manuscripts*, p. 82.

26 Wages are added to this list where Marx claims 'wages and private property are identical'. *Ibid.* p. 81. Likewise, wealth. *The Holy Family*, p. 51. This list is still not complete.

27 *1844 Manuscripts*, pp. 67–8.
28 *Ibid.* p. 81.
29 *Ibid.* p. 129.

CHAPTER 25: *The labor theory of value: labor-power*

1 *Capita*, I, 39.
2 *Ibid.* p. 195.
3 Sweezy, *The Theory of Capitalist Development*, p. 12.
4 *Capital*, I, 10.
5 Rubel, *Karl Marx, essai de biographie intellectuelle*, pp. 10–11.
6 *Capital*, I, 570–1.
7 For Marx, 'Political Economy conceals the estrangement inherent in the nature of labor by not considering the direct relations between the worker (labor) and production'. *1844 Manuscripts*, p. 71. As a result, 'labor', for the political economists, does not convey these relations.
8 *Capital*, I, 167.
9 *Theories of Surplus-Value*, pp. 168–9. For Engels' account of why 'labor-power' was substituted for 'labor', see his 'introduction' to Marx's 'Wage Labor and Capital', *Selected Writings*, I, 67ff. A good discussion of the effect of the transition to the concept of 'labor-power' on economic analysis can be found in John Strachey's much underestimated work, *The Nature of Capitalist Crisis* (New York, 1935), pp. 177ff.
10 *Capital*, I, 584.
11 Marx quotes from Hegel to underline this point: 'I may make over to another the use, for a limited time, of my particular bodily and mental aptitudes and capabilities; because, in consequence of this restriction, they are impressed with a character of alienation with regard to me as a whole. But by the alienation of all my labor-time and the whole of my work, I should be converting the substance itself, in other words, my general activity and reality, my person, into the property of another.' *Capital*, I, 168.
12 *Ibid.* p. 170.
13 *Capital*, III, 191. See too, Introduction, *Political Economy*, p. 239.
14 *Theories of Surplus-Value*, p. 381. By using the term 'forgets' here, Marx is suggesting this is something Ricardo really knows. He seems to have believed that Ricardo was at least partly aware of the internal tie between social conditions and the categories used to describe them.
15 Productive activity in feudalism, for example, which is 'not yet grasped in its generality and abstraction', brings other results. For Marx, the labor of serfs 'is still bound to a particular natural element as its matter, and it is therefore only recognized in a particular mode of existence determined by nature. It is therefore still only a specific, particular alienation of man, just as its product is conceived only as a specific form of wealth, due more to nature than to labor itself.' *1844 Manuscripts*, p. 96.
16 Quoted in M. Rubel, 'Fragments sociologiques dans les inédits de Marx', *Cahiers internationaux de sociologie*, XXII (1957), 129.
17 Introduction, *Political Economy*, p. 300: By defining all wealth-producing activity as 'labor in general', Adam Smith finds 'an abstract

expression for the simplest relation into which men have been mutually entering as producers from time of yore, no matter under what form of society', but as well for the special kind of society in which there is indifference to particular kinds of labor, where people pass easily from one kind of work to another. This, Marx says, 'implies the existence of a highly developed aggregate of different species of concrete labor, none of which is any longer the predominant one . . . the most general abstractions commonly arise only where there is the highest concrete development, where one feature appears to be jointly possessed by many, and to be common to all. Then it cannot be thought of any longer in one particular form.' *Ibid.* pp. 298–9.

18 *Capital,* I, 73.

19 Engels, we will recall, distinguished between 'work' and 'labor' as follows: 'The labor which creates use-values, and counts qualitatively, is *Work,* as distinguished from Labor; that which creates value and counts quantitatively, is *Labor* as distinguished from Work.' *Ibid.* p. 47. The 'value' referred to in the second half of this statement is 'exchange-value'.

CHAPTER 26: *Value as alienated labor*

1 *Capital,* III, 795, 372.

2 *Selected Correspondence,* p. 106.

3 Marx also says that 'value in general is a form of social labor'. *Theories of Surplus-Value,* p. 52. See too, his claim that the substance of commodities is labor – 'That is why they are value'. *Ibid.* p. 201. Engels provides a still more striking statement of this equation in replying to the question, 'What is the value of labor?' 'Value itself', he says, 'is nothing more than the expression of the socially necessary human labor materialized in an object. Labor can therefore have no value. It would be just as possible to speak of the value of labor and to try to determine it, as to speak of the value of value, or to try to determine the weight not of a body, but of heaviness itself.' *Anti-Dühring,* p. 224. Yet, many Marxists continue to speak about the 'value of labor'. See, for example, Leon Trotsky's *The Living Thoughts of Karl Marx* (New York, 1963), p. 19. In all this, great care must be taken not to confuse labor with labor-power, which does have a value equal to the amount of labor-time required to produce the means of subsistence people need in reproducing it.

4 One early – and rather surprising – exception is Edward Bernstein, who claims that Marxian value is what is left of a commodity after everything but labor has been abstracted. Edward Bernstein, *Evolutionary Socialism,* trans. Edith Harvey (London, 1909), p. 35. The same thought continues to crop up, in critical as well as in expository works, but, to my knowledge, has never been adequately explained.

5 *Letters to Dr Kugelmann,* p. 73.

6 *Capital,* I, 80. In his chapter on economics in *Anti-Dühring,* a chapter drafted by Marx, Engels begins with the question, 'Whence comes this surplus-value?' That there is value and its equation with labor are taken for granted. *Anti-Dühring,* pp. 227–8.

7 *Capital,* III, 608. The rest of nature is similarly dismissed: 'Since

exchange-value is a definite social manner of expressing the amount of labor bestowed upon an object, nature has no more to do with it than it has in fixing the course of exchange.' *Capital*, I, 82.

8 *Capital*, III, 618–19.

9 *Capital*, I, 371, 388. Even the qualification that the labor theory of value only takes account of socially useful labor exhibits the afore-mentioned link. Marx says 'nothing can have value, without being an object of utility. If the thing is useless, so is the labor, and therefore creates no value.' *Ibid.* p. 41. In short, labor which does not produce items people want to use is no labor at all; wanting to use what is produced is part of the core social relation conveyed by the concept 'labor'.

10 *Selected Correspondence*, p. 106.

11 *Capital*, I, 81.

12 *Theories of Surplus-Value*, p. 134. Value may also be seen as what finally happens under capitalist conditions of production to the powers workers expend in production, the result of what was referred to earlier as the transfer of species powers to objects.

13 *Capital*, I, 74.

14 The value form of the product in bourgeois production, according to Marx, 'stamps that production as a particular species of social pro-duction, and thereby gives it its special historical character'. *Ibid.* p. 81.

15 *Selected Correspondence*, p. 106. The same qualification that rules out the past rules out the future. Consequently, though labor-time serves as the measure of exchange under socialism, it is wrong to view this, as Joan Robinson does for example, as an instance where the labor theory of value has been put into practise. Joan Robinson, *An Essay on Marxian Economics* (London, 1963), p. 23.

16 *Capital*, I, 60.

17 *Theories of Surplus-Value*, p. 381. See too, *Capital*, I, 80.

18 The minimized distinction between skilled and unskilled labor, which some critics have tried to explode as a major fault in Marx's value theory, receives its proper perspective once we accept that what is being measured is the qualitatively undifferentiated labor of aliena-tion. Marx admits that the labor-power involved in skilled labor has a greater value than that involved in unskilled labor, but says this is based on the greater labor-time necessary to reproduce the former. Skilled labor is simply a compound of unskilled labor, the sum of all the unskilled labor that has gone into its creation. Since these two kinds of labor, when exercised under capitalist conditions of produc-tion, do not differ significantly in their degree of alienation (recall all the elements of this Relation), Marx can legitimately hold them up for measurement by the same standard.

19 'Wage-Labor and Capital', *Selected Writings*, I, 82.

20 'Wages, Price and Profit', *ibid.* p. 375; *Capital* III, 175. Market-value is sometimes the value of commodities produced under average con-ditions and which make up most commodities produced in a sphere. *Ibid.*

21 'Wages, Price and Profit', *Selected Writings*, I, 384. Marx states clearly that 'The assumption that the commodities of the various spheres of production are sold at their value merely implies, of

course, that their value is the center of gravity around which their prices fluctuate, and their continual rises and drops tend to equalize'. *Capital*, III, 175.

22 *Ibid*. p. 192; *Selected Correspondence*, pp. 129–32.

23 As indicated in the text, a similar role is given to competition among capitalists in bringing an average rate of profit to spheres of production which have different rates of surplus-value. *Capital*, III, 156, 192–3. To comprehend profit, Marx would have us treat the capitalist class as a whole. *Theories of Surplus-Value*, p. 285. So much for Böhm-Bawerk's 'Great Contradiction', which points to the average rate of profit existing between industries employing equal amounts of capital as being incompatible with Marx's belief that only labor produces value. Like so much of the criticism of Marx's economics, this one is directed against a position Marx never held, simply dismissing all his comments to the contrary. That Böhm-Bawerk's criticism has acquired, through constant repetition, the stature it has is a clear indication of the level on which most Marxian exegesis stands. See Ludwig v. Böhm-Bawerk, *Karl Marx and the Close of his System*, trans. Alice A. MacDonald (London, 1890), pp. 26ff. Böhm-Bawerk is not an 'ordinary' critic, but, as a later writer rightly noted, 'the lion of the anti-Marxists'. William Blake, *An American Looks at Karl Marx* (New York, 1939), p. 415.

24 *Letters to Dr Kugelmann*, pp. 73–4.

25 Introduction, *Political Economy*, p. 294.

26 *Capital*, III, 174. For Engels' comments, see his 'Supplement to *Capital*, III', in *Capital*, III, 872ff.

27 Introduction, *Political Economy*, pp. 300–1.

28 *Pre-Capitalist Economic Formations*, pp. 80–1.

29 *Capital*, I, 80. This notion of the dual connection between labor and value is contrasted with its absence among capitalist economists. Marx says, 'it is the weak point of the classical school of Political Economy that it nowhere, expressly and with full consciousness, distinguishes between labor, as it appears in the value of a product and the same labor as it appears in the use-value of that product'. *Ibid*. Because they do not grasp labor as alienated productive activity, they do not feel any need to make allowance for the distinctive qualities of such labor which appear in its product, value.

30 Marx says, 'A use-value . . . has value only because human labor in the abstract has been embodied or materialized in it.' *Ibid*. p. 38.

31 *Political Economy*, pp. 42–3.

32 Introduction, *Political Economy*, p. 279.

33 *Ibid*. p. 43. Marx comments, 'It is one of the chief failings of classical economy that it has never succeeded, by means of its analysis of commodities and, in particular, of their value, in discovering that form under which value becomes exchange-value'. *Capital*, I, 80–1. That form is the use-value of commodities.

34 *Ibid*. pp. 42–3.

35 *Ibid*. p. 36.

36 A satisfactory intellectual history, which my work has no pretence of being, would have to trace 'surplus-value' at least as far back as the 'produit net' of the physiocrats.

37 *Selected Correspondence*, p. 232.

38 See, for example, his criticism of Smith and Ricardo in *Theories of Surplus-Value*, p. 40. Besides working with the general form of surplus-value, the other original contributions Marx believes he made in *Capital*, I, are demonstrating the double character of labor and uncovering the relations hidden in the 'irrational' form of wages. *Selected Correspondence*, 232. However, in the Preface to *Capital*, I, Marx indicates that more important still is his treatment of value itself: 'The value-form, whose fully developed shape is the money-form is very elementary and simple. Nevertheless, the human mind has for more than 2,000 years sought to get to the bottom of it, whilst on the other hand, to the successful analysis of much more composite and complex forms, there has been at least an approximation.' *Capital*, I, 7–8.

39 *Ibid.* p. 80. The concepts of 'use-value' and 'exchange-value' in the works of other labor theory of value economists – in so far as they are there at all – do not get beyond the simple notions of how an article is used and that for which it is exchanged.

40 Joan Robinson, *On Re-reading Marx* (Cambridge, 1953), pp. 22–3.

41 Joseph Schumpeter, *Capitalism, Socialism, and Democracy* (New York, 1947), p. 23.

CHAPTER 27: *The metamorphosis of value*

1 *Capital*, III, 807. See too, *ibid.* p. 806.

2 *Selected Correspondence*, p. 106.

3 *Capital*, I, 571. Our grasp of the connection between Marx's understanding of capital and the theory of alienation is aided by the inclusion of the term 'alienation' in many of his treatments of capital, as for example, when he refers to it as 'the alienation of the condition of social production . . . from the real producers'. *Capital*, III, 259. See too, *ibid.* p. 428.

4 *Ibid.* pp. 794–5. For an even fuller 'definition' which was written much earlier, see 'Wage-Labor and Capital', *Selected Writings*, pp. 84–5. See too, *Pre-Capitalist Economic Formations*, pp. 97 ff.

5 *Grundrisse*, p. 412.

6 *Capital*, I, 153, 571.

7 *Capital*, III, 806.

8 *Grundrisse*, p. 175.

9 *Political Economy*, p. 51; *Capital*, III, 378.

10 *Political Economy*, p. 51. For a good account of money both as capital and as a commodity, see Ernest Mandel's scholarly work, *Traité d'économie marxiste* (Paris, 1962), Chapters 3, 4, and 8.

11 Marx says, 'By possessing the property of buying everything, by possessing the property of appropriating all objects, money is the object of eminent possession . . . Money is the pimp between man's need and the objects, between his life and his means of life. But that which mediates my life for me, also mediates the existence of other people for me. For me it is the other person.' *1844 Manuscripts*, p. 137. I have broken my general rule of using only late sources for these chapters, because this aspect of money as a commodity, which fits logically into the current discussion, is so much better treated in Marx's early writings.

12 *Ibid.* p. 139.

13 *Capital*, II, 358. The 'power' aspect of money will be further developed in the next chapter as part of the discussion of the fetishism of commodities.

14 *Capital*, I, 87. Elsewhere, Marx maintains, 'In order to sell a thing, nothing more is required than its capacity to be monopolized and alienated'. *Capital*, III, 619.

15 *Ibid.* p. 345.

16 *Ibid.* p. 344.

17 *Ibid.* p. 342.

18 *Ibid.* p. 334.

19 For discussions of alienation which could have come directly out of the *1844 Manuscripts*, see *Grundrisse*, pp. 356, 715–16.

20 If the new emphasis accorded 'alienation' does not affect Marx's commitment to the theory of alienation, it does make evident certain differences between this concept and that of 'estrangement'. What have been treated as synonyms can now be seen as having somewhat different emphases: 'alienation', generally – and particularly in Marx's later writings – lays more stress on what it is that man has given up and its subsequent relations to the donor; while 'estrangement' tends to stress what is left, the state of the individual upon and after giving. The full sense of both concepts, whenever they are used, remains the whole set of alienated relations which was constructed earlier.

21 *Letters to Dr Kugelmann*, p. 74. Marx states that volume II of *Capital* is his attempt to chart the various forms taken by value in the process of circulation. *Capital*, III, 807. Though subtitled 'The Process of Capitalist Production as a Whole', volume III continues the mapping work of volume II. Given all that is covered by the metamorphosis of value, it is evident that the present chapter has skimmed very lightly over the subject. I have been content here as before to make clear the links between Marx's economics and the theory of alienation, and have not reconstructed more of the complexity he uncovered than was necessary to serve this purpose.

CHAPTER 28: *The fetishism of commodities*

1 For an excellent account of the fetishism of commodites, see Lucien Goldman, 'la Reification', *Recherches dialectiques* (Paris, 1959).

2 The fetishism of commodities is also explained by a reference to what Marx observes in religion. In religion, he says, 'the productions of the human brain appear as independent beings endowed with life and entering into relations both with one another and with the human race. So it is in the world of commodities with the products of men's hands'. *Capital*, I, 72. In one particularly explosive broadside, Marx speaks of the fetishism of commodities as 'this false appearance and illusion, this mutual independence and ossification of the various social elements of wealth, the personification of things and conversion of production relations into entities, this religion of everyday life'. *Capital*, III, 809. Mention has already been made of this development, which is also called 'reification' (*Verdinglichung*), in the discussion of product alienation.

3 *Capital*, I, 72.

4 *Ibid.* p. 74n.
5 *Ibid.* p. 76.
6 *Ibid.* p. 72.
7 *Capital,* III, 801.
8 *Capital,* I, 592; *Capital,* III, 284. Marx quotes with approval the English economist Hodgskin's remark that 'Capital is a sort of cabalistic word like church and state or any other of these general terms which are invented by those who fleece the rest of mankind to conceal the hand that shears them'. Marx, *Theories of Surplus-Value,* ed. S. W. Ryazanskaya and R. Dixon, III (Moscow, 1971), 536.
9 *Capital,* III, 797.
10 *Theories of Surplus-Value,* p. 122; see too, *Capital,* III, 804.
11 *Ibid.*
12 *Ibid.* p. 383.
13 *Ibid.* p. 384. In keeping with Marx's conception of qualities as relations, the same results are given as follows: 'the social relation is consummated in the relation of a thing, of money to itself'. *Ibid.* In the end, it even appears as if 'interest were the typical product of capital, the primary matter, and profit, in the shape of profit of enterprise, were a byproduct of the process of reproduction'. *Ibid.*
14 *Ibid.* p. 798. See too, *ibid.* p. 803.
15 *Ibid.* p. 809. The 'Trinity Formula' provides a fitting conclusion to volume III, for the task Marx set out to do in *Capital* is now completed (volume IV was projected as a comparative study of other labor theories of value). Value has been successfully traced from its origins in alienated labor through its various forms in the economy to their misrepresentations in the minds of men. The works he hoped to write on other areas of social life remain unwritten, but in the 'Trinity Formula' Marx aptly summarizes his conclusions on the economc life of the alienated inhabitants of capitalism. It is only because he does not recognize the problem at which Marx directed these comments that G. D. H. Cole finds volume III 'petering out rather than coming to an end'. G. D. H. Cole, *A History of Socialist Thought,* II (London, 1954), 298.
16 *Capital,* III, 810.
17 Marcuse, *Reason and Revolution,* pp. 280–1.
18 On one occasiqn, Marx refers to the relations of social labor appearing to individuals 'as what they really are, material relations between persons and social relations between things'. *Capital,* I, 73.
19 *Gesamtausgabe,* I: 3, 531.

CHAPTER 29: *Class as a value Relation*

1 *1844 Manuscripts,* p. 103.
2 *The German Ideology,* p. 7.
3 *1844 Manuscripts,* pp. 109–10.
4 *Ibid.* p. 109. Even the distinction between spheres is dispensed with when Marx, referring to 'politics, art, literature, etc.', says that industry 'can be conceived as part of that general movement, just as that movement can be conceived as a particular part of industry, since all human activity hitherto has been labor – that is, industry – activity estranged from itself'. *Ibid.* p. 110. As with 'mode of production',

'industry' offers an example of a concept ordinarily limited to economics that Marx feels he can use when referring to other areas of life as well.

5 *The Holy Family*, p. 162.

6 Of capitalism, Marx says, 'Finally, there came a time when everything that men considered as inalienable became an object of exchange, of traffic and could be alienated. This is the time when the very things which till then had been communicated but never exchanged; given, but never sold; acquired, but never bought – virtue, love, conviction, knowledge, conscience, etc. – when everything, in short, passed into commerce. It is the time of general corruption, of universal venality, or, to speak in terms of political economy, the time when everything, moral or physical, having become a marketable value, is brought to the market to be assessed at its truest value.' *The Poverty of Philosophy*, p. 36.

7 *1844 Manuscripts*, p. 82.

8 Marx himself uses the expression 'value Relation' (*Wertverhaltnis*) to refer to part of the broader social conditions which underlie value and, hence, are conveyed in its concept – in this instance, to the opposition between capital and wage-labor. *Grundrisse*, p. 592.

9 *Ibid.* p. 75. See too, *The German Ideology*, p. 76.

10 *1844 Manuscripts*, p. 68. Competition is also referred to as 'liberation from the standpoint of the bourgeoisie'. *Die Deutsche Ideologie, Werke*, III, 395.

11 Marx declares such 'mutual exploitation' to be the 'general relation of all individuals to one another'. *Ibid.* It is capitalism's version of the necessary appropriation of man by man.

12 The individual in such a society is also said to be 'withdrawn into himself, wholly preoccupied with his private interest and acting in accordance with his private caprice'. 'Zur Judenfrage', *Werke*, I, 366.

13 *The German Ideology*, p. 58.

14 *Capital*, III, 85.

15 *The German Ideology*, p. 58.

16 *Ibid.* p. 77.

17 *1844 Manuscripts*, pp. 61–2. Marx adds that 'Customs, character, etc., vary from one estate to another and seem to be one with the land to which they belong'. *Ibid.* p. 62.

18 Nor, equally, could their private property ever be completely separated from them. Thus Marx says of feudalism, 'No matter, then, what we may think of the parts played by the different classes of people themselves in this society, the social relations between individuals in the performance of their labor appear at all events as their own mutual personal relations, and are not disguised under the shape of social relations between the products of labor'. In illustration, Marx notes that 'Compulsory labor is just as properly measured by time, as commodity producing labor; but every serf knows that what he expends in the service of his lord is a definite quantity of his own personal labor-power'. *Capital*, I, 77.

19 *The German Ideology*, p. 77. This blindness for social relations may also be included among the criteria for Marx's use of 'class', though, as we saw, Marx was willing to use this concept if only a few of the various criteria which applied were present.

20 *The Holy Family*, p. 157.
21 *Ibid*. pp. 156–7.
22 *The German Ideology*, p. 75.
23 *Ibid*. p. 77.

CHAPTER 30: *State as a value Relation*

1 *1844 Manuscripts*, p. 103.
2 'Zur Judenfrage', *Werke*, I, 353.
3 *1844 Manuscripts*, p. 103; *The German Ideology*, p. 72.
4 Marx points out that in feudal times people working for a lord were not just his property, but were 'bound to him by ties of respect, allegiance, and duty. His relation to them is therefore directly political, and has likewise a human, intimate side.' *1844 Manuscripts*, p. 62.
5 *Die Deutsche Ideologie, Werke*, III, 227–8.
6 *The German Ideology*, p. 75.
7 *Ibid*. Elsewhere, Marx says, 'And out of this very contradiction between the interest of the individual and that of the community the latter takes an independent form as the state, divorced from the real interest of individual and community, and at the same time as an illusory communal life'. *Ibid*. p. 23.
8 *Ibid*. p. 24.
9 The interdependence of state and class is brought out clearly in Marx's claim that, 'If the modern state wished to end the impotence of its administration, it would be obliged to abolish the present conditions of private life. And if the state wished to abolish these conditions of private life it would have also to put an end to its own existence, for it exists only in relation to them.' 'Kritische Randglossen', *Werke*, I, 402.
10 *The German Ideology*, pp. 23–4.
11 *Ibid*. p. 24.
12 Marx says, 'The illusory community, in which individuals have up till now combined, always took on an independent existence in relation to them, and was at the same time, since it was the combination of one class over against another, not only a completely illusory community, but a new fetter as well'. *Ibid*. pp. 74–5. What this fetter restrains man from doing is seen in the very next sentence: 'Only in community with others has each individual the means of cultivating his gifts in all directions: only in the community therefore is personal freedom possible.' *Ibid*.
13 *The Communist Manifesto*, p. 15.
14 'Eighteenth Brumaire', *Selected Writings*, I, 300.
15 In Marx's notes for 'The Civil War in France', it is made clear – clearer than in the finished draft – that the great accomplishment of the Commune was not that it destroyed the bourgeois state, but that it destroyed state rule. Of the state, Marx says, 'It has sprung into life against them. By them it was broken, not as a peculiar form of governmental (centralized) power, but as its most powerful, elaborated into seeming independence from society expression.' Quoted in Ralph Miliband, 'Marx and the State', *The Socialist Register, 1965* (New York, 1965), p. 296.

16 N. Poulantzas and R. Miliband 'The Problem of the Capitalist State, *Ideology in Social Science*, ed. R. Blackburn (New York, 1973).

17 *Capital* I, 10, 85, 592; *Capital* III, 284, 857–8; *1844 MSS*, 79, 109. 109.

18 *Letters to Dr Kugelmann*, p. 23.

19 It may be useful in this regard to mention that a new journal, *Kapitalistate*, has been started with the main purpose of bringing together current Marxist work from all over the world on the subject of the capitalist state. The three issues which have appeared as of winter 1975 suggest that over time this journal may provide a lot of material for the kind of analysis I have called for.

CHAPTER 31: *Religion as a value Relation*

1 *1844 Manuscripts*, p. 103.

2 *Capital*, I, 79.

3 For Marx, religion functions as 'the general theory of this world, its encyclopedic compendium, its logic in popular form, its spiritual *point d'honneur*, its enthusiasm, its moral sanction, its solemn complement, its general basis of consolation and justification . . . Religion is the sigh of the oppressed creature, the sentiment of a heartless world, and the soul of soulless conditions. It is the opium of the people. 'Zur Kritik der Hegelschen Rechtsphilosophie', *Werke*, I, 378.

4 *1844 Manuscripts*, p. 123.

5 *Ibid.* pp. 169–70. He maintains further that 'When man is not, his characteristic expression also cannot be human, and so neither could thought be grasped as an expression of man as a human and natural subject endowed with eyes, ears, etc., and living in society, in the world, and in nature'. *Ibid.* p. 169.

6 *Capital*, I, 79. See too, 'Zur Judenfrage', *Werke*, I, 376.

7 *The Holy Family*, p. 88.

8 *1844 Manuscripts*, p. 168.

9 *Capital*, I, 72.

10 *1844 Manuscripts*, p. 70.

11 'Zur Judenfrage', *Werke*, I, 353. Marx claims, 'Religion is simply the recognition of man in a roundabout fashion; that is, through an intermediary. Just as Christ is the intermediary to whom man attributes all his own divinity and all his religious bonds, so the state is the intermediary to which man confides all his non-divinity, all his human freedom.'

12 *1844 Manuscripts*, p. 70. Marx states that through god, the activity of man's imagination, brain and heart 'operate on him as an alien, divine, and diabolical activity'. *Ibid.* p. 73.

13 *Ibid.* p. 79. A vivid picture of the role of the priest and of religious alienation generally is found in Marx's treatment of the religious transformation of one of literature's 'noble' prostitutes in *The Holy Family*, pp. 230–4.

14 *1844 Manuscripts*, p. 116. In treating priests and other religious 'workers' Marx is more concerned with functions than in guessing about motives. For him, 'Religion is the opium of the people', and it does not matter how many priests are sincere and how many not. Nevertheless, his tone in dealing with this subject suggests that among those who have to gain from religion hypocrisy is widespread.

15 *Capital*, I, 79. Elsewhere, he states, 'Religion is for us the illusory sun

which to man seems to circle around him until he realizes that he himself is the center of his own turning.' 'Zur Kritik der Hegelschen Rechtsphilosophie', *Werke*, III, 379.

16 *1844 Manuscripts*, p. 123. Marx says, 'Since the real existence of man and nature has become practical, sensuous and perceptible – and since man has become for man as the being of nature, and nature for man as the being of man – the question about an alien being, about a being above nature and man – has become impossible in practise.' *Ibid.* pp. 113–14.

17 *Ibid.* p. 114.

18 Thus, alienation cannot be attacked piecemeal, but requires an all-out 'structural' assault. See Franz Pappenheim's brief though interesting discussion of this point in *The Alienation of Modern Man* (New York, 1959), Chapter 5. Again, I want to stress that it makes no sense on this view to speak of alienation coming to an end and religion, property, governments, classes, or any of its other facets continuing to exist, or of any of these facets being abolished without the whole panoply disappearing. So, for example, when Leszek Kolakowski states that it is too optimistic to believe that alienation will end with the abolition of private property, he has dispensed with Marx's notions and supplied ones of his own. Leszek Kolakowski, 'Karl Marx and the Classical Definition of Truth', in *Revisionism*, ed. Leopold Labedz (London, 1962), p. 187.

CHAPTER 32: *Marx's critique of bourgeois ideology*

1 *Theories of Surplus-Value*, III, 536.

2 'Wages, Price and Profit', *Selected Writings*, I, 384. It may be useful in this connection to re-read my discussion of the distinction between appearance and essence in Chapter 6.

3 *Capital*, III, 817.

4 See Chapter 11.

5 C. B. MacPherson, *The Political Theory of Possessive Individualism* (Oxford, 1962).

6 *Capital*, I, 372–3.

7 J. Mepham, 'The Theory of Ideology in *Capital*', *Radical Philosophy*, no. 2 (Summer 1972), 15.

8 There has been an enormous increase in the amount of work done on Marx's critique of bourgeois ideology. Besides the writings of Mac-Pherson and Mepham already mentioned, other works that are well worth consulting on this subject include: the chapter on ideology in Lefebvre, H., *The Sociology of Marx*, trans. N. Guterman (New York, 1968); L. Althusser, 'Ideology and Ideological State Apparatuses', *Lenin and Philosophy*, trans. B. Brewster (New York, 1971); J. Habermas, 'Technology and Science as "Ideology"', *Toward a Rational Society*, trans. J. J. Shapiro (Boston, 1970); R. Lichtman, 'Marx's Theory of Ideology', *Socialist Revolution*, no. 23 (April 1975); R. Blackburn, 'A Brief Guide to Bourgeois Ideology', *Student Power*, ed. R. Blackburn and A. Cockburn (London, 1969). For those who might be inclined to organize a study group around these relatively short readings, which is something I strongly recommend, let me suggest that you begin with Blackburn (his is the simplest piece and contains the most concrete examples) and conclude with

Althusser and Habermas (their pieces are the most complex and in many ways most suggestive of new lines of thought).

CHAPTER 33: *A critical evaluation*

1 Marx, 'Letter to Ruge', *Writings of the Young Marx on Philosophy and Society*, trans. and ed. L. O. Easton and K. H. Guddat (New York, 1967), p. 212.

2 *Selected Correspondence*, p. 110.

3 Thorstein Veblen, 'The Economics of Karl Marx: II', in *The Place of Science in Modern Civilization and Other Essays* (New York, 1961), p. 441.

4 *The Holy Family*, p. 52.

5 This is apparent in such claims as, 'The question is not what this or that proletarian, or even the whole of the proletariat at the moment considers its aim. The question is what the proletariat is, and what, consequent on that being, it will be compelled to do.' *Ibid.* p. 53.

6 Quoted by Marx, *ibid.* p. 51.

7 In this work, Engels writes, 'Although the average English worker can hardly read, let alone write, he nevertheless has a shrewd notion of where his own interest and that of his country lie. He knows, too, where the selfish interest of the bourgeoisie lies, and what he may expect from the middle classes.' Engels, *The Condition of the Working Class in England*, trans. W. O. Henderson and W. H. Chaloner (Oxford, 1958), p. 128.

8 Marx does not seem to have had much contact with workers other than those who attended political and protest meetings, that is, 'revolutionaries' like himself. Besides being more concerned with socialist politics than the mass of the proletariat, such workers were generally a grade above their peers in the kind of jobs they held, being chiefly skilled and self-employed workers. For example, the most active members of the Workers' Educational Society, in which Marx played the dominant role during the early part of his stay in London, were Heinrich Bauer (shoemaker), Joseph Moll (watchmaker), Karl Pfander (painter), George Eccarius (tailor) and Frederick Lessner (tailor). Lessner, 'Before 1848 and After', *Reminiscences*, p. 151. Though Marx could not help but be aware that his working class acquaintances were exceptions among their class, being so limited in his contacts lent itself to making false generalizations, and one trait all class conscious workers share is the reasoning ability that enabled them to acquire this consciousness.

9 For an illuminating discussion of the possible role of sexual repression in helping to produce such irrationality, see Wilhelm Reich, *Mass Psychology of Fascism*, trans. T. P. Wolfe (New York, 1946), pp. 19–28, 122–43.

10 Erich Fromm, *Fear of Freedom* (London, 1942), pp. 1–19.

11 Useful discussions of character structure can be found in Wilhelm Reich, *Character Analysis*, trans. T. P. Wolfe (New York, 1961), Part II; and in Hans Gerth and C. Wright Mills, *Character and Social Structure* (London, 1961), Parts I and II.

12 A fuller statement of my views on class consciousness is found in 'Toward Class Consciousness Next Time: Marx and the Working Class', *Politics and Society* (Fall 1972). For a more detailed description and evaluation of Reich's contribution to this subject,

see my articles 'The Marxism of Wilhelm Reich, or the Social Function of Sexual Repression', in *The Unknown Dimension: European Marxism since Lenin*, ed. D. Howard and K. Klare (New York, 1971), and 'Introduction', in Wilhelm Reich, *Sex-Pol: Marxist Writings, 1929–1934* (New York, 1973).

13 Another recent attempt to revise Marx's conceptual scheme in this area can be seen in the central distinction Marcuse draws (though barely suggested in Marx's writings) between 'true' and 'false' needs. Herbert Marcuse, *One-Dimensional Man* (Boston, 1964), p. 6. Rather than having to overcome or undermine barriers rooted in the worker's character structure, Marcuse restates the socialist's dilemma in terms of a struggle between the alienated and human needs in all of us. Focusing on this broad distinction, however, leaves the change producing levers both within and without the human personality dissembled. The same reconstruction leads Marcuse to what I consider a misplaced emphasis on those elements in the population in whom liberating needs are dominant (that is students and some Third World peoples) as agents of revolution.

14 H. Marcuse, *Soviet Marxism* (New York, 1961), p. 222.

15 Sidney Webb, *The Decay of Capitalist Civilization* (London, 1923), p. 220. In 1922, the labor theory of value was already spoken of as one of the 'venerable fallacies' of Marxism. N. Carpenter, *Guild Socialism* (London, 1922), p. 237.

16 The existing confusion over the term 'alienation' has reached the point that many people use it to register simple dissatisfaction or, worse, feelings of social maladjustment. Empirically minded sociologists have even set out to measure 'it'. For an attempt to remove the normative element in alienation and measure what is left, see Melvin Seeman, 'On the Meaning of Alienation', *American Sociological Review*, xxiv (1959), 786. It is understandable that out of this confusion the cry should go up to abandon the term 'alienation' altogether. See Pierre Naville, 'Alienation and the Analysis of the Modern World', *The Review*, iv, 1 (1962), 56. And if 'alienation' creates more problems than it solves, it may be best to abandon the term. However, as evidenced by this entire study, I am not convinced that this is, or at least need be, the case.

APPENDIX I: *In defense of the philosophy of internal relations*

1 Stuart Hampshire, *Thought and Action* (London, 1959), p. 17.

2 According to Hampshire, failure to comply with this requirement of communicability results in not having any means of pinpointing something, nor of recognizing it, nor of saying what makes it what it is, nor of contradicting a statement in which it appears, nor of investigating its history, nor of distinguishing between truth and falsity. *Ibid.* pp. 18ff.

3 P. F. Strawson, *Individuals* (London, 1965), pp. 15, 247.

4 *Ibid.* pp. 23, 25.

5 *Ibid.* pp. 26–8.

6 *Ibid.* 44–5. Strawson's discussion of 'sophisticated' and 'unsophisticated' particulars is another indication of the degree to which he relies on internal relations to bolster his argument against the existence of such relations. *Ibid.*

7 A. J. Ayer, *The Concept of a Person* (London, 1964), p. 33. Ayer continues, 'Thus, it may be maintained that it is possible for there to be a language which does not recognize the distinction between particulars and universals, or that physical objects must of necessity be the primary particulars in any universe of discourse which is comparable to our own'. *Ibid*. This is a helpful warning against closing our minds to new uses of language by making *a priori* assumptions from our own as to what must be the case.

8 For a useful account of the difficulty thinkers in the British empiricist tradition have in coming to grips with Marx's epistemology, see Charles Taylor's 'Marxism and Empiricism', *British Analytical Philosophy*, pp. 233ff. Empiricists hold that knowledge consists of impressions made on our minds by the external world, and that the form of these impressions is necessarily the same for all people. On this view, what we know about the world is entirely built upon these impressions, conception coming after perception. Consequently, different ways of viewing the world are thought to be reducible to the perceptible units that are the basic elements in each. But if conceptualization occurs at the time of perception, then the units into which we break down different world views are not commensurable. Thinking that they are makes it difficult to admit that Marx – unlike most of us – actually conceived of each element in the real world, upon perception, as a Relation.

9 Ayer, *The Concept of a Person*, p. 34.

10 *Ibid*.

11 *Ibid*. p. 32.

12 H. Popitz, *Der Entfremdete Mensch* (Basel, 1953), p. 113.

13 George Lukács, *Geschichte und Klassenbewusstein* (Berlin, 1968), pp. 168–9; Sartre, *The Problem of Method*, pp. 27–8.

APPENDIX II: *Response to my critics: more on internal relations*

1 The main reviews of *Alienation* that criticize the philosophy of internal relations are found in *Social Theory and Practise* (Spring 1973), *Social Research* (Spring 1973), *Contemporary Sociology* (Spring 1973), *Soviet Studies* (July 1972), *Radical Philosophy* (Spring 1974), and *Canadian Journal of Philosophy* (March 1974). Though similar objections have appeared elsewhere, these are the major reviews to which I am responding in this essay. Readers interested in following the discussion through some of the more favourable reactions to my interpretation of Marx's philosophy should also see *New York Review of Books* (9 March 1972), *Science and Society* (Summer 1972), *American Political Science Review* (Fall 1972), and *Political Studies* (June 1972).

2 'Die Moralisierende Kritik,' *Werke* IV, 339.

3 This schema for setting apart different views on totality was first suggested by Karel Kosik in *la Dialectique du concret*, trans. from German by Roger Dangeville (Paris, 1970), p. 35. There are important differences, however, in what Kosik and I understand of the second and third notions of totality presented here.

4 *1844 Manuscripts*, p. 15.

5 For a fuller exposition of the different moments in Marx's method, see my article, 'Marxism and Political Science: Prolegomenon to a Debate on Marx's Method', *Politics and Society* (Summer 1973).

Bibliography of works cited

WORKS BY MARX AND ENGELS

Karl Marx. *Capital,* trans. Samuel Moore and Edward Aveling, vol. I. Moscow, 1958.
Capital, vol. II. Moscow, 1957.
Capital, vol. III. Moscow, 1959.
A Contribution to the Critique of Political Economy, trans. N. I. Stone. Chicago, 1904.
Economic and Philosophic Manuscripts of 1844, trans. T. B. Bottomore, in Fromm, Erich, *Marx's Concept of Man.* New York, 1963.
Economic and Philosophic Manuscripts of 1844, trans. Martin Milligan. Moscow, 1959.
Economic and Philosophic Manuscripts of 1844, trans. Ria Stone. n.p., 1949.
Frühe Schriften, vol. I. Stuttgart, 1962.
Grundrisse der Kritik des Politischen Okonomie. Berlin, 1953.
Letters to Dr Kugelmann. London, 1941.
Writings of the Young Marx on Philosophy and Society, ed. and trans. L. O. Easton and K. H. Guddat. New York, 1967.
The Poverty of Philosophy. Moscow, n.d.
Pre-Capitalist Economic Formations, ed. E. J. Hobsbawm and trans. Jack Cohen. New York, 1965.
Theories of Surplus-Value, trans. G. A. Bonner and Emile Burns. London, 1951.
Theories of Surplus-Value, ed. S. W. Ryazanskaya and R. Dixon, trans. Jack Cohen and S. W. Ryazanskaya, vol. III. Moscow, 1971.

Karl Marx and Frederick Engels. *Briefwechsel,* vol. II. Berlin, 1949.
On Colonialism. Moscow, n.d.
The Communist Manifesto, trans. Samuel Moore. Chicago, 1945.
The German Ideology, trans. R. Pascal. London, 1942.
Gesamtausgabe, ed. V. Adoratsky, abt. I, vols. 2–3. Berlin, 1932.
The Holy Family, trans. R. Dixon. Moscow, 1956.
Kleine Okonomische Schriften. Berlin, 1955.
Selected Correspondence, ed. and trans. Dona Torr. London, 1941.
Selected Writings, vols. I–II. Moscow, 1951.
Uber Erziehung und Bildung, ed. P. N. Grusdew. Berlin, 1960.
Werke, vols. I, III, IV. Berlin, 1959–61.

Frederick Engels. *The Condition of the Working Class in England,* trans. W. O. Henderson and W. H. Chaloner. Oxford, 1958.
The Dialectics of Nature, trans. Clement Dutt. Moscow, 1954.
Germany: Revolution and Counter-Revolution. London, 1933.

Herr Eugen Dühring's Revolution in Science [Anti-Dühring], trans. Emile Burns. London, n.d.

WORKS RELATING TO MARX AND MARXISM

Acton, H. B. *The Illusion of the Epoch.* London, 1962.
Althusser, Louis. 'Ideology and Ideological State Apparatuses', *Lenin and Philosophy*, trans. B. Brewster. New York, 1971.
'l'Objet du *Capital*', *Lire le Capital*, vol. II, ed. by the author. Paris, 1965.
Pour Marx. Paris, 1966.
Ash, William. *Marxism and Moral Concepts.* New York, 1964.
Avineri, Shlomo. *The Social and Political Thought of Karl Marx.* Cambridge, 1968.
Axelos, Kostas. *Marx penseur de la technique.* Paris, 1961.
Berlin, Isaiah. *Karl Marx.* London, 1960.
Two Concepts of Liberty. Oxford, 1958.
Bernstein, Edward. *Evolutionary Socialism,* trans. Edith Harvey. London, 1909.
Bigo, Pierre. *Marxisme et humanisme.* Paris, 1953.
Blackburn, R. 'A Brief Guide to Bourgeois Ideology', *Student Power,* ed. R. Blackburn and A. Cockburn. London, 1969.
Blake, William. *An American Looks at Karl Marx.* New York, 1939.
Bober, Mandel. *Karl Marx's Interpretation of History.* Cambridge, 1950.
Böhm-Bawerk, Ludwig v. *Karl Marx and the Close of his System,* trans. Alice A. MacDonald. London. 1890.
Calvez, J. Y. *la Pensée de Karl Marx.* Paris, 1956.
Carew-Hunt, R. N. *The Theory and Practice of Communism.* London, 1963.
Carpenter, N. *Guild Socialism.* London, 1922.
Cathrein, Victor. *Socialism,* trans. Victor Gettleman. New York, 1962.
Cole, G. D. H. *A History of Socialist Thought,* vol. II. London, 1954.
Dunayevskaya, Raya. *Marxism and Freedom.* New York, 1958.
Eastman, Max. *Marx and Lenin: The Science of Revolution.* New York, 1922.
Fromm, Erich. *Marx's concept of Man.* New York, 1963.
Garaudy, Roger. *Théorie matérialiste de la connaissance.* Paris, 1953.
Goldman, Lucien. *Recherches dialectiques.* Paris, 1959.
Gurvitch, Georges. *Etudes sur les classes sociales.* Paris, 1966.
Habermas, J. 'Technology and Science as "Ideology" ', *Toward a Rational Society,* trans. J. J. Shapiro. Boston, 1970.
Hirsch, Max. *Democracy versus Socialism.* New York, 1901.
Hook, Sidney. *From Hegel to Marx.* Ann Arbor, 1962.
Marx and the Marxists. Princeton, 1955.
Towards the Understanding of Karl Marx. New York, 1933.

322   *Bibliography*

Jordan, Z. A. *The Evolution of Dialectical Materialism*. New York, 1967.

Kamenka, Eugene. *The Ethical Foundations of Marxism*. London, 1962.

Kolakowski, Leszek. 'Karl Marx and the Classical Definition of Truth', *Revisionism*, ed. Leopold Labedz. London, 1962.

Kosik, Karel. *la Dialectique du concret*, trans. Roger Dangeville. Paris, 1970.

Landshut, S. and Mayer, J. P. *Karl Marx, der Historische Materialismus. Die Frühschriften*, vol. I. Leipzig, 1932.

Lefebvre, Henri. *Logique formelle – logique dialectique*. Paris, 1947.
The Sociology of Marx, trans. N. Guterman. New York, 1968.

Lenin, V. I. *Collected Works*, vol. XXXVIII (Philosophical Notebooks). Moscow, 1961.

Levy, H. *A Philosophy for a Modern Man*. London, 1938.

Lichtheim, George. *Marxism*. London, 1965.

Lichtman, Richard. 'Marx's Theory of Ideology', *Socialist Revolution*, no. 23 (April 1975).

Lindsay, A. D. *Karl Marx's 'Capital'*. London, 1925.

Lukács, George. *Geschichte und Klassenbewusstein*. Berlin, 1923.

MacPherson, C. B. *The Political Theory of Possessive Individualism*. Oxford, 1962.

Mandel, Ernest. *Traité d'économie marxiste*. Paris, 1962.

Mao Tse-Tung. *On Contradiction*. Peking, 1952.

Marcuse, Herbert. *One-Dimensional Man*. Boston, 1967.
Reason and Revolution. Boston, 1964.
Soviet Marxism. New York, 1961.

McLellan, David. *The Young Hegelians and Karl Marx*. London, 1969.

Mepham, John. 'The Theory of Ideology in Capital', *Radical Philosophy*, no. 2 (Summer 1972).

Mészáros, Ivan. *Marx's Theory of Alienation*. London, 1970.

Meyer, A. G. *Marxism: The Unity of Theory and Practise*. Ann Arbor, 1963.

Miliband, Ralph. 'Marx and the State', *The Socialist Register, 1965*. New York, 1965.

Mills, C. Wright. *The Marxists*. New York, 1962.

Naville, Pierre. *le Nouveau léviathan*, vol. I. Paris, 1967.
'Alienation and the Analysis of the Modern World', *The Review*, IV, 1 (1962).

Ollman, Bertell. 'Introduction' to Wilhelm Reich, *Sex-Pol: Marxist Writings, 1929–1934*. New York, 1973.
'Marxism and Political Science: Prolegomenon to a Debate on Marx's Method', *Politics and Society* (Summer 1973).
'The Marxism of Wilhelm Reich, or the Social Function of Sexual Repression', in D. Howard and K. Klare (eds), *The Unknown Dimension: European Marxism since Lenin*. New York, 1971.

'Marx's Use of "Class"', *American Journal of Sociology*, LXIII (March 1968).

'Toward Class Consciousness Next time: Marx and the Working Class', *Politics and Society* (Fall 1972).

Pannekoek, Anton. *Lenin as Philosopher*, trans. by the author. New York, 1948.

Pappenheim, Franz. *The Alienation of Moaern Man*. New York, 1959.

Pareto, Vilfredo. *les Systèmes socialistes*, vol. II. Paris, 1902.

Plamenatz, John. *German Marxism and Russian Communism*. London, 1961.

Man and Society, vol. II. London, 1965.

Popitz, H. *Der Entfremdete Mensch*. Basel, 1953.

Popper, Karl. *The Open Society and its Enemies*, vol. II. London, 1962.

Poulantzas, N. and Miliband, R. 'The Problem of the Capitalist State', *Ideology in Social Science*, ed. R. Blackburn, New York, 1973.

Robinson, Joan. *An Essay on Marxian Economics*. London, 1963.

On Re-reading Marx. Cambridge, 1953.

Rubel, Maximilien. 'la Charte de la Première Internationale', *le Mouvement social*, no. 51 (April–June 1965).

'Fragments sociologiques dans les inédits de Marx', *Cahiers internationaux de sociologie*, XXII (1957).

'Introduction à l'éthique marxienne', *Pages choisies pour une éthique socialiste*. Paris, 1948.

Karl Marx, essai de biographie intellectuelle. Paris, 1957.

'les Premières lectures économiques de Karl Marx (II)', *Etudes de marxologie*, Cahiers de l'I.S.E.A., série 5, no. 2 (October 1959).

'la Russie dans l'oeuvre de Marx et Engels: leur correspondance avec Danielson', *la Revue socialiste* (April 1950).

Schaff, Adam. *A Philosophy of Man*. London, 1963.

Schumpeter, Joseph. *Capitalism, Socialism, and Democracy*. New York, 1947.

Seeman, Melvin. 'On the Meaning of Alienation', *American Sociological Review*, XXIV (1959).

Selsam, Howard. *Socialism and Ethics*. New York, 1943.

Sève, Lucien, *Marxisme et théorie de la personnalité*. Paris, 1969.

Shaw, George Bernard. *Bernard Shaw and Karl Marx*, ed. R. W. Ellis. New York, 1930.

Sheed, F. J. *Communism and Man*. London, 1938.

Strachey, John. *The Nature of Capitalist Crisis*. New York, 1935.

Sweezy, Paul. *The Theory of Capitalist Development*. New York, 1964.

Taylor, Charles. 'Marxism and Empiricism', *British Analytical Philosophy*, ed. Bernard Williams and Alan Montefiore. London, 1966.

Thier, Erich. *Das Menschenbild des Jungen Marx*. Gottingen, 1957.

Trotsky, Leon. *The Living Thoughts of Karl Marx*. New York, 1963.

Tucker, Robert. *Philosophy and Myth in Karl Marx*. Cambridge, 1964.

Veblen, Thorstein. 'The Economics of Karl Marx: II', *The Place of Sci-*

ence in Modern Civilization and other Essays. New York, 1961.
Venable, Vernon. *Human Nature: the Marxian View.* New York, 1945.
Webb, Sidney. *The Decay of Capitalist Civilization.* London, 1923.

Marxismusstudien, ed. Iring Fetscher. Tübingen, 1954–69, vols. I–VI.
Reminiscences of Marx and Engels. Moscow, n.d.
Socialist Humanism, ed. Erich Fromm. New York, 1965.

OTHER WORKS

Ayer, A. J. *The Concept of a Person.* London, 1964.
Barry, Brian. *Political Argument.* London, 1965.
Bradley, F. H. *Appearance and Reality.* London, 1920.
Buber, Martin. 'Productivity and Existence', *Identity and Anxiety,* ed.
    Maurice R. Stein and others. Glencoe, 1960.
Dietzgen, Joseph. *The Positive Outcome of Philosophy,* trans. W. W.
    Craik. Chicago, 1928.
Feuerbach, Ludwig. *Samtliche Werke,* ed. v. Wilhelm Bolin and Fried-
    rich Jodl, vol. II. Stuttgart, 1959.
    Das Wesen des Christentums, vol. II. Berlin, 1956.
Fromm, Erich. *Fear of Freedom.* London, 1942.
Gerth, Hans, and Mills, C. Wright. *Character and Social Structure.*
    London, 1961.
Hampshire, Stuart. *Thought and Action.* London, 1959.
Hegel, G. W. F. *The Logic of Hegel,* trans. William Wallace, from *The
    Encyclopaedia of the Philosophical Sciences.* Oxford, 1965.
    The Phenomenology of Mind, trans. J. B. Baillie. London, 1964.
    Samtliche Werke, ed. Karl Rosenkranz, vol. III. Stuttgart, 1927.
James, William. *The Will to Believe and Other Essays in Popular Phi-
    losophy.* New York, 1956.
Leibniz, G. W. *Nouveaux essais sur l'entendement humain.* Paris,
    1966.
    Monadologie. Paris, 1952.
Reich, Wilhelm. *Character Analysis,* trans. T. P. Wolfe. New York,
    1961.
    Mass Psychology of Fascism, trans. T. P. Wolfe. New York, 1946.
Sartre, Jean-Paul, *The Problem of Method,* trans. Hazel E. Barnes.
    London, 1963.
Spinoza, B. *Ethics,* trans. A. Boyle. London, 1925.
Strawson, P. F. *Individuals.* London, 1965.
Whitehead, Alfred N. *The Concept of Nature.* Ann Arbor, 1957.
    Process and Reality. London, 1929.

Index of names and ideas*

'ability to calculate advantages'
(Veblen), 245
abstraction: as dialectical category,
13, 33, 61–2 *passim*, 134–5,
139, 143, 152, 163, 164, 225,
228, 231, 232, 274–5, 289 n4,
297 n3, 306 nn5 and 17
force (method) of, 61–3; *see*
individuation within alienation:
the individual as, 134–5, 139,
143, 152, 301 n9
labor as, 134, 143–4, 170–3,
175–7, 177–8, 182–3, 309 n30
value as, 175–8, 179–80, 184–5,
209
class as, 204–5
law as, 164–5
other, 134, 139, 152, 197, 221,
246, 294 n8
abstrahieren: trans. of, ix
activity, 80, 81, 97–119, 121, 137,
204–5, 214, 248, 298 nn2 and
4; *see* appropriation
life, 99, 109–14 *passim*, 118, 133,
152, 202, 289 n11, 293–4 n23
natural, 79–80, 110–13, 151, 152,
298–9 n9
species (human, social), 82, 98–9,
109–19, 151, 152, 158, 297
n10, 299 (Chap. 16) n5, 302
n8, 303 n20

productive, *see* work
alienated, *see* labor, alienation
Acton, H. B. 7 10, 278 n11, 278–9
n21
alienation, 47, 90, 110, 118, 120,
131–233 *passim*, 248–55 *passim*, 263, 265, 271, 300–18
passim; see estrangement
concept of, 132, 160, 162, 193,
194, 254, 301 n14, 303 n14,
304 n1, 311 n20, 318 n16
theory of, xi, 74, 120, 131–5, 166,
169, 178, 185, 219, 233, 250–5,
263, 271, 297 n3, 301 n14, 310
n3, 311 n20
of labor, 136–42, 147, 148, 149,
151, 158, 160, 161, 162, 164,
165, 166–201 *passim*, 210, 229,
267, 302 nn2 and 3, 302 n13,
308 n18, 312 n15
from product, 122, 141–7, 169,
177–8, 181, 191, 202–3, 221,
224, 226, 251, 252, 301 n9,
302–3 *passim*
from others, 147–50, 155, 169,
181, 183, 191, 203–17 *passim*,
222, 224, 225, 226, 250, 251–2,
312–14 *passim*
from species, 150–2, 169, 304 n3
political, 202, 212–20, 227, 251,
314–15 *passim*

---

* In line with the main thesis of this book regarding Marx's philosophy of
internal relations, I have noted each 'significant' appearance in the text of
Marx's more important concepts. A reader who looks up all references to
capital, money, labor, etc. (together with immediate cross-references)
should be able to reconstruct, at least in broad outline, Marx's analysis of
capitalism as seen from this particular vantage point. He will also have a
fuller sense of the concepts, 'capital', 'money', 'labor', etc. than I have
been able to offer even in the pages devoted to these subjects. The sub-
sections for entries have been ordered with this dual aim in mind, though
the numbering within each subsection is consecutive. Attention has also
been given to include the specialized terms with which I expound Marx's
philosophy of internal relations. Finally, footnote references only appear
in the index if they involve a substantive point.

Cambridge Studies in the History
and Theory of Politics

TEXTS

Liberty, Equality, Fraternity, by James Fitzjames Stephen. Edited with an introduction and notes, by R. J. White

Vladimir Akimov on the dilemmas of Russian Marxism 1895–1903. An English edition of a 'A Short History of the Social Democratic Movement in Russia' and 'The Second Congress of the Russian Social Democratic Labour Party', with an introduction and notes by Jonathan Frankel

Two English Republican Tracts, Plato Redivivus or, A Dialogue Concerning Government (c. 1681), by Henry Neville and *An Essay upon the Constitution of the Roman Government (c. 1699),* by Walter Moyle. Edited by Caroline Robbins

J. G. Herder on Social and Political Culture, translated, edited and with an introduction by F. M. Barnard

The Limits of State Action, by Willhelm von Humboldt. Edited, with an introduction and notes, by J. W. Burrow

Kant's Political Writings, edited with an introduction and notes by Hans Reiss; translated by H. N. Nisbet

Marx's Critique of Hegel's 'Philosophy of Right', edited with an introduction and notes by Joseph O'Malley; translated by Annette Jolin and Joseph O'Malley

STUDIES

1867: Disraeli, Gladstone and Revolution, The Passing of the Second Reform Bill, by Maurice Cowling

The Conscience of the State in North America, by E. R. Norman

The Social and Political Thought of Karl Marx, by Shlomo Avineri

Men and Citizens: A Study of Rousseau's Social Theory, by Judith Shklar

Idealism, Politics and History: Sources of Hegelian Thought, by George Armstrong Kelly

The Impact of Labour 1920–1924. The Beginning of Modern British Politics, by Maurice Cowling